PERSISTENCE, PRIVILEGE, AND PARENTING

PERSISTENCE, PRIVILEGE, AND PARENTING

THE COMPARATIVE STUDY OF INTERGENERATIONAL MOBILITY

TIMOTHY M. SMEEDING,
ROBERT ERIKSON, AND MARKUS JÄNTTI

EDITORS

Russell Sage Foundation • New York

BP 53

The Russell Sage Foundation

The Russell Sage Foundation, one of the oldest of America's general purpose foundations, was established in 1907 by Mrs. Margaret Olivia Sage for "the improvement of social and living conditions in the United States." The Foundation seeks to fulfill this mandate by fostering the development and dissemination of knowledge about the country's political, social, and economic problems. While the Foundation endeavors to assure the accuracy and objectivity of each book it publishes, the conclusions and interpretations in Russell Sage Foundation publications are those of the authors and not of the Foundation, its Trustees, or its staff. Publication by Russell Sage, therefore, does not imply Foundation endorsement.

Library of Congress Cataloging-in-Publication Data

Persistence, privilege, and parenting : the comparative study of intergenerational mobility / Timothy M. Smeeding, Robert Erikson, and Markus Jäntti, editors.
  p. cm.
  Includes bibliographical references and index.
  ISBN 978-0-87154-031-7 (alk. paper)
1. Social mobility. 2. Generations—Economic aspects. 3. Families—Longitudinal studies.
4. Cost and standard of living. I. Smeeding, Timothy M. II. Jäntti, Markus, 1966– III.
Erikson, Robert, 1938–
HT612.P47 2011
305.5′13—dc23

2011016973

The paper used in this publication meets the minimum requirements of American National Standard for Information Sciences—Permanence of Paper for Printed Library Materials. ANSI Z39.48-1992.

Text design by Suzanne Nichols.

RUSSELL SAGE FOUNDATION
112 East 64th Street, New York, New York 10065
10 9 8 7 6 5 4 3 2 1

7/9/13

Contents

Contributors

Timothy M. Smeeding is director of the Institute for Research on Poverty and Distinguished Professor of Public Affairs at the University of Wisconsin–Madison.

Robert Erikson is professor of sociology at the Swedish Institute for Social Research, Stockholm University.

Markus Jäntti is professor of economics at the Swedish Institute for Social Research, Stockholm University.

Jo Blanden is lecturer in economics at the University of Surrey and research associate at the Center for Economic Performance, London School of Economics.

Miles Corak is professor of economics in the Graduate School of Public and International Affairs at the University of Ottawa.

Lori J. Curtis is professor in the Department of Economics at the University of Waterloo, Ontario.

Matthew Di Carlo is senior fellow of the Albert Shanker Institute.

Greg J. Duncan is Distinguished Professor in the Department of Education at the University of California, Irvine.

John Ermisch is professor of economics at the Institute for Social and Economic Research at the University of Essex (United Kingdom).

Gøsta Esping-Andersen is Icrea Academia Professor at the Universitat Pompeu Fabra in Barcelona.

David B. Grusky is professor of sociology at Stanford University, director of the Center for the Study of Poverty and Inequality at Stanford University, and co-editor (with Paula England) of the Stanford University Press Social Inequality Series.

Robert Haveman is the John Bascom Emeritus Professor of Economics and Public Affairs and research affiliate of the Institute for Research on Poverty at the University of Wisconsin–Madison.

John Jerrim is research officer in the Department of Quantitative Social Science at the Institute of Education, University of London.

Jan O. Jonsson is professor of sociology at the Swedish Institute for Social Research at Stockholm University and responsible for the Swedish Level-of-Living Survey (LNU).

Ariel Kalil is professor at the Harris School of Public Policy Studies at the University of Chicago, director of the Center for Human Potential and Public Policy, and a developmental psychologist.

Bertrand Maître is research officer at the Economic and Social Research Institute, Dublin.

John Micklewright is professor of quantitative social science in the Department of Quantitative Social Science at the Institute of Education, University of London.

Carina Mood is assistant professor of sociology at the Swedish Institute for Social Research, Stockholm University.

Brian Nolan is professor of public policy in the School of Applied Social Science, University College Dublin.

Fabian T. Pfeffer is Faculty Research Fellow at the Survey Research Center and a faculty associate at the Population Studies Center at the Institute for Social Research, University of Michigan.

Shelley Phipps is professor of economics at Dalhousie University, currently holding the Maxwell Chair in Economics; fellow of the Canadian Institute for Advanced Research (Social Interactions, Identity and Well-Being Group); and program director for Children, Family, and Work-Life Issues for the Canadian Labor and Skills Research Network.

Reinhard Pollak is research fellow at the Social Science Research Center (WZB) in Berlin.

Chiara Pronzato is assistant professor in the Department of Economics at the University of Turin, Italy.

James P. Smith is the RAND Chair in Labor Markets and Demographic Studies.

Kjetil Telle is head of research at the Section for Social and Demographic Research, Statistics Norway.

Sander Wagner is research assistant in the Department of Political and Social Sciences at Universitat Pompeu Fabra, Barcelona, Spain.

Jane Waldfogel is professor of social work and public affairs at the Columbia University School of Social Work and visiting professor at the Centre for Analysis of Social Exclusion at the London School of Economics.

Elizabeth Washbrook is research associate with the Centre for Multilevel Modelling at the University of Bristol.

Christopher T. Whelan is professor of sociology and head of the School of Sociology, University College Dublin.

Kathryn Wilson is professor of economics at Kent State University.

Kathleen M. Ziol-Guest is postdoctoral associate in the Department of Policy Analysis and Management at Cornell University, and senior researcher at Statistics Norway.

Julie M. Zissimopoulos is research associate professor in the Titus Family Department of Clinical Pharmacy and Pharmaceutical Economics and Policy, and associate director of the Schaeffer Center for Health Policy and Economics at the University of Southern California.

Acknowledgements

T he volume was supported and financed by the Institute for Research on Poverty (IRP), the Russell Sage Foundation (RSF), and the European Commission Network of Excellence, EQUALSOC (Economic Change, Quality of Life and Social Cohesion). Markus Jäntti and Timothy Smeeding want to thank Russell Sage for their chance to formulate and plan this volume during their 2007–2008 terms as RSF visiting scholars. All are indebted to the IRP staff for hosting a formulary conference and helping with editorial work and preparation of the manuscript, especially Deborah Johnson, David Chancellor, Dawn Duren, Coreen Williams, and Robin Snell. And we are indebted to April Rondeau and Suzanne Nichols at RSF for shepherding the volume along and chasing down its global list of authors when need be. The editors also want to thank all the author teams for their contributions, as well as two anonymous referees for their excellent comments, which greatly improved the volume.

Chapter 1

Introduction

TIMOTHY M. SMEEDING, ROBERT ERIKSON,
AND MARKUS JÄNTTI

T HE ABUNDANT evidence in the economic, demographic, and sociological literature of the association between parents' and children's
social positions makes it very clear that children's chances for a
good life are highly dependent on their social origins or socioeconomic
status (SES). More-educated, richer, two-earner couples at higher levels
of social and economic status have children later in life and do so in more
stable marriages. As a result, they have fewer children and can therefore
invest heavily in their children's upbringing. In contrast, younger parents
with less education, lower incomes, and larger numbers of children, as
well as lone parents and those in unstable relationships, are more limited
in the extent to which they can guarantee good lives for their children. For
instance, at the turn of the twenty-first century, and assuming that income
was shared equally within a household, U.S. parents in the highest
income quintile had the resources to spend $50,000 per year on a child,
while those in the bottom income group could afford to spend only $9,000
per year for food, housing, and all goods and services. The differences
were smaller for every other rich Organization for Economic Co-operation
and Development (OECD) nation studied (Moynihan, Smeeding, and
Rainwater 2004).

Family economic condition is not the only influence on the distribution
of life chances. The public sector in rich countries is concerned with promoting an equal start, and equal opportunities to succeed, for all children,
rich and poor alike. Policies to provide education, health care, and income
support are in place in all rich nations and may contribute to reaching
these goals. But some societies are more likely than others to equalize
opportunities. In many rich nations, growing inequalities of income and
wealth are widely expected to reduce opportunities for the less well-to-do,
while increasing them for the children of wealthier and higher-income parents. Indeed, evidence suggests that life chances are unequally distributed

1

in all rich nations, although the extent of these inequalities in life chances varies across countries. In this volume, we find that inequalities in economic status are quite persistent across generations, especially among children of low-income parents and, most especially, in the United States (Jäntti et al. 2006).

Why This Volume and Why Now?

This volume examines several ways in which inequality, advantage, and disadvantage are transmitted across generations and points to policy responses that might be deployed to improve social and economic mobility in an era of rising inequality. The chapters have been carefully chosen to shed light on the degree to which the social and economic mobility of children differs between countries and how those differences relate to public-sector provision and private family life. Although we cannot offer a full accounting of differences across all nations, we can assess many cross-national differences and the most likely drivers of those differences.

The volume takes a step toward answering these questions:

- What are the main transmission channels for mobility and immobility (stasis) across generations?

- How much of a role do inheritances play, and when do they play a role? Which inheritances—human (environment, behavior habits, genetic factors) or nonhuman (bequests, gifts)—are most important in promoting or retarding mobility? Or do both sets matter?

- What can social policy, especially education policy, do to affect changes in levels of social and economic mobility?

Comparable cross-national perspectives are more advantageous than those that concentrate on only one country because comparative studies can sometimes be interpreted as "natural experiments." That is, we observe levels of mobility in rich societies with very different levels of underlying inequality and with different policy stances toward subsidization of mobility-enhancing policies, taxation, and redistribution policy. It is likely that some of these differences in policies are not primarily driven by objectives related to mobility, and so quasi-experimental conditions are present.

The goal of this volume is to set a benchmark for the current understanding of how various aspects of mobility and inequality appear across countries with different levels of inequality and to add to our understanding of why mobility differs between countries, given different social structures and levels of inequality and poverty. Our conceptual framework for making cross-national comparisons is loosely based on a life-course approach. Parental heredity, early childhood upbringing, and the preschool and education systems affect the future earnings capacity of children, as well as adult earnings outcomes. Along the way, parental money transfers for meeting selective strategic needs of children (such as tuition and housing) and the social welfare state structure of each nation also help shape outcomes by the time children reach adulthood.

Each chapter discusses two or more countries and is thus explicitly cross-national in origin and focus. Each also focuses on some aspect of intergenerational mobility (IGM)—income, education, wealth, occupation, and so on. Some chapters are based on internationally comparable data sets; others summarize a broad set of technical papers on a specific aspect of IGM. The chapters are written by both sociologists and economists, and some reflect on both disciplinary approaches to intergenerational mobility. While these authors do not offer definitive answers to the questions posed earlier, we believe that they do help us decide which avenues of deeper exploration are most promising in unraveling the puzzles before us, especially those related to the effect of public policy on mobility.

We begin this introductory essay with a look at overall levels and trends in inequality and discuss the current evidence on mobility. We then provide an overview of the questions we pose and the answers given in the chapters that follow, highlighting the ways in which various factors affect children's chances for success over the life course. We should emphasize that the chapters are descriptive. In their attempts to illuminate the pathways through which advantage and disadvantage are transmitted over the life course, these analyses are not causal. In particular, they do not attempt to pin down the exact mechanisms by which some children succeed better than others. But they do trace the dimensions along which mobility differs within and across nations. We end with ideas for future research.

Trends in Inequality

The United States is the most economically unequal rich nation on Earth and has been so for at least the last forty years. Other Anglo-Saxon nations come in second, with Canada and the United Kingdom being somewhat below the United States in terms of overall inequality (figure 1.1). Nordic nations, such as Finland and Sweden, have had the least inequality but seem lately to approach other European nations that are in a middle position, such as Germany and the Netherlands. Only France has shown a trend toward declining inequality over the past few decades. While there has been some convergence of inequality across nations in recent years, the patterns shown here reflect those in the most harmonized cross-national data from the Luxembourg Income Study (LIS)[1] and earlier reviews (Brandolini and Smeeding 2009; Gottschalk and Smeeding 1997 [2001]; Jencks et al. 2010). The inequality of top incomes, taken from income tax records spanning the last century, also shows more or less the

Figure 1.1   Gini Index (Percentage) of Disposable Income

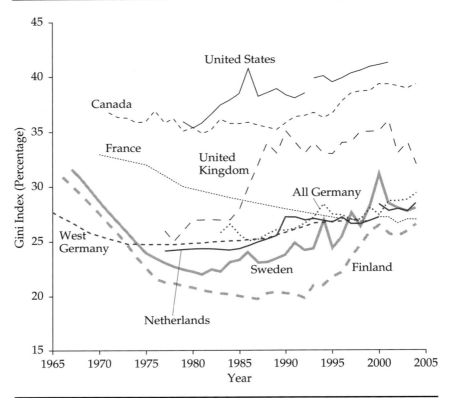

Source: Brandolini and Smeeding (2009), reproduced with permission.
Note: The Gini index varies from 0, complete equality, to 1, complete inequality.

same overall rankings (Atkinson, Piketty, and Saez 2010). Hence, the pattern of inequality orderings across nations is relatively fixed, but the trend is generally upward—since the early 1980s in some nations and in the later 1990s and 2000s in almost all others.

High income inequality may be easier to tolerate, and perhaps even be justified, if it is accompanied by a great deal of mobility across and within generations. But recent research in economics suggests that higher inequality may be related to less, not more, mobility (see, for example, Solon 2004). A worrisome consequence of rising economic inequality, then, is the possibility that its long-run effect is to reduce intergenerational mobility (Sawhill 2010). Families clearly have a strong interest in investing in the future social and economic well-being of their children. Although some of these investments may not require financial resources—such as reading to one's children when they are young—many obviously do, including payments for quality child care, purchases of books and computers, living in higher-priced neighborhoods with access to good public schools, assistance with college costs, and financial support for young adults to help them get started in their independent economic lives once their education is completed. As the length of the period to adulthood has grown in all rich nations, the positive effects of financial ability to help offspring have grown as well (Furstenberg 2010).

As financial resources have become more unequally distributed in a number of countries over the last three decades, and as prices for certain key child investment goods—such as high-quality child care, private schooling, and tertiary education—have increased, the differences in the capacities of rich and poor families to invest in their children also have become more unequal. It follows that unless these inequities are offset by public policies designed to moderate them, the children of the rich will have a better chance of staying rich in the future, and the children of the poor will have less chance of escaping poverty or low socioeconomic status.

This view is relatively new. The traditional view from the 1970s and earlier was that the role of family background in economic status in the United States, and more broadly in rich countries, was minor. This view was in part based on work by Gary Becker and Nigel Tomes (1979, 1986), which suggested a correlation or elasticity in log resources (earnings or income) between fathers and sons of around .10. In the early 1990s, this assumption was called into question by the work of Gary Solon (1992), David Zimmerman (1992), and others. In the United Kingdom, Anthony Atkinson (1981) had much earlier provided evidence of a substantially higher correlation. According to these newer estimates, the intergenerational income elasticity in the United States was at least .40. This result has been confirmed most recently in comparative work by Markus Jäntti and his colleagues (2006), Miles Corak (2004), and by two recent and very thorough reviews and meta-analyses of the evidence extant (Björklund and Jäntti 2009; Blanden 2009). Similar results referred to social mobility: Peter Blau and Otis Dudley Duncan (1967) claimed that social mobility in the United States was greater than in the United Kingdom, while Robert Erikson and John Goldthorpe (1985) showed that social fluidity (intergenerational occupational mobility) was much the same in the two nations.[2]

Trends in Mobility

While the trend in inequality is clear, trends in intergenerational correlations of income and earnings are still in some dispute; some historical and recent studies claim that mobility in the United States has declined (see, for example, Ferrie 2005; Levine and Mazumder 2007). Other more recent studies claim that there has been no change in the pattern of intergenerational mobility since the 1970s (Lee and Solon 2009). Still, it is hard to make a case that opportunity in America has *increased* since 1979—an era of high and rising inequality (Sawhill 2010). Indeed, if intergenerational mobility is being driven by cumulative forces of advantage and disadvantage over the life course, mobility outcomes may have become worse for the current generation of children because of increasingly higher inequality (DiPrete and Eirich 2006).

Among sociologists, the focus is on occupational mobility, and here Richard Breen and Ruud Luijkx (2005; see also Breen 2004) find that social fluidity has increased in France, Ireland, Sweden, Poland, Hungary, and the Netherlands, while they find no change in Germany and Britain. Breen and his colleagues (2009) likewise find decreasing associations between social origin and educational attainment in Sweden, the Netherlands, Britain, Germany, and France.

Although there is some evidence that parental investments in children have become more unequal over the past thirty years, analysis of the best multigenerational data available in the United States—from the Panel Study of Income Dynamics (PSID)—does not show a clear decline in inter-generational income mobility between children born in the 1950s and those born in the late 1970s, just before inequality began to rise (Lee and Solon 2009).[3] Part of the problem may be data-driven and based on meas-urement error. The individuals in the cohort born during the period of ris-ing inequality are only in their early thirties—still a bit too young to provide reliable estimates of lifetime income, especially when education and other forces have increased the amount of time it takes to reach adult-hood. Another distinct possibility is that the gradual but steady thirty-year rise in inequality in the United States is still too recent (or too small) to have the predicted effects on mobility (figure 1.1). Thus, it is difficult at the pres-ent time to assess change in mobility trends within the United States.

The situation in other countries is almost the same. For instance, in the United Kingdom successive birth cohorts have allowed for comparisons of intergenerational mobility across time. And these comparisons are equivocal on the changes in mobility, with sociologists claiming stasis (Erikson and Goldthorpe 2010) while economists argue that mobility may have declined (Blanden and Machin 2008) or remained constant (Nicoletti and Ermisch 2007).

The Cross-National Approach to Intergenerational Mobility Research

Current research on levels and trends in intergenerational income mobil-ity within nations is still in its infancy. It will take at least another decade or longer before we can assess comparable data within and across coun-tries to determine the trend in mobility since the onset of rising inequal-ity. But another way to understand mobility is through the prism of comparative cross-national studies, which are harmonized to the extent possible so that differences across nations (for instance, differences in school performance) can be established with some degree of certainty, not only in adulthood but also earlier in life.

Cross-national research on the share of family background in adult economic status has established that in almost all developed economies there is substantial intergenerational persistence of income. As we have seen, many other countries have less inequality than the United States, but do they have more or less mobility as well? Using comparable national data sets, Markus Jäntti and his colleagues (2006) find that the United States has the least income mobility, followed closely by the United Kingdom. Mobility up from the bottom of the distribution is especially low in the United States, while persistence at the top of the distribution is equally as high in the United States and the United Kingdom. In contrast, Finland, Denmark, Sweden, and Norway show a high degree of mobility and relatively low persistence across the income distribution.

How is income inequality correlated with mobility between one generation and the next (IGM)? A clear but not entirely consistent relationship between the two does show up in cross-national comparisons. Comparisons of national studies by Jo Blanden (2009) and Anders Björklund and Markus Jäntti (2009) suggest that inequality, measured at the parental level, and mobility, as measured by the intergenerational associations among nations in incomes or earnings, have overall rank correlations of .55 to .60, therefore establishing that, *on average*, inequality and IGM are correlated. But one can find both high and low mobility associated with various specific levels of inequality.

Figure 1.2 simplifies and summarizes the relationship between income inequality (measured by the Gini coefficient of income in the parental generation) and IGM elasticity—a measure of the strength of the relationship between the incomes of parents and the incomes of their grown children, which is inversely related to mobility. The figure includes eleven industrialized countries where both measures are now available, providing the accepted wisdom on which the chapters in this volume are based. The IGM data are drawn from a review of cross-national estimates of intergenerational mobility by Björklund and Jäntti (2009) supported by very similar estimates by Blanden (2009).

The inequality in income data comes from figure 1.1 and from the authors' own calculations in the studies reviewed by Björklund and Jäntti (2009) and Blanden (2009). It is important to note that the inequality estimates in table 1.1 are based on the level extant in the 1970s, when the parents' generation was economically active. It is also important to note that inequality then was at its lowest point in the past sixty years (since 1950) in almost all of these nations (Brandolini and Smeeding 2009).

As figure 1.2 suggests, the relationship between inequality and intergenerational elasticity is moderately positive across the eleven countries. One way of obtaining more insight into this relationship is to compare

Figure 1.2   Estimates of Intergenerational Income Mobility and Inequality for Fathers and Sons for Eleven Developed Countries

	Low parental inequality	Medium parental inequality	High parental inequality
High-medium persistence (low or medium mobility)		Germany	France Italy United Kingdom United States
Low persistence (high mobility)	Finland Norway Sweden	Denmark	Australia Canada

Source: Authors' calculations based on Blanden (2009) and Björklund and Jäntti (2009).
Notes: See table 1.1 for classifications of high, medium, and low. Japan is not included because of lack of data.

the degree of mobility in countries at similar levels of inequality. In figure 1.2, for example, it might be particularly instructive to consider a comparison between the United States and United Kingdom versus Australia and Canada. These countries have Gini coefficients between .30 and .37, but the income elasticity in the United Kingdom (.42) or the United States (.45) is more than double that in Canada or Australia (roughly .25 in each nation). There is less chance for comparison at the other end of the scale, as Finland, Norway, and Sweden have both low inequality and low persistence (that is, high mobility). Another two countries, Denmark and Canada, show intermediate levels of inequality, but Denmark has much higher rates of mobility. These countries contrast markedly with a third group of four countries that generally have high to medium levels of inequality but relatively low levels of intergenerational income mobility (Italy, the United States, France, and the United Kingdom). This is especially true of the United States and the United Kingdom, which show particularly low rates of mobility given their levels of inequality.[4]

How does intergenerational mobility compare with *current* levels of inequality? Table 1.1 uses the cross-national harmonized data from the Luxembourg Income Study (LIS) and from Andrea Brandolini and Timothy Smeeding (2009) to compare patterns of mobility (from figure 1.2) with inequality of current adult offspring income, as well as earlier parental (pre-1980) inequality.

Table 1.1   Comparing Mobility and Inequality

Nation	Persistence Elasticity[a] (Mobility–Immobility)	Inequality[b] (Pre-1980)	Inequality (1980 to 2004)
Finland	Low	Low	Low
Sweden	Low	Low	Low
Norway	Low	Low	Low
Denmark	Low	Medium	Low
Canada	Low	High	High
Australia	Low	High	High–Medium
Germany	Medium	Medium	Medium
United Kingdom	High	High	High
France	High	High	Medium
United States	High	High	High
Italy	High	High	High

Source: Authors' compilation based on Björklund and Jäntti (2009); Brandolini and Smeeding (2009); Blanden (2009); and Luxembourg Income Study (LIS) (n.d.).
[a]The higher the persistence elasticity, the lower the mobility: "low" = < .3; "medium" = .3 to .4; and "high" = > .4.
[b]The higher the Gini coefficient, the higher the household inequality: "low" = Gini of .20 to .25; "medium" = Gini of .26 to .30; "high" = Gini of .32 to .37.

There is a remarkable level of persistence over time in these relationships across nations, even if we know inequality has risen in all of them, save France, over the period in question. In fact, comparisons of inequality in both periods suggest a divergence between the four most mobile nations (the Nordic countries) and the three least mobile countries (the United States, the United Kingdom, and Italy). Germany has remained in the middle of both distributions; France has experienced declining inequality but low mobility; and Canada and Australia have low mobility for nations with high- to middle-level inequality.

The reason why it is important to emphasize this finding here is that many of the chapters in this volume, driven by differences in data sources, explore IGM in very different periods. Some view IGM over a lifetime, but others examine only outcomes among children whose parents were observed in the late 1990s and early 2000s. Hence, differences in generations observed are part of the story we tell here and the fact that *across*-country inequality rankings are not much changed is important (though levels *within* nations do differ over time).

Channels for Transmitting Persistence or Mobility

The channels through which intergenerational associations flow are less well known and more difficult to investigate. What factors matter for intergenerational persistence, and how do they compare across nations? Family, individuals' efforts, and the public sector are at the source of the differences we observe, but all three are intertwined in each nation. Family is important throughout the IGM process—especially in the early formative years, when mobility-related differences in test scores first appear—in part because it helps shape the habits and socio-behavioral traits that affect effort. The state can play a role, for example, by promoting universal early childhood education or by ensuring access to high-quality health care and providing income and social support.

Arguably, the association of the incomes of adult siblings—so-called sibling correlations—best captures the full effect of family background influences on outcomes such as higher education, since these capture parental factors that might affect offspring outcomes but are unrelated to parental income. Comparative research in this area is less well developed than that on IGM. But on this measure also, the U.S. results suggest that the impact of family background is large relative to its impact in other countries (Solon 1999).

A substantial body of literature suggests the theoretical mechanisms that affect the strength of the parent-child income or earnings association at various stages of the life course (see, for example, Grawe and Mulligan 2002). And recently there has been some serious discussion of the indirect influences of parents on children, such as intergenerational health trajectory determinants (Eriksson, Bratsberg, and Raaum 2005; Case and Paxson 2006).[5]

There are also many studies that empirically examine the importance of "mediating" factors to help overcome the advantages or disadvantages of inherited socioeconomic position at birth. These include those factors that are especially relevant and well accepted for policy, such as schools and education (Checchi, Ichino, and Rustichini 1999; Raaum, Sorensen, and Salvanes 2003). Socioeconomic background influences educational attainment in two ways: children from higher socioeconomic levels perform better at school, and they choose more academic educational tracks, even given previous performance (Boudon 1974; Erikson et al. 2005). The degree to which educational attainment is related to social background seems in recent years to have decreased in many European countries (Breen et al. 2009). One possible reason for this development may be the increase in the number of Europeans with tertiary education. Since the association between social origin and social class as an adult is lower among those with tertiary education than among those with less schooling, increasing numbers with higher education leads to a lower association between class origins and class destinations (Breen and Jonsson 2005). Indeed, Robert Haveman and Timothy Smeeding (2006) find that in all of the rich countries studied here, succeeding generations have increased levels of tertiary education, with the exception of Germany and the United States.[6]

Several studies include policy factors designed to limit the gradient in direct intergenerational money transfers, such as inheritance taxes. These transmission channels also include those factors that are not so immediately amenable to policy intervention and that depend on parenting, such as assortative mating (Ermisch, Francesconi, and Siedler 2006), and contextual factors, such as neighborhoods (Page and Solon 2003; Raaum, Sorenson, and Salvanes 2003, 2005; Lindahl 2010). In addition, gender differences in mobility are of great interest over and above assortative mating as more women develop labor market careers and incomes in advanced nations and increasingly become majorities among college students and graduates (Buchmann, DiPrete, and McDaniel 2008). Indeed, Oded Galor (2011) suggests that the rising demand for human capital being met by men and especially women is the major determinant of decreased fertility in rich nations.

At the present time, we cannot address all of these channels in the same data sets across two or more nations. But the studies mentioned here suggest that there may be significant differences in the effectiveness of the public institutions that different countries deploy in their efforts to provide equal opportunities to individuals born into families at different points along the income distribution. These differences may be due to institutional design, cost of investments in children, effective limits to parental choices, or other forces. For example, some countries may intervene earlier in the lives of disadvantaged individuals, and early intervention may be particularly effective. Or countries may differ in the sheer size of their social welfare expenditures or in the distribution of expenditures across various areas of social welfare, such as health or education. This could make a difference if expenditures in some areas are more effective than others in promoting mobility by promoting stability of parental incomes and low-cost access to mobility-enhancing institutions such as education and training. Finally, the effectiveness of institutions designed to promote mobility may depend in part on the amount of inequality they have to cope with. For example, a universal preschool program may be more or less effective depending on the differences in the private resources available to families and the abilities of high-SES parents to navigate their children to higher-quality preschools. Neighborhood differences in the quality of "universal" elementary and secondary education might work in the same way.

The Chapters in This Volume

The chapters are arranged in five parts, the first being longer-term framing studies. The next three parts follow the life course with a chapter on early childhood education, a set of three chapters that look at the role of education in promoting or retarding mobility, and then a chapter on the effects of intergenerational monetary transfers on mobility. The final chapter introduces the role of social and labor market institutions, which describe the context within which IGM takes place.

All of the chapters are based on harmonized cross-national data. Some use different measures of parental position and child outcomes: sociological (class, occupation), economic (wealth, earnings, income, parental education), and developmental (educational attainment, cognitive test scores). Some chapters include both economic and sociological measures (for example, chapters 2 and 4), and many of them combine economic and developmental approaches. The chapters in this volume therefore offer a rich and multidisciplinary set of approaches and tentative answers to the questions posed here.

Longer-Term Framing Studies of Parental SES and Adult-Child Outcomes

One good starting point for assessing the overall role of parents in intergenerational mobility is to look at studies that compare outcomes for adult children to outcomes for their parents who were observed twenty-five to thirty years ago. While multicountry studies, such as the one conducted by Jäntti and his colleagues (2006), are useful in this regard, they cannot possibly go into the depth that more nuanced treatments of pairs of countries can undertake. Chapters 2 through 5 make comparisons between three sets of countries to try to uncover the mechanisms found in the United States compared to the United Kingdom (chapter 2), Canada (chapter 3), and Germany (chapter 4). Each takes a different twist on the subject. In chapter 2, Jo Blanden, Kathryn Wilson, Robert Haveman, and Timothy Smeeding specify an empirical model of mobility based on both men's and women's earnings. Miles Corak, Lori Curtis, and Shelley Phipps look in chapter 3 at both patterns of income mobility and the public opinion surveys that help explain them in Canada versus the United States. Fabian Pfeffer suggests in chapter 4 that wealth rather than income is the primary provocateur of mobility differences between the United States and Germany. Finally, in chapter 5 Jan Jonsson, David Grusky, Reinhard Pollak, Matthew Di Carlo, and Carina Mood add an explicit sociological approach by examining the transfer of occupational status in the United States, Sweden, Germany, and Japan.

In chapter 2, Blanden and her co-authors use cross-national research to study the mechanisms underlying estimates of IGM in the United States and the United Kingdom, using harmonized data from the two nations. They deploy the PSID to allow analysis of the variables from earlier work (Blanden, Gregg, and Macmillan 2007), and vice versa. This integration allows them to study several pathways by which parental status is related to offspring status, including education, labor market attachment, occupation, marital status, and health. They find that these intergenerational linkages differ between the two nations in systematic ways. The findings suggest that in the United States, limited access to highly rewarded educational qualifications severely limits mobility, while the rigidity of the structure of occupational prestige and professional standing and training reduces mobility in the United Kingdom. In effect, they find that the two nations with similar levels of mobility and inequality appear to have different drivers of persistence and thus may require somewhat different policy solutions.

In chapter 3, Corak and his co-authors have compiled a comprehensive comparative study of the relationship between family economic background and adult outcomes in the United States and Canada. First, they discuss the implication in the existing literature that there are significant differences in the degree of intergenerational economic mobility between these two countries, with relative mobility being lower in the United States. Indeed, they find that the differences are the result of lower mobility at the very top and the very bottom of the earnings distribution. Next, they ask whether these differences reflect different underlying values of the citizens in these countries. Findings from comparable public opinion polls suggest that this is generally not the case. The citizens of both countries have a similar understanding of a successful life, one that is rooted in individual aspirations and freedom. They also have similar views on how these goals should be attained, but with one very important exception: Americans are more likely to see the public sector as hindering them in attaining their goals rather than helping them. Finally, Corak and his colleagues assess how the investments made in these countries affect the future of children through the family, the labor market, and public policy. Using a number of representative household surveys, they find that the configuration of all three sources of investment and support for children differs significantly across nations. Most importantly, they find that disadvantaged American children live in much more challenging circumstances where public policy does not play as strong a role in determining outcomes, as is the case in Canada.

Pfeffer argues in chapter 4 that research on intergenerational mobility typically conceptualizes and measures family background as any combination of parental education, parental occupation, and family income but overlooks family wealth, or net worth. Wealth is a dimension of economic well-being that is characterized by particularly large inequalities, and thus its neglect is troubling. Severe inequalities in familial wealth may well create unequal opportunities for children over and above those created by other socioeconomic characteristics of families. Recent research has begun to document strong and independent effects of parental wealth on children's educational opportunities in the United States (see, for example, Spilerman 2000).[7] Pfeffer extends this research by documenting the role of wealth (as compared to parental income or parental education) for the entire status-attainment process, including not only educational outcomes for children but also their own income and occupational attainment as adults. In assessing the degree to which the association between parental wealth and attainment differs by national context, he finds that the link between wealth inequality and inequality in opportunities differs between the United States and Germany, but that wealth outperforms parental income in explaining differences in mobility in both nations.

Jan Jonsson and his co-authors study intergenerational persistence in the United States, Sweden, Germany, and Japan using occupations as the fundamental building block. Although studies of social mobility conventionally use gradational scales (occupational prestige, socioeconomic status) or occupational aggregates (macro-class models), these authors add a "pure" occupational (micro-class) mechanism, whereby opportunities and associations of occupational inheritance drive intergenerational processes. They then use this model to examine cross-nationally common and divergent features of immobility, as well as trends in mobility. They find that all three forms of reproduction exist in all countries. Although the importance of macro-class and gradational reproduction has long been appreciated by mobility analysts, the results reported here indicate that occupational or micro-class immobility is also a prominent feature of contemporary mobility regimes. Unlike the other three chapters in part 1, chapter 4 reveals increasing mobility in all countries but no common pattern, suggesting that no single type of mobility increases in a similar way across countries. Instead, the model shows that declining intergenerational associations are produced in country-specific ways. These findings are consistent with those of Blanden and her colleagues, who compare only the United States and the United Kingdom. And they are consistent with the findings of Corak and Piraino (2010), who focus on fathers' and sons' employers and occupational characteristics (within Canada only).

Taken together, these chapters help frame the discussion of differences across generations as they present new information on patterns of transmission of intergenerational persistence across nations. They also find that despite similar levels of persistence across some nations, there may well be different factors operating to produce the observed differences. Most of all, they leave a great deal of room for the studies of intermediate mechanisms affecting children, as well as their outcomes as adults, in the following chapters.

Early Childhood and Preschool Factors

There is a belief that the most important influences on adult conditions are exerted early in life and mainly by parents (Heckman 2006, 2011; Knudsen et al. 2006). Parental income, heredity, habits, and aspirations affect children and therefore both educational and adult outcomes. But policy can perhaps intervene to level the playing field by promoting high-quality early childhood education among the most disadvantaged. In the United States, much attention has been paid in the past few years to the importance of early childhood education in leveling differences between the children of parents from various social classes (Heckman 2006). In part 2, we have two chapters that address early life deprivation issues.

The first is by Jane Waldfogel and Elizabeth Washbrook and addresses the early childhood education question. They compare the United States and the United Kingdom and find that each has very different public policy environments around early childhood education and benefits for low-income families. Both countries have implemented substantial, but different, reforms in these areas in the last decade. They document the income-related gaps in school readiness among two recent nationally representative cohorts of children from both nations and show that substantial income-related differences in cognitive ability are apparent among preschool-age children in both countries. Waldfogel and Washbrook then identify the reasons why low-income children fall behind and the areas in which interventions to close gaps may be most effective. The factors they consider are demographic characteristics, parenting behaviors, maternal and child health, and exposure to child care settings.

This chapter also briefly summarizes the relationship between income and early cognitive outcomes across the two countries for two cohorts born a decade apart: it documents the income-related gaps in school readiness for a cohort born in the early 1990s and then repeats the analysis for a cohort born in the early 2000s. Paying careful attention to comparability issues, Waldfogel and Washbrook explore how the overall degree of social inequality differs across the two countries and whether these differences have widened or narrowed following the period of reform. Contrasting the relative importance of these factors across the two countries allows them to draw some conclusions as to the extent to which the drivers of low-income children's lower levels of school readiness are common across the two countries, despite the very different public policy environments in the United Kingdom and the United States. They conclude that the United Kingdom has moved ahead of the United States in early childhood education for the most disadvantaged children.

In chapter 7, Greg Duncan, Kjetil Telle, Kathleen Ziol-Guest, and Ariel Kalil describe income dynamics in the United States and Norway and estimate associations between low childhood income and adult attainments, measured as late as age thirty-seven. Outcomes include years of completed schooling, adult earnings, and percentage of adult years with any unemployment. Inputs focus on low income during early childhood, that is, between a child's prenatal year and fifth birthday—which, as mentioned earlier, may be the most consequential period for children's life chances—as well as at later ages. Using data from the U.S. PSID and Norwegian Registries, Duncan and his colleagues describe cross-country distributional differences and estimate the relationship between adult outcomes and family economic conditions in early childhood, middle childhood (ages six to ten), and adolescence (ages eleven to fifteen). Correlations between childhood income and adult outcomes are generally weaker in the Norwegian data. In both data sets, these authors find statistically significant unfavorable associations between early childhood poverty and adult earnings. But these differences are much larger in the United States than in Norway. They close with a tantalizing discussion about the possibility that these results are related to the Scandinavian egalitarian welfare state's ability to mitigate the role of family background and the potentially correlated economic constraints imposed by low income in the family of origin. In the United States, where no such system exists, outcomes are poorer in all respects.

Education

Many economists and sociologists believe that schooling is a central mechanism for promoting inequality. The problems inherent in the idea of an education-based meritocracy have been intensively discussed in the United Kingdom (Young 1958; Goldthorpe 2003). Additional rungs of the education ladder beyond early childhood could also promote higher mobility (see, for example, Sawhill 2006; Sawhill and McLanahan 2006). But the evidence to date in the United States finds that there is less mobility and more persistence in the level and trend of educational mobility when viewed at the tertiary level—in matriculation to college or university—but especially in terms of college graduation rates (Haveman and Smeeding 2006).

Two chapters in part 3 address these differences, each with a focus on pre-tertiary education as a mediating treatment that can influence parental advantages or disadvantages. In chapter 8, John Ermisch and Chiara Pronzato show that parents' education is an important, but hardly exclusive, part of the common family background that generates a positive correlation between the educational attainments of siblings. Taken alone, the correlation between the educational attainments of parents and those of their children overstates considerably the causal effect of parents' education on the education of their children. The estimates based on Norwegian mothers of twins (which are then compared to similar U.S. children) indicate that an additional year of either mother's or father's education increases their children's education by as little as one-tenth of a year. Hence, there is hope that public intervention in the education process can help modify outcomes based on parental status alone. There is some evidence that the mother's effect is larger among less-educated parents and the father's effect is larger among better-educated parents, and that father's education has a larger effect than that of mother's in both the United States and Norway. But the difference in the estimated parental pathways is much larger and statistically significant in the United States. One explanation for a smaller maternal effect is that better-educated mothers work more in paid employment and spend less time interacting with their children, but Ermisch and Pronzato find no evidence to support this hypothesis. Indeed, children of otherwise identical Norwegian mothers (on a number of criteria, including both parents' education) who work *more* in paid employment complete *more* years of education. Finally, these authors find that mother's education is more important for daughters than for sons.

John Jerrim and John Micklewright argue in chapter 9 that literature on the transmission of socioeconomic status from parents to children does not typically pay much attention to gender differences in either generation. Parents clearly pass on a measure of their advantage or disadvantage to their children that affects both cognitive and behavioral outcomes. But whether fathers pass on more or less than mothers, and whether it is sons or daughters who benefit more, is rarely the focus. By contrast, Jerrim and Micklewright consider each parent and their different links to outcomes, examining the associations between fathers and sons, fathers and daughters, mothers and sons, and mothers and daughters. Using data from the 2003 round of the Program for International Student Assessment (PISA), they relate children's cognitive ability as recorded in standardized tests of mathematics, science, and reading skills at age fifteen to the years of education of mothers and of fathers. Using "effect" without implying causality, they find that it is more common for father's education to have a greater effect than mother's education. Second, this appears to be particularly true for sons, although there are plenty of countries that are counterexamples. Third, there seems to be more variation across countries in the gender differences in the parents' generation than the children's. Fourth, there is some suggestion that mothers' education has more effect on their daughters' ability than on their sons', yet the difference is often small. Fifth, it seems that we should consider not only the relative importance of each parent's education but also how they combine. The results suggest that parents' education typically combines positively; mother's education and father's education (assortative mating) appear complementary in their effect on the child's ability.

Direct Monetary Transfers

Another neglected intergenerational transfer mechanism not well integrated into the mobility literature cited here is direct monetary transfers, whether in the form of inter vivos gifts or inheritances at the death of parents or grandparents (Wolff 2003). These include monetary and other inheritances, but also direct access to jobs or occupations (see Corak and Piraino 2010) and help paying for key investment goods for the younger generation, such as higher education or housing. Money that parents give their adult children may therefore be important for financing children's education to allow them to avoid debt, for buying a first home, for relaxing credit constraints, or for overcoming a transitory income shock. Financial transfers may extend economic disparities across generations if the wealthy transfer considerable resources to their children but middle-class and poor households do not.

In chapter 10, Julie Zissimopoulos and James Smith examine annual gifts of money from parents to adult children in the United States and ten European countries, using the 2004 waves of the Health and Retirement Study (HRS) and the Survey of Health, Aging, and Retirement in Europe (SHARE). Utilizing the long panel of the HRS, they also study the long-term behavior of parental monetary giving to children across families and within a family. They find that in all countries many parents give money to children, but many also do not. In Europe, the average amount given is low, about 500 euros annually per child. The amount given varies positively with parental socioeconomic status, but negatively with public social expenditures, suggesting an insurance role for the welfare state. In the short term, parents in the United States give money to a child to compensate for low earnings or to satisfy an immediate need, such as schooling. Over sixteen years, U.S. parents gave an average of about $38,000 to all their children, or about five times as much as the annual donations in Europe. Further, 5 percent gave over $140,000, and a large fraction gave persistently. Overall, the annual amount of money that parents give their adult children in any country is not enough to substantively affect the distribution of resources within or between families in the next generation, although the strategic timing of transfers for schooling or housing may have a significant impact on an individual child's future outcomes.

Annual parental transfers for college-age children in school in the United States are substantially higher than average transfers to all children. The effect of parental transfers for higher education on intergenerational mobility in the United States depends in part on whether this financing is essential in the schooling decision. The findings are consistent with those of Haveman and Smeeding (2006), who find that children of high-income parents are more likely to graduate from college and to graduate without debt. In Australia, Canada, and Europe, where public financing of higher education is almost universal, tuition costs are less of a factor. (For a comparison of the cost of tertiary education in the United States and Canada, see Belley, Frenette, and Lochner 2010.)

The magnitude of inter vivos transfers over time is simply not large enough by itself to affect the distribution of resources within or between families in the next generation in any nation. But the timing and level of financial transfers—for example, to smooth consumption after an income shock or to finance higher education—may have a significant impact on the longer-term welfare of a child. For instance, annual parental transfers for college-age children in the United States were 50 percent of average college tuition costs in 2005, and 30 percent of average tuition plus room and board expenses in that year.

Social and Labor Market Institutions

The literature on intergenerational income mobility provides few clues about the role of welfare state or institutional labor market features on mobility across generations, possibly because the main effects would be indirect, such as the influence of parental leave and child care on maternal labor supply. Bernt Bratsberg and his colleagues (2007) show evidence that the Nordic countries have been comparatively effective in reducing the mobility disadvantages associated with having a low-earning father (although they have done less to diminish the advantages of being rich). This may be because of Norwegian welfare state institutions. Yet the same evidence could with equal plausibility be ascribed to the highly compressed wage structure within the Nordic countries, which benefits low-wage workers in particular. Intergenerational mobility therefore takes place within a set of social, political, and economic institutions that may accentuate or attenuate persistence across generations.

Brian Nolan, Gøsta Esping-Andersen, Christopher Whelan, Bertrand Maître, and Sander Wagner are among the first to address this question in a cross-national context. Their chapter aims to identify how welfare state institutions more broadly might affect patterns of intergenerational mobility, particularly emphasizing their role in alleviating the adverse effects of poverty and disadvantage. In theory, policies and institutions, as well as macroeconomic and historical context, have been identified as crucial in shaping patterns of social mobility. But apart from education, empirical research has contributed little in the way of concrete evidence on how these institutions affect transmission. One of the basic problems that efforts to identify the causal "smoking gun" face is that it is very difficult to know whether lower inequality in and of itself promotes mobility, or whether it is the same institutions and policies that underpin lower inequality that also influence mobility. In the latter scenario, low inequality and high mobility (see figure 1.2) are the joint outcome of some underlying combination of factors. National education, labor market, tax, and social protection features that influence cross-sectional inequality might have—and may indeed be designed to have—a direct effect on mobility as well. Equalizing opportunities has always been an important element in policies to reduce inequality. In most countries, this has primarily been pursued by democratizing access to education. But there are clearly other aspects of the welfare state—such as social security, labor market regulation, health care, housing, and family policies—that can influence mobility. Unfortunately, we have almost no empirical research that addresses this question. Nolan and his colleagues conclude by asking what research strategies have the greatest potential for increasing our understanding of the impact of welfare state institutions. One avenue would be to focus on specific barriers to mobility and how public policy can reduce them (see, for example, Jencks and Tach 2006). Another complementary strategy is to compare different countries over time, measuring trends in different aspects of mobility and relating these to variations in institutions and policies.

Next Steps: The Direction of Future Research

This volume contributes to a better understanding of the nature of the persistence of economic and social status across generations. It is clear that parental influences matter, both early on and later in life. Education plays a large role in outcomes, but in ways that vary across nations. Although the United States tends to display less mobility compared to other nations, it is important to bear in mind that many U.S. policies and institutions are likely to increase mobility from what it would have been in their absence. It should be noted that most of the findings reported here are tentative in that they point to various possible factors that account for cross-national differences in mobility.

In particular, future research should use data for more nations and data with cross-nationally comparable tests of cognitive and noncognitive abilities and academic achievement to examine the importance of parental background for these important child outcomes. Such studies could help us identify the relevance to adult outcomes of mobility-relevant skills formed at various points during an individual's development, the role played by parental resources in those outcomes, and whether policy influences these mobility-enhancing factors at various stages of the life course. Using data like these, plus administrative data in countries where they are available, we believe that it would be possible to undertake a small number of strategically selected cross-national studies to estimate correlations of test scores and other childhood outcomes with parental income and/or socioeconomic status at various points along the life course and address various factors that impede or enhance mobility. This is the next step in cross-national mobility research.

Notes

1. See "LIS Key Figures" at: http://www.lisproject.org/key-figures/key-figures.htm (accessed January 20, 2011).

2. "Social fluidity" was earlier called "relative mobility" and is best understood as the association between social origins and social destinations in terms of social class. Social fluidity is typically measured as a set of odds ratios and is thus abstracted from the mobility that follows when the origin distributions differ from the destination distributions. For more details, see Erikson and Goldthorpe (1992, 56).
3. However, see Mazumder (2007) and Aaronson and Mazumder (2008), who reach different conclusions.
4. One anomaly in these figures is the downward trend in inequality in France coupled with the high level of persistence (low level of IGM) found there.
5. Health is not explicitly dealt with except as it frames the mobility patterns we observe. Only one chapter in the volume (chapter 2) models health status, and it appears to have only a minor influence on the overall outcomes in each nation studied.
6. Also, labor markets in different countries reward educational qualifications differently, owing to relative supply and demand and labor market institutions that limit or expand the level of earnings for any given set of qualifications.
7. In chapter 10, Julie Zissimopoulos and James Smith present several ways in which wealth can be transferred across generations at strategic times in children's lives.

References

Aaronson, Daniel, and Bhashkar Mazumder. 2008. "Intergenerational Economic Mobility in the United States, 1940 to 2000." *Journal of Human Resources* 43(1): 139–72.

Atkinson, Anthony B. 1981. "On Intergenerational Income Mobility in Britain." *Journal of Post-Keynesian Economics* 3(2): 194–218.

Atkinson, Anthony B., Thomas Piketty, and Emmanuel Saez. 2010. "Top Incomes in the Long Run of History." In *Top Incomes: A Global Perspective*, edited by Anthony B. Atkinson and Thomas Piketty. Oxford: Oxford University Press.

Becker, Gary S., and Nigel Tomes. 1979. "An Equilibrium Theory of the Distribution of Income and Intergenerational Mobility." *Journal of Political Economy* 87(6): 1153–89.

———. 1986. "Human Capital and the Rise and Fall of Families." *Journal of Labor Economics* 4(3): S1–39.

Belley, Philippe, Marc Frenette, and Lance Lochner. 2010. "Post-Secondary Attendance by Parental Income: Comparing the United States and Canada." Working paper 2010-3. London, Ontario: University of Western Ontario, CIBC Centre for Human Capital and Productivity.

Björklund, Anders, and Markus Jäntti. 2009. "Intergenerational Mobility and the Role of Family Background." In *Oxford Handbook of Inequality*, edited by Wiemer Salverda, Brian Nolan, and Timothy Smeeding. Oxford: Oxford University Press.

Blanden, Jo. 2009. "How Much Can We Learn from International Comparisons of Intergenerational Mobility?" Working paper 111. London: London School of Economics, Center for the Economics of Education.

Blanden, Jo, Paul Gregg, and Lindsey Macmillan. 2007. "Accounting for Intergenerational Income Persistence: Noncognitive Skills, Ability, and Education." *Economic Journal* 117(519): 43–60.

Blanden, Jo, and Stephen Machin. 2008. "Up and Down the Intergenerational Ladder in Britain: Past Changes and Future Prospects." *National Institute Economic Review* 205(1): 101–16.

Blau, Peter M., and Otis Dudley Duncan. 1967. *The American Occupational Structure.* New York: Wiley.

Boudon, Raymond. 1974. *Education, Opportunity, and Social Inequality: Changing Prospects in Western Societies.* New York: Wiley.

Brandolini, Andrea, and Timothy Smeeding. 2009. "Cross-National Patterns of Inequality." In *The Oxford Handbook of Inequality*, edited by Wiemer Salverda, Brian Nolan, and Timothy Smeeding. Oxford: Oxford University Press.

Bratsberg, Bernt, Knut Roed, Oddbjørn Raaum, Robin Naylor, Markus Jäntti, Tor Eriksson, and Eva Österbacka. 2007. "Nonlinearities in Intergenerational Earnings Mobility: Consequences for Cross-Country Comparisons." *Economic Journal* 117(519): C72–92.

Breen, Richard, ed. 2004. *Social Mobility in Europe.* Oxford: Oxford University Press.

Breen, Richard, and Jan Jonsson. 2005. "Inequality of Opportunity in Comparative Perspective: Recent Research on Educational Attainment and Social Mobility." *Annual Review of Sociology* 31: 223–43.

Breen, Richard, and Ruud Luijkx. 2005. "Social Mobility in Europe Between 1970 and 2000." In *Social Mobility in Europe*, edited by Richard Breen. Oxford: Oxford University Press.

Breen, Richard, Ruud Luijkx, Walter Müller, and Reinhard Pollak. 2009. "Non-persistent Inequality in Educational Attainment: Evidence from Eight European Countries." *American Journal of Sociology* 114(5): 1475–1521.

Buchmann, Claudia, Thomas DiPrete, and Anne McDaniel. 2008. "Gender Inequalities in Education." *Annual Review of Sociology* 34: 319–37.

Case, Anne, and Christina Paxson. 2006. "Children's Health and Social Mobility." *Future of Children* 16(2): 151–73.

Checchi, Daniele, Andrea Ichino, and Aldo Rustichini. 1999. "More Equal but Less Mobile? Education Financing and Intergenerational Mobility in Italy and in the United States." *Journal of Public Economics* 74(3): 351–93.

Corak, Miles, ed. 2004. *Generational Income Mobility in North America and Europe.* Cambridge: Cambridge University Press.

Corak, Miles, and Patrizio Piraino. 2010. "The Intergenerational Transmission of Employers." Discussion paper 4819. Bonn, Germany: Institute for the Study of Labor (IZA).

DiPrete, Thomas, and Greg Eirich. 2006. "Cumulative Advantage as a Mechanism for Inequality: A Review of Theory and Evidence." *Annual Review of Sociology* 32: 271–97.

Eriksson, Tor, Bernt Bratsberg, and Oddbjørn Raaum. 2005. "Earnings Persistence Across Generations: Transmission Through Health?" Memorandum 35/2005. Oslo, Norway: University of Oslo, Department of Economics.

Erikson, Robert, and John H. Goldthorpe. 1985. "Are American Rates of Social Mobility Exceptionally High? New Evidence on an Old Issue." *European Sociological Review* 1(1): 1–22.

———. 1992. *The Constant Flux: A Study of Class Mobility in Industrial Societies.* Oxford: Clarendon Press.

———. 2010. "Income and Class Mobility Between Generations in Great Britain: The Problem of Divergent Findings from the Data Sets of Birth Cohort Studies." *British Journal of Sociology* 61(2): 211–30.

Erikson, Robert, John H. Goldthorpe, Michelle Jackson, Meir Yaish, and David R. Cox. 2005. "On Class Differentials in Educational Attainment." *Proceedings of the National Academy of Sciences* 102(27): 9730–33.

Ermisch, John, Marco Francesconi, and Thomas Siedler. 2006. "Intergenerational Mobility and Marital Sorting." *Economic Journal* 116(513): 659–79.

Ferrie, Joseph P. 2005. "History Lessons: The End of American Exceptionalism? Mobility in the United States Since 1850." *Journal of Economic Perspectives* 19(3): 199–215.

Furstenberg, Frank F. 2010. "On a New Schedule: Transitions to Adulthood and Family Change." *Future of Children* 20(1): 67–87.

Galor, Oded. 2011. "The Demographic Transition: Causes and Consequences." *Cliometrica*. DOI: 10.1007/s11698-011-0062-7.

Goldthorpe, John H. 2003. "The Myth of Education-Based Meritocracy." *New Economy* 10(4): 234–39.

Gottschalk, Peter, and Timothy M. Smeeding. 1997. "Cross-National Comparisons of Earnings and Income Inequality." *Journal of Economic Literature* 35(2): 633–87. (Reprinted in *The Economics of the Welfare State*, edited by Nicholas Barr [Cheltenham: Edward Elgar, 2001])

Grawe, Nathan D., and Casey B. Mulligan. 2002. "Economic Interpretations of Intergenerational Correlations." *Journal of Economic Perspectives* 16(3): 45–58.

Haveman, Robert, and Timothy M. Smeeding. 2006. "The Role of Higher Education in Social Mobility." *Future of Children* 16(2): 125–50.

Heckman, James J. 2006. "Skill Formation and the Economics of Investing in Disadvantaged Children." *Science* 312(June 30): 1900–902.

———. 2011. "The American Family in Black and White: A Post-Racial Strategy for Improving Skills to Promote Equality." Discussion paper 5495. Bonn, Germany: Institute for the Study of Labor (IZA).

Jäntti, Markus, Bernt Bratsberg, Knut Røed, Oddbjørn Raaum, Robin Naylor, Eva Österbacka, Anders Björklund, and Tor Eriksson. 2006. "American Exceptionalism in a New Light: A Comparison of Intergenerational Earnings Mobility in the Nordic Countries, the United Kingdom, and the United States." Discussion paper 1938. Bonn, Germany: Institute for the Study of Labor (IZA).

Jencks, Christopher, Ann Owens, Tracey Shollenberger, and Queenie Zhu. 2010. "How Has Rising Economic Inequality Affected Children's Educational Outcomes?" Working paper. Cambridge, Mass.: Harvard University, Kennedy School of Government and Department of Sociology (August 14).

Jencks, Christopher, and Laura Tach. 2006. "Would Equal Opportunity Mean More Mobility?" In *Mobility and Inequality: Frontiers of Research from Sociology and Economics*, edited by Samuel Morgan, David Grusky, and Gary Fields. Stanford, Calif.: Stanford University Press.

Knudsen, Eric I., James J. Heckman, Judy L. Cameron, and Jack P. Shonkoff. 2006. "Economic, Neurobiological, and Behavioral Perspectives on Building America's Future Workforce." *Proceedings of the National Academy of Sciences* 103(27): 10155–62.

Lee, Chul-In, and Gary Solon. 2009. "Trends in Intergenerational Income Mobility." *Review of Economics and Statistics* 91(November): 766–72.

Levine, David I., and Bhashkar Mazumder. 2007. "The Growing Importance of Family and Community: An Analysis of Changes in the Sibling Correlation in Earnings." *Industrial Relations* 46(1): 7–28.

Lindahl, Lena. 2010. "A Comparison of Family and Neighborhood Effects on Grades, Test Scores, Educational Attainment, and Income Evidence from Sweden." *Journal of Economic Inequality* 1–20. DOI: 10.1007/s10888-010-9144-1.

Luxembourg Income Study (LIS). n.d. *Luxembourg Income Study* [database]. Available at: http://www.lisproject.org (accessed May 12, 2011).

Mazumder, Bhashkar. 2007. "Trends in Intergenerational Mobility." *Industrial Relations* 46(1): 1–6.

Moynihan, Daniel Patrick, Timothy M. Smeeding, and Lee Rainwater. 2004. *The Future of the Family*. New York: Russell Sage Foundation.

Nicoletti, Cheti, and John F. Ermisch. 2007. "Intergenerational Earnings Mobility: Changes Across Cohorts in Britain." *B.E. Journal of Economic Analysis and Policy* 7(2, Contributions): article 9.

Page, Marianne, and Gary Solon. 2003. "Correlations Between Brothers and Neighboring Boys in Their Adult Earnings: The Importance of Being Urban." *Journal of Labor Economics* 21(October): 831–55.

Raaum, Oddbjørn, Erik Sorensen, and Kjell G. Salvanes. 2003. "The Impact of Primary School Reform on Educational Stratification: A Norwegian Study of Neighborhood and School Mate Correlations." *Swedish Economic Policy Review* 10(2): 142–69.

———. 2005. "The Neighborhood Is Not What It Used to Be." *Economic Journal* 116(1): 278–300.

Sawhill, Isabel. 2006. "Opportunity in America: The Role of Education." Brookings policy brief. Washington, D.C.: Brookings Institution Press.

———. 2010. "Do We Face a Permanently Divided Society?" Paper presented to the Tobin Conference. Boston (May 2).

Sawhill, Isabel, and Sara McLanahan. 2006. "Opportunity in America, Introducing the Issue." *The Future of Children* 16(2): 3–17.

Solon, Gary. 1992. "Intergenerational Income Mobility in the United States." *American Economic Review* 82(3): 393–408.

———. 1999. "Intergenerational Mobility in the Labor Market." In *Handbook of Labor Economics,* vol. 3A, edited by Orley Ashenfelter and David Card. Amsterdam: North-Holland.

———. 2004. "A Model of Intergenerational Mobility Variation over Time and Place." In *Generational Income Mobility in North America and Europe,* edited by Miles Corak. Cambridge: Cambridge University Press.

Spilerman, Seymour. 2000. "Wealth and Stratification Processes." *Annual Review of Sociology* 26: 497–524.

Wolff, Edward N. 2003. "The Impact of Gifts and Bequests on the Distribution of Wealth." In *Death and Dollars,* edited by Alicia H. Munnell and Annika Sundén. Washington, D.C.: Brookings Institution Press.

Young, Michael. 1958. *Rise of the Meritocracy.* London: Thames and Hudson.

Zimmerman, David J. 1992. "Regression Toward Mediocrity in Economic Stature." *American Economic Review* 82(3): 409–29.

PART I

LONGER-TERM FRAMING STUDIES OF PARENTAL SES AND ADULT-CHILD OUTCOMES

Chapter 2

Understanding the Mechanisms Behind Intergenerational Persistence: A Comparison of the United States and Great Britain

JO BLANDEN, KATHRYN WILSON,
ROBERT HAVEMAN, AND TIMOTHY M. SMEEDING

NUMEROUS U.S. and European studies in economics and sociology have attempted to measure and compare the extent of social mobility across nations with different economic systems, occupational hierarchies, and values.[1] Much of the economics research is reviewed in Gary Solon (2002), Miles Corak (2006), Anders Björklund and Markus Jäntti (1997, 2009), and Jo Blanden (forthcoming). Recent cross-national studies by sociologists and demographers are also relevant, including Robert Erikson and John Goldthorpe (2002), Richard Breen and Jan Jonsson (2005), and Emily Beller and Michael Hout (2006).

Research from both traditions provides evidence that the overall level of social mobility in the United States and the United Kingdom,[2] once thought to be greater than elsewhere, is little different and arguably lower than that in other rich Western nations.[3] The economics estimates also indicate an underlying positive relationship between income inequality and intergenerational income persistence.[4] Sociologists and demographers find that intergenerational persistence is linked to social class measured by occupation or parental education.[5]

In this study, we build on this cross-national research from both traditions, using harmonized data to study the mechanisms underlying estimates of relative intergenerational mobility in the United States and Great Britain. We examine several pathways by which parental status is related to offspring status, including education, labor market attachment, occupation, marriage, and health. We begin by describing our methodology and data and then present results for men and women separately, before summarizing our results and offering some thoughts on the nature of the interventions that may be effective for increasing mobility in the two nations.

Conceptual Framework

Our empirical decomposition of the parent-offspring linkage is based on the intergenerational human capital investment framework proposed by Gary Becker and Nigel Tomes (1986). In this model, parents are altruistic and benefit from both their own consumption and that of their offspring. The earnings (wages) of offspring depend on their innate ability (which, by assumption, is positively correlated with parental ability and earnings because of genetic transmission and environmental culture) and the value of their human capital (for example, their educational attainment). Parents forgo some of their own consumption in order to invest in offspring human capital; investment faces diminishing marginal returns and (by assumption) the returns to parental investment are positively related to offspring ability.

With smoothly functioning capital markets, parents equate the market interest rate on borrowing with the present value of the marginal return to investing in offspring. If borrowing is not possible, the opportunity cost of investing (for example, parents' reductions in their own consumption) is increased. With or without credit constraints, the level of investment in children—and hence offspring income—depends on both offspring ability (by assumption) and parental income. And with credit constraints, the link between parental and offspring income is stronger.

In this context, we would expect some societies to have greater intergenerational mobility than others. Comparing two otherwise identical societies, the Becker-Tomes model would suggest greater mobility in the country with (1) the more smoothly functioning capital market; (2) weaker intergenerational transmission of education and occupation preferences; (3) more equal quality of schooling for children; and (4) more homogenous levels of education, which limit the inherent advantages of dual highly educated parents in providing guidance, mentoring, and financial support to their children.

Our decomposition approach separates total intergenerational persistence into the relationship between parental income and the child's characteristics (for example, education, health, and occupation) and the monetary returns to those characteristics. This framework has clear parallels with the Becker-Tomes model; investments are to some extent influenced by parental income, and this, combined with the return on those investments, determines the final link between incomes across generations.

Our empirical analysis will be guided by common observations regarding important differences in the education, health care, and labor market processes in these two nations. For example, the model highlights the linkage between parents' income and offspring's wages through offspring human capital (for example, education and health). Differences in the education systems between the two countries are large, especially at the tertiary level. For example, while the United Kingdom allocates about 1.3 percent of its GDP to the support of tertiary schooling, the United States allocates more than double this level. Nearly two-thirds of U.S. spending is private, while about two-thirds of British tertiary spending is public.[6] The model combines this linkage with the returns to human capital, implying that nations with fewer constraints on market wage differences and hence large and growing earnings and income inequality are likely to have high rates of return on human capital investment, relative to nations with less innovation and more rigid labor markets.

These considerations pose several interesting questions. Is the connection between parental resources and offspring schooling closer in the United States than in the United Kingdom, as the reliance on private spending for tertiary schooling in the United States would imply? Is the offspring-earnings return to schooling in the United Kingdom greater than that in the United States, as the constrained supply of tertiary resources would suggest? Or does the less restrictive labor market and relatively high and faster-growing wage and income inequality in the United States suggest higher returns to education there than in the United Kingdom?

Health status is also an element of human capital. Although health status is in part behavioral (for example, smoking), the vastly different health systems in the two nations factor into the health status of individuals as well. The Organization for Economic Co-operation and Development reports that, in the United States, 25 percent of above-median-income people forgo health care because of cost, while only 8 percent of their counterparts in the United Kingdom forgo care. For those with less than median income, the percentages are 52 percent and 9 percent for the two countries, respectively.[7] Access to health care for youths in the United States is largely dependent on parental health insurance and public programs such as Medicaid; lower-income youths have less and lower-quality health care than those from higher-income families. This implies a positive relationship between parental income and offspring earnings through the health status and health care access linkage.

The framework also suggests that differences between the two countries in occupational structure are relevant to understanding intergenerational linkages. Historically it was commonly believed that class was less subject to intergenerational transmission in the United States than in Europe (see, for example, the writings of Tocqueville, Marx, and Engels). However, empirical evidence suggests that any difference that was present in the past had been closed by the second half of the twentieth century (Erikson and Goldthorpe 1985; Long and Ferrie 2007). Nonetheless, there is still a perception among some sociologists (for example, Devine 1997) that social class background has a greater influence on life chances in the

United Kingdom compared with the United States. In addition, recent work by Jan Jonsson and his colleagues (2009) uses the United States as an exemplar nation for weak "big-class" identification, such that social class matters less for inheritance than it does in other nations.[8] Is offspring occupation more closely linked to parental economic status in the United Kingdom compared to the United States? Is the association between earnings and occupational prestige also larger?

Is it possible that the linkage between parental and offspring status also operates through the marriage market? Both nations have seen major changes in marital and cohabitation status over recent decades. The United States has higher marriage rates, but also higher divorce rates, than the United Kingdom. In addition, the median age of marriage is lower in the United States.[9] Is the link between parental income and marriage opportunities for offspring greater in the United States than in the United Kingdom? Is the return to marriage in the United Kingdom smaller than it is in the United States, as the difference in rates between the two nations would suggest?

Our exploration of the linkages suggested by this framework may also point to broad strategies for increasing social mobility. For example, if constrained resource allocation to education leads to a closer link between parental resources and offspring schooling, perhaps an education strategy that targets children from low-income families will be effective in increasing social mobility. Or if occupational status explains a large share of the level of economic persistence between parents and offspring, perhaps policies to increase access to professional occupations should be considered. In the same way, the magnitude of other linkages that we explore may point to different policy strategies.

It should be noted that we are not able to model or control for many types of difference across families that also affect mobility. These are captured mainly by the independent effect of parental income and the error terms in our estimates. For instance, if parental income is important for the educational attainment and economic well-being of children because of inherited and learned cognitive skills, we still cannot capture the parents' neighborhood choices or the socio-emotional (noncognitive) effects of parental and home culture on child outcomes. There are no data sources or complete structural models by which we can compare all aspects of parental inputs to child outputs from cradle to adulthood. Hence, the best we can do is to attempt to isolate various channels by which status is transmitted from parent to child. We return to this later.

Estimation Methods

The standard approach to measuring intergenerational mobility (IGM) follows from estimating the regression model shown in equation 2.1:

$$\ln Y_i^{child} = \alpha + \beta \ln Y_i^{parent} + \mu_i \qquad (2.1)$$

where the estimated beta ($\hat{\beta}$) expresses the degree of intergenerational persistence (with the degree of IGM $= 1 - \hat{\beta}$). For example, if $\beta = 0.4$, it is estimated that, on average, 40 percent of the difference between the incomes of parents is reflected in the difference in income of their offspring.

We also report an alternative measure of intergenerational persistence: the correlation of parents' and children's incomes. This adjusts for differences in income variance between the two generations. As before, the extent of mobility can be thought of as measured by $1 - r$.

$$r = Corr_{y^p,y^c} = \beta \left(\frac{SD^{y^p}}{SD^{y^c}} \right) \qquad (2.2)$$

The intergenerational correlation provides a measure of rank mobility between the generations and provides an interesting comparison with the intergenerational elasticity. As argued by Anders Björklund and Markus Jäntti (2009), it provides a measure that is not mechanically affected by changes in inequality across generations.

Simple Decomposition

Following the procedures in Blanden, Gregg, and Macmillan (2007), we then decompose the intergenerational β into two parts:

1. A measure of the extent to which parental income is related to a pathway factor (for example, education)[10]:

$$ED_i^{child} = \alpha_{ed} + \lambda_{ed} \ln Y_i^{parent} + \varepsilon_{1i} \qquad (2.3)$$

2. A measure of the payoff of a pathway factor for the offspring:

$$\ln Y_i^{child} = \omega_1 + \rho_{ed} ED_i^{child} + v_{1i} \qquad (2.4)$$

The overall intergenerational elasticity is then decomposed by the formula:

$$\beta = \lambda_{ed} \rho_{ed} + Cov\left(v_{1i}, \ln Y_i^{parent}\right) / Var\left(\ln Y_i^{parent}\right) \qquad (2.5)$$

The first term of equation 2.5, $\lambda_{ed}\rho_{ed}$, is the component of β explained by (in this case) education; the second term is the unexplained component of β. This simple framework measures the unconditional strength of the education linkage between parental and offspring incomes, without considering the interaction of education with other pathways by which parental and offspring status are linked.

While this unconditional example illustrates our decomposition framework using a single pathway variable, our empirical analysis considers five intervening "pathway factors"—offspring education, labor market attachment, marital status, health, and occupation. In this context, there are interactions between the pathway variables, and these need to be accommodated in the estimation.

To take account of the influence of the different interacting pathways, we adopt two approaches. First, we model the pathways through *sequential addition* to the offspring-earnings equation (see equation 2.7). Second, we estimate a *double decomposition* model that compares the conditional and unconditional relationships between parental income and the individual pathways.

Sequential Analysis

The sequential addition approach is best understood by considering a model that includes two pathway variables—say, education and occupation. In a first step, we calculate the unconditional relationships between each pathway variable and parental income; neither of these estimated relationships reflects the linkage between parental income and the other pathway variable. For education, we use equation 2.3.

$$ED_i^{child} = \alpha_{ed} + \lambda_{ed} \ln Y_i^{parent} + \varepsilon_{1i} \tag{2.3}$$

An analogous unconditional relationship is between parental income and offspring occupation.

$$Occ_i^{child} = \alpha_{occ} + \lambda_{occ} \ln Y_i^{parent} + \varepsilon_{2i} \tag{2.6}$$

We then estimate a regression equation that relates offspring earnings to both of the pathway factors, offspring education and occupation:

$$\ln Y_i^{child} = \omega_2 + \gamma_{ed} ED_i^{child} + \gamma_{occ} Occ_i^{child} + v_{2i} \tag{2.7}$$

With these two pathways, it follows that a decomposition analogous to equation 2.5 is:

$$\beta = \lambda_{ed}\gamma_{ed} + \lambda_{occ}\gamma_{occ} + Cov\left(v_{2i}, \ln Y_i^{parent}\right) \Big/ Var\left(\ln Y_i^{parent}\right) \tag{2.8}$$

The extent to which the education effect is modified by the inclusion of occupation depends on the strength of the relationship between education and occupation, the impact of occupation on offspring earnings, and the association of parental income and offspring's education.

In the full sequential addition analysis, we estimate four different versions of equation 2.7, leading to four different decompositions of β. The first considers only the education pathway. Although educational attainment is measured at age thirty, this outcome is primarily a consequence of choices made in the late teens and even before. In the second specification, we add two variables reflecting early life cycle choices—early marriage (before age twenty-two) and early labor market attachment (ages twenty-two to twenty-five). Comparing the decomposition from this second specification of equation 2.7 with those from the first (equation 2.4) reveals the extent to which the addition of these early life cycle variables adds to our understanding of the pathway linkages. This comparison also reveals the extent to which the education channel observed in the first decomposition is working through the additional early life cycle pathways. The third specification adds variables measured at around age thirty, including labor market attachment at ages twenty-six to twenty-nine and marriage, health, and occupation at age thirty. Our final specification adds occupation at age thirty-four. By adding these variables in a discrete time-sequenced ordering, we are able to estimate the maximum explanatory effect of each group prior to observing the extent to which this effect is explained through the relationships of each group with later pathways.

Double Decomposition Analysis

In this approach, also designed to capture the interactions between the variables, we compare the conditional and unconditional relationships between parental income and the pathways. Again using the two-variable education-occupation example, we begin with the unconditional relationships between parental income and offspring education and offspring occupation, as seen in equations 2.3 and 2.6.

$$ED_i^{child} = \alpha_{ed} + \lambda_{ed} \ln Y_i^{parent} + \varepsilon_{1i} \tag{2.3}$$

$$Occ_i^{child} = \alpha_{occ} + \lambda_{occ} \ln Y_i^{parent} + \varepsilon_{2i} \tag{2.6}$$

One reasonable conjecture is that children with higher parental income have better occupations because they do better in education. In this case, we would add offspring education to equation 2.6:

$$Occ_i^{child} = \sigma_{occ} + \delta_{occ} \ln Y_i^{parent} + \varphi ED_i^{child} + \varepsilon_{3i} \tag{2.9}$$

Combining equations 2.3 and 2.9 with the parameters estimated in the conditional earnings function (equation 2.7), the decomposition would now be written as:

$$\beta = \lambda_{ed}\gamma_{ed} + \lambda_{ed}\phi\gamma_{occ} + \delta_{occ}\gamma_{occ} + Cov\left(v_{2i}, \ln Y_i^{parent}\right) \Big/ Var\left(\ln Y_i^{parent}\right) \qquad (2.10)$$

The part of β that was attributed to occupation ($\lambda_{occ}\gamma_{occ}$) in equation 2.8 is now redistributed into two parts. The *indirect effect* of education through occupation is $\lambda_{ed}\phi\gamma_{occ}$, measuring the extent to which children with higher family incomes obtain more education and therefore better jobs. The *direct effect* of occupation is $\delta_{occ}\gamma_{occ}$, indicating that even among those with the same education level, higher parental income is associated with occupational advantages. Hence, we label this approach a "double decomposition" and use it as our most complete specification.

Both the sequential and double decomposition analyses are based on some assumptions about the ordering of individual decisions and the relationship between them. It is assumed that variables that are entered into the model earlier are exogenous to those entered later. For example, this means that education is determined independently of occupation, but that occupation depends on educational achievement. This may not be the case if individuals choose an education program with a specific career goal in mind. However, we believe that the broad educational and occupation groups specified make this endogeneity problem less likely than if we were using more specific occupations and qualifications, such as "law degree" and "lawyer."

The United States and Great Britain: Data and Variables

We use two prominent longitudinal survey data sources: the 1970 British Cohort Study (BCS) for Great Britain and the Panel Study of Income Dynamics (PSID) for the United States. The BCS began with a target sample of the population of individuals born in a week in April 1970 (around 18,000), and it has a usable sample of 7,665 for our intergenerational income analysis. The gap between the target and usable samples is largely due to attrition; by the age thirty-four survey, the number of observations had fallen to 9,665. The PSID includes the cohort born between 1960 and 1970, yielding a sample size of 1,448.

We devote a great deal of effort to making the two data sets as comparable as possible across all of the important variables for the analysis. Our measure of parental economic status is average gross parental income, measured when the child was age ten and age sixteen in both countries. Because parental income in the BCS is reported in categories, we group

Table 2.1   Pathway Variables

	U.S. Data	British Data
Education at age thirty	High school graduate	O level or equivalent
	Some college	A level
	College completion	Degree or equivalent
Early marriage	Year of first marriage age twenty-two or younger	Year of first marriage is before 1992
Labor market (ages twenty-two to twenty-five, ages twenty-six to twenty-eight)	Percentage of years working less than 500 hours and not attending school	Percentage of years where less than six months are spent in full-time work or full-time education
	Percentage of years working 1,500 hours or more or primary role is student	Percentage of years with twelve months of full-time work or at least six months of full-time education
Health at age thirty	Excellent	Excellent
	Poor or very poor	Poor or fair
Marriage	Married at age thirty	Married at age thirty
Occupation at age thirty	Seven-category occupation code based on NS-SEC	Seven-category occupation code based on NS-SEC
Occupation at age thirty-four	Seven-category occupation code based on NS-SEC	Seven-category occupation code based on NS-SEC

Source: Authors' compilation.

PSID income into categories that are comparable to those in the BCS, and use midpoints in both cases. Parental income is used rather than parental earnings because it captures the effect of public cash transfer benefits on the level of available parental resources. Moreover, parental earnings are not reported in the BCS.[11] We measure offspring economic status by average earnings at ages thirty and thirty-four, since these are the adult ages for which surveys are available for the BCS.

Our pathway variables are shown in table 2.1, and like the parental and offspring economic status variables, the definitions and measures of these variables are harmonized. For the United States, offspring education is measured at age thirty and classified as less than high school graduate, high school graduate, attended college, graduated from college, and attended graduate school; for Great Britain, education is classified as less than O level, O level or equivalent, A level, or degree or equivalent.[12]

We have transformed PSID occupation data into the eight-category version of the National Statistics Socio-Economic Classification (NS-SEC) system; the BCS includes the NS-SEC classification code.[13] For both countries, occupation is measured at ages thirty and thirty-four.[14] Two measures of labor market attachment are used. The first captures the percentage of years during the ages of twenty-two to twenty-five and twenty-six to twenty-nine when the offspring are primarily not in the labor market and not in school, while the second is the percentage of years from ages eighteen to twenty-eight during which the offspring are engaged in full-time (or close to full-time) work or education. In both surveys, self-reported health status (excellent, good, fair, or poor) measures the health of the offspring at age thirty. Being married at age thirty and age of first marriage are used as indicators of the marital status of the offspring (table 2.2).

Assumptions and Limitations

Our procedures require us to make several assumptions regarding the process through which parental economic position is transmitted to offspring. These assumptions are implicit in our choice of pathways to explore in decomposing the estimated βs. Here we mention only the most important of these assumptions and some of the other limitations associated with our methodology.

Omitted Pathways

Although the pathways we analyze are guided by economic theory, they are also constrained by data limitations. There are many other potential pathways by which parental income may influence offspring earnings, including inherited cognitive and noncognitive abilities, wealth, and neighborhood effects. In our approach, we assume that the linkages of these unmeasured pathways are not correlated with the included pathways and are therefore captured in the unexplained component of β. However, any relationship between unobserved and included pathways leads to estimates of the included pathway effects that are biased. For example, we do not include measures of cognitive and noncognitive ability, and if these are positively correlated with the pathways that are included, then the magnitude of the contributions of the included pathways to persistence are inflated.[15]

Two mitigating factors blunt this concern regarding our ability to meet the identification requirements for consistent estimation. First, Lalaina Hirvonen (2010) shows that the problem of bias is reduced when more pathway covariates are included in the estimation. Hence, rather than focusing on a single pathway, we examine a number of different pathways simultaneously, thereby reducing potential bias.[16] Second, given that our interest is in international comparisons, we further weaken this condition by assuming that the correlations between the omitted variables

Table 2.2   Descriptive Statistics for Pathway Variables in Earnings Regressions

	U.S. Men	U.S. Women	British Men	British Women
At least high school graduate/O levels	88.7%	91.2%	74.1%	75.5%
At least some college/ A levels	53.0	56.8	43.7	45.5
Graduate college/degree	29.1	27.4	23.4	23.4
Education missing	1.4	1.3	6.4	3.3
Married at age twenty-two or less	31.3	46.8	5.4	12.9
Missing married at twenty-two	17.3	18.0	5.2	3.3
Ages twenty-two to twenty-five, no work/education	22.9	25.2	5.8	13.9
Ages twenty-two to twenty-five, full-time work/education	64.5	58.3	88.1	70.9
Ages twenty-six to twenty-nine, no work/education	7.5	19.4	2.8	12.5
Ages twenty-six to twenty-nine, full-time work/education	84.5	63.7	71.5	51.8
Missing labor market information	2.3	0.4	6.2	3.2
Married at age thirty	66.7	63.5	38.3	47.5
Missing married at thirty	2.0	0.3	7.6	4.0
Health excellent at thirty	34.2	27.2	33.2	33.9
Health poor (plus "fair" for U.K. respondents) at thirty	4.2	7.1	13.0	11.7
Health missing at thirty	3.8	1.9	6.2	3.2
Higher managerial and professional level at thirty	16.3	11.8	15.4	7.4
Lower managerial and professional level or higher at thirty	40.0	43.3	45.7	44.9
Intermediate or higher at thirty	49.0	63.6	55.6	70.4
Small employers and own account or higher at thirty	58.9	69.9	56.6	71.1
Lower supervisory and technical level or higher at thirty	71.7	72.2	77.7	77.9
Semiroutine or higher at thirty	85.9	86.3	88.2	92.6
Missing occupation at thirty	12.5	16.3	9.2	12.3
Higher managerial and professional level at thirty-four	17.7	9.7	22.4	12.8
Lower managerial and professional level or higher at thirty-four	41.0	41.2	51.9	49.9
Intermediate or higher at thirty-four	51.2	63.9	59.3	70.5
Small employers and own account or higher at thirty-four	60.3	69.6	63.1	72.3

(Table continues on p. 40.)

Table 2.2   *Continued*

	U.S. Men	U.S. Women	British Men	British Women
Lower supervisory and technical or higher at thirty-four	73.9	70.9	81.1	77.7
Semiroutine or higher at thirty-four	88.3	86.9	90.4	94.1
Missing occupation at thirty-four	5.4	10.7	19.5	22.9
Sample size	647	801	3,899	3,766

Source: Authors' calculations based on data from the Panel Study of Income Dynamics (PSID) (2011) for the United States, and the British Cohort Study (BCS) (n.d.) for Great Britain.
Note: The means of the variables are the means of the observations that are not missing. This is appropriate because in the main analysis missing values are replaced with these mean values.

and pathway variables have the same magnitude in both nations. Thus, as long as the model captures the same pathways and error biases in both nations, our results will be robust with respect to cross-national differences in effects.

Independence of Linkages

We make two assumptions concerning the independence of the linkages. First, we assume that the link between parental income and any offspring pathway attainment is independent of the linkage between parental income and other pathway attainments. Second, we assume that the returns to pathway attainments are constant and independent of parental income. Both of these assumptions are essential to enable us to perform the decomposition.

Measures of Economic Status

We focus on parental income as our measure of family background and on average earnings at ages thirty to thirty-four as the final outcome measure for adult children. It is more common in the literature to measure the association between earnings across the two generations (Björklund and Jäntti 2009). That is not possible here as the British data do not contain separate information on parental earnings. In some ways, parental income is a more appropriate variable because it includes the impact of taxes and transfers, which clearly matter for available parental resources. We study the asymmetric relationship between parental income and child's earnings because we believe that individual earned income better reflects offspring adult attainment than offspring household income. Later, we examine the robustness of our model to the use of offspring household income as the dependent variable.

Table 2.3   Comparison of Individual Earnings Persistence Across Countries

	United States	Great Britain
βs (elasticities)		
Men	0.385 (0.047)	0.269 (0.016)
Women	0.349 (0.050)	0.341 (0.025)
Partial correlations		
Men	0.301 (0.037)	0.275 (0.017)
Women	0.241 (0.035)	0.220 (0.016)

Source: Authors' calculations based on data from the Panel Study of Income Dynamics (PSID) (2011) for the United States, and the British Cohort Study (BCS) (n.d.) for Great Britain.
Note: Standard errors in parentheses.

Measurement error in parental income leads to a downward-biased estimate of β (Solon 1992). In our case, the British estimate may be relatively more downward-biased because of greater transitory variation in parental income than in the United States.[17]

Classical measurement error in the dependent variable does not lead to any bias in the estimated β. However, if measurement error is related to parental income, then its effects might be quite different. Steven Haider and Gary Solon (2006) note that income at young ages is likely to be a particularly poor measure of permanent income for the most educated members of the sample. We measure offspring earnings at ages thirty and thirty-four, which may understate permanent income for college graduates. If offspring education and parental income are related, then measuring offspring income at a young age will lead to a downward-biased estimate of intergenerational persistence. Again, our results will be most seriously affected if the magnitude of this bias is different across the two nations.

Estimation Results

In table 2.3, we report the total βs measured as the elasticity of individual offspring earnings with respect to parental family income from estimates of equation 2.1. All of these estimates are highly statistically significant. For males, the U.S. β is .385, and in Great Britain the elasticity for men is lower at .269. The finding of lower mobility in the United States is consistent with some (but not all) of the recent research on this topic (Blanden forthcoming).[18] The stark contrast between the U.S. and British results for males is reduced when the intergenerational partial correlation is considered (.301 for the United States and .275 for Great Britain); it appears that some of the difference in β is due to the very rapid growth in male earnings inequality in the United States over the period of study.[19] The extent of persistence for women appears to be similar in the United States and

Great Britain by both measures, although the partial correlation is much lower than the β owing to the wide dispersion of women's earnings in both nations.[20]

Sequential Decomposition Analysis for Males

Tables 2.4 and 2.5 summarize our sequential decomposition analysis for U.S. and British men, respectively. Column 1 includes only a single pathway—offspring education. This specification explains rather more of the observed persistence in the United States than in Great Britain, 56 percent compared to 35 percent; because β is larger in the United States, the absolute difference is even larger. In the second specification (column 2), we add the early marriage and early labor market attachment variables. These add very little to the explanation of persistence.[21] In the third specification (column 3), offspring occupation, health, and marriage at age thirty are included along with offspring labor market attachment in the late twenties. The additional labor market attachment variables have a similar relative impact in both nations, explaining 4 percent of β in the United States and 3 percent in Great Britain. The marriage and health variables have very little explanatory power. In both the United States and Great Britain, however, offspring occupation has a large and positive linkage between parental income and offspring earnings, explaining 20 percent of β in the United States and one-quarter in Great Britain. Occupation is clearly correlated with education in both nations; the addition of offspring occupation reduces the share of persistence accounted for by education by fifteen to twenty percentage points (57 percent to 36 percent) in the United States and from 35 percent to 20 percent in Great Britain.

Column 4 is our complete sequential analysis, with offspring occupation at age thirty-four added to the other pathway linkages. This additional linkage also accounts for an important portion of the persistence—12 percent in the United States and 21 percent in Great Britain. Again, some of this explanatory effect is working through education and occupation at age thirty as the contributions of these variables fall. It is noteworthy that adding the offspring occupation linkages substantially increases the proportion of β explained by the model for Great Britain, whereas in the United States adding these linkages only marginally increases the total fraction of persistence that is explained. The addition of the offspring occupation linkages in the United States tends to absorb explanatory power that had been attributed to the education linkage, without contributing substantially to the overall level of persistence that is explained.[22]

In appendix tables 2A.1 and 2A.2, we present the detailed estimates that lie behind these sequential decompositions for men. The first pair of columns indicates the λ coefficients from the series of regressions linking the pathway variables to log parental income. The second pair of columns

Table 2.4 Sequential Models: U.S. Men

	(1) Part of Total β	(1) Percentage of Total β	(2) Part of Total β	(2) Percentage of Total β	(3) Part of Total β	(3) Percentage of Total β	(4) Part of Total β	(4) Percentage of Total β
Explained components of total β								
Education	0.217	56.3%	0.220	57.2%	0.139	36.2%	0.122	31.7%
Early marriage			0.011	2.9	0.010	2.6	0.011	2.9
Labor market attachment, ages twenty-two to twenty-five			-0.006	-1.7	-0.010	-2.6	-0.010	-2.5
Labor market attachment, ages twenty-six to twenty-nine					0.017	4.4	0.016	4.1
Marriage and health at thirty					0.004	1.0	0.005	1.4
Occupation at thirty					0.076	19.7	0.054	13.9
Occupation at thirty-four							0.044	11.6
Explained β	0.217	56.3	0.225	58.4	0.235	61.3	0.242	63.0
Unexplained β	0.168	43.7	0.160	41.6	0.149	38.7	0.142	37.0
Total β	0.385		0.385		0.385		0.385	

Source: Authors' calculations based on Panel Study of Income Dynamics (PSID) (2011).

Table 2.5 Sequential Models: British Men

	(1) Part of Total β	(1) Percentage of Total β	(2) Part of Total β	(2) Percentage of Total β	(3) Part of Total β	(3) Percentage of Total β	(4) Part of Total β	(4) Percentage of Total β
Explained components of total β								
Education	0.093	34.7%	0.095	35.5%	0.053	19.8%	0.037	13.6%
Early marriage			−0.0007	−0.3	−0.0003	−0.1	−0.004	−0.1
Labor market attachment, ages twenty-two to twenty-five			0.013	4.7	0.007	2.7	0.008	2.9
Labor market attachment, ages twenty-six to twenty-nine					0.009	3.4	0.009	3.1
Marriage and health at thirty					0.004	1.5	0.0034	1.3
Occupation at thirty					0.065	24.2	0.044	16.5
Occupation at thirty-four							0.057	21.1
Explained β	0.094	34.7	0.107	39.9	0.137	51.0	0.155	57.7
Unexplained β	0.175	65.3	0.162	60.1	0.131	48.6	0.112	41.9
Total β	0.269		0.269		0.269		0.269	

Source: Authors' calculations based on British Cohort Study (BCS) (n.d.).

presents the γ coefficients from the single regression of log offspring earnings on the set of included pathway variables (see equation 2.7). In the third pair of columns, we summarize the relative effect of these two linkages as the ratio of λ to γ (λ/γ); a ratio greater than unity indicates that the parent income–offspring pathway linkage (λ) dominates the earnings payoff from the offspring pathway effect (γ).[23] The final columns show the percentage of β explained by each pathway variable, as summarized in tables 2.3 and 2.4.

The greater contribution of the education pathway to explaining total β in the United States is primarily due to the greater "returns" to schooling in the United States relative to Great Britain. Parental income's influence on educational attainment is relatively similar across the two countries, as shown in the first two columns of table 2A.1. However, the earnings return to education in the second set of columns is much larger in the United States than in Great Britain, particularly the returns for a college degree. This is seen in the appendix table by the markedly smaller (λ/γ) ratios of education variables in the United States relative to Great Britain.[24] The detailed estimates for the other pathway variables do not show a clear pattern.

An alternative way to look at the results is to compare the absolute amount of persistence that is explained, using the "Part of Total β" column. If we consider these results for the full sequential model, they reveal that the absolute explanatory power of the pathways is rather similar across the two nations, apart from the education pathway. One possible interpretation is that mobility between the two nations would be equal were it not for the higher returns to education in the United States. This interpretation, however, is somewhat problematic because of the difficulties in comparing the absolute levels of mobility across nations. Moreover, this interpretation ignores the insights of the partial correlation measure of mobility, which reveals that once differences in changing inequality are taken into account, there is a rather narrower gap in mobility between the two nations. For this reason, we prefer to concentrate on the relative proportions explained.

In summary, for U.S. men, the linkage between parental income and offspring earnings is largely accounted for by the offspring-education pathway, whereas in Great Britain offspring occupation plays a much stronger role. The difference in the strength of the education pathway is due to relative differences in the returns to education in the two countries rather than relative differences in the influence of parental income on educational attainment.

Sequential Decomposition Analysis for Females

Tables 2.6 and 2.7 summarize the sequential pathway results for women. In both countries, the pathway variables we analyze explain substantially

Table 2.6 Sequential Models: United States Women

	(1) Part of Total β	(1) Percentage of Total β	(2) Part of Total β	(2) Percentage of Total β	(3) Part of Total β	(3) Percentage of Total β	(4) Part of Total β	(4) Percentage of Total β
Explained components of total β								
Education	0.194	55.7%	0.163	46.8%	0.094	27.0%	0.087	24.9%
Early marriage			0.019	5.5	-0.007	-1.9	-0.008	-2.2
Labor market attachment, ages twenty-two to twenty-five			0.078	22.4	0.032	9.1	0.031	9.0
Labor market attachment, ages twenty-six to twenty-nine					0.06	17.3	0.054	15.5
Marriage and health at thirty					-0.004	-1.0	-0.003	-0.8
Occupation at thirty					0.077	22.1	0.059	17.0
Occupation at thirty-four							0.050	14.4
Explained β	0.194	55.7	0.260	74.7	0.253	72.6	0.272	77.8
Unexplained β	0.155	44.3	0.088	25.3	0.096	27.4	0.077	22.2
Total β	0.349		0.349		0.349		0.349	

Source: Authors' calculations based on Panel Study of Income Dynamics (PSID) (2011).

Table 2.7　Sequential Models: British Women

	(1)		(2)		(3)		(4)	
	Part of Total β	Percentage of Total β	Part of Total β	Percentage of Total β	Part of Total β	Percentage of Total β	Part of Total β	Percentage of Total β
Explained components of total β								
Education	0.175	51.5%	0.158	46.4%	0.075	22.0%	0.054	15.8%
Early marriage			0.003	0.7	-0.002	-0.6	-0.001	-0.4
Labor market attachment, ages twenty-two to twenty-five			0.054	15.7	0.007	2.0	0.007	2.0
Labor market attachment, ages twenty-six to twenty-nine					0.061	18.0	0.057	16.8
Marriage and health at thirty					-0.0003	-0.1	-0.001	-0.3
Occupation at thirty					0.097	28.6	0.070	20.6
Occupation at thirty-four							0.071	21.0
Explained β	0.175	51.5	0.214	62.8	0.203	70.0	0.257	75.5
Unexplained β	0.163	48.5	0.127	37.2	0.138	30.0	0.083	24.5
Total β	0.341		0.341		0.341		0.341	

Source: Authors' calculations based on British Cohort Study (BCS) (n.d.).

more of total β for females than they do for males.[25] Also, as compared to that of males, the general pattern of effects of the different pathways for females is roughly similar in the two nations.

In both nations, the education-only specification (column 1) explains over one-half of the observed persistence. For males, only in the United States does education have this large explanatory effect. In moving from column 1 to column 2, the female decompositions suggest a large explanatory role for early labor market attachment, especially relative to the explanatory power of this linkage for males. In both nations, female offspring from higher-income families tend to have a stronger early labor market attachment than those from lower-income families, and this tie with the world of work is reflected in their earnings in their midthirties. The third and fourth specifications (columns 3 and 4) indicate that part of this impact occurs because women from higher-income families (relative to lower-income families) also have stronger labor market ties in their late twenties and higher-status occupations in their midthirties.

In the final specification for females, about 75 to 80 percent of intergenerational persistence is explained by this set of sequential linkages in both the United States and Great Britain. The general finding for males that the linkage between parental income and offspring earnings is primarily accounted for by education in the United States and by occupation in Great Britain is also seen for females in the two countries, but the differences for females are not as large. Finally, while the full pathway effect of labor market attachment is relatively small for males (about 2 percent of total β in the United States and 6 percent in Great Britain), it is substantially greater for females in both countries. In both countries, more than 19 percent of total β for females is explained by this pathway. A strong relationship between offspring labor market attachment and family income and a large payoff to work experience combine to produce this pattern. It is reasonable to speculate that differences in the timing of childbearing for women from higher- and lower-income families account for the importance of this pathway.

Double Decomposition Analysis

In the results for the sequential decomposition analyses, the conditional contribution of the offspring education pathway is likely to be understated because some portion of the joint effect of family income on both education and occupation is reflected in the estimated percentage of β explained that is attributed to occupation.

Tables 2.8 and 2.9 show the results of our double decomposition estimates. The first two columns of each table repeat the overall results on the percentage of β explained by the various pathways from the sequential

Table 2.8 Double Decomposition Using Education Pathway—Men

	Total Effect ($\lambda\gamma$)		Effect Through Education ($\lambda_{ed}\varphi\gamma$)		Direct Effect ($\delta\gamma$)	
	Part of Total β	Percentage of Total β	Part of Total β	Percentage of Total β	Part of Total β	Percentage of Total β
Explained components of total β, United States						
Education	0.122	31.7%	0.122	31.7%		
Early marriage	0.011	2.9	0.006	1.5	0.005	1.4%
Labor market attachment, ages twenty-two to twenty-five	-0.010	-2.5	-0.008	-2.2	-0.001	-0.4
Labor market attachment, ages twenty-six to twenty-nine	0.016	4.1	0.008	2.0	0.008	2.1
Marriage and health at thirty	0.005	1.4	0.006	1.5	-0.001	-0.2
Occupation at thirty	0.054	13.9	0.037	9.6	0.016	4.3
Occupation at thirty-four	0.045	11.6	0.030	7.9	0.014	3.7
Explained β	0.242	63.0	0.201	52.2	0.041	10.6
Unexplained β	0.142	37.0				
Total β	0.385	100.0				

(Table continues on p. 50.)

Table 2.8   *Continued*

	Total Effect ($\lambda\gamma$)		Effect Through Education ($\lambda_{ed}\varphi\gamma$)		Direct Effect ($\delta\gamma$)	
	Part of Total β	Percentage of Total β	Part of Total β	Percentage of Total β	Part of Total β	Percentage of Total β
Explained components of total β, Great Britain						
Education	0.037	13.6%	0.037	13.6%	−0.002	−0.1%
Early marriage	−0.0004	−0.1	−0.0002	−0.1		
Labor market attachment, ages twenty-two to twenty-five	0.008	2.9	−0.0007	−0.2	0.008	3.1
Labor market attachment, ages twenty-six to twenty-nine	0.008	3.1	0.001	0.4	0.007	2.7
Marriage and health at thirty	0.0034	1.3	0.0021	0.5	0.001	0.8
Occupation at thirty	0.044	16.5	0.0241	9.0	0.020	7.5
Occupation at thirty-four	0.057	21.1	0.0272	10.1	0.029	11.0
Explained β	0.156	58.3	0.0893	33.2	0.067	25.0
Unexplained β	0.112	41.7				
Total β	0.269					

Source: Authors' calculations based on Panel Study of Income Dynamics (PSID) (2011) for the United States and British Cohort Study (BCS) (n.d.) for Great Britain.

Table 2.9   Double Decomposition Using Education Pathway—Women

	Total Effect		Effect Through Education		Direct Effect	
	Part of Total β	Percentage of Total β	Part of Total β	Percentage of Total β	Part of Total β	Percentage of Total β
Explained components of total β, United States						
Education	0.087	24.9%	0.087	24.9%		
Early marriage	−0.008	−2.2	−0.005	−1.3	−0.003	−0.9%
Labor market attachment, ages twenty-two to twenty-five	0.031	9.0	0.001	0.4	0.030	8.5
Labor market attachment, ages twenty-six to twenty-nine	0.054	15.5	0.041	11.8	0.013	3.7
Marriage and health at thirty	−0.003	−0.8	0.001	0.3	−0.004	−1.2
Occupation at thirty	0.059	17.0	0.027	7.7	0.032	9.3
Occupation at thirty-four	0.050	14.4	0.020	5.6	0.031	8.8
Explained β	0.271	77.8	0.172	49.3	0.099	28.4
Unexplained β	0.077	22.2				
Total β	0.349	100.0				

(Table continues on p. 52.)

Table 2.9 *Continued*

	Total Effect		Effect Through Education		Direct Effect	
	Part of Total β	Percentage of Total β	Part of Total β	Percentage of Total β	Part of Total β	Percentage of Total β
Explained components of total β, Great Britain						
Education	0.054	15.8%	0.054	15.8%		
Early marriage	-0.001	-0.4	-0.0007	-0.2	-0.0006	-0.2%
Labor market attachment, ages twenty-two to twenty-five	0.007	2.0	0.0021	0.6	0.005	1.4
Labor market attachment, ages twenty-six to twenty-nine	0.057	16.8	0.039	11.4	0.018	5.4
Marriage and health at thirty	-0.001	-0.3	0.0015	0.4	-0.002	-0.7
Occupation at thirty	0.070	20.6	0.037	10.8	0.033	9.8
Occupation at thirty-four	0.071	21.0	0.037	10.7	0.035	10.3
Explained β	0.257	75.5	0.169	49.6	0.091	25.9
Unexplained β	0.083	24.5				
Total β	0.341					

Source: Authors' calculations based on data from Panel Study of Income Dynamics (PSID) (2011) for the United States and British Cohort Study (BCS) (n.d.) for Great Britain.

decomposition, found in column 4 of tables 2.4 to 2.7. The remaining areas of the tables break down this pattern into the part of the effect of occupation that is not mediated by the relationship between parental income and education (the "direct effect" of occupation— $\delta_{occ}\gamma_{occ}$) and the part that is mediated by the relationship between parental income and education (the "indirect effect" of occupation—$\lambda_{ed}\phi\gamma_{occ}$) (see equation 2.10). This indirect effect reflects the extent to which children with higher family incomes obtain more education and therefore better jobs.

Again, there is a very stark division across gender lines. For the men, almost all of the explained β works through the education mechanism in the United States; in total, .201 of the .242 of explained β is through education either directly or indirectly through education's effect on occupation. Although education has an important role to play in Great Britain, there is a much greater direct effect from parental income on the occupation variables. Just over half of explained β (.089 of .156) is directly or indirectly through education, with the remaining portion almost entirely from occupation. For women, the magnitude of the indirect and direct effects is similar in both nations; around two-thirds of the explanatory power is mediated through education, with one-third coming independently from the other pathways.

Some Robustness Tests

The results we have presented are our preferred comparisons of IGM between the United States and Great Britain and of the mediating pathways from parental income to offspring earnings that help us to perceive the underlying sources of intergenerational persistence. In addition to these results, we tested a number of other specifications and definitions; here we summarize some of these findings.

Measure of Income

As already discussed, the economics literature (as reviewed by Björklund and Jäntti 2009) has tended to concentrate on individual earnings as the primary measure of offspring's outcomes. However, total family income is perhaps more pertinent for living standards. Appendix table 2A.3 reports estimates for both intergenerational elasticity and correlation between family incomes across generations. For both men and women, persistence is greater in the United States than in Great Britain, and in the United States persistence is much greater for women than for men.

Appendix table 2A.4 reports the summary of the pathway estimation using family income. For these estimations, we must take into account the differences in the dependent variables; in Great Britain earnings and income are current weekly or monthly measures, whereas in the United

States they are annual. This means that in Great Britain income is observed for more individuals than earnings. It also means that those who were not working at either of the survey dates tend to have lower family incomes.[26]

The results for men are very similar when the model is estimated with family income rather than earnings. For women, however, much less of β is accounted for when family income is used; in the earnings model, about three-quarters of β is accounted for, whereas in the family income model only 51.7 percent (the United States) and 60.6 percent (Great Britain) of β is accounted for. Not surprisingly, the marriage pathway is more important for family income IGM than for earnings IGM, accounting for about 7 percent of β. These results suggest the importance of marriage in understanding income IGM for women. To take this work further, we would include some variables that describe the human capital of partners.

Observations with Zero Earnings

The earnings variable is the average of earnings at age thirty and at age thirty-four. In the results shown earlier, we use earnings only in years when there are positive earnings. A potential issue in evaluating the level of IGM for women is the number of observations reporting trivial amounts of earned income, particularly for the United States, where earnings are measured on an annual basis. We dropped both the bottom 1 percentile and the bottom 5 percent of earnings in the female samples, with virtually no effect on the total β. For Great Britain, the β fell from .340 to .333 and .300, respectively, with these changes; for the United States, the β changed from .349 to .312 and .326, respectively.

Measure of Occupation

The NS-SEC occupation code is matched to the British data using occupation and information on managerial and supervisory duties—as it is designed to do. In the United States, it was assigned based on three-digit occupation information. If there is error in the assignment of these codes, the coefficient estimates for occupation in the United States could be biased downward. In addition to errors in assignment, a second potential issue with using the NS-SEC for the United States is that it may not capture occupational differences as well in the United States as in European countries (see Erikson and Goldthorpe 1992).

One way to address these issues is to use the three-category classification of SEC code (rather than the eight-category version). This reduces the possibility of measurement error because any incorrect assignment to the more narrowly defined categories would not be expected to be as much of an issue for the broader classification codes; however, using the broader classification also eliminates information if the categories are correctly assigned. When the model is estimated using the three-category SEC occupation codes, the percentage of β accounted for by the occupation pathways in the United States falls (from 25.5 to 14.6 percent for men and from 31.4 to 25.1 percent for women).[27] For Great Britain, the magnitude of the changes is extremely similar (the proportion explained by occupation falls from 38 to 29 percent for men and from 42 to 37 percent for women); the implication is that any bias due to misclassification is approximately equal in both nations. While certainly not conclusive, this suggests that the relatively lower effect of the occupation pathway in the United States is not driven by measurement error.

Education-Only Model

One of our core findings so far is that education is relatively more important than occupation in transmitting intergenerational inequality in the United States, in contrast to its relative importance in Great Britain. One concern might be that the education variables are not strictly comparable across nations. If education is poorly measured in Great Britain, then, once again, this could lead to an underestimate of the importance of education. To address this concern, appendix table 2A.5 uses a more detailed breakdown of qualifications that more adequately reflects the U.K. education system, and this increases the proportion of β accounted for by education by less than one percentage point for each gender.

Conclusions

Our analysis has explored the linkages between parental and offspring economic position that lead to social persistence or immobility in a cross-national framework. Our estimates rely on a rich history of research on social mobility in both economics and sociology. Using harmonized U.S. and British data and a common econometric model, we explore several pathways that link offspring to their parents' status—offspring education, labor market attachment, occupation, marital status, and health status. For each of these pathways, we estimated both the tie between parental income and the pathway outcome (offspring education, labor market attachment, and so on) and the earnings payoff to the offspring of the attainment level achieved.

We analyzed these patterns for both men and women and found a striking consistency across the key mechanisms that help explain intergenerational mobility in the two nations. In the United States, the pathway through offspring education is more important, primarily because of the higher returns to education and skills (for a good review of various aspects of these differences, see Machin 2009; on the United States, see Katz and Autor 1999; Goldin and Katz 2008). By contrast, we find that the linkage through occupation is substantially more important in the United Kingdom than in the United States for both genders.

Consistent with the higher returns to educational attainment in the United States, labor market attachment is a more important pathway in the United States than in the United Kingdom, especially for women. For both genders, health and marital status have relatively little explanatory power in understanding the linkage between parental income and off-spring earnings.

The consistency of these education and occupation linkages across both genders suggests that structural factors related to cultural behaviors, labor market operation, and the characteristics of educational systems play a large role in understanding and supporting social mobility in these countries. Having said this, however, we note that the linkage of parental to offspring status through attachment to labor market work is a more important explanation for female persistence relative to male persistence, especially in the United Kingdom. There were large changes in labor market opportunities for women during the 1970s and 1980s, when the females in our sample were children; labor market attachment was more closely related to parental income for females in our sample than for males, and thus a more important driver of intergenerational persistence.

Our research findings are consistent with both evidence and conventional wisdom regarding the structure of—and policy concerns in—both the United States and the United Kingdom. In the United States, high and growing earnings inequality, driven largely by earnings increases among the most highly educated and trained U.S. workers, has driven up the rate of return to additional higher schooling. Similarly, the stagnation in college graduation rates in the United States has increased the returns for those who do graduate. Although our results suggest that the bias does not seem to have increased, the youths gaining qualifications and benefiting from these increasing returns are from the nation's better-off families, raising the issue of equity and access in U.S. education. These patterns increase the linkage between parental income and offspring earnings, as well as the level of intergenerational persistence.[28]

In the United Kingdom, the close tie between origin social class and later occupation is viewed by many as indicating that qualified youths from lower-income families are constrained from entering higher-level and professional occupations. This concern is discussed widely and accepted in popular literature as well as in government white papers (see Panel on Fair Access to the Professions [PFAP] 2009).[29] These perceptions are consistent with the results found here—namely, that links between family background and later occupation are a key driver of intergenerational persistence in the United Kingdom. Of course, one important way to open access to the high-income and high–social class jobs is to provide more equal access to schooling and training for these occupations. While our findings in Great Britain point to encouraging more equal access to upper-class jobs, equalizing educational opportunity and attainment is nonetheless an essential component of enhancing mobility.

If our evidence regarding the important roles of the education system in the United States and the structure of occupations and classes in the United Kingdom is correct, it suggests that policy approaches designed to increase social mobility should also differ somewhat between these two countries. Indeed, recent proposals in the two countries appear to reflect these different emphases. In 2010 the United States passed legislation designed to increase educational attainment from preschool to university, especially for youths from the bottom half of the income distribution. Income-conditioned subsidies for both university and community college attendance are a part of this policy package. In addition, states such as Georgia and Texas have led the way in an attempt to increase attendance and graduation for the highest-ranked secondary school graduates at their state institutions of higher learning, and they have also focused on issues of access and graduation for lower-income students.

In the United Kingdom, a new report on fair access to professions (PFAP 2009) is recommending that greater attention be paid to professional (occupational) attainment and the social exclusivity of many highly esteemed professions. The claim is that top jobs and professions have not only expanded but have also become more socially exclusive over the past several decades (Macmillan 2009).

In both countries, then, policymakers appear to be tailoring proposals that reflect the underlying process of intergenerational social mobility documented by our analysis—stimulating educational attainment (college attendance and graduation) especially for youths from families with modest means in the United States, and opening up both the education and occupational structure in the United Kingdom.

The authors are grateful to the Sutton Trust, the Russell Sage Foundation, and their respective universities and institutes for support of this project. We also want to thank Dawn Duren and Deborah Johnson for manuscript preparation and two anonymous referees, Bhash Mazumder, Robert Erikson, and Madison conference participants for comments on the earlier draft. And finally, we hold harmless all of these, accepting full responsibility for any and all errors of omission and commission. Comments and reactions are most welcome.

Appendix

Table 2A.1   United States and British Men, Detailed Decomposition Results

Factors	Parent Income Influence on Factor (λ)		Return to Factor (γ)		Ratio (λ/γ)		Decomposition of Total β: Percentage Variation Explained	
	United States	Great Britain	United States	Great Britain	United States	Great Britain	United States	Great Britain
High school graduate/O levels	0.095 (.020)	0.148 (.013)	0.187 (.084)	0.040 (.018)	0.51	3.73	4.6%	2.2%
Attend college/A levels	0.304 (.030)	0.211 (.015)	0.061 (.070)	0.024 (.019)	4.95	8.61	4.9	1.9
College graduate/degree	0.239 (.027)	0.181 (.013)	0.357 (.073)	0.142 (.022)	0.67	1.27	22.2	9.5
Education total							31.7	13.6
Ages twenty-two to twenty-five, no labor/education	−0.002 (.019)	−0.034 (.006)	0.079 (.124)	−0.193 (.067)	−0.03	0.17	0.0	2.4
Ages twenty-two to twenty-five, full-time work/education	−0.032 (.017)	0.019 (.007)	0.297 (.133)	0.063(.050)	−0.11	0.30	−2.5	0.5
Ages twenty-six to twenty-nine, no labor/education	−0.015 (.012)	−0.016 (.004)	−0.093 (.204)	−0.241 (.072)	0.17	0.07	0.4	1.4
Ages twenty-six to twenty-nine, full-time work/education	0.025 (.016)	0.011 (.004)	0.568 (.144)	0.416 (.059)	0.04	0.03	3.7	1.6
Labor market attachment total							4.5	6.0

Married at age twenty-two or younger	−0.156 (.026)	−0.022 (.007)	−0.072 (.063)	0.016 (.030)	2.17	−1.34	2.9	−0.1
Married at age thirty	−0.008 (.030)	0.016 (.015)	0.061 (.063)	0.074 (.014)	−0.13	0.21	−0.1	0.4
Health poor	−0.010 (.012)	−0.022 (.010)	−0.426 (.132)	−0.042 (.037)	0.02	0.53	1.1	0.4
Health excellent	0.068 (.030)	0.062 (.015)	0.022 (.055)	0.022 (.015)	3.06	0.10	0.4	0.5
Marriage and health total							4.3	1.2
Occupation 2 or better at thirty	0.089 (.022)	0.089 (.011)	0.086 (.099)	0.055 (.022)	1.04	1.62	2.0	1.8
Occupation 3 or higher at thirty	0.156 (.029)	0.204 (.015)	−0.063 (.106)	0.105 (.025)	−2.49	1.94	−2.6	8.0
Occupation 4 or higher at thirty	0.191 (.029)	0.211 (.015)	0.416 (.132)	−0.052 (.077)	0.46	−4.05	20.7	−4.1
Occupation 5 or higher at thirty	0.169 (.029)	0.208 (.015)	−0.374 (.117)	0.070 (.075)	−0.45	2.98	−16.4	5.3
Occupation 6 or higher at thirty	0.168 (.026)	0.148 (.012)	0.213 (.109)	0.114 (.026)	0.79	1.30	9.3	6.3
Occupation 7 or higher at thirty	0.085 (.020)	0.069 (.010)	0.040 (.107)	−0.040 (.029)	2.13	−1.74	0.9	−1.0
Occupation at age thirty total							13.9	16.5
Occupation 2 or better at thirty-four	0.116 (.023)	0.129 (.012)	0.217 (.094)	0.183 (.021)	0.53	0.71	6.5	8.8
Occupation 3 or higher at thirty-four	0.176 (.030)	0.182 (.014)	−0.047 (.101)	0.171 (.030)	−3.76	1.07	−2.1	11.5
Occupation 4 or higher at thirty-four	0.192 (.031)	0.172 (.014)	0.157 (.127)	−0.096 (.053)	1.22	−1.79	7.9	−6.0
Occupation 5 or higher at thirty-four	0.209 (.030)	0.173 (.014)	−0.062 (.115)	0.013 (.048)	−3.35	13.02	−3.4	1.0
Occupation 6 or higher at thirty-four	0.191 (.027)	0.114 (.011)	0.115 (.105)	0.170 (.030)	1.66	0.67	5.7	7.2
Occupation 7 or higher at thirty-four	0.094 (.020)	0.049 (.008)	−0.121 (.107)	−0.070 (.034)	−0.77	−0.70	−3.0	−1.3
Occupation at age thirty-four total							11.6	21.1
Total percentage variation explained							63.1	58.3

Source: Authors' calculations based on Panel Study of Income Dynamics (PSID) (2011) for the United States and British Cohort Study (BCS) (n.d.) for Great Britain.

Note: The omitted comparison factors for each categories are: high school dropout/no O levels, part-time worker, occupation = 7, and health "good" or "very good." The categorical variables are coded as "at least" high school, and so on. Standard errors are in parentheses.

Table 2A.2 United States and British Women, Detailed Decomposition Results

Factors	Parent Income Influence on Factor (λ)		Return to Factor (γ)		Ratio (λ/γ)		Decomposition of Total β: Percentage Variation Explained	
	United States	Great Britain	United States	Great Britain	United States	Great Britain	United States	Great Britain
High school graduate/O levels	0.095 (.020)	0.148 (.013)	0.187 (.084)	0.040 (.018)	0.51	3.73	4.6%	2.2%
High school graduate/O levels	0.099 (.016)	0.143 (.014)	0.036 (.102)	0.029 (.022)	2.74	4.89	1.0%	1.2%
Attend college/A levels	0.250 (.026)	0.209 (.016)	−0.022 (.066)	0.113 (.023)	−11.44	1.85	−1.6	6.9
College graduate/degree	0.218 (.024)	0.195 (.013)	0.406 (.076)	0.134 (.026)	0.54	1.46	25.4	7.6
Education total							24.9	15.8
Ages twenty-two to twenty-five, no labor/education	−0.101 (.022)	0.082 (.012)	−0.139(.114)	−0.147 (.047)	0.73	0.54	4.0	−1.4
Ages twenty-two to twenty-five, full-time work/education	0.050 (.018)	0.031 (.007)	0.341 (.122)	−0.057 (.035)	0.15	−1.44	4.9	−0.7
Ages twenty-six to twenty-nine, no labor/education	−0.066 (.017)	−0.044 (.008)	−0.210 (.136)	−0.440 (.044)	0.31	0.10	4.0	5.7
Ages twenty-six to twenty-nine, full-time work/education	0.066 (.021)	0.046 (.010)	0.605 (.098)	0.820 (.036)	0.11	0.06	11.5	11.1
Labor market attachment total							24.5	18.8
Married at age twenty-two or younger	−0.148 (.025)	−0.079 (.009)	0.051 (.063)	0.025(.026)	−2.90	−1.98	−2.2	3.4

Married at age thirty	0.073 (.027)	0.010 (.016)	−0.198 (.069)	−0.084 (.018)	−0.37	−0.11	−4.1	−0.2
Health poor/fair	−0.030 (.010)	−0.034 (.010)	−0.223 (.141)	0.028 (.027)	0.14	−1.19	1.9	−0.3
Health excellent	0.049 (.024)	0.045 (.015)	0.095 (.061)	0.018 (.018)	0.51	2.52	1.3	0.2
Marriage and health total							−3.0	3.1
Occupation 2 or better at thirty	0.075 (.017)	0.068 (.008)	0.034 (.111)	0.155 (.037)	2.18	0.44	0.7	3.1
Occupation 3 or higher at thirty	0.195 (.025)	0.179 (.015)	0.311 (.084)	0.153 (.024)	0.63	1.17	17.4	8.1
Occupation 4 or higher at thirty	0.193 (.024)	0.161 (.014)	0.131 (.134)	0.221 (.110)	1.47	0.73	7.2	10.5
Occupation 5 or higher at thirty	0.181 (.023)	0.156 (.014)	−0.365 (.238)	−0.150 (.114)	−0.50	−1.05	−19.0	−6.9
Occupation 6 or higher at thirty	0.176 (.022)	0.116 (.013)	0.090 (.222)	0.132 (.041)	1.95	0.88	4.5	4.5
Occupation 7 or higher at thirty	0.098 (.098)	0.044 (.008)	0.220 (.114)	0.106 (.040)	0.45	0.41	6.2	1.4
Occupation at thirty total							17.0	21.6
Occupation 2 or better at thirty-four	0.087 (.016)	0.080 (.010)	0.283 (.117)	0.124 (.032)	0.31	0.64	7.0	2.9
Occupation 3 or higher at thirty-four	0.216 (.025)	0.150 (.014)	−0.087 (.080)	0.213 (.027)	−2.49	0.71	−5.4	9.4
Occupation 4 or higher at thirty-four	0.220 (.024)	0.142 (.013)	0.188 (.138)	0.074 (.079)	1.17	1.93	11.9	3.1
Occupation 5 or higher at thirty-four	0.189 (.024)	0.140 (.013)	0.013 (.295)	0.003 (.086)	14.97	47.45	0.7	0.1
Occupation 6 or higher at thirty-four	0.183 (.023)	0.114 (.012)	0.003 (.280)	0.115 (.047)	59.71	0.99	0.2	3.9
Occupation 7 or higher at thirty-four	0.120 (.018)	0.038 (.007)	0.002 (.104)	0.144 (.046)	75.94	0.26	0.1	1.6
Occupation at thirty-four total							14.4	21.0
Total percentage variation explained							70.3	75.5

Source: Authors' calculations based on Panel Study of Income Dynamics (PSID) (2011) for the United States and British Cohort Study (BCS) (n.d.) for Great Britain.

Note: The omitted comparison factors for each categories are: high school dropout/no O levels, part-time worker, occupation = 7, and health "good" or "very good." The categorical variables are coded as "at least" high school, and so on. Standard errors are in parentheses.

Table 2A.3   Comparison of Family Income Persistence Across Countries

	United States	Great Britain
βs (elasticities)		
Men	.355 (.042)	.294 (.020)
Women	.472 (.035)	.280 (.018)
Partial correlations		
Men	.315 (.038)	.240 (.016)
Women	.437 (.033)	.240 (.015)

Source: Authors' calculations based on Panel Study of Income Dynamics (PSID) (2011) for the United States and British Cohort Study (BCS) (n.d.) for Great Britain.
Note: Standard errors in parentheses.

Table 2A.4   Offspring Family Income

	United States Men		British Men		United States Women		British Women	
	Part of Total β	Percentage of Total β	Part of Total β	Percentage of Total β	Part of Total β	Percentage of Total β	Part of Total β	Percentage of Total β
Explained components of total β								
Education	0.116	30.4%	0.027	9.3%	0.101	20.8%	0.043	15.4%
Early marriage	0.024	6.4	0.001	0.3	-0.004	-0.8	-0.001	-0.5
Labor market attachment, ages twenty-two to twenty-five	-0.002	-0.5	0.012	4.1	0.019	4.0	0.021	7.4
Labor market attachment, ages twenty-six to twenty-nine	0.011	3.0	0.011	3.6	0.020	4.2	0.007	2.4
Marriage and health at thirty	0.003	0.7	0.077	2.6	0.033	6.8	0.021	7.3
Occupation at thirty	0.034	8.8	0.036	12.3	0.045	9.3	0.032	11.4
Occupation at thirty-four	0.043	11.3	0.042	14.1	0.036	7.4	0.023	8.1
Employment at thirty and thirty-four			0.033	11.3			0.026	9.1
Explained β	0.229	60.0	0.169	57.7	0.251	51.7	0.169	60.6
Unexplained β	0.153	40.0	0.124	42.3	0.234	48.3	0.111	39.6
Total β	0.381		0.294		0.485		0.280	

Source: Authors' calculations based on Panel Study of Income Dynamics (PSID) (2011) for the United States and British Cohort Study (BCS) (n.d.) for Great Britain.

Table 2A.5 Robustness Check on British Education Measures

Alternative Education Measures	Parental Income Influence on Factor (λ)		Return to Factor (γ)		Ratio (λ/γ)		Percentage Variation Explained	
	Men	Women	Men	Women	Men	Women	Men	Women
Low academic qualifications (below O level)	.071 (.010)	.073 (.011)	−.001 (.052)	−.082 (.074)	−71.5	−0.90	−0.03%	−1.8%
Low vocational qualifications (below O level equivalent)	.094 (.011)	.090 (.011)	.125 (.057)	.183 (.080)	0.75	0.49	4.4	4.8
Vocational qualification (O level equivalent)	.108 (.012)	.113 (.013)	−.025 (.041)	−.162 (.062)	−4.3	−0.70	−1.02	−5.4
O level qualification	.142 (.014)	.143 (.014)	.084 (.029)	.242 (.048)	1.69	0.59	4.4	10.2
Post-school level vocational qualification	.193 (.015)	.206 (.016)	.056 (.028)	.171 (.048)	3.46	1.21	4.0	10.4
A level	.208 (.015)	.209 (.016)	.095 (.035)	.065 (.057)	2.18	3.30	7.4	4.02
Degree-level vocational qualification	.185 (.015)	.202 (.015)	−.020 (.034)	.137 (.048)	−9.40	1.48	−1.4	8.1
Degree	.179 (.013)	.195 (.013)	.268 (.025)	.380 (.037)	0.67	0.51	17.8	22.8
Education total							35.6	52.2

Source: Authors' calculations based on Panel Study of Income Dynamics (PSID) (2011) for the United States and British Cohort Study (BCS) (n.d.) for Great Britain.
Note: Standard errors in parentheses.

Notes

1. This chapter combines rich traditions in both disciplines and emerging cross-national comparative research. In Europe, cross-national sociological research in social mobility began in the 1950s, led by David Glass (1954) in England and Gosta Carlsson (1958) and Kaare Svalastoga (1959) in Sweden. They were followed by American researchers in the 1960s and 1970s, including Otis Duncan and Robert Hodge (1963); Peter Blau and Duncan (1967); Duncan, David Featherman, and Beverly Duncan (1972); and William Sewell and Robert Hauser (1975). Comparative and cross-national researchers made major contributions in the 1980s; see Breen (1985) and Erikson and Goldthorpe (1992). The economics literature began later and was pioneered by Anthony Atkinson (1970, 1980, 1981), Atkinson and François Bourguignon (1982), and Atkinson, Bourguignon, and Christian Morrisson (1992). Gary Becker and Nigel Tomes (1986) formalized the economics approach, leading to the important studies by Gary Solon (1992) and David Zimmerman (1992). The most important comparative economic mobility paper in economics using carefully harmonized data was by Markus Jäntti and his colleagues (2006).

2. Our particular data excludes Northern Ireland and so refers to Great Britain. In general, previous studies have referred to the whole United Kingdom. We try to be accurate with reference to this distinction.

3. This result derives from both methodological and data advances, especially the use of more permanent measures of family economic status than those used in the early literature (Mazumder 2005). Evidence on the relative position of these two nations is mixed, though most studies rank the United States as slightly less mobile than the United Kingdom (see, for example, Blanden 2009; Björklund and Jäntti 2009).

4. Research in economics also suggests that the United States has the least income mobility from the bottom quintile, with 42 percent of sons from this lowest parental category ending up in the same quintile (Jäntti et al. 2006). The United Kingdom and the United States do not differ appreciably from Denmark and Sweden in the mobility of sons in the middle quintiles. However, in both the United Kingdom and the United States, sons who begin in the top quintile are less likely to emigrate to the lowest quintile compared to the Scandinavian countries.

5. For example, recent sociological research by Richard Breen and his colleagues (2009, 2010) and Breen and Jan Jonsson (2005, 2007) explores the linkages between education and class mobility as well as equality of opportunity and gender.

6. See OECD, "Country Statistical Profile 2010," available at: http://stats.oecd.org/Index.aspx?DataSetCode=CSP2010 (accessed January 15, 2011).

7. See OECD, "Country Statistical Profile 2009," available at: http://stats.oecd.org/Index.aspx?DatasetCode=CSP2009 (accessed January 15, 2011).

8. Jonsson and his colleagues (2009) contrast two schools of thought in the social mobility literature: a graduation approach, which regards socio-economic status as essential for inheritance, and a "big-class" approach in which it is the broad occupation group that is transmitted. Our measure of occupational status is of the "big-class" type.

9. See OECD Family Database, "SF3.1: Marriage and Divorce Rates," http:// www.oecd.org/dataoecd/4/19/40321815.pdf (last updated December 20, 2010; accessed January 15, 2011).

10. In our estimation, the pathway variables are specified as categorical; for ease of exposition, we write them here as continuous variables.

11. We included in our sample all individuals with at least one observation of parental income and at least one observation of adult earnings. A total of 8,992 of the BCS observations have information on individual earnings at ages thirty or thirty-four, and 13,503 have information on parental income at offspring ages ten or sixteen. We do not distinguish between one- and two-parent families in measuring parental economic position. Jo Blanden (2005) looks in detail at the impact of attrition on the measurement of mobility in the BCS. The evidence presented there suggests that attrition and nonresponse tends to lead to final samples with slightly higher parental and child status than average. By including all observations with information on parental earnings at ages ten or sixteen, we have mitigated these problems as much as possible. Evidence on the PSID (Fitzgerald, Gottschalk, and Moffitt 1998) similarly suggests that the children who do not attrite come from better backgrounds. These authors consider the impact of attrition in the twenties on estimates of intergenerational mobility and find that these do tend to bias persistence slightly upward. However, it should be noted that these results are based on older cohorts than those who are considered here, and patterns may therefore be different.

12. According to the International Standard Classification of Education (ISCED) code, these differentiations reflect similar educational attainment in the two countries (see tables 1 and 2 at: http://www.oecd.org/dataoecd/11/ 18/2765339.xls; accessed March 1, 2010).

13. The NS-SEC classification codes are shown in appendix tables 2A.1 and 2A.2. The PSID three-digit occupation codes were converted to the NS-SEC by manually comparing each of the three-digit occupation codes with the criteria for the NS-SEC codes. We are thankful to Lawrence Miller for his assistance in converting the data. The NS-SEC is based broadly on the Goldthorpe social class schema; see Rose and Pevalin (2005). The eighth category of the NS-SEC is never worked/long-term unemployed. As we focus on those with some employment, this category is not used in our analysis.

14. Due to the nature of our data, the categorical variables are defined as "at least high school," "at least some college," and "college" (with the same approach used for occupation). If exclusive dummies were used, this would lead to ambiguity in the expected relationship between parental income and the middle categories; for example, those with high school education are well

educated compared to those with no high school but poorly educated compared to those with "some college" or "completed college."

15. We exclude these variables because they are not available in the PSID. However, some measures of this type are available in the BCS and were considered by Blanden, Gregg, and Macmillan (2007), who show that most of the effects of cognitive and noncognitive abilities are minimized once education is included in the analysis.

16. Hirvonen (2010, 22) states: "Ultimately, the problem of omitted variable bias is likely to impair the results, yet including more covariates in the equation should also decrease the degree of the total inconsistency in the estimates. Normally, the more variables are involved in the equation, the higher the propensity for them to net out the effect of bias."

17. The BCS asks parents to provide information on the "combined gross income of the child's mother and father" on either a weekly or monthly basis; in the U.S. PSID, income is captured by adding up all sources of reported income from the previous year.

18. In their explicit international comparison, Bernt Bratsberg and his colleagues (2007) find mobility in the United States to be lower than in the United Kingdom. This is supported by the literature reviews of Jo Blanden (forthcoming) and Anders Björklund and Markus Jäntti (2009). Miles Corak (2006) reads the literature differently, ranking the countries the other way around, although the difference is not great.

19. As noted by Blanden, Gregg, and Macmillan (2010), the impact of measurement error is different across the two measures of persistence; r is less downward-biased by measurement error in parental income than is β, but r is downward-biased by measurement error in the child's earnings.

20. Oddbjørn Raaum and his colleagues (2007) find a similar pattern across the United States, the United Kingdom, and the Nordic countries; although there are differences in the extent of mobility in men's earnings, mobility for women's earnings are rather similar.

21. In the United States, the mediating relationship with early labor market attachment has an unexpected negative relationship between parental income and offspring full-time labor market work. The relationship through early marriage is also negative for British men.

22. Moving from the column 1 to the column 4 specification increases the explained portion of persistence from 56 percent to 63 percent; in Great Britain, the increase is from 35 percent to 58 percent.

23. In a rough way, the ratio provides some insight into the "meritocracy with equal opportunity" versus "aristocracy" debate. A ratio greater than unity suggests that the opportunity to acquire human capital (broadly defined), rather than a large labor market payoff to human capital, is primarily what causes persistence.

24. The country differences in returns to schooling are consistent with the findings of George Psacharopoulos and Harry Patrinos (2004), although we

should add one caveat: if life-cycle bias as described by Haider and Solon (2006) is more pronounced in the United Kingdom than in the United States, this could lead to a lower estimate of the returns to education there.

25. As noted, unlike for males, the levels of intergenerational persistence are similar between the countries for females (β = .349 in the United States and .341 in Great Britain).

26. Unless this difference is accounted for, it will be picked up in the missing occupation category and counted as "unexplained variation." To overcome this problem for Great Britain, we include employment at the two survey dates as an additional pathway.

27. The overall percentage of β explained falls from 63.0 to 59.5 percent for men and from 77.8 to 74.5 percent for women in the United States. In this specification, while occupation accounts for a lower percentage of β, the portion accounted for by education increases relative to the base model (from 31.7 to 39.0 percent for men and from 24.9 to 26.5 percent for women), indicating that some of the education pathway effects are through occupation opportunities within these broader occupation codes, particularly for men. The other pathways remain largely unchanged. Full results are available from the authors upon request.

28. The growth in earnings inequality in the United States, with the top earners becoming increasingly distant from the central part of the earnings distribution, is frequently noted in the United States (see Haveman 1996; Burtless 1990). The concentration of college enrollment and graduation among youths from higher-income families in the United States is also well documented (see Haveman and Wilson 2006; Haveman and Smeeding 2006).

29. Recently, the Conservative Party shadow secretary of state for education stated that his party would not seek to increase the number of grammar schools, stating the "uncomfortable truth that our schools are entrenching social advantage." In reporting on his speech, the *Telegraph* noted that his position reflected a belief that social persistence is also due to "prejudice or discrimination from the privileged classes, who conspire to ensure that those who are not part of their group will find it almost impossible to break into it." This position, the newspaper stated, is widely shared. "There's No Way Up," *Telegraph*, May 20, 2007, available at: http://www.telegraph.co.uk/news/uknews/1552095/Theres-no-way-up.html (accessed December 4, 2009).

References

Atkinson, Anthony B. 1970. "On the Measurement of Inequality." *Journal of Economic Theory* 2(3): 244–63.

———. 1980. "On Intergenerational Income Mobility in Britain." *Journal of Post-Keynesian Economics* 3(2): 194–218.

———. 1981. "The Measurement of Economic Mobility." In *Essays in Honor of Jan Pen*, reprinted in *Social Justice and Public Policy*. Cambridge, Mass.: MIT Press.

Atkinson, Anthony B., and François J. Bourguignon. 1982. "The Comparison of Multidimensioned Distributions of Economic Status." *Review of Economic Studies* 49: 183–201.

Atkinson, Anthony B., François J. Bourguignon, and Christian Morrisson. 1992. *Empirical Studies of Earnings Mobility*. Chur, Switzerland: Harwood Academic Publishers.

Becker, Gary, and Nigel Tomes. 1986. "Family Capital and the Rise and Fall of Families." *Journal of Labor Economics* 4(3, part 2): S1–39.

Beller, Emily, and Michael Hout. 2006. "Intergenerational Social Mobility: The United States in Comparative Perspective." *The Future of Children* 16(2): 19–36.

Björklund, Anders, and Markus Jäntti. 1997. "Intergenerational Income Mobility in Sweden Compared to the United States." *American Economic Review* 87(5): 1009–18.

———. 2009. "Intergenerational Income Mobility and the Role of Family Background." In *The Oxford Handbook of Economic Inequality*, edited by Wiemer Salverda, Brian Nolan, and Timothy M. Smeeding. Oxford: Oxford University Press.

Blanden, Jo. 2005. "Essays on Intergenerational Mobility and Its Variation over Time, Place, and Family Structure." Ph.D. diss., University College London.

———. 2009. "How Much Can We Learn from International Comparisons of Social Mobility?" Invited paper written for the Sutton Trust Summit on Social Mobility. Surrey, U.K. (March).

———. Forthcoming. "Cross-Country Rankings in Intergenerational Mobility: A Comparison of Approaches in Economics and Sociology." *Journal of Economic Surveys*.

Blanden, Jo, Paul Gregg, and Lindsey Macmillan. 2007. "Accounting for Intergenerational Persistence: Noncognitive Skills, Ability, and Education." *Economic Journal* (conference volume, March): C43–60.

———. 2010. "Intergenerational Persistence in Income and Social Class: The Impact of Within-Group Inequality." Working paper 10/230. Bristol, U.K.: University of Bristol, Centre for Market and Public Organisation.

Blau, Peter M., and Otis Duncan. 1967. *American Occupational Structure*. New York: Free Press.

Bratsberg, Bernt, Knut Røed, Oddbjørn Raaum, Robin Naylor, Markus Jäntti, Tor Eriksson, and Eva Österbacka. 2007. "Nonlinearities in Intergenerational Earnings Mobility: Consequences for Cross-Country Comparisons." *Economic Journal* 117(519): C72–92.

Breen, Richard. 1985. "A Framework for Comparative Analyses of Social Mobility." *Sociology* 19(1): 93–107.

Breen, Richard, and Jan O. Jonsson. 2005. "Inequality of Opportunity in Comparative Perspective: Recent Research on Educational Attainment and Social Mobility." *Annual Review of Sociology* 31: 223–43.

———. 2007. "Explaining Change in Social Fluidity: Educational Equalization and Educational Expansion in Twentieth-Century Sweden." *American Journal of Sociology* 112(6): 1775–810.

Breen, Richard, Ruud Luijkx, Walter Müller, and Reinhard Pollak. 2009. "Non-persistent Inequality in Educational Attainment: Evidence from Eight European Countries." *American Journal of Sociology* 114(5): 1475–521.

———. 2010. "Long-Term Trends in Educational Inequality in Europe: Class Inequalities and Gender Differences." *European Sociological Review* 26(1): 31–48.

British Cohort Study. n.d. London: Centre for Longitudinal Studies, Institute of Education. Available at: http://www.cls.ioe.ac.uk/studies.asp?section=0001 00020002 (accessed May 17, 2011).

Burtless, Gary. 1990. "Earnings Inequality over the Business and Demographic Cycles." In *A Future of Lousy Jobs? The Changing Structure of U.S. Wages,* edited by Gary Burtless. Washington, D.C.: Brookings Institution Press.

Carlsson, Gosta. 1958. *Social Mobility and Class Structure.* Lund: CWK Gleerup.

Corak, Miles. 2006. "Do Poor Children Become Poor Adults? Lessons from a Cross-Country Comparison of Generational Earnings Mobility." *Research on Economic Inequality* 13: 143–88.

Devine, Fiona. 1997. *Social Class in America and Britain.* Edinburgh: Edinburgh University Press.

Duncan, Otis D., David L. Featherman, and Beverly Duncan. 1972. *Socioeconomic Background and Achievement.* New York: Seminar Press.

Duncan, Otis D., and Robert W. Hodge. 1963. "Education and Occupational Mobility." *American Journal of Sociology* 68(6): 629–44.

Erikson, Robert, and John H. Goldthorpe. 1985. "Are American Rates of Social Mobility Exceptionally High? New Evidence on an Old Issue." *European Sociological Review* 1(1): 1–22.

———. 1992. *The Constant Flux: A Study of Class Mobility in Industrial Societies.* Oxford: Clarendon.

———. 2002. "Intergenerational Inequality: A Sociological Perspective." *Journal of Economic Perspectives* 16(3): 31–44.

Fitzgerald, John, Peter Gottschalk, and Robert Moffitt. 1998. "An Analysis of the Impact of Sample Attrition on the Second Generation of Respondents in the Michigan Panel Study of Income Dynamics." *Journal of Human Resources* 33(2): 300–344.

Glass, David V., ed. 1954. *Social Mobility in Britain.* London: Routledge.

Goldin, Claudia, and Lawrence F. Katz. 2008. *The Race Between Education and Technology.* Cambridge, Mass.: Harvard University Press.

Haider, Steven J., and Gary Solon. 2006. "Life-Cycle Variation in the Association Between Current and Lifetime Earnings." *American Economic Review* 96(4): 1308–20.

Haveman, Robert. 1996. *Earnings Inequality: The Influence of Changing Opportunities and Choices.* Washington, D.C.: American Enterprise Institute.

Haveman, Robert, and Timothy Smeeding. 2006. "The Role of Higher Education in Social Mobility." *The Future of Children* 16(2): 125–50.

Haveman, Robert, and Kathryn Wilson. 2006. "Economic Inequality in College Matriculation and Graduation." In *Economic Inequality in Higher Education,* edited by Stacy Dickert-Conlin and Ross Rubenstein. New York: Russell Sage Foundation.

Hirvonen, Lalaina. 2010. "Accounting for Intergenerational Earnings Persistence: Can We Distinguish Between Education, Skills, and Health?" Working paper 2/2010. Stockholm: Stockholm University, Swedish Institute for Social Research.

Jäntti, Markus, Bernt Bratsberg, Knut Røed, Oddbjørn Raaum, Robin Naylor, Eva Österbacka, Anders Björklund, and Tor Eriksson. 2006. "American Exceptionalism in a New Light: A Comparison of Intergenerational Earnings Mobility in the Nordic Countries, the United Kingdom, and the United States." Discussion paper 1938. Bonn, Germany: Institute for the Study of Labor (IZA).

Jonsson, Jan O., David B. Grusky, Matthew Di Carlo, Reinhard Pollak, and Mary C. Brinton. 2009. "Microclass Mobility: Social Reproduction in Four Countries." *American Journal of Sociology* 114(January): 977–1036.

Katz, Lawrence F., and David H. Autor. 1999. "Changes in the Wage Structure and Earnings Inequality." In *Handbook of Labor Economics,* edited by Orley Ashenfelter and David E. Card. Amsterdam: North-Holland/Elsevier.

Long, Jason, and Joseph Ferrie. 2007. "The Path to Convergence: Intergenerational Occupational Mobility in Britain and the United States in Three Eras." *Economic Journal* 117(519): C67–71.

Machin, Stephen. 2009. "Education and Inequality." In *The Oxford Handbook of Economic Inequality,* edited by Wiemer Salverda, Brian Nolan, and Timothy M. Smeeding. Oxford: Oxford University Press.

Macmillan, Lindsey. 2009. *Social Mobility and the Professions.* Bristol, U.K.: University of Bristol, Centre for Market and Public Organisation. Available at: http://www.bris.ac.uk/cmpo/publications/other/socialmobility.pdf (accessed March 1, 2010).

Mazumder, Bhashkar. 2005. "The Apple Falls Even Closer to the Tree Than We Thought: New and Revised Estimates of the Intergenerational Inheritance of Earnings." In *Unequal Chances,* edited by Samuel Bowles, Herbert Gintis, and Melissa Osborne Groves. Princeton, N.J.: Princeton University Press.

Panel Study of Income Dynamics (PSID) [public use dataset]. 2011. Produced and distributed by the Institute for Social Research, Survey Research Center, University of Michigan, Ann Arbor, Michigan. Available at: http://psidonline.isr.umich.edu (accessed May 17, 2011).

Panel on Fair Access to the Professions (PFAP). 2009. *Unleashing Aspiration: The Final Report of the Panel on Fair Access to the Professions.* Available at U.K. Cabinet Office: http://www.bis.gov.uk/assets/biscore/corporate/migratedd/publications/p/panel-fair-access-to-professions-final-report-21_july09.pdf (accessed May 11, 2011).

Psacharopoulos, George, and Harry Patrinos. 2004. "Returns to Investment in Education: A Further Update." *Education Economics* 12(2): 111–34.

Raaum, Oddbjørn, Bernt Bratsberg, Knut Røed, Eva Österbacka, Tor Eriksson, Markus Jäntti, and Robin A. Naylor. 2007. "Marital Sorting, Household Labor Supply, and Intergenerational Earnings Mobility Across Countries." *B.E. Journal of Economic Analysis and Policy* 7(2, Advances): 1–49.

Rose, David, and David J. Pevalin. 2005. "The National Statistics Socio-Economic Classification: Origins, Development and Use." *National Statistics*. Available at: http://www.statistics.gov.uk/methods_quality/ns_sec/downloads/NS-SEC_Origins.pdf (accessed March 1, 2010).

Sewell, William H., and Robert M. Hauser. 1975. *Education, Occupation, and Earnings: Achievement in the Early Career*. New York: Academic Press.

Solon, Gary. 1992. "Intergenerational Income Mobility in the United States." *American Economic Review* 82(3): 393–408.

———. 2002. "Cross-Country Differences in Intergenerational Earnings Mobility." *Journal of Economic Perspectives* 16(3): 59–66.

Svalastoga, Kaare. 1959. *Prestige, Class, and Mobility*. Copenhagen: Gyldendal.

Zimmerman, David J. 1992. "Regression Towards Mediocrity in Economic Status." *American Economic Review* 82(3): 409–29.

Chapter 3

Economic Mobility, Family Background, and the Well-Being of Children in the United States and Canada

MILES CORAK, LORI J. CURTIS,
AND SHELLEY PHIPPS

A MONG THE many things the citizens of the United States and Canada
share in common is a perspective that informs and defines their
self-image and social goals. In particular, the histories and cultures
of these two countries have been shaped by newcomers seeking opportunities and better lives. The idea of "equality of opportunity," in which
inherited aspects of family background play a secondary role to individual
motivation, talents, and energy in determining economic success, is an
important part of this common heritage and makes "land of opportunity"
a common defining metaphor.

Yet there are very important differences in economic outcomes on the
two sides of the forty-ninth parallel. The United States is richer, with a per
capita income in 2007 that was almost 20 percent higher than in Canada
(Organization for Economic Co-operation and Development [OECD]
2009). But it is also more unequal. In the United States, households at the
top decile of the income distribution have almost six times as much as
those at the bottom decile, a ratio that is the third-highest among thirty
OECD countries. In Canada, this ratio is just over four; essentially at the
OECD average, Canada ranks eighteenth among the thirty countries (OECD
2008, 51, table 1.A2.2).

The research literature addressing these similarities and differences
has a long history, with perhaps the most comprehensive recent analysis
published under the title *Small Differences That Matter* (Card and Freeman
1993). Our research addresses one difference that has been uncovered since
the publication of this book: economic mobility across the generations—

the tie between family economic background and the adult attainments of children—is not the same in these countries. This fact informs public policy concerns about equality of opportunity and the functioning of the labor market, as well as policies dealing with education, health care, immigration, and support to families with children (Haskins and Sawhill 2009; *New York Times* 2005; Sawhill and Morton 2008; Wessel 2005).

A general consensus has developed that relative mobility of earnings across the generations is greater in Canada than in the United States. Americans are much more likely than Canadians to occupy the same place in the earnings distribution as their parents. Taking these average indicators of the degree of stickiness between family background and adult economic outcomes of children as its starting point, our examination is predicated on the idea that the Canada–United States comparison is analytically valuable because of the degree of similarity in many features of these societies. As such, a cross-country comparison can suggest causal mechanisms and highlight the role of public policy and institutions in determining the overall degree of generational mobility within each country.

The chapter proceeds by addressing three questions: Is there something to explain? If there is, does it reflect differences in values and the meaning of the social goals they underlie? And finally, if values associated with the meaning of equality of opportunity are the same, then are there differences in the investments made in children that could account for the different outcomes?

We summarize the findings in the existing literature that there are significant differences in the degree of intergenerational economic mobility between these two countries, with the United States characterized by a significantly lower average degree of relative mobility. Our review suggests that these differences reflect the fact that family background is more strongly related to the adult outcomes of children—that intergenerational mobility is lower—at the very top and the very bottom of the earnings distribution in the United States.

Findings from comparable public opinion polls suggest that these differences should not be characterized as the result of fundamentally different values over the meaning of equality of opportunity, and hence of different social choices that in some sense are optimal for each country. The citizens of both countries have a very similar sense of a good and successful life being one that is rooted in individual aspirations and freedom. Americans differ from Canadians, however, in being more likely to see government as hindering rather than helping them in achieving these goals.

These two countries draw different boundaries between the roles of family, market, and the public sector in investing in the capacities of children. Using a number of representative household surveys, we find that the configuration of all three sources of investment and support for children differs significantly: disadvantaged children live in much more challenging familial circumstances in the United States, their parents have more difficulty in maintaining a strong foothold in labor markets characterized by greater inequalities, and the role of the welfare state is not as strong in determining their outcomes as it is in Canada. As a result, we also conclude that the differences in generational mobility documented for past cohorts of young people—those who came of age as adults during the 1990s—will continue to exist for the next cohort: those who are about to enter adulthood in the 2010s.

Comparable Estimates of Earnings Mobility Across the Generations

The empirical framework for the measurement of the degree of intergenerational earnings mobility is in large part informed by the following equation:

$$Y_{i,t} = \alpha + \beta Y_{i,t-l} + \varepsilon_{i,t} \qquad (3.1)$$

Y represents the outcome of interest—generally permanent income measured in natural logarithms—i indexes families, and t indexes generations. Thus, the adult earnings of a child from a particular family, $Y_{i,t}$, are related to the average earnings of the members of a similar age cohort, α, plus a deviation from the average that consists of two parts. The first part reflects the fraction of parental advantage inherited by the child, as indicated by $\beta Y_{i,t-1}$; the second, $\varepsilon_{i,t}$, reflects all other influences not correlated with parental earnings.

This is an exercise in description, not causation. The empirical challenge is to obtain an accurate estimate of β, which represents, when earnings are measured in natural logarithms, the intergenerational elasticity of earnings. This is an overall average indicator of the degree to which inequality is transmitted across the generations and as such might be an interesting statistic to describe an economy, much in the way that the Gini coefficient is used to summarize inequality at a point in time.

The intergenerational elasticity, however, is more challenging to estimate than the Gini coefficient; ideally, it requires data from a longitudinal study of a large, nationally representative sample of individuals and families. Miles Corak (2006) points out that a comprehensive reading of the available empirical literature does not lead to any substantive conclusions about the relative size of β across countries if no account is taken of how the measurement and life-cycle errors outlined by Gary Solon (1992), David Zimmerman (1992), Nathan Grawe (2006), and Steven Haider and Solon (2006) are addressed. Not all studies are created equal in this regard, and the derivation of robust and comparable estimates of the intergenerational elasticity must take this into account before drawing any conclusions.

Corak (2006) offers a set of internationally comparable estimates drawn from this literature that recognizes differences in study designs. The meta-analysis of the literature upon which these findings are based could reasonably suggest a range of estimates for the United States of between .40 at the low end and .52 at the upper end. But this still is outside a comparable set of bounds for Canada, which range from .16 to .21 (Corak 2006, 152, table 1).

An important contribution to the accurate estimation of the intergenerational elasticity in father-son earnings for the United States is offered by Bhashkar Mazumder (2004, 2005) in research that is distinguished by the development of data involving a linkage between survey data and administrative data on earnings.[1] His analysis of samples for parents that span up to fifteen years leads to an estimate of the intergenerational elasticity of earnings between fathers and sons as high as .613, with an associated standard error of .096 (Mazumder 2005, 248, table 7). The nature of the data and the age cohorts used in this study make it directly comparable to the Canadian. Using administrative data associated with the Canadian income tax system, Corak and Andrew Heisz (1999, 513, table 3) use paternal earnings over a five-year period and find the intergenerational elasticity to be .23, with a standard error of .003. What is striking is that the sample selection rules used in these two studies are very close to being the same. Mazumder (2004, 2005) examines a young cohort of men who were fifteen to twenty years old in 1983—having been born between 1963 and 1968—and who were living with their parents in that year. These young men were at least twenty-seven years of age when their earnings were measured in 1995 to 1998. Corak and Heisz (1999) examine a cohort of men who were age sixteen to nineteen in 1982—having been born between 1963 and 1966—and who filed an income tax return while living at home between 1982 and 1986. These young men were at least twenty-seven years of age when their earnings were measured between 1993 and 1995.

On this basis, the difference in the degree of relative intergenerational mobility is higher than suggested in Corak (2006), being about three times as great in Canada as in the United States. Just as importantly, however, these two studies are based on sufficiently large sample sizes to permit analyses of differences in mobility at different points in the parental earnings distribution.

It is these differences that cause the cross-country differences in average mobility; they are summarized in figures 3.1 and 3.2 for sons born, respectively, to top-decile and bottom-decile fathers. Over one-quarter (26 percent) of the sons born to top-earning fathers grew up to be adults who were also in the top 10 percent of their earnings distribution. It is also notable that these sons were more likely in Canada than in the United States to drop to the very bottom of their earnings distribution, where

Figure 3.1   **Earnings Deciles of Sons Born to Top-Decile Fathers: Canada and the United States**

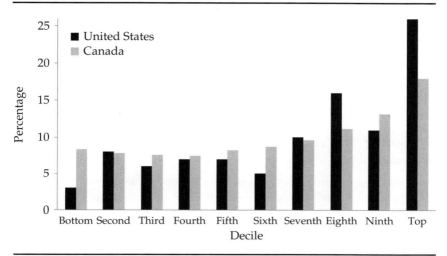

Source: Authors' calculations based on data from Corak and Heisz (1999, 520, table 6); Mazumder (2004, 93, table 2.2).

Figure 3.2   **Earnings Deciles of Sons Born to Bottom-Decile Fathers: Canada and the United States**

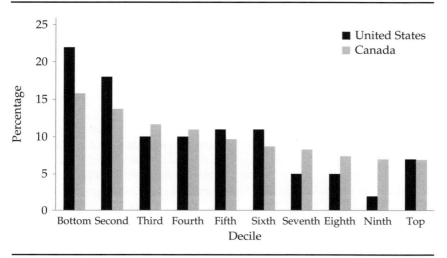

Source: Authors' calculations based on data from Corak and Heisz (1999, 520, table 6); Mazumder (2004, 93, table 2.2).

8.4 percent of Canadian sons found themselves in the bottom, compared to just 3 percent of U.S. sons.

If downward mobility is less likely in the United States, so is upward mobility. Twenty-two percent of sons born to bottom-decile American fathers remained in the bottom as adults, and a further 18 percent moved up only one decile. In Canada, almost 16 percent (15.8 percent) remained in the bottom, with 14 percent moving up one decile. In fact, on the basis of the full transition matrices reported in Mazumder (2004) and Corak and Heisz (1999), bottom-decile sons in Canada were as likely to move to the top half of the earnings distribution as third-decile Americans.

Economic Mobility and Equality of Opportunity

Although these differences in generational economic mobility are significant, in both a substantive and a statistical sense, they do not necessarily imply differences in equality of opportunity. Christopher Jencks and Laura Tach (2006) and John Roemer (2004) address this issue, pointing out in particular that complete equality of opportunity is not indicated by an intergenerational elasticity of zero—or entries in a transition matrix that are all the same. In this sense, it is not as if Canada, in some optimal sense, is further along than the United States. The existing differences could very well be optimal for each country, reflecting underlying values and the social choices that respect them.

Roemer (2004, 50) is particularly clear on this point. His definition of equality of opportunity "views inequities of outcome as indefensible, ethically speaking, when and only when they are due to differential circumstances." The issue, of course, is how to define "circumstances." Children resemble their parents for all kinds of reasons, some of which tend to be persistently rewarded in the labor market. To paraphrase Roemer, there are three successively broader fields, or circumstances, that would give rise to successively broader definitions of equality of opportunity and hence state intervention.

At one extreme is the influence of social connections and family income in facilitating access to important resources that influence capabilities and the chances that children will succeed. Most citizens in the rich countries might agree with the notion that equality of opportunity would be promoted if the influence of inherited wealth, connections, and outright nepotism in determining access to health care, education, and jobs was eliminated.

Roemer also suggests, at the other extreme, that most citizens would disagree with the suggestion that the influence of inherited ability should be eliminated in order to promote equality of opportunity. After all, even the most generationally mobile countries in the OECD have not completely eliminated the intergenerational link in earnings.

But between these extremes, societies may legitimately make different choices concerning the extent to which parent-child correlations in outcomes are in accord with a level playing field. Child outcomes are also influenced by the monetary and nonmonetary investments that parents make in their children, investments that influence their skills, beliefs, and motivation. These investments reflect parents' degree of altruism and their efficacy in translating time and money into long-run outcomes. Different sets of values lead to different policy recommendations dealing with the extent of state intervention and public provision of goods that compensate or substitute for parental and familial investments of this more subtle sort.

As such, we should be cautious in drawing normative conclusions from observed statistical differences. Policy recommendations cannot be drawn from the sort of cross-country comparison we have offered without providing additional information about the social values that give meaning to "equality of opportunity" and defining the legitimate methods to attain it.

For this reason, we draw on Corak (2010) to inform our analysis with results from two public opinion polls conducted in 2009 that address a host of issues related to economic mobility and equality of opportunity. Among other things, this study asks a representative sample in both countries a question meant to uncover the meaning given to equality of opportunity. In the United States, respondents were asked the following question:

> The term "American Dream" means different things to different people. Here are some ways some people have described what the American Dream means to them. On a scale of one to ten, please tell me how accurately each statement describes what you consider the American Dream to be. One would mean this statement does not describe the American Dream at all. A ten would mean this statement describes the American Dream almost perfectly.

The term "American Dream" does not have a comparable counterpart in Canadian discussions of public policy and self-identity. The parallel question for the Canadian survey was determined on the basis of input from polling experts in both countries and piloted on a small sample of Canadians. It was posed as:

> Americans often talk about attaining the "American Dream" to describe what it means to have a good life in their country. This means different things to different people. Here are some ways some Americans have described what the American Dream means to them. On a scale of one to ten, please tell me how accurately each statement describes what you would consider the "Canadian Dream" to be. One would mean the statement does

Figure 3.3   Defining the American Dream in the United States and Canada: Percentage Responding Eight or Higher on a Ten-Point Scale

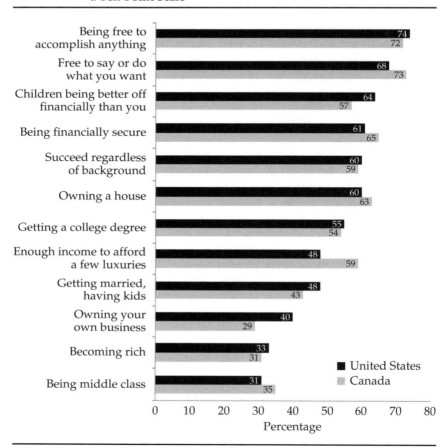

Source: Corak (2010, figure 5), reproduced with permission.

not describe what it means at all. A ten would mean the statement describes it perfectly.

Given that it may still be reasonable to question whether the two prompts are entirely equivalent, the answers to the questions are very similar and are presented in figure 3.3, which shows the proportion of the sample answering eight or higher on a ten-point scale.[2] Americans and Canadians have for the most part the very same ranking of these alternatives, and indeed in very much to the same degree. The two options that garner the greatest consensus—in the neighborhood of 70 percent—refer to aspects of individual freedom. Financial security follows next, with about 60 percent of the samples giving the financial welfare of children, financial security, and house ownership a score of eight or higher out of ten. Although there are some differences, the general message from this information is that there are strong similarities between the two countries in what the good life means and, most importantly, that it is associated with individual freedoms.

Corak (2010) points out that the citizens of these countries also have similar views concerning the factors that determine economic mobility. Both Americans and Canadians feel strongly that individual attributes, like hard work and schooling choices, lead to upward economic mobility. In both countries, factors external to the individual—those that are outside of his or her control—rank much lower.

The most notable difference between the two countries concerns the role of government as a means of influencing economic mobility. Corak (2010) reports that the question "Generally speaking, do you think the government does more to help or more to hurt people trying to move up the economic ladder?" does not garner majority support one way or the other in either of the countries. But 46 percent of Canadians feel that government does more to help than to hurt, compared to 36 percent of Americans. On the other hand, 46 percent of Americans feel that government does more to hurt versus 39 percent of Canadians.[3] These differences are wider than any other differences in responses to all the questions addressed to these two groups of citizens.

All of this suggests that while the citizens of the two countries may think of a good life for themselves and their children in the same way, their expectations concerning how to achieve this goal—and in particular the role of the state—may differ.

Two Portraits of Child Well-Being

How different are the investments that these countries make in their children? Are child well-being and child outcomes different as a result of these investments? And consequently, to what extent can we expect the degree of generational mobility observed for the current generation of young adults to continue for the next generation?

We respond to these questions by loosely organizing a descriptive analysis of the well-being of children and the situation in which they are growing up around the framework developed by Solon (2004). The portraits we paint are also informed by a wide literature on the influence of early childhood development on long-run outcomes, as exemplified by Eric Knudsen and his colleagues (2006), but these are portraits and not rigorous causal analyses. Our description uses a number of nationally representative surveys and is addressed to a group of children who were newborns to thirteen years of age just before the year 2000.[4] These children, who grew up during the 1990s and the first years of the new millennium, will be the next generation of adults in the coming decade or two. In other words, they are the cohort who, when they become young adults, will be the subject of the next wave of intergenerational mobility studies.

To paraphrase Solon (2004), we can imagine the adult outcomes of children being determined by three broad forces: the family, the labor market, and government policy. Families have different capacities and resources for investing in their children, and they face different incentives to do so according to their socioeconomic status and according to the institutions in their country. The degree to which inherent family traits and family-specific investments are passed on to the next generation reflects a wide range of influences, some specific to the national context.

But the capacity and the incentives to invest in children are also influenced by how families interact and interface with the labor market and public programs. An increase in the cost of human capital investment, such as in market-based provision of child care, private primary schooling, or college tuition fees, leads to lower human capital investment. At the same time, a higher return to human capital creates an incentive for more investment. Solon takes the rate of return to education as an indicator of the degree of inequality in the labor market and shows that societies with labor markets characterized by more cross-sectional inequality— that is, a higher return to education—are less generationally mobile.

Public policy can both accentuate and dampen the influence of labor market inequality. Solon also shows that generational mobility is promoted by "progressive" public programs—those that are of relatively more benefit to the relatively less well off. Thus, it is not simply the level of public expenditures that is important, but also the ways in which those expenditures are distributed according to socioeconomic status. Indeed, Solon's use of the term "public programs" means more than just public transfers or publicly provided child-directed programs. The term should be understood as referring to all aspects of public actions that influence the relationship between families and the labor market, which in addition to expenditures include the structure of taxation and regulations.

Parents, Families, and Family Life

Parents and families are central to the well-being of children in both the here and now and over the longer term as they grow into adulthood. Children require more than just the material sustenance that money can buy; they also need the nonmaterial care flowing from the time they share with their parents and other caregivers. The findings in this section sketch the circumstances that might offer both opportunities and challenges for parents to meet the monetary and nonmonetary needs of their children.

Age, ethnic background, and immigrant status in a rough way all signal the extent and types of networks that parents have and how well established they may be in the labor market. In particular, younger mothers are typically less secure economically insofar as they have not had time to finish an education, have not found a secure job, and face much higher rates of unemployment than older mothers. Besides monetary support, parents also offer their children time. Research indicates that, even after controlling for economic status, outcomes for children whose mothers were very young at the time of their birth are on average not as good as outcomes for children with older mothers. Young mothers may face a host of stresses associated with a lack of parenting experience and family support. Indeed, family structure is often cited as one of the most important determinants of child attainments. Living in a small family with two biological parents may offer the highest odds of setting a child off on a successful path; living with a single parent and in a large family may offer the lowest.

Research also shows that the mother's education is a very strong correlate of child well-being and outcomes. But this association is strongest for mothers with low levels of education. Having a mother with very low education is linked with significantly worse outcomes for children, but high levels of parental education are not any more significantly tied to better outcomes than are intermediate levels. As a result, differences between Canada and the United States in the postsecondary attainments of parents may not be particularly important for children.[5]

All of these characteristics and resources may influence parenting style. Given the centrality of parents in the lives of young children, positive parent-child interaction is often viewed as very important for child development and well-being, with many studies noting that parenting styles are highly correlated with child-health outcomes.[6] Mothers' physical and mental health is thought to have a strong association with child health status. Healthy mothers are thought to be most capable of adopting a parenting style of most benefit to their children.

For all of these reasons, we begin by presenting information on the age and education of mothers, as well as on other aspects of family size and structure.

Canadian and American children are about the same age, but their mothers are not. Canadian mothers are noticeably more likely to be ages thirty-five to forty-four (48.9 percent) than American mothers (39.1 percent). Almost 9 percent of American mothers are less than twenty-four years of age, but in Canada only half that proportion fall into this age group. The same general pattern holds for fathers present in the household.

This corresponds to the fact that there are differences across the countries with respect to the age at which women gave birth. Teenage births are more common in the United States. Table 3.1 shows that in Canada 2.1 percent of children thirteen years or younger were born to teenage mothers and that in the United States this figure—at 8.3 percent—is almost four

Table 3.1   The Characteristics of Families and Parents in Canada and the United States for Children Thirteen Years of Age or Younger in the Late 1990s

	Canada	United States
Proportion of children born to teenagers	2.1%	8.3%
Proportion of children born to black mothers	1.7	15.7
Proportion of children born to immigrants	17.2	14.3
Current marital status of mothers		
Married or common law	84.1	76.9
Single, divorced, or separated	8.9	13.0
Single, never married	6.0	9.1
Family size[a]		
No siblings	19.3	19.9
One sibling	46.0	40.0
Two siblings	24.5	24.6
Three or more siblings	10.2	15.6
Family size in single-parent families[b]		
No siblings	32.9	23.9
One sibling	41.8	33.9
Two siblings	18.7	24.5
Three or more siblings	6.6	17.7
Education attainment of mothers[c]		
Less than high school	12.1	12.9
High school diploma	17.6	31.3
Some postsecondary	27.5	16.3
Postsecondary certificate	25.0	14.5
University or college degree	17.7	25.1
Education attainment of single mothers[d]		
Less than high school	20.6	19.3
High school diploma	14.6	34.5
Some postsecondary	34.4	18.3
Postsecondary certificate	22.0	14.5
University or college degree	8.4	13.4

Source: Authors' calculations using weighted data from National Longitudinal Survey of Children and Youth (Statistics Canada n.d.) and the National Survey of American Families (Urban Institute n.d.).
[a]All children age thirteen or younger.
[b]All children age thirteen or younger living in single-mother families.
[c]All children age thirteen or younger with a mother present.
[d]All children age thirteen or younger living in single-mother families.

times as high. These differences are still noticeable when slightly older mothers are considered. Almost one in seven Canadian children (15.3 percent) were born to mothers age twenty to twenty-four years, but almost one in four American children (24.6 percent) have mothers in this age group at birth. As a result, there are proportionally many more very young mothers in the United States.

Canadian and American children live in very different types of families. In Canada, children are much more likely to be living with a mother who is currently married and even more likely to be living with both of their biological parents. In the United States, children are more likely to be living with stepparents or in single-mother families. Just over 84 percent of Canadian children live with mothers who are currently married (both legal and common law), while 77 percent of American children are in the same situation. In Canada, about 9 percent of children live with mothers who are single because they are divorced or separated, and a further 6 percent live with mothers who were never married. Both of these proportions are higher in the United States.

But the current marital status of the mother hides some important differences in the nature of families between the two countries. In Canada, 78 percent of children age thirteen and younger live with both biological parents—a substantially greater proportion than in the United States, where only 65 percent of children do so. As such, there is a larger difference in the proportion of children living with two biological parents than there is in the proportion living with a currently married mother. This implies that more children in the United States live with stepparents. Over 7 percent of American children have a stepparent, compared to 5.5 percent of Canadian children.

American single mothers tend to be younger than their Canadian counterparts, and they are more likely to have given birth as teenagers. Almost 15 percent of American single mothers are less than twenty-five years of age, compared to about 11 percent in Canada. The bulk of Canadian single mothers—more than four out of every ten—are between thirty-five and forty-four years of age. This is a substantially higher proportion than in the United States. Furthermore, a much higher fraction of U.S. children age thirteen and younger who are living with single mothers were born when she was a teenager (15 percent) than is the case for their counterparts in Canada (10 percent).

In Canada, single-mother families are smaller than other families; the most common size in both countries is a mother and two children. Over 40 percent of children in single-mother families in Canada have one sibling, and about 34 percent in the United States. But having no siblings is also common in these types of families, albeit more so in Canada than in the United States. Fully one in three Canadian children who live with a single mother have no siblings, compared to one in four in the United

States. At the same time, a greater fraction of American children with a single parent live in families of three or more children. Children in single-mother families in the United States are slightly more likely than other children to have two or more siblings. In contrast, Canadian children in single-mother families are much less likely than children in other families to have two or more siblings.

The fraction of parents who have not completed high school in Canada and the United States is about the same, but in Canada a larger fraction have gone on to some form of postsecondary education. About 12 to 13 percent of mothers have not completed high school. In Canada, however, 27.5 percent of mothers have some postsecondary education, while 17.6 percent have a high school diploma. Almost the reverse is true in the United States: 16.3 percent have some postsecondary education, and almost one-third have a high school diploma.

Having a postsecondary certificate or diploma (other than a university degree) is more likely among Canada mothers, while in the United States mothers are more likely to have degrees. This difference may reflect differences across the two countries in the structure of the education systems, with certificates being more commonly granted by Canadian community colleges, which are outside the university system. This pattern is much the same when the fathers present in the household are compared.

Education levels are considerably lower for single mothers compared to married mothers. They are much more likely to have very low levels of education and much less likely to have high levels. But the differences between the two countries mirror the patterns for all mothers. One-fifth of children in single-mother families are living with a mother who does not have a high school diploma. Single mothers are half as likely to have completed a university degree as married mothers, but this fraction is higher in the United States.

Not presented in table 3.1 are our data showing that, while parents on both sides of the border report themselves to be in good health, single mothers and low-income mothers report lower health status, particularly in the United States, where one in five single mothers say that they are in poor or fair health. Nine out of ten single mothers in Canada report being in good or better health, while one in ten report fair or poor health. In the United States, the proportion of single mothers reporting fair or poor health is twice as large at 21.3 percent. In addition, the mental health of single mothers and low-income mothers is significantly inferior to that of other mothers. In Canada, about one in twenty single mothers and low-income mothers have experienced a mental health problem that persisted for at least an entire week, about 7 percent have felt depressed for all or most of a week, and about 5 percent report having been "unable to shake the blues" or not feeling happy. This is significantly greater than the 2 to 3 percent of Canadian mothers overall who feel the same way. The same

general patterns hold in the United States, with about double the proportion of single mothers and low-income mothers reporting mental health
problems all or most of the time relative to mothers overall.

It is difficult to obtain comparable measures of parenting style across
these two countries with the surveys available to us. One comparable
indicator of parent-child interaction is the extent to which children are
read to. This falls short of characterizing the nature of the parenting
style, but the data do show that approximately 64 percent of Canadian
children and 46 percent of American children are read to daily. One-
quarter of Canadian children and one-half of American children are
read to between one and six days per week. Children who are never read
to constitute nearly 10 percent of the group of Canadian children between
the ages of zero and five; the comparable number in the United States is
7 percent.

The proportion of children who are never read to is higher in single-
mother families, and particularly in low-income families, in both countries. Fewer children in these families are read to daily in comparison with
all children, although a higher proportion of these children in Canada are
read to daily than is the case with comparably situated children in the
United States: 54.4 percent versus 36.4 percent of low-income children,
and 58.9 percent versus 37.6 percent of the children of single mothers.

Work and Child Care Arrangements

Parental participation in the labor market is both cause and effect of child
care arrangements. Parents who choose or need to work must find alternative arrangements for their children, and the availability of care outside
of the home offers opportunities to work or to work more hours.

In this section, we begin by noting that Canadian mothers of the cohort
of children under study have higher rates of labor force participation than
American mothers, but mothers and fathers who are in the labor force
work longer hours in the United States. On this basis alone, it is not immediately apparent how labor market engagement influences the overall
demand for child care or how differences in social policy and family
structure influence work patterns.

However, there are very clear differences between the two countries in
child care policies and social support. Parental benefits are much more
generous in Canada. In 1998, Canadian mothers who had worked a minimum of seven hundred hours over a fifty-two-week period received fifteen weeks of maternity benefits equivalent to 55 percent of past earnings.
Another ten weeks of leave could be taken under the same conditions by
either the mother or the father of a newborn, though generally this parental
benefit was taken up by mothers. Thus, in Canada, new mothers who had
sufficient work experience were being provided with the opportunity to

stay home for up to twenty-five weeks after the birth of their child. In 2001 this package of benefits, administered by the federal government through the national unemployment insurance program, was extended to one year. Maternity benefits are much more limited in the United States. Parents are entitled to twelve weeks of leave without pay if they work in a company with more than fifty people. This covers only about half of women in the workforce. Also, the United States offers a tax deduction for child care if it facilitates employment.

National child care programs are not offered in either country. In Canada, child care is organized provincially, with some provinces offering universal programs and others subsidizing certain child care facilities or offering subsidies or tax deductions to parents. In the United States, child care is publicly provided for some vulnerable children under the Head Start program, and at the federal level there is limited funding for low-income working families through the Child Care Development Fund Block Grant created in 1996. It has been estimated that only about 12 percent of eligible children are receiving this support. These funds can be used for child care services, and a state can also waive fees for families below the poverty line.

Families engage with labor markets in very different ways in these two countries, and the institutional context set by public policy is also very different. In the United States, more mothers either work full-time or not at all. Almost 30 percent of mothers in the United States are not in the paid labor force; in Canada, just under one-quarter do not work. At the same time, four out of every ten American children have mothers who work forty or more hours per week, the most common arrangement. Only one-quarter of Canadian children have mothers who work forty or more hours per week. Lower hours of maternal employment are much more common in Canada, where about half of children have mothers who are employed less than forty hours per week. This is the case for fewer than one-third of children in the United States. In both countries, it is relatively rare for mothers to work more than fifty hours per week, but at the same time it is not uncommon. Over 7 percent of children in the United States and 5 percent in Canada have mothers who work these very long hours (see table 3.2).

In both countries, the workweek is much longer for fathers than it is for mothers, with fathers in the United States in the late 1990s working more than their Canadian counterparts. Not working at all is rather uncommon for fathers in both countries, and fathers are also not as likely as mothers to be employed part-time. In both Canada and the United States, about one-half of fathers work forty to forty-nine hours per week. Working even longer hours is significantly more common in the United States, where almost 40 percent of fathers work fifty hours per week or more, compared to about 30 percent in Canada.

Table 3.2   Distribution of Weekly Hours of Work for Mothers, Fathers, and Single Mothers of Children Age Thirteen and Younger in Canada and the United States

	Mothers		Fathers		Single Mothers	
	Canada	United States	Canada	United States	Canada	United States
Not working	24.8	29.0	5.5	4.0	31.9	20.2
One to twenty-nine hours	24.8	16.9	2.9	2.2	18.6	13.7
Thirty to thirty-nine hours	25.1	13.8	11.6	4.8	23.6	17.6
Forty to forty-nine hours	20.3	32.8	51.7	50.4	21.0	39.3
Fifty or more hours	5.0	7.4	28.2	38.6	4.9	9.1

Source: Authors' calculations using weighted data from National Longitudinal Survey of Children and Youth (Statistics Canada n.d.) and the National Survey of American Families (Urban Institute n.d.).
Note: Expressed as column percentages of all children thirteen years or younger in each family type.

More detailed calculations show that, as a result of the patterns documented in table 3.2, one in ten children of married couples in the United States have parents who together work over one hundred hours per week. This high commitment to paid work is much less common in Canada, where it occurs for only two out of every one hundred children. The most common arrangement in the United States is for parents to work from eighty to ninety-nine hours per week. In contrast, Canadian parents most commonly work between sixty and seventy-nine hours per week.

In the United States, single mothers are more likely to be working than married mothers. Only about one-fifth of single mothers do not work any hours per week, but this is the case for almost one-third of married mothers. In Canada, these proportions are almost exactly reversed. Furthermore, just over 48 percent of single mothers work more than forty hours per week in the United States, almost double the Canadian proportion.

On the flip side of these employment patterns are differences in care arrangements for infants and toddlers, preschoolers, and school-age children (as documented in table 3.3). The majority of infants and toddlers in Canada are cared for by their parents; in the United States the majority are in some other type of care. Fifty-six percent of all children up to two years of age are cared for exclusively by their parents in Canada, compared to 40.7 percent in the United States. This difference probably reflects the very different maternity and parental leave policies in Canada for

Table 3.3   **Child Care Arrangements in Canada and the United States**

	Canada	United States
Children zero to two years of age[a]		
Parental care	55.9%	40.7%
Child care center	6.4	13.3
Cared for by a relative	16.0	30.0
Cared for by a nonrelative	21.0	15.5
Children three to four years of age[a]		
Parental care	45.4	23.1
Child care center	12.4	34.3
Cared for by a relative	15.2	21.3
Cared for by a nonrelative	25.1	12.6
Children five to ten years of age[a]		
Parental care	54.6	40.7
Child care center	2.7	5.9
Before- or after-school program	5.2	13.6
Cared for by a relative	17.5	22.2
Cared for by a nonrelative	17.0	12.0
Children five to ten years of age in single-mother families[b]		
Parental care	48.1	27.7
Child care center	3.7	5.6
Before- or after-school program	7.7	17.7
Cared for by a relative	18.9	30.9
Cared for by a nonrelative	17.6	12.4

Source: Authors' calculations using weighted data from National Longitudinal Survey of Children and Youth (Statistics Canada n.d.) and the National Survey of American Families (Urban Institute n.d.).
Note: Totals do not add up to 100 as not all child care options are presented.
[a]Expressed as a percentage of children in the particular age category.
[b]Expressed as a percentage of children five to ten years of age in single-mother families.

working mothers of newborn children. The labor force participation of mothers with children younger than one year of age is much higher in the United States and no different than it is for mothers as a whole. In the United States, 29.8 percent of women with an infant—or virtually the same fraction as all mothers—report that they do not work. In Canada, 35.6 percent of mothers with newborns report not working versus 24.8 percent of all mothers.[7]

Over three-quarters of American preschoolers are in some type of non-parental care arrangement, while only about half of Canadian three- and four-year-olds are in this situation. Preschoolers in the United States are on average three times more likely to be cared for in formal child care centers than preschoolers in Canada. These facts imply that the longer work hours of mothers and fathers create more of a demand for nonparental care than the higher overall labor market participation in Canada, a tendency consistent with the flexible work arrangements that permit more part-time employment among Canadian mothers.

The majority of children five to ten years of age in Canada receive parental care only (54.6 percent). The figure is significantly lower but still substantial in the United States at 40.7 percent. Proportionately more five- to ten-year-olds attend before- and after-school programs in the United States—about 14 percent versus only about 5 percent in Canada. In both countries, only a small fraction of children—just over 3 percent in the United States and 2 percent in Canada—look after themselves when their parents are working.

The final panel of table 3.3 illustrates that there are substantial differences in the care arrangements of five- to ten-year-olds in single-mother families, with about a twenty-percentage-point difference in the fraction receiving nonparental care. Fifty-two percent of the five- to ten-year-olds of these parents in Canada are in this situation, as are 72 percent of American children in this age group with single mothers. At the same time, care by a relative is more common for the children of single mothers who are receiving nonparental care in the United States than it is in Canada, with nearly one-third in this situation in the United States compared with one-fifth in Canada. As with all children, the children of American single mothers are more likely to attend before- and after-school programs. More Canadian children, however, are separately cared for by a non-relative (17.6 percent versus 12.4 percent), either inside or outside the child's home.

It is possible that child care has a wide variety of opposing impacts on child well-being. High-quality care might mitigate some of the disadvantages of limited early nurturing in dysfunctional families, for example, but a reduction in the period of time during which young children can be breast-fed might have a detrimental impact on their long-term health and well-being. One of the difficulties inherent in assessing the overall impact of child care is that the substitution of nonparental care for parental care has the potential to either increase or decrease the emotional and physical resources available to a child. If the availability of child care increases the ability of family members to work, for example, the ramifications may be both positive and negative for a child.

In her detailed description of child care arrangements in Canada, Tracey Bushnik (2006) documents that the use of child care increased most notably in Quebec from 1995 to 2003. Michael Baker, Jonathan Gruber, and Kevin Milligan (2008) find evidence in the National Longitudinal Survey of Children and Youth (NLSCY) data that a number of outcome measures worsened for children in two-parent families in Quebec. These results may be attributable to a variety of causes involving either the nature of the child care itself or the increases in the labor market activity of mothers that were observed as a result of the introduction of the universal child care program.[8]

Family Income, Low Income, and Inequality

Children in the United States are on average significantly more affluent than those in Canada. After taxes and government transfers, the resources available to the average child in the United States amounts to $35,667 versus $27,222 in Canada, a difference of $8,445, or 31 percent. On the basis of the methods used in the calculations, this difference is equivalent to $16,890 for a family of four.[9]

Labor market earnings are the major source of income in both countries, but there are marked differences in the structure of government transfers available to families with children in the two countries. Almost nine out of every ten children in Canada live in a family receiving some form of transfer income. The proportion of children in Canada receiving transfer income (including, for example, child tax benefits, both regular and maternity or parental employment insurance benefits, and social assistance) is close to double that in the United States (87.5 percent versus 45.8 percent). Those families receiving transfers get an average of $3,107 per child in Canada and $2,883 in the United States.[10]

In Canada, fully 85 percent of children in two-parent families receive some form of income support from the government, but this proportion is only 35 percent in the United States. These proportions are higher in both countries for children living in single-parent families. Virtually all (99.7 percent) of these children are in receipt of some amount of income transfer in Canada, compared to 83 percent in the United States.

Despite considerably higher average incomes, children in the United States are much more likely to be living in low-income households. During 1999, 26.7 percent of U.S. children, versus 17.1 percent of Canadian children, lived below a low-income threshold of one-half of median income.[11] On average, the depth of low income is also greater in the United States. The average child in a low-income household was 41.7 percent below the low-income threshold in the United States, but 26.5 percent below in Canada. This gap amounted to $6,268 in the United States and $3,213 in Canada.

These differences are the result of the fact that transfer payments reduce the rate of low income in Canada significantly more than in the United States. In fact, labor markets lead to roughly similar rates of low income in both countries. About the same fraction of children would be in a low-income household on the basis of solely parental labor market earnings: 27.1 percent in Canada compared with 30 percent in the United States. The depth of low income would be greater in Canada. On average, low-income Canadian children would be 60.3 percent below the low-income threshold, while American children would be 50.9 percent below.

Although 63.2 percent of low-income Canadian children live in families reporting some labor market earnings, for only 30.3 percent are earnings the major source. This is in contrast with low-income children in the United States, where earnings are the major source of income for 77.6 percent. Earnings are a smaller share of total income in Canada because rates of labor force participation are lower for low-income parents and because government transfers are more significant. In Canada, 36.8 percent of low-income families with children report zero earnings, while in the United States this is so for only 11.7 percent. Virtually all (99.9 percent) Canadian low-income families with children receive some form of transfer payment. Receipt of transfer income is also the norm in the United States, with 93.1 percent of low-income families with children reporting that they receive some amount of support, but the amount is not as high.

In both Canada and the United States, children are significantly more likely to be in the bottom of the countrywide income distribution. About 15 percent of children in each country are found in the bottom 10 percent of the income distribution for the entire population, and only about 5 to 6 percent are in the top 10 percent. Although children in the two countries fit into their respective country income distributions in much the same way, the gap between a child at the top and one at the bottom is much larger in the United States. The child in the top 10 percent of the U.S. income distribution has on average over fourteen times as much income as a child in the bottom 10 percent. In Canada the income of a child in the top 10 percent is seven and a half times the income of a child in the bottom 10 percent. The differences are also significant when the average middle-income child is compared to the average child in the bottom tenth. In the United States, the child in the middle of the income distribution has 4.6 times as much income as a child in the bottom; in Canada the middle-income child has only 2.7 times as much.

These differences reflect the fact that the income distribution in the United States is much more unequal than in Canada, with a larger fraction of individuals having a much higher than average income and a larger fraction having a much lower than average income. As figure 3.4 illustrates, this also implies that the incomes of a strong majority of Canadian children would place them in the lower-middle portion of the U.S. income distribution. About two-thirds of Canadian children (64.2 percent) have incomes that would rank them above the bottom tenth of the income distribution but no higher than the middle. Only 24.4 percent of Canadian children have incomes sufficient enough to place them in the top half of the U.S. distribution, compared with 38.9 percent of American children. The chances that a Canadian child will be in the top tenth of the U.S. income distribution are only 1.5 percent versus 5.2 percent for American

Figure 3.4   Distribution of Children in Canada and the United States in the U.S. Income Distribution

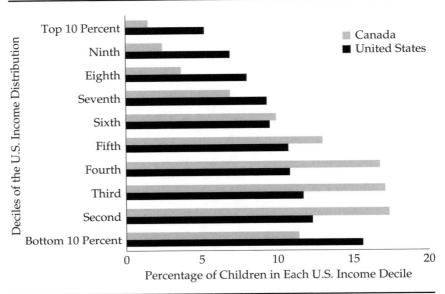

Source: Authors' calculations using 1999 Current Population Survey for the United States (U.S. Bureau of the Census 1999) and 1998 Survey of Labour and Income Dynamics for Canada (Statistics Canada 2000).

children. At the same time, Canadian children are less likely to have an income placing them in the bottom of the U.S. income distribution. Only 11.4 percent of Canadian children would find themselves in the bottom 10 percent, a situation faced by 15.6 percent of U.S. children.

Other indicators of material well-being also point to the fact that Canadian children live in less extreme circumstances. Over three-quarters (76 percent) of Canadian families with young children own the home in which they live. In the United States, 63 percent of families with children own their homes. Rates of homeownership are much lower for low-income families in both countries. In Canada, four in ten low-income families own the home in which they live, and in the United States 3.6 of every ten do so.

As well as being a proxy for wealth, homeownership may indicate a greater overall level of stability. Frequent residential moves, for example, have been shown to be a correlate of poorer outcomes for children. James Coleman (1988) treats residential moves as a marker for the disruption of the social capital and networks available to the family and child. In our data, over half of children between the ages of two and thirteen moved at least once in their lifetime, with the proportion being higher in the United States and higher among low-income children. In Canada, 57.6 percent of children experienced a change of residence, compared with 65.4 percent in the United States. At the same time, close to seven out of ten low-income Canadian children (68 percent) changed residence at some point in their lives compared to three-quarters (74 percent) of low-income American children.

Living conditions are more crowded in the United States, particularly for low-income children, where 70 percent share a bedroom and only 6.5 percent live in homes with extra bedrooms. In Canada, 57.4 percent of low-income children share a room, and about 9 percent live in homes with more bedrooms than children or adults in the house.

Early Childhood Outcomes and the Prospects for Economic Mobility

These configurations of forces—family structure and family life, caregiving arrangements and participation in the labor market, and financial resources from the market and the state in both an absolute and a relative sense—all come together to determine the relationship between a child's socioeconomic status and well-being in the here and now as well as capacities for succeeding in life in the future. A series of intermediate outcomes links family background to adult outcomes. In particular, mental and physical health, as well as cognitive development and readiness to learn, have all been shown to vary with social and economic background. In this section, we document differences in these outcomes between Canada and the United States and speculate on the prospects for economic mobility in the two countries.

It is not possible to sketch a direct causal link between the differences in resources available to children in these two countries and the early outcomes that influence their long-term prospects. But if there is a relationship, our portrait of child well-being in Canada and the United States would suggest that differences in the prospects of the children on the two sides of the border should be evident even at the early ages that are the focus of our analysis. The cohorts of young children under study—particularly the relatively less well off—were being raised in more challenging family circumstances in the United States. Younger, less well educated parents—who are more likely to also be single parents and who must obtain a larger fraction of their income from employment yet have less flexibility in their choice of child care arrangements and hours of work—find themselves in more stressful situations. The challenges of providing for both the monetary and nonmonetary needs of their children are greater for those at the bottom of the income ladder in the United States. In fact, the absolute disadvantages faced by these children are more severe than the situation of their relatively disadvantaged counterparts in Canada.

If these patterns had also held a generation ago, it might not be surprising that bottom-decile sons in Canada are as likely to move to the top half of the earnings distribution as third-decile Americans. These differences in absolute advantage reflect not just more challenging family situations but also the stronger presence of a more unequal labor market in American family life. This unequal labor market is not met with as large a counterweight through public programs, such as child care and leave policies, tax-transfer programs, and broad-based public provision of health care and public education of relatively more advantage to the disadvantaged. In this sense, all three elements of Solon's (2004) model—family, labor markets, and public policy—offer less support to those at the bottom of the income distribution in the United States than in Canada.

The suggestion would be that the gap in the degree of generational economic mobility between these two countries described for a previous generation of young adults in the existing empirical literature is likely not to be narrowed for the children growing up during the 1990s, those who will come of age in the next decade or so. This is not a statement on the current configuration of public policy in the United States to the extent that it has changed for the cohort of children born since 2000. But if this speculation has any validity, then we should already begin to see differences in the outcomes relevant for economic mobility among the children who are the subject of our analysis. Consequently, we focus on three related outcomes that interact to set a trajectory for a child and offer both risks and opportunities for long-run success: mental and physical health, cognitive outcomes and readiness to learn, and early education outcomes.

Empirical research has documented a strong positive association between income and health in adulthood and the antecedents for this relationship in childhood. Poor health in childhood is likely to exert a long-run influence through two channels: directly through its influence on the person's health as an adult, and indirectly through its effects on schooling and the accumulation of other experience. An understanding of the relationship between family background and income, on the one hand, and health in childhood, on the other, may therefore signal the nature of the long-term prospects for children living in low-income families and hence the probable degree of their economic mobility.

At the risk of overstating the case, the study of the income-health gradient benefits from an expected direction of causation, since child health is not likely to determine child socioeconomic status. The correlation may still be capturing other factors, but the case is certainly stronger than what can be said of adult health. Income-health gradients have been documented with Canadian as well as American data and exist in Canada despite the presence of universal public health insurance coverage of doctor and hospital services (Case, Lubotsky, and Paxon 2002; Currie and Stabile 2003;

Oreopoulos et al. 2008; Phipps 2002; Smith 2009). A widening gap in the health of children of low and high socioeconomic status as they age has been observed and is hypothesized to stem from one of two factors: either low-income children are less able to adapt to and recover from adverse health "shocks" than are other children, so that the impacts of health events persist and accumulate for them, or low-income children respond similarly to single negative health events in the long term but are subject to a greater incidence of shocks over time.[12]

Table 3.4 shows that the mental health of children varies strongly with socioeconomic status in both the United States and Canada. Canadian and American mothers report that 70 percent of their children are never nervous, high-strung, or tense. Approximately one-fourth of their children sometimes exhibit these tendencies, and three in one hundred children do so often. Although there are no significant differences noted between the United States and Canada for any type of household, children in single-mother or low-income families in both countries are less likely to never be nervous, high-strung, or tense relative to children in all families. The difference is 9 percent in Canada and 6 percent in the United States. In Canada, these children are nearly twice as likely as all children to exhibit these tendencies often.

About 60 percent of mothers in both Canada and the United States report that their children have never experienced concentration problems. As with nervousness and tension, no differences are apparent across countries, but children in single-parent and low-income households in both countries are 10 percent more likely than are all children to have concentration difficulties.

At the same time, Canadian children are reported to be happier than American children. Seventy-five percent of Canadian children and 66 percent of American children, according to their mothers, are never miserable, unhappy, tearful, or distressed. About one-fourth of Canadian children and one-third of American children are reported to sometimes be in this state, and 1 percent and 2 percent of Canadian and American children, respectively, are reported to be so often. The percentage of children who are often unhappy or distressed is slightly higher among low-income and single-mother families in each country, but there are no significant differences in rates for these family types between the two countries. Children in single-mother families are less likely than other children to never be miserable or unhappy. In Canada, these children are nearly 15 percent less likely than other children to never be unhappy; the comparable gap in the United States is 7 percent.

The physical health of children also varies across these two countries. American mothers are more inclined to report that their children are in only fair or poor health. Approximately 60 percent of children in each country are reported to be in excellent health, and 29.2 percent in Canada

Table 3.4   Mental Health Indicators for Children Thirteen Years and Younger in Canada and the United States

	Canada			United States		
	All Families	Single-Mother Families	Low-Income Families	All Families	Single-Mother Families	Low-Income Families
Nervous, high-strung, or tense						
Never or not true	71.2%	62.5%	67.2%	71.6%	66.7%	67.3%
Sometimes or somewhat true	25.7	31.7	28.8	25.1	28.2	27.4
Often or very true	3.0	5.8	4.0	3.2	5.1	5.3
Child cannot concentrate for long						
Never or not true	60.0	48.5	51.4	57.5	47.9	51.1
Sometimes or somewhat true	33.1	40.4	39.5	34.3	39.3	35.8
Often or very true	6.9	11.2	9.1	8.2	12.8	13.1
Miserable, unhappy, tearful, or distressed						
Never or not true	74.5	60.2	71.0	66.3	59.7	62.8
Sometimes or somewhat true	24.5	37.9	27.9	31.9	37.8	34.0
Often or very true	0.9	1.9	1.1	1.9	2.5	3.2

Source: Authors' calculations using weighted data from National Longitudinal Survey of Children and Youth (Statistics Canada n.d.) and the National Survey of American Families (Urban Institute n.d.).

Notes: Table entries are column percentages of all children thirteen years or younger, except for the middle panel, which refers to children between the ages of six and eleven. The responses to survey questions were "never," "sometimes," or "often" in Canada, and "not true," "somewhat true," or "very true" in the United States.

Table 3.5   **Indicators of Physical Health for Children in the United States and Canada**

	All Families		Single-Mother Families		Low-Income Families	
	Canada	United States	Canada	United States	Canada	United States
Child's health status[a]						
Excellent	58.1%	57.2%	52.4%	48.6%	52.4%	47.7%
Very good	29.2	26.4	31.5	27.8	29.7	25.8
Good	11.1	12.3	14.1	16.4	14.9	19.0
Fair	1.4	3.5	1.8	6.4	2.5	6.6
Poor	0.2	0.5	0.2	0.8	0.5	1.0
Physician visits during the year	83.6	77.4	86.5	77.9	84.0	69.9
Hospitalizations during the year	4.5	7.9	5.2	8.1	5.9	8.7

Source: Authors' calculations using weighted data from National Longitudinal Survey of Children and Youth (Statistics Canada n.d.) and the National Survey of American Families (Urban Institute n.d.).
Note: Expressed as a proportion of children thirteen years and younger in each family type.
[a]Health status as reported by the mother.

and 26.4 percent in the United States are reported to be in very good health. At 4 percent versus 1.6 percent, more than twice as many children in the United States are reported to be in fair or poor health as in Canada. Although children in single-mother families are worse off relative to all children in both countries, Canadian children in these families fare better than their American counterparts, with 2 percent versus 7 percent reported being in fair or poor health. A similar pattern emerges with respect to low-income children: 3 percent in Canada and 7.6 percent in the United States are reported to be in either fair or poor health (see table 3.5).

More Canadian than American children visit the doctor in a given year; the opposite is true of visits to nurses. Nearly 84 percent of Canadian children and 77 percent of American children make physician visits. Children in Canada on average make a greater number of visits to physicians: 3.3 versus 2.7 per year. Nurse visits are higher in the United States: 35 percent of children in the United States and 19 percent of Canadian children receive care from a nurse. The average number of nurse visits per child is also greater in the United States. These patterns probably have a good deal to do with the universal provision of health care in Canada. Similar patterns are not seen, for example, with respect to visits to dentists, which in general are not covered by public health insurance in either country. Almost 80 percent of children ages three to thirteen in both Canada and the United States make dental visits.

In general, Canadian children in single-mother and low-income families are as likely as other children to see a physician. But while this pattern holds true in the United States for children from single-mother households, a slightly smaller proportion of American children from low-income households, relative to all children, see a doctor during the year. In general, the average numbers of doctor visits are alike across the different groups in each country, although in Canada the children of single mothers and children in low-income families make slightly more visits than do all children.[13] Interestingly, this is not the case for visits to a dentist. In Canada, only two-thirds of children from low-income families, and three-fourths from single-mother families, visit a dentist, compared—as mentioned—to almost 80 percent for children regardless of family type. In addition, there are no significant differences in these rates across the two countries.

American children have higher rates of hospitalization. About 4.5 percent of Canadian children versus 8 percent of American children are hospitalized during the year, a fact that may seem surprising given the higher rate of physician visits in Canada. It may be that visits to physicians prevent some hospitalizations, that the relatively poorer health of children in the United States leads to higher rates of hospitalization, or that there is more rationing of care in Canada. Although patterns of hospitalization for different family types are relatively similar within each of the two countries, the children of low-income parents are slightly more likely to experience a hospitalization than are other children. In Canada, 5.9 percent stay overnight in the hospital versus 4.5 percent of all children; in the United States, 8.7 percent of low-income children, in comparison with 7.9 percent of all children, are hospitalized during the year. The between-country differences are significant for all groups.

Mental and physical health are important in their own right, but also because they may influence cognitive and learning outcomes. In fact, early learning and vocabulary development varies significantly across the countries, with four- and five-year-old Canadian children scoring significantly higher on a comparable test of school readiness. Canadian four-year-olds have an average raw score on the Peabody Picture Vocabulary Test that is 10.3 percent above that of four-year-old children in the United States. The gap for five-year-olds is smaller, at 6.2 percent, but still favors Canadian children.

According to the reports of mothers in the two countries, similar proportions of children between the ages of six and thirteen are doing well at school, although a slightly higher proportion of Canadian children are doing very well (44 percent versus 38 percent). Mothers in the United States report a higher percentage of children with average performance:

28 percent versus 23 percent in Canada. As with mothers' assessments of health, the most notable difference between Canadian children and American children is at the bottom of the scale. The proportion of U.S. children performing below the middle or near the bottom in school is twice what it is in Canada (7 percent versus 3.4 percent). The schooling results for single-mother or low-income children are not quite as good as for other children in both countries, although the same basic patterns emerge from mothers' reports. Specifically, 5.8 percent of the children of single mothers are performing poorly in school in Canada, in comparison with 10.7 percent in the United States. The difference for low-income children is not as stark but is still significant between the two countries: 5.3 percent in Canada and 8.3 percent in the United States are performing poorly or very poorly in school.

Granted, these indicators lack complete objectivity. After all, in both countries well over two-thirds of the children are reported by their mothers to be doing better than average in school. Although this result is not unique to these data or this study, it is the differences between the two countries that are important. Furthermore, these differences hold up in more comprehensive tests of older children. For example, the Third International Mathematics and Science Study (TIMSS) offers information on how children ages twelve and thirteen years compare across countries on standardized math and science tests. According to these results, Canadian children perform substantially better on average in mathematics and somewhat better in science than do children in the United States. Both Canadian and American children are above the international mean for the math and science test scores. For the United States, the standardized mean math score is 501.6, while for Canada it is about one-third of a standard deviation higher, at 530.8. The Canadian standardized mean score for science is slightly higher, at 533.1, but the American science score, 514.9, is also higher than its math score. According to these measures, Canadian children are doing substantially better in math and somewhat better in science than American children.[14]

Along most of these dimensions—mental and physical health, early learning, and academic performance in primary school—Canadian children, but particularly Canadian children from single-parent or low-income families, have on average better outcomes than their American counterparts. As such, this picture lines up with the differences in the resources available to these children through family, markets, and public policy, and this would suggest that the foundation for economic mobility is already being laid in the years before these children become teenagers and make decisions concerning higher education and employment. It is thus very likely that the differences in the degree of generational mobility documented for young adults who came of age during the 1990s will continue at least for another generation of young adults.

Conclusions

This study of the relationship between family economic background and adult outcomes in the United States and Canada suggests that there are important similarities and differences between these two countries. International comparisons of the average degree of generational earnings mobility suggest that Canada is more mobile than the United States, but a closer look at studies that use particularly high-quality data that are directly comparable across this pair of countries shows that the difference is even larger than implied by the broad international literature. On average, Canada is up to three times more mobile than the United States. Furthermore, these differences arise from differences in the extremes of the earnings distribution: there is notably less mobility at the very top and the very bottom of the American income ladder. For this reason, we focus our more detailed comparative analysis not just on the average child but also on the relatively disadvantaged, and we try to chart the prospects for upward mobility in these two countries.

These cross-country differences in outcomes are not a reflection of different societal preferences or different interpretations of the meaning of equality of opportunity. In fact, it is valuable to compare these two particular relatively rich countries because they are so much alike. Both countries value the ideal of equality of opportunity, and both define it in terms of individual freedoms but also individual responsibilities. Americans, however, are more inclined to view government as hindering rather than helping this process.

This is reflected in the actual resources available to children. We offer a descriptive overview of these resources organized loosely around a model of intergenerational economic mobility that highlights the role of families, labor markets, and public policies in determining the degree of mobility and explaining differences between jurisdictions. The family context in which children are raised in the United States is more challenging than in Canada, raising the risk that the capabilities of some children will not be fully developed. American labor markets are also more unequal, raising the stakes for child outcomes, both elevating opportunities and heightening risks. Finally, public policy is less "progressive" in the United States and does not compensate in the same degree for family background and labor market inequality.

The portrait we paint of young children across these three dimensions underscores the fact that childhood outcomes differ before children reach their teen years and may direct them down pathways that will lead to different adult outcomes. Mental and physical health, school readiness, and some education outcomes are all more developed in Canada. But this portrait also highlights some particularly relevant institutional differences in public policy between the countries that merit closer attention as the underlying causes.

First, the universal provision of accessible health care in Canada plays a role in the preventative care of children, reducing the number and severity of health shocks that could lead to more severe difficulties. But in both countries issues of access are subtly associated with economic and social barriers that limit visits to health care providers, ability to pay for prescriptions, and knowledge as to how to navigate the health care system. The anecdotal evidence provided by Janny Scott (2005) with respect to U.S. adults' ability to access and respond to care providers probably rings true for children on both sides of the border.

Second, the flexibility available to parents in making child care choices and deciding upon hours of work differs between the two countries, whose very different policies offer different opportunities for parents in balancing the demands of family and workplace, particularly in the early years of a child's life. Canadian mothers and fathers would appear to have more flexibility as a result of significant policy changes in the mid-1990s that extended paid leave during the year after a child's birth as well as the legislative right to return to their jobs. There seems also to be more use of part-time employment in Canada. In the United States, the limited nature of parental leave policies leads to a polarization in family decisions: relatively well-off families can afford either to use private child care or to have the mother withdraw from the labor market, while at the other extreme single mothers have fewer options and are much more likely to continue working. This discussion leaves aside important issues of the quality of the care arrangements, an area of continued research.

The third public policy issue stems from labor market inequalities and the role of tax-transfer programs. Left to their own devices, labor markets lead to roughly the same level of income poverty in these two countries, though there is more affluence on average in the United States and greater inequality. Although the average Canadian child is not as affluent as the average American child, the poorest Canadian is not as poor in an absolute sense as Americans at the bottom of the income distribution. Public income transfers play a much more important role in reducing poverty among children in Canada, where virtually all families receive some measure of public support.

It is important to reemphasize that much of our analysis refers to a particular cohort of young people—those who were young teens at the turn of the century and who will soon be coming of age as adults. Demographics, labor markets, and public policy have all changed significantly over the course of the last decade. These changes may have a bearing on how younger cohorts of children fare as adults. But given the configuration of these forces during the period relevant for the cohort we study, essentially the 1990s and early 2000s, our analysis suggests that the next wave of intergenerational mobility studies—which will be based on this very group—are likely to find that the degree of mobility remains greater in Canada than in the United States.

The authors are affiliated, respectively, with the University of Ottawa, Ottawa, Canada; the University of Waterloo, Waterloo, Canada; and Dalhousie University, Halifax, Canada. Corak also acknowledges his affiliation with the Institute for the Study of Labor (IZA) and the Centre for Research and Analysis of Migration (CReAM). This research was supported financially by the Pew Charitable Trusts and the Social Sciences Humanities Research Council of Canada through a Standard Research Grant to Corak. The support of the Statistics Canada Halifax Research Data Centre, which facilitated access to some of the Canadian surveys used in the analysis, and the research assistance of Stephanie Andrews, Ali Akba Ganghro, and Lynn Lethbridge is also gratefully acknowledged. The comments and suggestions of participants, particularly those of Julia Isaacs, at the working conference on "Intergenerational Mobility Within and Across Nations" sponsored in part by the Russell Sage Foundation and organized by the Institute for Research on Poverty at the University of Wisconsin–Madison in September 2009, and at the fall 2009 meetings of the Association for Public Policy and Management held in Washington, D.C., as well as those by the editors and two referees, are acknowledged with appreciation. A more detailed version of this chapter is available as Corak, Curtis, and Phipps (2010).

Notes

1. Mazumder (2004) links the Survey of Income and Program Participation (SIPP) to Social Security Administration summary earnings data, offering high-quality earnings information on up to 1,600 father-and-son pairs.
2. The 95 percent confidence interval for the U.S. survey is plus-or-minus 3.4 percentage points at sample proportions of 50 percent, falling to plus-or-minus 2.0 percent at 10 and 90 percent. These bounds are similar in Canada, with the 95 percent interval being plus-or-minus 3.0 percent at a proportion of 50 percent. With respect to this particular question, the option "Getting a college degree" was changed in the Canadian version to "Getting a university degree."
3. The remaining 15 to 18 percent responded either "both," "depends," or "neither."
4. For a detailed discussion of the data sources and our use of them, see Corak, Curtis, and Phipps (2010).
5. One exception to this pattern, however, is schooling outcomes, which tend to be strongly influenced by higher levels of maternal education. All this being said, it is again important to recognize that, since the publication of Behrman and Rosenzweig (2002), the causal mechanism from mother's edu-

cation to child outcomes is the subject of debate. For a comprehensive overview of this literature, see Holmlund, Lindahl, and Plug (2008).

6. Parenting styles are sometimes classified as being, at one extreme, permissive, and at the other, authoritarian. It has been suggested that the style of greatest benefit to children involves neither of these but rather a positive-authoritative interaction. While still acknowledging the importance of parenting style, other researchers have pointed out that attributing causality to correlations can be difficult. Parenting style may be as much a response to children's behavior as a cause of it (Burton, Phipps, and Curtis 2002; Cadman et al. 1991).

7. This said, while more young children in the United States are in nonparental care, the overall pattern in the type of care is fairly similar in the two countries. In both countries, an infant is most likely to be cared for by a parent. In the United States, care by a relative is the second most likely situation; care by relatives or nonrelatives is about equally likely in Canada. A child care center is the least likely care arrangement for an infant or toddler in both countries.

8. The authors also caution that the impacts may represent short-term, transitional impacts, not long-term impacts, and that the potential exists for families to choose child care as a result of benefits that are not fully observable in the data.

9. The difference in the median living standard is not as great, but it is still significant. The median child has access to $27,442 in the United States and $22,703 in Canada, a difference of $4,739, or 21 percent. All monetary values are expressed in 1998 Canadian dollars, with all income information drawn from two surveys explicitly designed for the purpose: the 1998 Canadian Survey of Labour and Income Dynamics (SLID) and the 1999 U.S. Current Population Survey (CPS).

10. This does not account for the value of in-kind benefits in the United States, nor for increases in the earned income tax credit (EITC) in recent years.

11. On the basis of the surveys used in this section, the median income in Canada for 1998 was $22,703, leading to a low-income threshold of $11,351; in the United States for 1999 it was $27,442, implying a low-income threshold of $13,721. These derivations are based on samples representing the entire population of each country, not just the children. One-half of median income is a threshold currently highlighted by the Luxembourg Income Study (LIS), a research network and data archive directed to international comparative research. Accordingly, our derivations follow this precedent, including the use of the square root of household size as the equivalence scale.

12. Janet Currie and Mark Stabile (2003) use the NLSCY to demonstrate support for the second hypothesis. At the same time, other research has demonstrated that low-income or less-educated individuals and their children may be hindered in utilizing health services by such economic and social barriers as the cost of transportation to visit health care providers, an inability to pay for prescriptions, and lack of knowledge as to how to navigate the health care system.

13. The relative similarities in the utilization of physician services within Canada and between the children of single mothers and all children in the United States may seem somewhat surprising in light of the earlier observation that low-income and single-mother children suffer on average from poorer health. This may be particularly true in Canada, where public health insurance should limit financial barriers to care; visit levels may therefore reflect other types of access barriers, such as transportation issues or gaps in knowledge regarding children's care needs and available services.

14. See the TIMSS website (http://ustimss.msu.edu) for more information.

References

Baker, Michael, Jonathan Gruber, and Kevin Milligan. 2008. "Universal Child Care, Maternal Labor Supply, and Family Well-being." *Journal of Political Economy* 116(4): 709–45.

Behrman, Jere R., and Mark R. Rosenzweig. 2002. "Does Increasing Women's Schooling Raise the Schooling of the Next Generation?" *American Economic Review* 92(1): 323–34.

Burton, Peter, Shelley Phipps, and Lori Curtis. 2002. "All in the Family: A Simultaneous Model of Parenting Style and Child Conduct." *American Economic Review* 92(1): 368–72.

Bushnik, Tracey. 2006. *Child Care in Canada.* Catalog no. 89-599-MIE-No 3. Ottawa: Statistics Canada.

Cadman, David, Peter Rosenbaum, Michael Boyle, and David R. Offord. 1991. "Children with Chronic Illness: Family and Parent Demographic Characteristics and Psycho-Social Adjustment." *Pediatrics* 87(6): 884–89.

Card, David, and Richard B. Freeman, eds. 1993. *Small Differences That Matter: Labor Markets and Income Maintenance in Canada and the United States.* Chicago: University of Chicago Press/National Bureau of Economic Research.

Case, Anne, Darren Lubotsky, and Christina Paxson. 2002. "Economic Status and Health in Childhood: The Origins of the Gradient." *American Economic Review* 92(1): 1308–34.

Coleman, James S. 1988. "Social Capital in the Creation of Human Capital." *American Journal of Sociology* 94 (supplement): S95–120.

Corak, Miles. 2006. "Do Poor Children Become Poor Adults? Lessons for Public Policy from a Cross-Country Comparison of Generational Earnings Mobility." In *Research on Economic Inequality,* vol. 13, *Dynamics of Inequality,* edited by John Creedy and Guyonne Kalb. Amsterdam: Elsevier Press.

———. 2010. *Chasing the Same Dream, Climbing Different Ladders: Economic Mobility in the United States and Canada.* Washington, D.C.: Economic Mobility Project/ Pew Charitable Trust.

Corak, Miles, Lori Curtis, and Shelley Phipps. 2010. "Economic Mobility, Family Background, and the Well-being of Children in the United States and Canada." Discussion paper 4814. Bonn, Germany: Institute for the Study of Labor (IZA).

Corak, Miles, and Andrew Heisz. 1999. "The Intergenerational Earnings and Income Mobility of Canadian Men: Evidence from Longitudinal Income Tax Data." *Journal of Human Resources* 34(3): 504–33.

Currie, Janet, and Mark Stabile. 2003. "Socioeconomic Status and Child Health: Why Is the Relationship Stronger for Older Children?" *American Economic Review* 93(5): 1813–23.

Grawe, Nathan D. 2006. "The Extent of Life-Cycle Bias in Estimates of Intergenerational Earnings Persistence." *Labour Economics* 13(5): 551–70.

Haider, Steven, and Gary Solon. 2006. "Life-Cycle Variation in the Association Between Current and Lifetime Earnings." *American Economic Review* 96(4): 1308–20.

Haskins, Ron, and Isabel Sawhill. 2009. *Creating an Opportunity Society.* Washington, D.C.: Brookings Institution Press.

Holmlund, Helena, Mikael Lindahl, and Erik Plug. 2008. "The Causal Effect of Parents' Schooling on Children's Schooling: A Comparison of Estimation Methods." Discussion paper 3630. Bonn, Germany: Institute for the Study of Labor (IZA).

Jencks, Christopher, and Laura Tach. 2006. "Would Equal Opportunity Mean More Mobility?" In *Mobility and Inequality,* edited by Stephen L. Morgan, David B. Grusky, and Gary S. Fields. Stanford, Calif.: Stanford University Press.

Knudsen, Eric I., James J. Heckman, Judy L. Cameron, and Jack P. Shonkoff. 2006. "Economic, Neurobiological, and Behavioral Perspectives on Building America's Future Workforce." *Proceedings of the National Academy of Sciences* 103(27): 10155–62.

Mazumder, Bhashkar. 2004. "The Apple Falls Even Closer to the Tree Than We Thought: New and Revised Estimates of the Intergenerational Inheritance of Earnings." In *Unequal Chances: Family Background and Economic Success,* edited by Samuel Bowles, Herbert Gintis, and Melissa Osborne. Princeton, N.J.: Princeton University Press/Russell Sage Foundation.

———. 2005. "Fortunate Sons: New Estimates of Intergenerational Mobility in the United States Using Social Security Earnings Data." *Review of Economics and Statistics* 87(2): 235–55.

New York Times. 2005. *Class Matters,* edited by correspondents of the *New York Times.* New York: Times Books/Henry Holt and Co.

Oreopoulos, Philip, Mark Stabile, Randy Walld, and Leslie L. Roos. 2008. "Short-, Medium-, and Long-Term Consequences of Poor Infant Health: An Analysis Using Siblings and Twins." *Journal of Human Resources* 43(1): 88–138.

Organization for Economic Co-operation and Development (OECD). 2008. *Growing Unequal? Income Distribution and Poverty in OECD Countries.* Paris: OECD.

———. 2009. "Economic, Environmental, and Social Statistics: Macroeconomic Trends: GDP per Capita." In *OECD Factbook 2009.* Available at: http://dx.doi.org/10.1787/540641728538.

Phipps, Shelley. 2002. "The Well-being of Young Canadian Children in International Perspective: A Functionings Approach." *Review of Income and Wealth* 48(4): 51–73.

Roemer, John E. 2004. "Equal Opportunity and Intergenerational Mobility: Going Beyond Intergenerational Income Transition Matrices." In *Generational Income Mobility in North America and Europe,* edited by Miles Corak. Cambridge: Cambridge University Press.

Sawhill, Isabel V., and John E. Morton. 2008. *Economic Mobility: Is the American Dream Alive and Well?* Washington, D.C.: Economic Mobility Project/Pew Charitable Trusts.

Scott, Janny. 2005. "Life at the Top in America Isn't Just Better, It's Longer." In *Class Matters,* edited by correspondents of the *New York Times.* New York: Times Books/Henry Holt and Co.

Smith, James P. 2009. "The Impact of Childhood Health on Adult Labor Market Outcomes." *Review of Economics and Statistics* 91(3): 478–89.

Solon, Gary. 1992. "Intergenerational Income Mobility in the United States." *American Economic Review* 82(3): 393–408.

———. 2004. "A Model of Intergenerational Mobility Variation over Time and Place." In *Generational Income Mobility in North America and Europe,* edited by Miles Corak. Cambridge: Cambridge University Press.

Statistics Canada. n.d. *National Longitudinal Survey of Children and Youth* (NLSCY). Available at: http://www.statcan.gc.ca/cgi-bin/imdb/p2SV.pl?Function=getSurvey&SDDS=4450&lang= en&db=imdb&adm=8&dis=2 (accessed May 17, 2011).

———. 2000. *Survey of Labour and Income Dynamics* (SLID), *1998.* Available at: http://www.statcan.gc.ca/cgi bin/imdb/p2SV.pl?Function=getSurvey&SurvId=3889&SurvVer=1&SDDS=3889&InstaId=15506&InstaVer=2&lang=en&db=imdb&adm=8&dis=2 (accessed May 17, 2011).

Urban Institute. n.d. *National Survey of American Families* (NSAF). Available at: http://www.urban.org/center/anf/nsaf.cfm (accessed May 17, 2011).

U.S. Bureau of the Census. 1999. *Current Population Survey* (CPS). Available at: http://www.icpsr.umich.edu/icpsrweb/ICPSR/studies/2825 (accessed May 17, 2011).

Wessel, David. 2005. "As Rich-Poor Gap Widens in the U.S., Class Mobility Stalls." *Wall Street Journal,* May 13.

Zimmerman, David J. 1992. "Regression Toward Mediocrity in Economic Structure." *American Economic Review* 82(3): 409–29.

Chapter 4

Status Attainment and Wealth in the United States and Germany

FABIAN T. PFEFFER

O UR EFFORTS to understand the channels through which socioeconomic advantage is transmitted across generations rely on a
crucial condition: we need to identify correctly the main ingredients
of advantage. In other words, we need comprehensive concepts and measures of social background. Most research on intergenerational mobility
draws on indicators of educational attainment, occupational status, and
income to describe the position of families and associated opportunities for
children. One important feature of the economic circumstances of families
that is less often included in these studies is family wealth, or net worth.
Wealth is a dimension of economic well-being that presents particularly
stark inequalities. Researchers have documented that the distribution of
wealth is far more unequal than the distribution of income (Keister and
Moller 2000; Wolff 2006) and that it is subject to especially strong racial and
ethnic inequalities (Oliver and Shapiro 1997; Scholz and Levine 2004; Hao
2007). Severe inequalities in family wealth may create unequal opportunities for children over and above the socioeconomic characteristics of
families traditionally included in research on intergenerational mobility.

A few contributions have detected independent effects of parental
wealth on children's educational opportunities for the United States. Dalton
Conley (1999, 2001) finds a strong association between a family's wealth
position and the educational attainment of its offspring. Parental wealth
appears to play a central role in conferring educational advantage on
children independent of other socioeconomic characteristics of families.
Although the important role of parental wealth for educational success has
been confirmed in other instances (see, for example, Morgan and Kim 2006;
Haveman and Wilson 2007; Belley and Lochner 2007), it seems fair to say
that the empirical study of intergenerational wealth effects is still in its
early stages compared to most other topics in the field of intergenerational

mobility research (for an overview, see Grawe 2008). The main reason for this circumstance lies in the fact that there are significantly fewer data sources available that include reliable indicators of wealth holdings.

The study of inequality in opportunities has a long history. For several decades, sociologists have studied this topic under a common framework—namely, *status attainment research*. Status attainment models have been developed in Peter Blau and Otis Dudley Duncan's seminal work, *The American Occupational Structure* (1967), to estimate the relative effects of different background characteristics on individuals' educational and occupational success. Blau and Duncan's approach to the study of the reproduction of social inequalities might be the single most replicated model that sociology has seen. Over several decades, it has been extended, modified, confirmed, and criticized (Campbell 1983; Ganzeboom, Treiman, and Ultee 1991). One especially persistent critique of these models comes from Samuel Bowles (1972) and Bowles and Herbert Gintis (2002), who have repeatedly suggested that standard status attainment models yield a biased picture of the determinants of attainment because they fail to include important socioeconomic background characteristics, particularly parental wealth. The first contribution of this chapter, then, is to update the classical status attainment model and investigate how wealth alters the conclusions about the central factors in the intergenerational transmission of advantage that researchers have drawn from this model. It does so by documenting the association between parental wealth and not only children's final educational status but also their early occupational attainment.[1]

So far, research on the relationship between parental wealth and offspring's life chances has been largely confined to the United States. We therefore do not know whether the relationship between wealth inequality and inequality in opportunities is unique to the United States or a hallmark of all industrialized nations.[2] Owing to the restricted availability of appropriate data, the only other nation for which we can use survey data to study intergenerational wealth effects of the kind considered here is Germany. In many ways, the German welfare state builds a rich contrast to the U.S. context and has served as a fruitful comparative case in much research on intergenerational mobility processes (see, for example, DiPrete 2002). With surprisingly similar levels of wealth inequality (see Jäntti, Sierminska, and Smeeding 2008; Wolff 2006), Germany is also an ideal case to investigate the importance of institutional arrangements in strengthening or attenuating the link between wealth inequality and inequality in opportunities. This chapter thus also attempts to provide a first institutional perspective on the importance of wealth for children's life chances. I offer theoretical arguments for why parental wealth may constitute an important ingredient of advantage in the United States and why the role of wealth in the status attainment process might be different in Germany.

Wealth As a "Transformative Asset"

For Aage Sørensen (2000), a person's social class position is based on the sum of assets that he or she controls through property rights. In this framework, wealth constitutes the central dimension of "class as life conditions" (see also Spilerman 2000). To understand why these life conditions based on wealth may translate into attainment opportunities for the next generation, it is helpful to draw on recent qualitative research from Thomas Shapiro (2004, 10) in which he proposes viewing parental assets as "transformative assets that lift [children] beyond their own achievement." Based on this framework and prior evidence, I posit that the transformation of monetary well-being into attainment opportunities can occur in three direct ways.

First, as Shapiro's ethnographic work vividly shows, the main wealth-building strategy in most families, the purchase of a home, is primarily driven by parents' assessment of the educational opportunities that residential neighborhoods and their schools offer to their children. By purchasing homes in certain neighborhoods, parents choose "life conditions" conducive to their children's educational success. I therefore hypothesize that parental wealth—the central component of which is housing wealth—serves as a genuine economic resource that funds access to valuable educational resources at the primary and secondary education levels. Advantages arising from parental wealth are thus not limited to what many economists in the field of wealth studies focus on—namely, bequests and inter vivos transfers (Kessler and Masson 1988)—but may instead accrue much earlier in the form of de facto purchases of educational resources.

Second, the purchasing function of parental wealth may be even more apparent at the postsecondary level. Significant tuition and living costs may often not be met by parents' disposable income but instead require families to draw on some form of savings or home equity–based lending. The need for economic support is by no means restricted to college access, but such support is equally important for college persistence and completion. Of course, there is a long-standing and controversial literature on the existence of credit constraints in college—that is, the question of whether perfect credit markets provide lending opportunities to those whose need for funding for postsecondary education cannot be met by their families (see Cameron and Taber 2004). Although the theory of credit constraints discusses the importance of parental wealth early on (Becker and Tomes 1986), the empirical literature in this field counts far more contributions that study the relationship between parental income and educational outcomes. Again, the reason is that much more data on income are readily available than data on wealth. More recent contributions, however, demonstrate that the empirical consideration of parental wealth suggests important credit constraints in access to college (Belley and Lochner 2007; Lovenheim, forthcoming). But even if credit markets could match the functions of parental wealth, the educational advantages associated with the latter may still extend beyond the attainment of a first college degree. Student debt—which is likely to be accumulated by students from less-wealthy families—has been shown to be associated with lower propensities to seek postgraduate education (see Millett 2003).

Third, the effects of parental wealth may extend beyond educational attainment to directly confer additional labor market advantages. Parental wealth can by hypothesized to take on an insurance function for both initial job search and early career mobility by providing "important real and psychological safety nets" (Shapiro 2004, 11). A *real safety net* for costly job searches prevents a low reservation wage at job market entry and its rapid decline in times of unemployment. In other words, such a safety net permits offspring to maintain job searches until a satisfying job offer is attained. This may be particularly important when freshly graduated college students face the challenge of paying off accumulated student debt. As a *psychological safety net,* parental wealth may additionally serve to expand the range of occupational options considered and facilitate the decision to apply for more competitive, high-status occupations.

The distinction between the purchasing and insurance functions of wealth should not be construed as strictly exclusive explanations of wealth effects on only education and only occupation, respectively. The insurance function of wealth may also play an important role for educational attainment insofar as it determines the discount rate applied to future labor market prospects and thereby influences the investment decisions involved in educational choices (such as, but not limited to, the decision to borrow for college).

Thus far, I have laid out several hypotheses on how parental wealth could exert direct effects on children's status attainment. However, the observed associations could also arise, at least in part, from unobserved— and potentially unobservable—characteristics of parents that are responsible for their propensity not only to accumulate assets but to foster the educational attainment of their children. I am alluding to a different perspective on wealth that considers it to be merely a less error-prone measure of "permanent income" and therefore a more adequate proxy for differential consumption patterns (see, for example, Burkhauser, Frick, and Schwarze 1997; Moon and Smolensky 1977). In neoclassical economics, different wealth positions simply indicate a postponement of consumption and therefore result from differential savings propensities. This framework also suggests a range of factors that may determine savings propensities, such as different levels of risk aversion, the discount rates of the future, and altruistic preferences for bequesting to one's offspring (see also Becker and Tomes 1986). All of these might be unobserved characteristics of parents that underlie the association between wealth and attainment. For instance, families' wealth positions may derive from their level of risk aversion, and risk aversion, in turn, might be transmitted to children (Dohmen et al., forthcoming), influencing their willingness to make long-term educational investments, such as college or graduate school, or to build steady career patterns in highly competitive occupations.[3] These and similar lines of reasoning would thus suggest that instead of *carrying* different behavioral implications for children, family wealth *derives* from different behaviors of parents that also account for the intergenerational transmission of advantage.

Although the hypotheses listed so far have been largely devised in reference to the United States, their importance can be assumed to differ by national context. In the following section, I outline how specific features of the U.S. and German education systems and welfare states may be expected to intensify or moderate the hypothesized intergenerational effects of wealth (see table 4.1). I should stress that this chapter does not investigate cross-national differences in the total degree of intergenerational mobility, but rather whether different components of social background, specifically parental wealth, are associated differently with children's opportunities. Hence, I do not posit reasons why one country may permit more or less intergenerational mobility, but rather why the association between wealth and attainment may be stronger in one country than the other.

Let us start with the ability to acquire access to educational resources through homeownership and home equity. Such access is made possible by the localized funding structure of public education in the United States, where property taxes are the main revenue for educational expenditures on the primary and secondary levels. By educational resources I do not primarily refer to school resources—which have, at best, small effects on educational outcomes (Hanushek 1986, 1997; but see also Hedges,

Table 4.1   Summary of Hypotheses

Theoretical Mechanism	United States	Germany
Homeownership and quality of neighborhood and schools	+	−
Direct monetary resource, specifically for higher education	+	−
Insurance function for educational decisionmaking and labor market entry and mobility	+	−
Unobserved parental characteristics	?	?

Source: Author's compilation.
Note: +/− denotes that the mechanism is hypothesized to be stronger, weaker, or similar when the two countries are compared.

Laine, and Greenwald 1994; Greenwald, Hedges, and Laine 1996)—but to advantageous contexts based on the composition of the student body and the neighborhood population (see Coleman et al. 1966). From this perspective, the most consequential feature of the localized funding structure of the U.S. education system might not be the resulting differences in school resources but the incentive it sets for wealthy parents to select into different neighborhoods. As mentioned earlier, Shapiro (2004) shows that, for wealthy parents, perceived school quality is indeed the main factor in choosing a neighborhood.

In Germany, school choice is no less of an issue in parents' strategies to secure educational opportunities for their children. However, educational resources show less variation across different neighborhoods than across different school types. Entry into the "right" track of the highly differentiated German education system is much less determined by residential choices than by parents' knowledge of and own prior success in navigating the complex pathways of the German system (see Pfeffer 2008).

On the postsecondary level, cross-national differences may be more readily apparent. High tuition costs are a salient feature of the U.S. system, and the financial aid system explicitly disregards some aspects of wealth in determinations of need-based aid. The German higher education system, in contrast, has traditionally been tuition-free (although this is changing). In addition, living costs are partly covered by a need-based aid system—which, however, also fails to take into account parental wealth. Overall, the lower total cost associated with attaining a postsecondary education should nevertheless make parents' savings or borrowing potential a less consequential resource in Germany.

Regarding occupational attainment, it can be noted that the degree to which parental wealth is required to provide a safety net for job searches and occupational mobility depends fundamentally on the existence of alternative public provisions of such an insurance function. For instance, Markus Gangl's (2004) work on the consequences of unemployment spells for future career trajectories shows that relatively generous unemployment benefits in Germany provide a real safety net for continued growth in occupational status, while such public provision does not exist to the same degree in the United States. In the latter case, parental wealth may provide a functional substitute for continuing job searches and maintaining reservation wages. In addition, the psychological benefit that young adults derive from their parents' wealth might be more consequential in the more volatile U.S. job market than is the case with the relatively static German labor market (Carroll and Mayer 1986).

Based on these fundamental differences in the institutional setup of the U.S. and German education and welfare systems, we should expect the overall relationship between wealth and status attainment to be stronger in the United States than in Germany. In the United States, parental wealth may take on important functions for educational and occupational success that are partly made dispensable in Germany by the public provision of education and social insurance (see also Conley and Gifford 2006). However, the possibility that intergenerational wealth effects may be driven by unobserved parental characteristics, as described earlier, makes this prediction (and the interpretation of results) more hazardous. The analyses reported here do not attempt to identify which of the hypothesized mechanisms drive the observed effects. They are instead meant to reveal an additional dimension of intergenerational mobility and to provide initial comparative evidence that will inspire further research into the underlying causal mechanisms of intergenerational mobility as it relates to wealth.

Data and Methods

It is notoriously difficult for children to report accurately on their parents' socioeconomic status, and it is virtually impossible to gather detailed information from them about their parents' asset holdings. Studies such as this one therefore need to rely on wealth data collected directly from parents. Worldwide, there are only three panel surveys available that not only have that information but also track the educational careers of children for a sufficient period to enable the observation of final educational and early occupational attainment: the U.S. National Longitudinal Survey of Youth (NLSY79), the U.S. Panel Study of Income Dynamics (PSID), and the German Socio-Economic Panel (GSOEP). The NLSY began in 1979 with a sample of approximately 12,700 adults between the ages of fourteen and twenty-two. Children born to female panel members are tracked in the NLSY79 Child and Young Adult Supplement (Center for Human Resource Research 2008). The PSID is the longest-running nationally representative panel study in the world. It began in 1968 with approximately 4,800 households, and it continues to interview all original sample members and split-off households, such as those of children (Brown and Schoeni 2007). The GSOEP is Germany's largest panel study, partly modeled after the PSID. It began in 1984 with 6,000 households living in the Federal Republic of Germany and was expanded to the former German Democratic Republic after the fall of the Berlin Wall (Wagner, Frick, and Schupp 2007).

The analytic sample consists of children of households that participated in the 1989 wave of the U.S. surveys and the 1988 wave of the German survey, which all included a full-fledged module to measure household wealth. Being of school age in those base years, these children have reached ages twenty-three to thirty-five in the latest available waves of the NLSY (2006, N = 2,497) and the GSOEP (2007, N = 745) and are ages twenty-four to thirty-six in the latest available PSID wave (2007, N = 1,665).

The measures of wealth in these surveys are fairly comprehensive and provide information separately for each asset type—namely, savings

Table 4.2   Distribution of Wealth in the United States and Germany

	NLSY (1989)	PSID (1989)	GSOEP (1988)
Gini coefficient	0.85	0.76	0.79
Wealth share of top 5 percent	56.9%	42.1%	33.0%
Wealth share of top 20 percent	83.1%	71.5%	73.2%

Source: Author's calculations based on data from National Longitudinal Survey of Youth (Center for Human Resource Research 2008), Panel Study of Income Dynamics (Brown and Schoeni 2007), and German Socio-Economic Panel (Wagner, Frick, and Schupp 2007).
Note: Based on analytic sample.

accounts, stocks, business holdings, real estate, home equity, and debts. Like previous research on intergenerational wealth effects, this analysis relies on a measure of *net worth* (total wealth minus debts). Table 4.2 gives a picture of the highly unequal distribution of family wealth. These inequality measures are reported for the analytic population—that is, households with school-age children in 1988 or 1989. They confirm what more recent cross-national comparisons of wealth distributions have also shown (see Wolff 2006; Jäntti et al. 2008): wealth is very highly unequally distributed in both the United States and Germany. In fact, the level of wealth inequality in the GSOEP sample lies between that based on the NLSY and the PSID when we compare the Gini coefficient of wealth and the share of wealth held by the top 20 percent of wealth holders. Only at the very top of the distribution does wealth seem to be more polarized in the United States compared to Germany. While the wealthiest 5 percent hold about one-third of all wealth in Germany, they appear to hold up to (PSID) or even more than (NLSY) half of all wealth in the United States (see also Jäntti et al. 2008).

For the empirical models, the net worth measure is assigned a ceiling value of $1 million (1989, purchasing power parity) and log-transformed to reduce skew. Cases of zero and negative wealth are set to $500. Additional analyses (not shown) test different floor values and include the amount of net debt as an additional indicator of a household's wealth position and yield the same substantive results. Remaining indicators of a family's socioeconomic standing are the highest number of years of education completed by either parent, the highest socioeconomic index score (SEI) (Frederick and Hauser 2008) of either parent's occupation, and the (natural logarithm of) family income averaged across five income years ("permanent income") and adjusted for household size ($1/hsize$).[4] Educational attainment is measured as the total number of years of education attained, and occupational attainment as the SEI score of the current main occupation. The choice of these measures is driven by an effort to replicate the classical variables used in status attainment research. Missing values on all variables are multiply imputed, drawing on the Stata ICE module (which applies regression switching methods; see Royston 2005).

Several methodological problems challenge the analysis of wealth data collected from large national surveys. First, nonresponse to asset questions is relatively high and may introduce substantial bias. While the data providers of the NLSY and PSID already provide imputations of missing wealth values (based on cross-wave interpolation and hot deck imputation, respectively), I collaborated with the data providers of the GSOEP to implement a similar multiple imputation strategy for the German data (see Frick and Pfeffer 2011). Second, the issue of measurement error in survey reports of socioeconomic standing—which looms especially large in data on wealth—is addressed by using measures from two points in time for all variables included in this analysis.[5] Third, although the wealth measures used in the three surveys are very similar (the GSOEP has historically been modeled after the PSID), it would be highly problematic to assume that the wealth survey items measure exactly the same across surveys and do so equally well (see Sierminska, Brandolini, and Smeeding 2008). For the United States, the use of two independent data sources is meant to yield further confidence in the stability of the findings. Additional sensitivity analyses also suggest that the cross-national comparison is robust to the possibility of different levels of wealth measurement error across these data sets.[6]

As described, this chapter draws on widely used methods of status attainment research. Status attainment models are structural equation models that estimate the direct and indirect effects of an individual's social background on his or her educational and occupational attainment. I follow the common practice of labeling these estimated coefficients "effects" while stressing that they are estimated under specific assumptions about potential causality and, for the reasons mentioned earlier, are not meant to yield direct causal evidence—a point that has been stressed from the outset by the creators of path analysis (Duncan 1966; Wright 1934). The visual display of the estimation results occurs via path diagrams in which directed arrows indicate direct effects and curved, undirected arrows indicate unanalyzed correlations. Path coefficients can be interpreted as standardized linear regression coefficients (directed arrows) and simple correlation coefficients (curved arrows). The inclusion and exclusion of any specific effect is based on considerations of model fit. The latter is not discussed in detail here; suffice to say that all of the presented models fulfill standard statistical criteria for satisfactory model fit (see appendix tables 4A.1 to 4A.3). The models estimated here also include a "measurement model." This part of the model not only specifies that each (latent) variable is measured by two variables observed at two different points in time, but also allows for measurement error in each variable as well as some selected correlations among these measurement errors. To further facilitate the focus on the substantive (structural) part of the models, there is no further discussion of the measurement part of the estimated models here, nor is it included in the path diagrams (but see appendix and notes 5 and 6).

Results

To assess how the inclusion of wealth alters conclusions drawn from status attainment models, I begin by replicating the standard model of status attainment, which includes only parental education, parental occupation, and family income as background characteristics. In a second step, I add the net worth measure and observe its effects on educational and occupational attainment as well as the resulting changes in the general structure of the intergenerational transmission of advantage. The resulting path diagrams are displayed in figures 4.1 and 4.2 for the United States and in figure 4.3 for Germany. All solid lines stand for statistically significant effects ($p < .05$), and a dashed line indicates an effect that does not reach statistical significance but is still included for illustrative purposes.

Wealth Effects in the United States

In the standard models of status attainment in the United States (figures 4.1 and 4.2), parental education exerts the strongest effects on children's attainment compared to other indicators of social background. This finding is more pronounced with the PSID data than with the NLSY data, but it corresponds well to the common result of most analyses of intergenerational mobility processes. Controlling for parental education, we see that parents' occupational status as indicated by the socioeconomic index also exerts significant effects on educational attainment and, at least in the PSID, has lingering direct effects on occupational attainment. The same holds true for household income, which exerts stable direct effects on educational and occupational outcomes in both data sets. The correlations among different background components are stronger in the PSID data. Overall, these base models yield rather comparable conclusions about the relative force of different social background components and match up well with the classical results of status attainment research (Blau and Duncan 1967; Sewell and Hauser 1975).

Of course, many other aspects of these models could be discussed here, but the focus of the analysis is on the question of how the overall structure of these models changes once wealth enters the picture. Figures 4.1(b) and 4.2(b) provide the answers, which can be summarized in the following way. First, the intergenerational effects of parental wealth are significant and strong. The size of the coefficients is in the broad range of that of other background effects (with the exception of the effects of parental education, which remain stronger in the PSID data).

Figure 4.1   Effect of Wealth on Standard Status Attainment Models: The United States (NLSY)

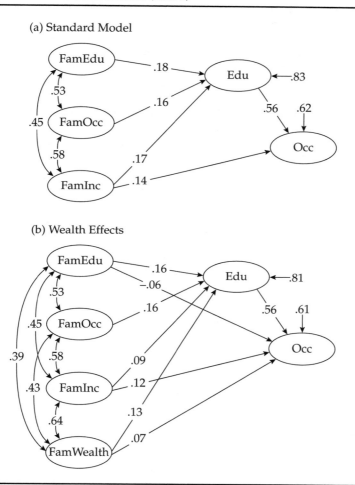

(a) Standard Model

(b) Wealth Effects

Source: Author's calculations based on National Longitudinal Survey of Youth (Center for Human Resource Research 2008).

Second, the direct effect of parental wealth on occupational attainment, when we control for its association with educational attainment, is also significant and about half the size of its direct effects on education. Other background effects on occupational attainment differ between the two data sources, with parental occupation exerting positive effects in the PSID and family income exerting positive effects and parental education,

Figure 4.2   Effect of Wealth on Standard Status Attainment Models: The United States (PSID)

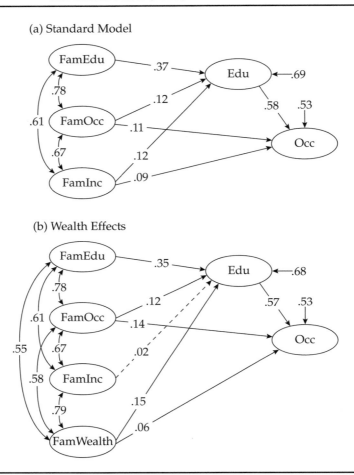

(a) Standard Model

(b) Wealth Effects

Source: Author's calculations based on Panel Study of Income Dynamics (Brown and Schoeni 2007).

surprisingly, showing negative effects (when we control for all other independent variables) in the NLSY.

Third, by adding parental wealth to the classical status attainment model, the effects of family income are reduced—even to statistical and substantive nonsignificance in the case of the PSID. This suggests that in prior research at least a part of the family income measure has functioned as a rough proxy measure for intergenerational wealth effects. Based on the PSID results, we might even be tempted to conclude that all income

Figure 4.3   Effect of Wealth on Standard Status Attainment Models: Germany (GSOEP)

(a) Standard Model

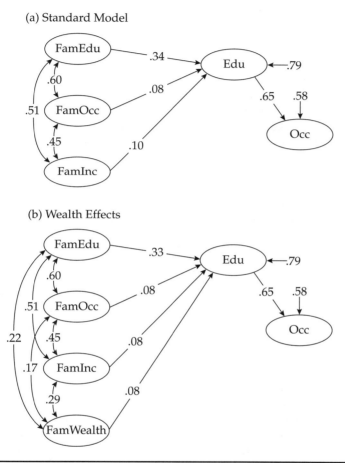

(b) Wealth Effects

Source: Author's calculations based on German Socio-Economic Panel (Wagner, Frick, and Schupp 2007).

effects are in fact wealth effects and subscribe to the claim, offered earlier, that wealth is just another and more reliable measure of permanent income. The NLSY results, however, suggest a more cautious conclusion. Here, I observe wealth effects while significant income effects remain. Possible explanations for this difference between the NLSY and PSID results are less likely to be found in different levels of measurement error, but may relate to differences in the age structure among parents in the two data sets.[7]

Overall, the suspected strong role of wealth in the intergenerational transmission of status is confirmed for the United States. Both educational and occupational outcomes are clearly associated with the value of parents' net worth when all the classical indicators of social background are held constant.

Wealth Effects in Germany

In the base model for Germany (figure 4.3), we again observe strong effects of parental education on educational attainment, which surpass the otherwise significant effects of parental occupation and family income. In contrast to the U.S. case, however, none of these background factors exerts direct effects beyond educational attainment on occupational destinations. In other words, the transmission of labor market advantage seems to be entirely mediated by educational attainment. This does not necessarily imply that the structure of intergenerational mobility would be in any way more "meritocratic" than in the United States. Instead, it means that higher-status parents succeed in passing along advantage to their children through higher levels of educational attainment. Beyond this, parents' socioeconomic resources do not—perhaps do not need to—contribute to status maintenance.

What changes when we add parental wealth to the picture? In figure 4.3(b), we observe a significant effect of parental wealth on educational attainment—incidentally of the very same size as the effects of parental occupational status and family income. Parental education remains the most crucial component of social background, and status reproduction still works through the transmission of educational advantage. This analysis is the first to provide empirical evidence for the relationship between wealth inequality and inequality in educational opportunity in Germany. Judging from the results, the role of parental wealth in intergenerational mobility merits at least as much attention as that of income and occupational background. Another reason why wealth inequality should be studied as an additional factor in intergenerational mobility in Germany is that, even more so than in the United States, it forms an independent dimension of social inequality that partly runs across existing lines of socioeconomic stratification, as indicated by the weaker correlation of wealth with other social background characteristics.

Cross-National Comparison

Finally, what have we learned about the relative centrality of parental wealth in the intergenerational transmission of status in these two countries? Comparing the sizes of the presented standardized regression coefficient within each data set, the most sensible conclusion is that of cross-national similarity in the relative importance of parental wealth as one ingredient of intergenerational advantage.[8] The effects of parental wealth on educational attainment are comparable in size to those of family income (in the NLSY and GSOEP) and family occupation (in all three data sets). They are significantly smaller than the effects of parental education, with the German intergenerational wealth effect, at about one-quarter of the parental education effect, in between the relative effect sizes estimated in the two U.S. data sets. The influence of wealth in status transmission extends beyond educational attainment in the United States, but not in Germany. This cross-national difference, however, is not peculiar to wealth effects. Instead, in Germany none of the included background characteristics show direct effects on occupational destinations once educational attainment has been taken into account.

Conclusions

The status attainment models presented here confirm that parental wealth exerts independent and strong effects on children's life chances in both the United States and Germany. Independently from classical measures of the socioeconomic standing of families—namely, parental education, occupation, and income—wealth emerges as an additional and reasonably powerful factor in the intergenerational transmission of advantage. Standard status attainment models, as they have been used over the last four decades, have therefore indeed neglected an important characteristic of parent households and partly failed to capture a central component of intergenerational status transmission. This shortcoming is not specific to the status attainment framework but rather characterizes a large part of mobility research. This chapter began by pointing out that gaining a better understanding of the channels of intergenerational mobility requires that mobility analyses incorporate the most relevant socioeconomic characteristics of parents. The results of this analysis suggest that wealth qualifies as one such characteristic.

One main contribution of this chapter is that, in revealing the similar role of parental wealth in educational attainment in the United States and Germany, it provides initial comparative evidence on intergenerational wealth effects. The size of wealth effects on children's educational opportunity is comparable in these two nations. Wealth effects on occupational attainment, controlling for the relationship between wealth and education, are observable only in the United States; in Germany these effects, like all other included background effects, are fully mediated by educational attainment.

How do these findings square with the theoretical expectations spelled out earlier? In offering three hypotheses on the causal processes that may underlie intergenerational wealth effects—in reference to neighborhood and school contexts, credit constraints, and social insurance—I argued that each of these processes could be more pronounced in the United States than in Germany. I have also cautioned, however, that these causal interpretations of the associations studied here are challenged by the possibility of unobserved heterogeneity. This caution is based on more than just the standard econometric suspicion of unobserved bias. It derives from economic theory, which proposes several behavioral traits as correlates of parents' wealth position.

The problem of unobserved heterogeneity, unfortunately, not only bars us from inferring support for the hypothesized causal mechanisms from the results presented here but also precludes the possibility of devising a final prediction and explanation of the cross-national differences and similarities in the intensity of intergenerational wealth effects. Are these unobserved characteristics of parents the main or even the only explanation for wealth effects on children's life chances, rendering the other suggested causal pathways negligible? At this point, the similarity of wealth effects across these two nations cannot rule out that possibility. Or does the relative importance of these unobserved characteristics differ by country? What if the wealthy and nonwealthy are distinguished by one set of characteristics in a nation of homeowners, like the United States (see Kurz and Blossfeld 2004), and by a different set of characteristics in a nation of savers, like Germany (Börsch-Supan et al. 2001)? Conceivably, the effects of unobserved behavioral differences might even run in different directions in these countries, offering a possible counterweight to the differences expected based on the causal mechanisms suggested earlier.

In short, the cross-national comparison presented here reveals the symptomatic challenge in identifying institutional influences on intergenerational mobility processes without observing the causal microlevel mechanisms underlying these processes. Comparative research that seeks to pin down the influence of institutional and macro-social structures is plagued by well-known structural difficulties (see Lieberson 1991), but the requirement that we obtain an empirical understanding of the causal pathways through which status is reproduced over generations in each nation is an especially thorny one.

The results of this analysis do establish that parental wealth plays a central role in the reproduction of inequality, a finding that future mobility research cannot afford to ignore. The analysis cannot, however, substantiate the claim that the institutional setup of education and social security systems may alter this role. To do so, the mechanisms that have been hypothesized to drive the observed effects must be subjected to empirical testing, a task that I attend to in a different part of my research.[9] Here I map out the necessary next steps that would lay the foundation for further illuminating the black box of intergenerational wealth effects. Although I hope that the status attainment models provided an accessible first overview of intergenerational wealth effects, these models entail the strong assumption of linear background effects on different status destinations.

Two important extensions of these models are necessary: the years of education measure that has fallen into disgrace with most sociologists will have to give way to the more meaningful measure of educational degrees, and not just for technical reasons. The theoretical hypotheses developed in this chapter apply to different stages of the educational attainment process. That is, neighborhood and school contexts may influence secondary attainment, while credit constraints should chiefly be at work at the postsecondary level. Similarly, the effects of parental wealth on occupational attainment might become more easily interpretable once we investigate how wealth is associated with different occupational class positions. The category of self-employment is but the most obvious case for which parental wealth may take on particularly important functions (see Evans and Jovanovic 1989; Fairlie and Robb 2008).

A second necessary departure from the linear world of status attainment research is to try to identify heterogeneity in the effects of wealth across its distribution. The observed wealth effects might, for instance, be concentrated at the extremes of the wealth distribution. The lack of wealth especially has come to be understood as a position of particular disadvantage (Sherraden 1991; Haveman and Wolff 2005; Brandolini, Magri, and Smeeding 2010). The latter work also sparked much interest in asset-building policies among both academics and policymakers (see, for instance, Shapiro and Wolff 2001), which should remind us of the need to confront the thorny issues of causality before any policy-relevant conclusions—be it in favor of asset-building strategies or broader institutional reforms—can be formulated.

Finally, the comparative scope of this analysis may be expanded in the future. National panel studies from other countries that track the children of panel households either have been initiated much later than the panel studies used here or have begun collecting wealth data in later waves. With the necessary patience, however, researchers will be able to analyze the association between parental wealth and the educational and early occupational success of the panels' second generation in the United Kingdom (British Household Panel Study [BHPS], first collection of wealth data in 1995); Australia (Household Income and Labour Dynamics in Australia [HILDA], wealth data starting in 2002); and Switzerland (Swiss Household Panel [SHP], wealth data starting in 2009). In addition, by drawing on registry data, such an analysis may also include some Scandinavian countries (see Pfeffer and Hällsten 2011).

This research has been supported by a dissertation grant from the Institute for Research on Poverty at the University of Wisconsin–Madison as well as by grants from the Spencer Foundation and the German National Academic Foundation. The author thanks Robert M. Hauser, Erik O. Wright, and Markus Gangl, as well as the editors and reviewers, for helpful comments.

Appendix

Figure 4A.1   Full Status Attainment Model: NLSY

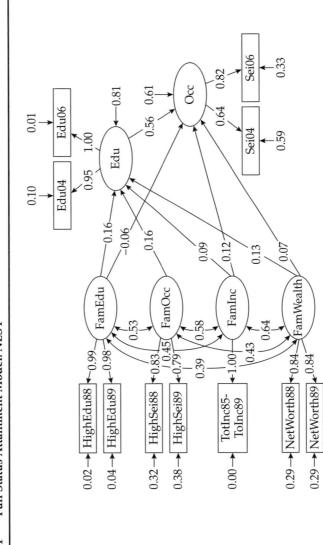

Fit statistics (N = 2,497): Chi^2 = 50.17, df = 27, p = .00435, RMSEA = .019, BIC = −161.0.
Correlations in measurement errors: HighSei89-NetWorth89, HighSei88-NetWorth88, HighSei88-TotInc, Edu04-Sei044.

Correlation Table

	Edu04	Edu06	Sei04	Seei06	Edu88	Edu89	Sei88	Sei89	Ltincadjln	Wealth88	Wealth89
Edu04	1.000										
Edu06	0.946	1.000									
Sei04	0.407	0.385	1.000								
Sei06	0.484	0.506	0.546	1.000							
Edu88	0.315	0.332	0.109	0.185	1.000						
Edu89	0.315	0.329	0.108	0.176	0.970	1.000					
Sei88	0.284	0.305	0.161	0.226	0.423	0.420	1.000				
Sei89	0.254	0.267	0.126	0.207	0.413	0.414	0.643	1.000			
Ltincadjln	0.325	0.335	0.219	0.256	0.445	0.443	0.429	0.453	1.000		
Wealth88	0.305	0.310	0.172	0.224	0.365	0.356	0.318	0.320	0.567	1.000	
Wealth89	0.288	0.302	0.186	0.223	0.353	0.349	0.330	0.344	0.597	0.806	1.000

Source: Author's calculations based on National Longitudinal Survey of Youth (Center for Human Resource Research 2008).

Figure 4A.2   Full Status Attainment Model: PSID

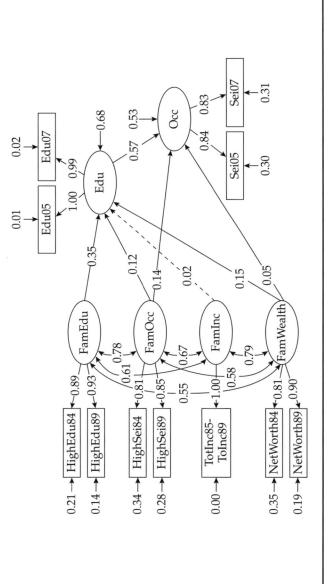

Fit statistics (N = 1,665): *Chi²* = 50.64, *df* = 28, *p* = .00584, RMSEA = .022, BIC = −157.1.
Correlations in measurement errors: HighEdu84-HighSei84, HighEdu84-Wealth84, Wealth84-HighSei84, Edu07-Occ07.

Correlation Table

	Edu05	Edu07	Sei05	Sei07	Edu84	Edu89	Sei84	Sei89	Ltincadjln	Wealth84	Wealth89
Edu05	1.000										
Edu07	0.988	1.000									
Sei05	0.550	0.546	1.000								
Sei07	0.562	0.568	0.696	1.000							
Edu84	0.483	0.481	0.373	0.339	1.000						
Edu89	0.494	0.490	0.359	0.342	0.826	1.000					
Sei84	0.410	0.409	0.328	0.319	0.629	0.597	1.000				
Sei89	0.399	0.403	0.312	0.302	0.579	0.604	0.690	1.000			
Ltincadjln	0.423	0.421	0.343	0.333	0.538	0.564	0.551	0.569	1.000		
Wealth84	0.360	0.361	0.284	0.245	0.446	0.416	0.445	0.418	0.632	1.000	
Wealth89	0.372	0.376	0.311	0.270	0.451	0.453	0.426	0.442	0.708	0.726	1.000

Source: Author's calculations based on Panel Study of Income Dynamics (Brown and Schoeni 2007).

Figure 4A.3   Full Status Attainment Model: GSOEP

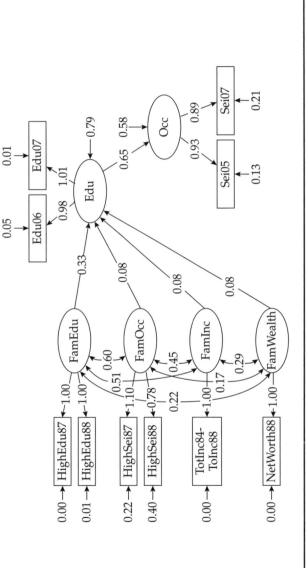

Fit statistics (N = 745): Chi^2 = 33.36, df = 24, p = .09679, RMSEA = .023, BIC = −125.4.
Correlations in measurement errors: HighEdu88-HighSei88, HighSei88-TotInc, Edu06-Occ06.

Correlation Table

	Edu06	Edu07	Sei06	Sei07	Edu87	Edu88	Sei87	Sei88	Ltinc	Wealth88
Edu06	1.000									
Edu07	0.984	1.000								
Sei06	0.605	0.613	1.000							
Sei07	0.560	0.582	0.830	1.000						
Edu87	0.426	0.441	0.292	0.284	1.000					
Edu88	0.425	0.441	0.289	0.280	0.994	1.000				
Sei87	0.376	0.376	0.219	0.231	0.664	0.660	1.000			
Sei88	0.268	0.268	0.159	0.158	0.468	0.472	0.857	1.000		
Ltinc	0.309	0.315	0.193	0.181	0.505	0.506	0.493	0.308	1.000	
Wealth88	0.209	0.202	0.165	0.159	0.221	0.215	0.188	0.134	0.288	1.000

Source: Author's calculations based on German Socio-Economic Panel (Wagner, Frick, and Schupp 2007).

Notes

1. Russell Rumberger (1983) has estimated status attainment models that include a net worth measure, but unfortunately they excluded other important socio-economic background characteristics, such as parental education and income. Although he did find significant and strong effects of net worth on both years of schooling and earnings attained, it is unclear whether those effects might partly arise from the exclusion of these other background indicators.

2. Florencia Torche and Seymour Spilerman (2006, 2009) demonstrate that parental wealth plays an important role in two late-industrializing countries. In both Mexico and Chile, they find strong effects of parents' asset ownership on different indicators of offspring's economic well-being. Spilerman (2004) also finds independent effects of a rudimentary proxy measure of parental wealth on educational attainment as well as a range of economic well-being measures among young Israelis.

3. I find this line of reasoning largely unconvincing because (a) given the fact that a large part of families' wealth is determined by bequests and inter-generational transfers, if anything, risk aversion would more likely be a mediator than a preceding confounder of the relationship between wealth and children's outcomes; and (b) risk aversion holds no promise for explaining the positive relationship between wealth and opportunities if we assume risk-averse families to be more likely to accumulate wealth while expecting risk-averse children to be less willing to invest in long educational and occupational careers (see Belzil and Leonardi 2009).

4. Adjusting income measures for household size is a widely shared practice for income measures (Canberra Expert Group 2001), but no such consensus has emerged yet for wealth variables (see Sierminska and Smeeding 2005). The decision whether to adjust wealth measures for household size mainly depends on the specific wealth component we study: some asset types can be considered more easily divisible, such as savings, while others retain their value largely independent of the number of children drawing from them, such as housing wealth. Since housing wealth makes up the largest part of the typical family's asset portfolio, I have decided against the household size adjustment of the net worth measure. It can also be noted, however, that further analyses (not shown here) that include a control for household size leave the net worth coefficient substantively unaltered.

5. For the social background variables, these are the years 1988+1989 (NLSY), 1984+1989 (PSID), and 1987+1988 (GSOEP); for children's outcomes, the years are 2004+2006 (NLSY), 2005+2007 (PSID), and 2006+2007 (GSOEP).

6. For instance, measurement error in the GSOEP wealth measure would have to be five to seven times the estimated U.S. level to make the intergenerational wealth effects in Germany disappear (detailed results available from the author).

7. There is no obvious reason why the wealth measure in the PSID should be more reliable than the NLSY wealth measure—certainly, neither the technical

literature (see Engelhardt 1998; Juster, Smith, and Stafford 1999) nor the measurement model of this analysis gives any such indication. Again, a sensitivity analysis that imposes equal levels of measurement error for both data sets yields the same results. Although there is also no apparent reason why the five-year income average in the PSID data should be a more error-prone indicator of permanent income than in the NLSY, I have replicated the PSID analyses with a ten-year average income measure, and the results also remain unchanged.

Instead, an important difference between the NLSY and PSID samples used here is the younger age of the NLSY mothers (despite looking at NLSY sample members as parent households a decade after the panel started). The NLSY families are therefore on average less wealthy than the PSID families, and their wealth and income are still less correlated (see appendix).

8. A more audacious interpretation, which I myself am not willing to follow, would assume the complete cross-national standardization of all measures included here and directly compare coefficient sizes across data sets. It can be noted, however, that even if one engaged in this comparison, it would hardly be evident that these two countries differed *radically* in the importance of wealth for educational attainment.

9. There is not sufficient space here to summarize the details of this project (see Pfeffer 2010), but I may nevertheless point the reader toward some of its results. Drawing on different empirical approaches that test for the presence of unobservable bias, I am able to lend more credence to the causal relationship between parental wealth and educational outcomes. Both the ensuing empirical assessment of the mediating mechanisms and, at closer sight, the cross-national comparison suggest an important and more fundamental insurance function of wealth in both nations, a function that is not replaced by existing educational policies and welfare state arrangements (see also Pfeffer and Hällsten 2011).

References

Becker, Gary S., and Nigel Tomes. 1986. "Human Capital and the Rise and Fall of Families." *Journal of Labor Economics* 4(3): S1–39.

Belley, Philippe, and Lance Lochner. 2007. "The Changing Role of Family Income and Ability in Determining Educational Achievement." *Journal of Human Capital* 1(1): 37–89.

Belzil, Christian, and Marco Leonardi. 2009. "Risk Aversion and Schooling Decisions." Working paper 28. Palaiseau, France: École Polytechnique.

Blau, Peter M., and Otis Dudley Duncan. 1967. *The American Occupational Structure.* New York: Free Press.

Börsch-Supan, Axel, Anette Reil-Held, Ralf Rodepeter, Reinhold Schnabelb, and Joachim Winter. 2001. "The German Savings Puzzle." *Research in Economics* 55(1): 15–38.

Bowles, Samuel. 1972. "Schooling and Inequality from Generation to Generation." *Journal of Political Economy* 80(3–2): S219–51.

Bowles, Samuel, and Herbert Gintis. 2002. "The Inheritance of Inequality." *Journal of Economic Perspectives* 16(3): 3–30.

Brandolini, Andrea, Silvia Magri, and Timothy M. Smeeding. 2010. "Asset-Based Measurement of Poverty." *Journal of Policy Analysis and Management* 29(2): 267–84.

Brown, Charles C., and Robert H. Schoeni. 2007. *A Panel Study of Income Dynamics, 1968–2007 (Waves I–XXXVII)*. Ann Arbor: University of Michigan, Survey Research Center.

Burkhauser, Richard V., Joachim R. Frick, and Johannes Schwarze. 1997. "A Comparison of Alternative Measures of Economic Well-being for Germany and the United States." *Review of Income and Wealth* 43(2): 153–71.

Cameron, Stephen V., and Christopher Taber. 2004. "Estimation of Educational Borrowing Constraints Using Returns to Schooling." *Journal of Political Economy* 112(1): 132–82.

Campbell, Richard T. 1983. "Status Attainment Research: End of the Beginning or Beginning of the End?" *Sociology of Education* 56(1): 47–62.

Canberra Expert Group. 2001. *Final Report and Recommendations*. Ottawa, Canada: Canberra Expert Group on Household Income Statistics.

Carroll, Glenn R., and Karl Ulrich Mayer. 1986. "Job-Shift Patterns in the Federal Republic of Germany: The Effects of Social Class, Industrial Sector, and Organizational Size." *American Sociological Review* 51: 323–41.

Center for Human Resource Research. 2008. *NLSY79 User's Guide*. Columbus: Ohio State University.

Coleman, James S., Ernest Campell, Carol Hobson, James McPartland, Alexander Mood, Frederick Weinfeld, and Robert York. 1966. *Summary Report from Equality of Educational Opportunity* (the Coleman Report). Washington: U.S. Government Printing Office.

Conley, Dalton. 1999. *Being Black, Living in the Red: Race, Wealth, and Social Policy in America.* Berkeley and Los Angeles: University of California Press.

———. 2001. "Capital for College: Parental Assets and Postsecondary Schooling." *Sociology of Education* 74(1): 59–72.

Conley, Dalton, and Brian Gifford. 2006. "Home Ownership, Social Insurance, and the Welfare State." *Sociological Forum* 21(1): 55–82.

DiPrete, Thomas A. 2002. "Life Course Risks, Mobility Regimes, and Mobility Consequences: A Comparison of Sweden, Germany, and the United States." *American Journal of Sociology* 108(2): 267–309.

Dohmen, Thomas J., Armin Falk, David Huffman, and Uwe Sunde. Forthcoming. "The Intergenerational Transmission of Risk and Trust Attitudes." *Review of Economic Studies.*

Duncan, Otis D. 1966. "Methodological Issues in the Analysis of Social Mobility." In *Social Structure and Mobility and Economic Development,* edited by Neil J. Smelser and Seymour Martin Lipset. Chicago: Aldine.

Engelhardt, Gary V. 1998. "Income and Wealth in the NLSY79." Unpublished paper, Darthmouth College, Department of Economics.

Evans, David S., and Boyan Jovanovic. 1989. "An Estimated Model of Entrepreneurial Choice Under Liquidity Constraints." *Journal of Political Economy* 97(4): 808–27.

Fairlie, Robert W., and Alicia M. Robb. 2008. *Race and Entrepreneurial Success: Black-, Asian-, and White-Owned Businesses in the United States.* Cambridge, Mass.: MIT Press.

Frederick, Carl, and Robert M. Hauser. 2008. "A Crosswalk for Using Pre-2000 Occupational Status and Prestige Codes with Post-2000 Occupation Codes." Unpublished paper, University of Wisconsin–Madison, Department of Sociology.

Frick, Joachim R., and Fabian T. Pfeffer. 2011. "Multiple Imputation of the 1988 GSOEP Wealth Data." Technical working paper. Berlin: German Institute for Economic Research (DIW Berlin).

Gangl, Markus. 2004. "Welfare States and the Scar Effects of Unemployment: A Comparative Analysis of the United States and West Germany." *American Journal of Sociology* 109(6): 1319–64.

Ganzeboom, Harry B. G., Donald J. Treiman, and Wout C. Ultee. 1991. "Comparative Intergenerational Stratification Research: Three Generations and Beyond." *Annual Review of Sociology* 17: 277–302.

Grawe, Nathan. 2008. *Wealth and Economic Mobility.* Economic Mobility Project. Available at: http://www.economicmobility.org/assets/pdfs/EMP_LitReview_Education.pdf (accessed September 14, 2008).

Greenwald, Rob, Larry V. Hedges, and Richard D. Laine. 1996. "The Effect of School Resources on Student Achievement." *Review of Educational Research* 66(3): 361–96.

Hanushek, Eric A. 1986. "The Economics of Schooling: Production and Efficiency in Public Schools." *Journal of Economic Literature* 24(3): 1141–77.

———. 1997. "Assessing the Effects of School Resources on Student Performance: An Update." *Educational Evaluation and Policy Analysis* 19(2): 141–64.

Hao, Lingxin. 2007. *Color Lines, Country Lines: Race, Immigration, and Wealth Stratification in America.* New York: Russell Sage Foundation.

Haveman, Robert, and Kathryn Wilson. 2007. "Access, Matriculation, and Graduation." In *Economic Inequality and Higher Education: Access, Persistence, and Success,* edited by Stacy Dickert-Conlin and Ross Rubenstein. New York: Russell Sage Foundation.

Haveman, Robert, and Edward N. Wolff. 2005. "The Concept and Measurement of Asset Poverty: Levels, Trends, and Composition for the United States, 1983–2001." *Journal of Economic Inequality* 2(2): 145–69.

Hedges, Larry V., Richard D. Laine, and Robert Greenwald. 1994. "Does Money Matter? A Meta-analysis of Studies of the Effects of Differential School Inputs on Student Outcomes." *Educational Researcher* 23(3): 5–14.

Jäntti, Markus, Eva Sierminska, and Timothy M. Smeeding. 2008. "How Is Household Wealth Distributed? Evidence from the Luxembourg Wealth

Study." In *Growing Unequal? Income Distribution and Poverty in OECD Countries,* edited by Organization for Economic Cooperation and Development. Paris: OECD.

Juster, F. Thomas, James P. Smith, and Frank Stafford. 1999. "The Measurement and Structure of Household Wealth." *Labour Economics* 6(2): 253–75.

Keister, Lisa A., and Stephanie Moller. 2000. "Wealth Inequality in the United States." *Annual Review of Sociology* 26: 63–81.

Kessler, Dennis, and Andre Masson, eds. 1988. *Modeling the Accumulation and Distribution of Wealth.* Oxford: Clarendon Press.

Kurz, Karin, and Hans-Peter Blossfeld, eds. 2004. *Home Ownership and Social Inequality in Comparative Perspective.* Stanford, Calif.: Stanford University Press.

Lieberson, Stanley. 1991. "Small Ns and Big Conclusions: An Examination of the Reasoning in Comparative Studies Based on a Small Number of Cases." *Social Forces* 70(2): 307–20.

Lovenheim, Michael F. Forthcoming. "The Effect of Liquid Housing Wealth on College Enrollment." *Journal of Labor Economics.*

Millett, Catherine M. 2003. "How Undergraduate Loan Debt Affects Application and Enrollment in Graduate or First Professional School." *Journal of Higher Education* 74(3): 386–427.

Moon, Marilyn, and Eugene Smolensky. 1977. *Improving Measures of Economic Well-being.* New York: Academic Press.

Morgan, Stephen L., and Young-Mi Kim. 2006. "Inequality of Conditions and Intergenerational Mobility: Changing Patterns of Educational Attainment in the United States." In *Mobility and Inequality: Frontiers of Research in Sociology and Economics,* edited by Stephen L. Morgan, David B. Grusky, and Gary S. Fields. Stanford, Calif.: Stanford University Press.

Oliver, Melvin L., and Thomas M. Shapiro. 1997. *Black Wealth, White Wealth: A New Perspective on Racial Inequality.* New York: Routledge.

Pfeffer, Fabian T. 2008. "Persistent Inequality in Educational Attainment and Its Institutional Context." *European Sociological Review* 24(5): 543–65.

———. 2010. "Wealth and Opportunity in the United States and Germany." Ph.D. diss., University of Wisconsin–Madison.

Pfeffer, Fabian T., and Martin Hällsten. 2011. "Wealth Effects in Three Mobility Regimes: The United States, Germany, and Sweden in Comparison." Paper presented at the Annual Meeting of the America n Sociological Association, Las Vegas (August 23, 2011).

Royston, Patrick. 2005. "Multiple Imputation of Missing Values: Update of ICE." *Stata Journal* 5(4): 527–36.

Rumberger, Russell W. 1983. "The Influence of Family Background on Education, Earnings, and Wealth." *Social Forces* 61(2): 755–73.

Scholz, John Karl, and Kara Levine. 2004. "U.S. Black-White Wealth Inequality." In *Social Inequality,* edited by Kathryn M. Neckerman. New York: Russell Sage Foundation.

Sewell, William H., and Robert M. Hauser. 1975. *Education, Occupation, and Earnings: Achievement in the Early Career.* New York: Academic Press.

Shapiro, Thomas M. 2004. *The Hidden Cost of Being African American: How Wealth Perpetuates Inequality.* Oxford: Oxford University Press.

Shapiro, Thomas M., and Edward N. Wolff, eds. 2001. *Assets for the Poor: The Benefits of Spreading Asset Ownership.* New York: Russell Sage Foundation.

Sherraden, Michael. 1991. *Assets and the Poor: A New American Welfare Policy.* Armonk, N.Y.: M. E. Sharpe.

Sierminska, Eva, Andrea Brandolini, and Timothy M. Smeeding. 2008. "Comparing Wealth Distributions Across Rich Countries: First Results from the Luxembourg Wealth Study." In *Household Wealth in Italy,* edited by Grazia Marchese, Luigi Cannari, and Giovanni D'Alessio. Rome: Banca d'Italia.

Sierminska, Eva, and Timothy Smeeding. 2005. "Measurement Issues: Equivalence Scales, Accounting Framework, and Reference Unit." In *Luxembourg Wealth Study Conference on the Construction and Usage of Comparable Microdata on Household Wealth, Perugia.* Rome: Banca d'Italia.

Spilerman, Seymour. 2000. "Wealth and Stratification Processes." *Annual Review of Sociology* 26: 497–524.

———. 2004. "The Impact of Parental Wealth on Early Living Standards in Israel." *American Journal of Sociology* 110(1): 92–122.

Sørensen, Aage B. 2000. "Toward a Sounder Basis for Class Analysis." *American Journal of Sociology* 105(6): 1523–58.

Torche, Florencia, and Seymour Spilerman. 2006. "Parental Wealth Effects on Living Standard and Asset Holdings: Results from Chile." In *International Perspectives on Household Wealth,* edited by Edward N. Wolff. Cheltenham, U.K.: Edward Elgar.

———. 2009. "Intergenerational Influences of Wealth in Mexico." *Latin American Research Review* 44(3): 75–101.

Wagner, Gert G., Joachim R. Frick, and Jürgen Schupp. 2007. "The German Socio-Economic Panel Study (SOEP): Scope, Evolution, and Enhancements." *Schmollers Jahrbuch* 127(1): 139–69.

Wolff, Edward N., ed. 2006. *International Perspectives on Household Wealth.* Cheltenham, U.K.: Edward Elgar.

Wright, Sewall. 1934. "The Method of Path Coefficients." *Annals of Mathematical Statistics* 5(3): 161–215.

Chapter 5

Occupations and Social Mobility: Gradational, Big-Class, and Micro-Class Reproduction in Comparative Perspective

JAN O. JONSSON, DAVID B. GRUSKY,
REINHARD POLLAK, MATTHEW DI CARLO,
AND CARINA MOOD

T HE PURPOSE of this chapter is to revisit the classical sociological questions about social mobility with a new cross-national data set and a new approach to analyzing mobility data. We first present a model of mobility that estimates the net amount of gradational, occupational, and big-class reproduction, and we then apply this model to examine cross-national variability in mobility and recent trends in mobility. This chapter thus adds to a small but growing collection of recent works that are reviving and reinventing the sociological approach to studying mobility (Beller and Hout 2006; Breen 2004; Breen and Jonsson 2005; Harding et al. 2005).

It may be useful to start off by reminding ourselves why sociologists care about mobility. There are two lines of questioning that have historically animated sociologists who study mobility: the formation of self-aware and politically active social groups (the "collective action" question), and the effects of social origins on life chances (the "equal opportunity" question). The first question may be understood as European in provenance, while the second has been embraced more frequently by U.S. scholars.

For mobility scholars oriented toward the collective action question, the presumption has long been that high levels of social mobility, manifested both within and across generations, undermine the formation of (homogeneous) social classes. When, for example, Werner Sombart (1906) considered why the United States did not take to socialism, he concluded that U.S. workers were disinclined to identify with their class or to act on its behalf because they were not counting on remaining within it for very long. It might be said that the main mobility project to which U.S. workers were oriented was that of individual advancement rather than collective advancement. The amount of social mobility may additionally affect the demographic and cultural composition of a social class. As John Goldthorpe (1980) has noted, when members of a class are drawn diversely from various social origins, the class then becomes too heterogeneous to develop a coherent classwide culture.

This focus on class formation, once the mainstay of the sociological interest in mobility, has arguably become less important in the field. In recent years, it has increasingly given way to an interest in equality of opportunity, as revealed by the extent to which children born into more- or less-privileged families have different opportunities for getting ahead. The mobility table tells us, in other words, how much children's starting point matters for their subsequent life chances.

This same interest in monitoring departures from equal opportunity would appear to motivate much mobility research within the discipline of economics as well. Insofar, then, as sociologists have shed their interest in questions of class formation, we can no longer draw sharp distinctions between the two disciplines in the motivations underlying intergenerational mobility analysis. The main disciplinary difference in the contemporary period is now principally found in the way those motivations are expressed. The ideal-typical economist explores departures from equal opportunity through the prism of economic standing and income mobility, while the ideal-typical sociologist explores such departures through the prism of social standing and social mobility.

Sociologists' interest in social standing and mobility has led them to focus almost exclusively on the intergenerational transmission of occupations. Indeed, sociologists are arguably obsessed with occupations, the now-famous claim being that occupations are the "backbone" of the stratification system (Blau and Duncan 1967; Parkin 1971). Although some economists (Björklund and Jäntti 1997; Nicoletti and Ermisch 2007) have also incorporated occupations into their mobility analyses (albeit indirectly), to do so remains comparatively rare within the economics tradition.

Why do sociologists make so much of occupations? The short answer is that, because occupations are deeply institutionalized in the labor market, they serve as a powerful omnibus indicator of the social world within which individuals work and live. At a dinner party, we tend to ask a new acquaintance, "What do you do?" because the response, almost invariably conveyed in the form of an occupation, provides at once evidence on life chances and capacities (skills and credentials, earnings capacity, networks), honor and esteem (prestige, socioeconomic status), and the social and cultural world within which interactions occur (consumption practices, politics, attitudes). We care, in other words, about occupations because they are pregnant with information on the life chances, social standing, and social world of their incumbents (see Weeden and Grusky 2005). The (largely untested) bias in this regard is that occupation is far more strongly correlated with these variables than is income.

The Three Forms of Reproduction

When occupations are treated as an omnibus indicator of social conditions, there are three main ways in which we can then examine how an individual's origin (as expressed in the mother's and father's occupations) influences her or his destination (as expressed in the individual's adult occupation). First, occupations can be *scaled* or *graded* in ways that signal the general desirability of the labor market position, with the origin-destination association then revealing the extent to which those born into families in which parents have desirable occupations are likely themselves to assume desirable occupations. This association between origin and destination desirability arises because parents at the top of the desirability distribution control the resources that make it possible for their children to get ahead. That is, their children can secure desirable occupations by virtue of (1) their access to the economic resources needed to obtain an elite education or capitalize on entrepreneurial opportunities, (2) their access to the social networks that provide information about or entry into the most rewarded occupations, and (3) their access to the skills and cultural resources that allow them to qualify for and succeed in such occupations. Although some sociologists have sought to measure desirability directly (Jencks, Perman, and Rainwater 1988), most unidimensional scales measure desirability only indirectly by asking respondents about the general "social standing" of occupations (prestige scales) or by indexing the occupational resources, such as education and income, that are presumed to signal overall desirability (socioeconomic scales). There is a long and lively history of debates among proponents of prestige scales (Goldthorpe and Hope 1974; Nakao and Treas 1992; Treiman 1977), socioeconomic scales (Duncan 1961; Ganzeboom, de Graaf, and Treiman 1992; Hodge 1981), and other closely related scales (Hauser and Warren 1997).

The second main way in which sociologists deploy occupations for the purpose of studying mobility is to aggregate them into *big social classes* and then examine the exchanges among these classes. The typical big-class scheme defines three, seven, or twelve categories (such as the salariat, craft workers, the petty bourgeoisie, farmers). Although most big-class schemes do not rely exclusively on occupational information for the purpose of defining classes (and may additionally rely on self-employment, industry, or job characteristics), in practice occupations have been understood as the most fundamental arbiter of class position (for an important exception, see Wright 1997).

The big classes so defined are assumed to transmit a constellation of working conditions, a social context that affects behavior and decision-making, and a cultural context that is an adjustment to this social context. Unlike the scaling tradition, the big-class tradition draws attention to the effects of class-specific resources, the claim being that children from two big classes of similar general desirability do not necessarily have the same mobility chances. Although craft workers and the petty bourgeoisie, for example, may be roughly similar in overall desirability, the children of craft workers should develop a taste and capacity for craft work while the children of the petty bourgeoisie should develop a taste and capacity for entrepreneurship. The big-class formulation additionally assumes that all children born into the same class (such as the salariat) have similar mobility chances even though their parents originate from very different detailed occupations (such as doctor, lawyer, or professor). These myriad detailed occupations are presumed to be similar enough in working conditions, employment form, or culture to preclude any need to differentiate them.

The contest between gradational and big-class approaches has often been acrimonious and, until recently, has obscured a third and equally fundamental way of deploying occupations for the purpose of mobility analysis. This third way, the *micro-class* approach, shares with the big-class approach the assumption that mobility regimes take on a discrete form and cannot be understood wholly in terms of a gradational imagery. This lumpiness assumes, however, an especially detailed form: the claim is that unit occupations (such as lawyer, policeman, secretary) are, at least in some societies, more deeply institutionalized than any big-class combinations of those occupations (such as craft workers or professionals). In the micro-class view, parents tend to "bring home" their occupations, and children accordingly learn occupation-specific skills, profit from occupation-specific networks, and develop occupation-specific aspirations. The daughter of an architect, to take but one example, may be socialized into appreciating the aesthetic features of buildings, exposed to drawing and programming skills that are relevant to the architectural practice, find that she has a comparative advantage in relevant subjects in school, and intern during the summer with a business partner of her parent. The probability that an architect's child will become an architect, a carpenter's child will become a carpenter, and a farmer's child will become a farmer is accordingly high (when compared to the corresponding probabilities for children from occupations of the same general desirability and same big class). The strong big-class reproduction that we long thought was revealed in mobility tables may instead be artifactual and express nothing more than the tendency for reproduction at the detailed occupational level.

Both of these forms of class models differ from gradational models in allowing for so-called inheritance effects. Because parents are understood to be transferring class-specific resources to their children (rather than more generalized ones), the main departure from equal opportunity under a class formulation takes the form of a tendency for class inheritance, not a tendency for mobility between occupations of roughly equal desirability, prestige, status, or income. When we tabulate social origin class with destination class, the inheritance effects show up as a particularly strong association in cells in the main upper-left to lower-right diagonal. The resulting statistical models thus fit a full set of inheritance terms, one for each class, and are less parsimonious than ones that estimate a single intergenerational income elasticity parameter or summarize the association in a tabular array in a single association term. Although an equality constraint on such inheritance terms could be imposed, it is not uncommon to hypothesize (and to find) that some classes have rather stronger holding power than others (Breen 2004; Erikson and Goldthorpe 1992; Jonsson et al. 2009).

It would, of course, be possible to presume that reproduction takes on an exclusively gradational, big-class, or micro-class form and to build a mobility model that then capitalizes on the imagery underlying that particular form. The field has indeed often proceeded in just this way—that is, big-class analysts have often insisted on building purist big-class models, while gradationalists have insisted on building purist gradational models. By contrast, the model that we have developed combines all three forms (big-class, micro-class, gradational) and thereby makes it possible to tease out the contribution of each.

How Does Social Reproduction Vary Across Countries?

In any given country, some types of social reproduction are deeply institutionalized, while others appear only in attenuated form. We advance here some hypotheses about the structure of such cross-national differences in reproduction.

The gradational form is likely to be relatively well developed in all countries for two reasons: desirable occupations tend to come with the resources that allow parents to assist their children in getting ahead, and undesirable occupations tend to be combined with reduced resources that then prevent parents from assisting with upward mobility projects for their children. There are nonetheless *some* differences across countries in the extent to which desirable occupations are bestowed with reproduction-enhancing resources. In a country that rewards desirable occupations with especially high income or wealth, parents in these occupations can "buy" reproduction more reliably, and the gradational effect accordingly is stronger. We are not suggesting that income inequality in and of itself automatically promotes gradational reproduction. Rather, the key question is the extent to which such inequality takes on a gradational form, a pattern in which desirable occupations are especially laden with income while undesirable occupations are especially poor. If, for example, a compensating differentials logic dominates, then the occupations that are highly paid tend to be less desirable on so-called intrinsic factors, and thus we might expect gradational reproduction to be reduced. Although there is a strong association in all countries between occupational income and other desirable occupational assets (such as prestige or autonomy), this association might well be attenuated in some countries, such as Sweden, in which occupational assets are provided more universally.[1]

We expect yet more substantial cross-national variability in the extent of big-class and micro-class reproduction. What determines whether these two forms of reproduction are weak or strong? The key consideration in this regard is whether a country's division of labor, wage bargaining systems, labor market, and educational and vocational institutions are organized in big-class or micro-class terms. If, for example, in a society the big-class form is built into its core institutions (such as collective bargaining arrangements), then a big-class identity is not only salient for parents but their life chances are decisively established at the big-class level. This identity is then transferred to their children with more reliability than in societies in which big classes are just statistical constructions that reflect mainly the tastes and theories of social scientists. By the same logic, in countries where occupations or micro-classes are highly institutionalized (such as Germany), we would expect social reproduction to follow micro-class lines.

Although we might think of big-class and micro-class reproduction as polar opposites and hence negatively related, it is not necessarily the case that reproduction is a zero-sum game and that societies must be organized exclusively at one and only one level. To the contrary, some countries are balkanized along both micro-class and big-class lines, whereas others evince little class structuration of either sort. If the amount of micro-class reproduction (high or low) is cross-classified against the amount of big-class reproduction (high or low), we accordingly arrive at four ideal-type mobility regimes. We suggest here that the United States, Japan, Sweden, and Germany may be understood as representatives of these ideal types (see also Grusky 2005; Jonsson et al. 2009).

Germany, for example, can be understood as a country in which both types of class reproduction are strong. The vocational training system (Müller and Gangl 2003) gives institutional backing to occupational distinctions and renders them salient to parents and children alike, whereas big-class reproduction is promoted by trade unions and employment regulation (Ebbinghaus and Visser 2000; Kocka 1981) that institutionalize the demarcation between white-collar salaried employees (Angestellte) and blue-collar workers (Arbeiter). By contrast, Japan is conventionally regarded as a country that has suppressed both big-class and micro-class forms of organization, with the firm instead serving as the main organizational form in the labor market (Ishida 1993; Nakane 1970).

The United States and Sweden can each be regarded as "mixed cases" in which one of the two forms of reproduction is present. The big-class form is, of course, characteristically Swedish in the sense that Swedish trade unions are organized at the big-class level, wage negotiations have likewise taken a centralized form, and Swedish political platforms are crafted to appeal to big-class constituencies (Esping-Andersen 1990; Korpi 1983). The micro-class form is poorly developed in Sweden, however, because of the historically early decline of the guilds. The U.S. case takes the obverse form in which occupational organization trumps big-class organization. Here craft and professional organizations are well developed, whereas overarching forms of big-class organization are viewed with some suspicion.

We assess these hypotheses by applying our multidimensional model of social mobility to over-time data from our four countries of interest. By examining gradational, big-class, and micro-class reproduction in each of these countries, we are able to establish whether and where cross-national differences occur. This approach allows us to go beyond conventional comparative analyses that conflate the various forms of reproduction and simply presume that cross-national differences, if any are found, will assume the same pattern regardless of form.

Mechanisms for Trend

The patterning of trend in social mobility has also been intensively debated and researched during the last decades (for a review, see Breen and Jonsson 2005). In the 1960s and 1970s, it was argued that the "natural development" of industrial societies led to a gradual decline in intergenerational reproduction, a decline that was assumed to occur in tandem with a decline in income inequality (Bell 1973; Blau and Duncan 1967; Treiman 1970). This upward trend in mobility was understood to be driven by (1) a long-term shift toward universalistic values and a corresponding decline in class-based discrimination by teachers or employers, (2) a rise in geographic mobility that further undermined class-based discrimination by preventing teachers or employers from knowing the class origins of their students or workers, and (3) the spread of a competitive market that obliged employers to emphasize merit over class origins in their hiring and recruitment decisions. More recently, some scholars have additionally suggested that class-based forms of organization are withering away and that class identities are becoming less salient, with these developments in turn weakening class-based reproduction (Pakulski 2005).

The evidence on such claims has been mixed. For example, Harry Ganzeboom, Ruud Luijkx, and Donald Treiman (1989) have concluded that there is a worldwide trend toward decreasing intergenerational association (at the big-class level), just as the modernization hypothesis would have it. The most recent collaborative effort in the big-class mobility tradition (see Breen 2004) also finds a decline in intergenerational association in several European countries, albeit not all of them. By contrast, Robert Erikson and John Goldthorpe (1992) have suggested that such fluctuations as can be found are largely trendless, and they emphasize that these changes are best understood as the consequence of quite idiosyncratic forces within each country, not the grand worldwide forces that modernization hypothesis stresses.

The studies mentioned all treat reproduction in generic terms rather than recognizing that it takes distinct forms (big-class, micro-class, gradational) and may be evolving in different ways for each. There are many reasons why trends may prove to be form-specific. For example, the standard convergence hypothesis suggests that idiosyncratic labor market forms are not sustainable over the long run as the forces of globalization and institutional isomorphism (such as European Union integration) play out. This formulation implies that the big-class politics of Sweden, the micro-class vocationalism of Germany, and the firm-based employment of Japan will gradually dissipate under the forces of globalization and integration. The convergence hypothesis is relevant here because it is precisely these idiosyncratic institutional forms that drive our hypotheses about why some countries have distinctively weak or strong micro-class or big-class effects. If these institutional forms are becoming less prominent or distinctive, then we might expect national idiosyncrasies in mobility to gradually wither away as well (see Goldthorpe 2002; Breen 2004).

Data, Variables, and the Definition of Classes

The data sources used here are presented in table 5.1. The variables drawn from these sources are father's and respondent's occupation, sex, age, and a small number of other variables needed to code micro-class (such as employment status and branch of industry). The data for Sweden come from the 1970, 1975, 1980, 1985, and 1990 censuses. The occupations of parents can be recovered in Sweden by linking individual respondents to their parents in the 1960 and 1970 censuses (see Erikson and Jonsson 1993).

The building block of our mobility tables is the micro-class scheme. Because we identify eighty-two micro-classes and are therefore analyzing eighty-two–by–eighty-two mobility tables, we need large samples of

Table 5.1   Data Sources for Intergenerational Mobility Analysis

Survey	Period	Ages	Birth Cohorts	Occupational Scheme[a]	Sample Size
Occupational Changes in a Generation I (OCG-I)	1962	30 to 64	1898 to 1932	1960 SOC	17,544
Occupational Changes in a Generation II (OCG-II)	1973	30 to 64	1909 to 1943	1960 to 1970 SOC	18,856
General Social Survey (GSS)	1972 to 2006	30 to 64	1908 to 1973	1970 to 1980 SOC	9,986
Survey of Social Stratification and Mobility (SSM)	1955 to 2005	30 to 64	1891 to 1975	Japanese SCO	6,703
Japan General Social Survey (JGSS)	2000 to 2002	30 to 64	1936 to 1972	Japanese SCO	1,917
German Social Survey (ALLBUS)	1980 to 2008	30 to 64	1916 to 1978	ISCO-68, ISCO-88	6,656
German Socio-Economic Panel (GSOEP)	1986, 1999, 2000	30 to 64	1922 to 1970	ISCO-68, ISCO-88	2,887
German Life History Study LV I–III	1981 to 1989	30 to 64	1921 to 1959	ISCO-68	1,234
ZUMA-Standard Demographic Survey	1976 to 1982	30 to 64	1912 to 1952	ISCO-68	2,928
International Social Justice Project (ISJP)	1991, 1996, 2000	30 to 64	1927 to 1970	ISCO-88	888
1970, 1975, 1980, 1985, and 1990 Swedish census (linked to 1960 and 1970 censuses)	1970 to 1990	30 to 35	1936–1960	NYK	1,244,740

Source Authors' compilation:

the sort that, in most countries, can only be created by pooling multiple data sets.[2] By virtue of these data requirements, we have been forced to make some compromises, such as including surveys that pertain to somewhat different time periods in each country. We can, however, control for some of these differences in our trend analyses.

The respondents' occupations are ascertained when they are between thirty and sixty-four years old. In Sweden, the respondents are much younger, ranging in age from thirty to thirty-five. This approach eliminates any overlapping respondents across time points. We have assessed elsewhere the effects of survey differences in age coverage (Jonsson et al. 2009) and found them to be trivial in their consequences. We have also reestimated many of our models using an expanded data set that includes older Swedish respondents and found only trivial changes in the estimates (relative to the results reported here).

We have sought to maximize the comparability of the occupation and class schemes by returning to the detailed occupational codes in each country and painstakingly coding them into our eighty-two-category scheme. This classification is designed to capture the socially defined boundaries in the division of labor (see Jonsson et al. 2009). We define the micro-class as "a grouping of technically similar jobs that is institutionalized in the labor market through such means as (a) an association or union, (b) licensing or certification requirements, or (c) widely diffused understandings . . . regarding efficient or otherwise preferred ways of organizing production and dividing labor" (Grusky 2005, 66). Although some compromises in the coding protocol were required because of our small sample size and because of cross-national differences in occupational classification, there is much evidence that, despite all such compromises, micro-class schemes of this sort capture some of the most profound institutional boundaries in the labor market (see Weeden and Grusky 2005). The full eighty-two-category scheme is presented in table 5.2, described in further detail in Jan Jonsson and colleagues (2009), and implemented with the protocol laid out at www.classmobility.org.

In our analyses, we examine micro-class reproduction by using the categories of table 5.2 in their original categorical form, while we examine gradational reproduction by assigning these categories to a prestige scale (using the scores developed by Nakao and Treas 1992).[3] We have chosen a prestige scale because we wish to apply a measure that signals relative desirability rather than occupational resources (such as education or income). Indeed, the resource distribution may well be shifting over time, most notably insofar as rising income inequality implies a stretching-out of that distribution. This type of shift complicates efforts to distinguish changes in the underlying scale from changes in the intergenerational association. There is good reason, however, to believe that judgments of prestige or desirability are quite resistant to change—hence our

Table 5.2 Micro-Classes Nested in Manual-Nonmanual Classes, Macro-Classes, and Meso-Classes

Nonmanual Class			Manual Class	
Professional-Managerial	Proprietors	Routine Nonmanual	Manual	Primary
Classic professions	Proprietors	Sales	Craft	Fishermen
Jurists		Real estate agents	Craftsmen, not elsewhere classified	Farmers
Health professionals		Agents, not elsewhere classified	Foremen	Farm laborers
Professors and instructors		Insurance agents	Electronics service and repair	
Natural scientists		Cashiers	Printers and related workers	
Statistical and social scientists		Sales workers	Locomotive operators	
Architects		Clerical	Electricians	
Accountants		Telephone operators	Tailors and related workers	
Authors and journalists		Bookkeepers	Vehicle mechanics	
Engineers		Office workers	Blacksmiths and machinists	
Managers and officials		Postal clerks	Jewelers	
Officials, government, and nonprofit organizations			Other mechanics	
Other managers			Plumbers and pipe-fitters	
Commercial managers			Cabinet-makers	
Building managers and proprietors			Bakers	
Other professions			Welders	
Systems analysts and programmers			Painters	
Aircraft pilots and navigators			Butchers	
Personnel and labor relations workers			Stationary engine operators	
			Bricklayers and carpenters	
			Heavy machine operators	
			Lower manual	
			Truck drivers	

Elementary and
secondary teachers
Librarians
Creative artists
Ship officers
Professional and technical,
not elsewhere classified
Social and welfare workers
Workers in religion
Nonmedical technicians
Health semiprofessionals
Hospital attendants
Nursery school teachers
and aides

Chemical processors
Miners and related workers
Longshoremen
Food processing workers
Textile workers
Sawyers
Metal processors
Operatives and related workers,
not elsewhere classified
Forestry workers
Service workers
Protective service workers
Transport conductors
Guards and watchmen
Food service workers
Mass transportation operators
Service workers, not elsewhere
classified
Hairdressers
Newsboys and deliverymen
Launderers
Housekeeping workers
Janitors and cleaners
Gardeners

Source: Authors' calculations based on original research. See appendix for data sources.

decision to condition on a prestige scale. We can then account for possible
changes in the amount of gradational reproduction in terms of changes in
the association between occupational desirability and the various occupational resources, such as income, that are associated with desirability.
Although we present results based on a prestige scale, we have additionally carried out side analyses with other gradational scales (devised by
Ganzeboom, de Graaf, and Treiman 1992; Siegel 1971). Because the prestige scale we use correlates quite highly with such alternative scales, the
main results we show do not hinge on the choice of scale.[4]

We next aggregated our eighty-two micro-classes into a big-class scheme.
Given the wide range of competing big-class models, we were disinclined
to rely exclusively on any one of them; instead, our preference was to build
a hybrid classification that represents the many and varied distinctions
adopted in the most popular class models. The manual-nonmanual divide
is the starting point for our scheme because it is one of the core barriers in
contemporary labor markets and incorporated into most (but not all) big-
class models. We further distinguish three big classes within the nonmanual sector (professional-managerial, proprietor, routine nonmanual)
and two big classes within the manual sector (manual, primary). We refer
to these five categories as "macro-classes." Finally, our macro-classes are
themselves subdivided into "meso-classes," yielding another ten categories (including, for example, classic professions, sales workers, and
craft workers). The end result of this classification exercise is eighty-two
micro-classes nested within ten meso-classes, five macro-classes, and the
manual-nonmanual division (see table 5.2 for a full listing).

These three types of big-class effects are layered over parameters
that capture reproduction at the micro-class and gradational levels. This
overlapping parameterization makes it possible to isolate effects at different big-class levels as well as distinguish such big-class effects from
those operating at the micro-class or gradational levels. The father-to-
child mobility table in figure 5.1 depicts this full set of overlapping
parameters and demonstrates how they capture affinities off the micro-
class diagonal, off the meso-class diagonal, and even off the macro-class
diagonal.

We can use this parameterization to tease out the net amount of reproduction of each type. This means, for example, that the inheritance parameter for lawyers reveals the extent to which the son of a lawyer is more
likely than someone else (from an equally desirable classic profession) to
become a lawyer. The inheritance effect for classic professions represents,
by contrast, the extent to which the mobile sons of lawyers (that is, those
who *do not* become lawyers) are likely to end up in some other classic profession (with the comparison group now being sons who come from outside the classic professions but are within the professional-managerial
macro-class). With this specification, we can therefore estimate inheritance

Figure 5.1   Nested Forms of Manual-Nonmanual and Macro-Class, Meso-Class, and Micro-Class Inheritance

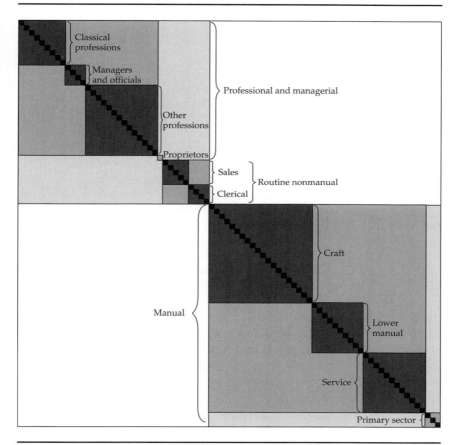

Source: Jonsson et al. (2009), reprinted with permission.

effects that are net of other confounded effects, allowing us to locate with some precision the main rigidities in the class structure.

The gradational effect, which is also included in our models, reflects the degree to which exchange follows a desirability gradient net of micro-class, meso-class, and macro-class inheritance. There are, of course, some mobility scholars who would rely exclusively on a gradational parameter to characterize exchange. By contrast, we treat it as a residual parameter, one that "mops up" some of the affinities that persist even after micro-class, meso-class, and macro-class reproduction are fully controlled. This parameter is therefore the only one governing flows in the white off-diagonal zones of figure 5.1 and is likewise the only one distinguishing off-diagonal exchanges within each meso class. If, for example, the son of a lawyer does not become a lawyer, we assume that his likelihood of ending up in some other classic profession is governed exclusively by the relative desirability of those professions. The lawyer is more likely under this specification to become an architect (roughly equal in status) than an accountant (rather lower in status).

We do not pretend that our specification, exhaustive though it may appear to be, is a complete specification of all exchange in our highly detailed cross-classification. The model is not intended to capture particularistic affinities (or disaffinities) between occupations that reflect the effect of tastes or skills that are not captured by a desirability effect. We have found, for example, an excess affinity between fishermen and ship officers that might be understood as reflecting seafaring tastes, skills, or networks. We elsewhere report more comprehensively on such affinities (Jonsson et al. 2009). Although our model does not capture such particularistic exchanges, it is not necessary to meticulously model the occupational topography given that our objective here is to identify the structure of reproduction and the most important and systematic departures from equal opportunity.

We should note, finally, that our analyses here pertain to men, an unfortunate restriction to which we were forced to resort because many of our data sources are male-only. As is frequently emphasized, women's mobility is complicated to model because, even more so than for men, the process of intergenerational transmission operates through both parents. We have presented elsewhere (Jonsson et al. 2009) selected results on women's mobility that set the stage for future analyses that will focus exclusively on women's mobility.

How Common Is Immobility?

We set up our core analyses by first reporting simple immobility rates for each of the four types of immobility featured in our analyses. These rates, displayed in figure 5.2, show that approximately two-thirds of all respondents do not cross the manual-nonmanual divide, a result that does not differ very much across countries. The conventional assumption that Sweden and Germany are class societies is better revealed at the macro-class level, as here we find that almost half of Swedish and German offspring remain in their macro-class of origin, an inheritance rate that is rather higher than what prevails in the United States (0.39) and Japan (0.41). The immobility percentages are, of course, lower still for meso-class inheritance. Here the United States is the most mobile country, while Japan and Germany are the least mobile. The final bar in figure 5.2 represents micro-class immobility. Although Germany comes in, as expected, with a relatively high micro-class immobility rate, it is notable that here again Japan's is yet higher.

Figure 5.2   Immobility by Country and Type of Immobility

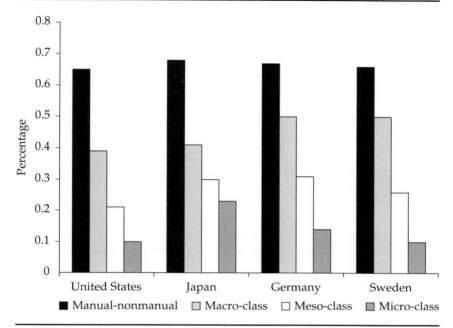

Source: Authors' calculations based on original research. See appendix for data sources.
Notes: We have defined an exhaustive meso-class scheme by treating "propri-etors" and the "primary sector" as meso-classes, and we have defined an exhaus-tive micro-class scheme by treating "proprietors" as a micro-class.

The Japanese result is remarkable given that occupations and occu-pational reproduction are not typically featured in analyses of Japanese society. We have examined (see Jonsson et al. 2009) whether this result simply reflects the large size of the primary sector in Japan. That is, because farming and fishing are high-immobility occupations, a country with many such occupations would tend to register much overall immobility. It turns out, however, that even outside the primary sector Japan's immobility rate is quite high, a result that suggests that occupations play a more fun-damental role in Japan than is typically appreciated.

Modeling Social Fluidity and Reproduction

For a proper test of the association between origin and destination, we turn to an analysis of *relative rates* of mobility (or "social fluidity"), an analysis that speaks to issues of equal opportunity. In such an analysis, the margin-als of the mobility table are fit, and the class and gradational parameters are therefore unaffected by the relative sizes of occupations. We expect differences across countries and generations in those relative sizes.

The model that we apply includes parameters for gradational, big-class, and micro-class reproduction. It takes the following form (in each country):

$$m_{ij} = \alpha \beta_i \gamma_j \varphi^{u_i u_j} \delta_{ij}^A \delta_{ij}^B \delta_{ij}^C \delta_{ij}^M \tag{5.1}$$

where i indexes origins and j destinations, m_{ij} refers to the expected value in the ij^{th} cell, α is the main effect, β_i and γ_j are row and column marginal effects, φ refers to the prestige effect, μ_i (origin) and μ_j (destination) are the prestige values assigned to each of the eighty-two micro-classes, and δ^A, δ^B, δ^C, and δ^M represent the manual-nonmanual, macro-class, meso-class, and micro-class effects, respectively. It is an important feature of the model that the δ parameters are fit simultaneously and therefore represent net effects. The manual-nonmanual parameter, for example, reflects the average density across the cells pertaining to manual or non-manual inheritance after accounting for the inheritance at the macro-class, meso-class, and micro-class levels (see Herting, Grusky, and van Rompaey 1997).

The prestige parameter, φ, captures the tendency of offspring to assume an occupation that is close (in desirability) to their origin occupation (see Hout 1988). If this parameter were omitted, the tendency for desirability-based clustering might show up as class reproduction. We want instead to identify reproductive effects that are not attributable to simple gradational differences between classes.[5]

We begin by presenting the results from a simple model that constrains all densities of social reproduction (gradational, big-class, micro-class) to be the same across countries. The resulting model, graphed in figure 5.3, provides evidence on the baseline structure of social reproduction.[6] The height of the bars represents the size of the inheritance effects, and hence the most striking feature of figure 5.3 is the extreme micro-diagonal clustering splitting the table into two triangles. This clustering appears at the top of the class structure, throughout the middle classes, and at the bottom of the class structure. Although the "middle regions" have sometimes been identified as a zone of considerable fluidity (Featherman and Hauser 1978), figure 5.3 conveys a picture of impressive micro-class inheritance even there.

These micro-class terms are overlaid on big-class terms that, while less substantial, are by no means trivial in size. The most prominent big-class parameter, the one pertaining to the manual-nonmanual divide, reveals itself as a cliff marking off both the manual and nonmanual quadrants. Within each quadrant, the remaining meso-class and micro-class effects are for the most part less prominent, thus creating the effect

Figure 5.3   The Contours of Reproduction

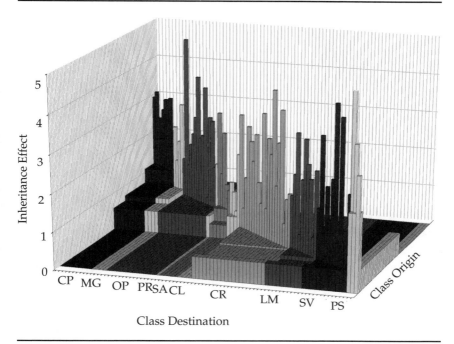

Source: Authors' figure based on original research. See appendix for data sources.
Note: Coefficients are drawn from model that standardizes sample size to ten-thousand cases in each country. CP = classical professions; MG = managers and officials; OP = other professions; PR = proprietors; SA = sales; CL = clerical; CR = craft; LM = lower manual; SV = service; PS = primary sector.

of nonmanual and manual plateaus. The manual-nonmanual divide is in this regard an especially prominent big-class barrier to equal opportunity.

The other big-class effects are less impressive in strength. We have shown elsewhere that big-class effects appear large in conventional big-class analyses because of omitted micro-class and gradational reproduction (Jonsson et al. 2009). That is, when the gradational and micro-class terms are omitted, the big-class effects loom far larger and create the appearance of substantial big-class reproduction—which is descriptively true, but largely a function of simple aggregation of occupational inheritance. This result is important because it implies that, insofar as one seeks to reduce inequality of opportunity (as manifested in class inheritance), it is necessary to address both micro-class and gradational reproduction.

Table 5.3   Immobility Parameters by Country and Type of Reproduction

Coefficients	United States	Japan	Germany	Sweden
Meso-class[a]	0.18	0.24	0.07*	0.16
Macro-class[a]	0.39	0.48*	0.66*	0.63*
Manual-nonmanual	0.66	0.51*	0.66	0.54*
Micro-class[a]	1.29	1.76*	1.82*	1.45*
Gradational[b]	1.03	1.06	1.37*	1.33*

Source: Authors' calculations based on original research. See appendix for data sources.
*Significantly different from the U.S. coefficient (at $\alpha = 0.05$).
[a]Parameter estimates averaged across all categories making up this type of class.
[b]Coefficients multiplied by 1,000.

Cross-National Variation in Social Reproduction

We next consider whether this pooled model conceals much cross-national variability in the structure of mobility. This question can be addressed by estimating a model that constrains all cross-national variability to be captured in a set of shift parameters for each immobility coefficient (Erikson and Goldthorpe 1992; Xie 1992). The core parameters from this model are presented in table 5.3 and then graphed in figure 5.4 (for model fit statistics, see appendix table 5A.1). For purposes of summary, we have not presented here the full set of either meso-class or micro-class estimates, and instead we have simply averaged across them. The meso-class entry for the United States, for example, implies that the average of the eight meso-class estimates is 0.18.[7]

The estimates in table 5.3 are only partly consistent with the conventional view that big classes are relatively well developed in Europe. Although the macro-class coefficients are indeed strong in Sweden and Germany, the other big-class coefficients (meso-class, manual-nonmanual) do not reveal any corresponding evidence of such European exceptionalism (for a similar conclusion, see Ishida 2010). The meso-class parameter is in fact significantly smaller in Germany than in the United States.

In our opening comments, we did not anticipate much variability in gradational reproduction, an expectation that is borne out in the quite similar gradational coefficients for the United States, Japan, and Sweden. However, the gradational effect for Germany and Sweden is especially strong, a result that suggests that desirable occupations in these countries have especially ample resources that allow children born into them to fare especially well. Although we can at this point merely speculate about the reasons for this result, we can note that in these two countries many high-status occupations require university degrees, meaning that it is likely

Figure 5.4   Immobility Parameters by Country and Type of Reproduction

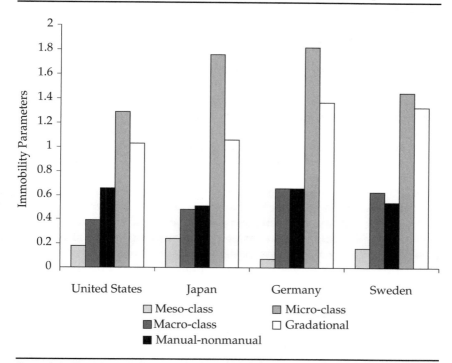

Source: Authors' compilation based on original research. See appendix for data sources.

that there is an unusually strong association between human capital and occupational prestige in these countries.

Is the variability in micro-class effects also consistent with our expectations? As shown in table 5.3 and figure 5.4, the micro-class effects are indeed weak in Sweden and strong in Germany (as predicted), but they are also surprisingly weak in the United States and surprisingly strong in Japan. We do not wish to exaggerate such cross-national variability in micro-class effects. In all four countries, the most extreme departures from equal opportunity occur at the micro-class level, and much of what was previously presumed to be big-class reproduction turns out instead to be a finer form of micro-class reproduction. We explicitly selected two countries, Japan and Sweden, that would not conventionally be regarded as home grounds for micro-class processes, yet we find for both that the micro-class form is quite prominent. Even in Japan, which has long been represented as a "de-occupationalized" regime, we find evidence of much micro-class reproduction. Likewise, micro-class reproduction is prominent in Sweden, even though it is typically featured in scholarly and popular accounts as a prototypical big-class regime.

Trends in Mobility and Fluidity

We suggested in our opening comments that a multidimensional mobility model is also useful in identifying where change is occurring. Are all countries experiencing the same pattern of change? Is big-class reproduction, for example, declining in all countries, just as postmodernists would have it? Or are trends playing out differently in different countries? Is there any evidence of a convergence in mobility regimes whereby each country is shedding its idiosyncratic features and moving toward some generic mobility form?

We take on these questions by disaggregating our mobility tables by period. Rather than insisting mechanically on the same periodization in each country, we have allowed for cross-national differences in periodization to accommodate idiosyncrasies in data availability and also, where possible, to reflect conventional national periodizations of social and economic history. We have pooled the U.S. data into four periods: the 1960s (1962 Occupational Changes in a Generation [OCG]), the 1970s (1973 OCG and 1972 to 1979 General Social Survey [GSS]), the 1980s (1980 to 1989 GSS), and the 1990s and beyond (1990 to 2006 GSS). The Japanese data are likewise pooled into four periods, but with slightly different break points: 1955 to 1965 ("early expansion"), 1975 to 1985 ("consolidation"), 1985 to 1995 ("the lost decade"), and 2000 to 2005 ("the contemporary period"). As noted earlier, the Swedish data consist of five periods pertaining to the quintannual censuses from 1970 to 1990 (with 1990 being the last census in Sweden). And finally, we have disaggregated the German data into three time periods: the 1970s (1976 to 1982), the 1980s (1983 to 1990), and the 1990s and beyond (1991 to 2008).

We should note that a methodological complication arises insofar as trends in mobility are driven by cohort effects and associated cohort replacement processes (Breen and Jonsson 2007). It is possible that patterns of mobility differ across the mobility tables defined by our periods principally because the mix of birth cohorts represented in these tables shifts as older cohorts age out of the labor market. However, an analysis based on age-by-cohort tables would, with the exception of Sweden, be too sparse given the data available to us, and we are therefore forced to resort to the common device of monitoring trend via period alone. Although the signal is perforce muted under this approach (because cohorts age out of the labor force only gradually), such muted trends are at least descriptively correct as an overall characterization of the extent of fluidity in each period (Breen and Jonsson 2007).

We begin our analysis by examining simple observed rates of immobility. As shown in figures 5.5 to 5.8, the case for across-the-board declines in

Figure 5.5   Immobility in the United States by Type of Immobility

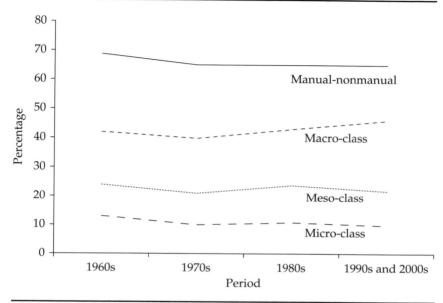

Source: Authors' calculations based on original research. See appendix for data sources.

Figure 5.6   Immobility in Japan by Type of Immobility

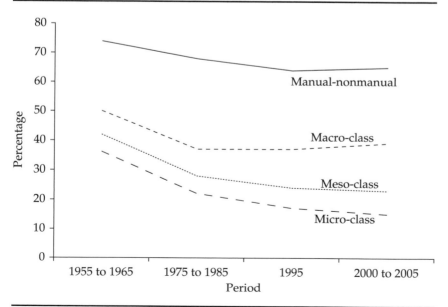

Source: Authors' calculations based on original research. See appendix for data sources.

Figure 5.7   Immobility in Sweden by Type of Mobility

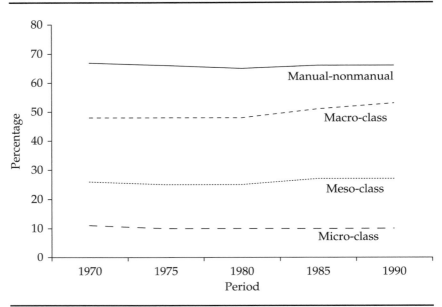

Source: Authors' calculations based on original research. See appendix for data sources.

Figure 5.8   Immobility in Germany by Type of Immobility

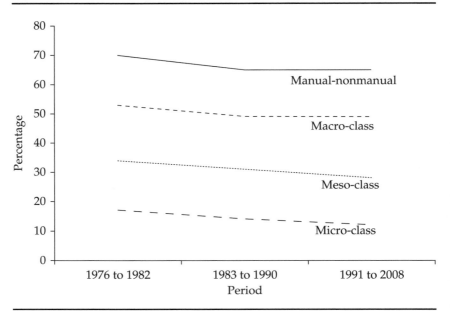

Source: Authors' calculations based on original research. See appendix for data sources.

immobility is most evident in the early years in the United States, Japan, and Germany. This result is typical of societies characterized by a rapid decline of the agricultural sector and a consequent "forced immobility" for farming children. There is more to this particular result, however, than mere forced immobility: when farmers are excluded from the analysis, the decline in immobility in the early period is less substantial in the United States, Japan, and Germany, but it is still prominent (analyses not presented here).

The trends after this early decline are neither as striking nor as consistent. In the United States, Japan, and Germany, the manual-nonmanual and macro-class trend lines prove resistant to further decline, and indeed there is more than a hint of increasing macro-class immobility. The latter is in fact the only visible trend in Sweden. The meso-class and micro-class trend lines reveal, by contrast, either trendless fluctuation (the United States), slight decline (Japan and Germany), or stability (Sweden).

Figures 5.5 to 5.8 imply that the objective experience of mobility remains, for the most part, quite common in all four countries. Although the manual-nonmanual divide is only rarely crossed (in all time periods and countries), it is common to experience all other types of mobility monitored here. Additionally, we find that absolute mobility rates change only slowly and that such patterns of change as obtained here do not show great similarity across countries. The "trendless fluctuation" narrative thus has some force in the context of absolute mobility rates.

Important as absolute rates of mobility are, they do not speak to the matter of equality of opportunity, and we therefore turn next to trends in social fluidity. We begin by carrying out an analysis of social fluidity, using the conventional form. That is, we first fit a gradational model that forces the association in a mobility table to follow a prestige (or desirability) gradient, and we then fit a big-class model that instead absorbs the association with a set of meso-class inheritance terms. These two models may be represented as follows (within each time period and country):

$$m_{ij} = \alpha \beta_i \gamma_j \varphi^{u_i u_j} \tag{5.2}$$

$$m_{ij} = \alpha \beta_i \gamma_j \delta_{ij} \tag{5.3}$$

where φ refers to the prestige effect, μ_i (origin) and μ_j (destination) are the prestige values assigned to each of the eighty-two micro-classes, δ_{ij} represents the full set of ten meso-class inheritance effects, and the marginal effects are defined as with equation 5.1. We appreciate that these are simplified models, but they nonetheless serve the function of setting up our own more complicated analyses with some instructive baselines.

Because the gradational model represented here captures all association with a single parameter, it is accordingly straightforward to allow that parameter to vary over time (separately within each country). For the meso-class model, the association is captured in ten inheritance terms, and we therefore proceed by fitting a shift effect that allows for a global increase or decrease in inheritance that applies equally to all ten terms. The tables are simply too sparse (except in Sweden) to attempt anything more elaborate. Although our model fits the full set of ten inheritance parameters in the base time period, for presentational purposes we report only the mean of those base parameters in table 5.4.[8] Also, because our disaggregated tables are so sparse, we have opted to further impose a linear constraint across periods on these shift effects, meaning that change is summarized with a single slope parameter indicating the amount of change per period. We have also estimated models that relax this constraint and fit separate shift effects for each period. The conclusions from such models are quite similar to those implied by our more parsimonious specification (and hence we do not report the nonlinear results here).[9]

As shown in the two upper rows of table 5.4, the conventional models all reveal a simple decline in association, although the trend in the Swedish meso-class model is small (but significant) while the point estimate for the U.S. meso-class model is somewhat larger but not significant. The decline in the father-to-son associations are in several cases noteworthy. In particular, the gradational effect in Japan decreased by some 30 percent over the entire time period ($0.31*3/3.12 = 0.298$), and non-negligible changes in the gradational effect register also for the other three countries. The decline in class inheritance is not as impressive, but in Japan and Germany it is reasonably large and significant. These types of results, which are quite commonly reported (see Breen 2004), inform the conventional view that there is an across-the-board decline in association (in at least most countries).

Is it the case, however, that *all* forms of reproduction are uniformly declining in all countries? We cannot take on this question without next turning to our full model, which allows us to distinguish trends for different types of reproduction. We proceed, as before, by fitting shift effects that are constrained to trend linearly, but now we impose this specification simultaneously on each of the five types of reproduction terms (gradational, nonmanual-manual, macro-class, meso-class, micro-class). The results from this specification are presented in the bottom panel of table 5.4 (see also the fit statistics in appendix table 5A.1).

The parameter estimates presented here, which again take the form of a base coefficient for the first time period and a slope coefficient representing per-period change, reveal very clearly that there is a great deal of decline in association. Of the twenty trend coefficients, seven are significant, and six of those seven are in turn negative. We are in this regard simply reproducing an already established result: the gradational and meso-class models with which we led off likewise implied that the origin-by-destination association is declining.

Table 5.4 Trends in Social Reproduction

Coefficients	United States		Japan		Germany		Sweden	
	Base	Change	Base	Change	Base	Change	Base	Change
Conventional change models								
Gradational	2.27	−0.15*	3.12	−0.31*	2.93	−0.18*	2.96	−0.15*
Meso-class	0.98	−0.09	1.41	−0.08*	1.51	−0.09*	1.13	−0.00*
Net change model								
Gradational	0.94	−0.05	0.29	0.12	1.38	0.02	1.61	−0.12*
Manual-nonmanual	0.73	−0.05*	0.50	0.00	0.73	−0.03	0.67	−0.06*
Macro-class	0.32	0.03	0.35	0.01	0.62	0.00	0.55	0.05*
Meso-class	0.21	−0.02	0.36	−0.11*	−0.02	−0.01	0.16	−0.00
Micro-class	1.48	0.01	2.18	0.02	2.02	−0.14*	1.61	−0.01*

Source: Authors' calculations based on original research. See appendix for data sources.
*Significantly different from zero (at α = .05).

The main virtue of our model, however, is that it allows us to further identify the *type* of reproduction that is weakening. For example, does this decline mainly take the form of weakening big-class reproduction, just as standard-issue postmodernist scholars would argue? Or are all forms of reproduction instead declining in some across-the-board fashion? The results of table 5.4 imply that both of these accounts are too simple and that mobility regimes are instead evolving in nation-specific ways. Although we find, for example, that big-class effects are indeed declining straightforwardly in the United States and Japan (as the postmodernists would suggest), there is no evidence of an equally strong big-class decline in either of our two European countries. The persisting strength of the big-class form in Europe is consistent with a standard European exceptionalist account.

The German case is fascinating because it shows strong evidence of decline in micro-class reproduction rather than big-class reproduction. The distinctive feature of Germany is, of course, its well-developed vocationalism and associated institutional support for micro-class reproduction. According to our model, such micro-class reproduction is withering away in Germany by roughly 13 percent per period ($e^{-.14} = 0.87$), implying that the net propensity for reproduction declines from 7.54 in the base period ($e^{2.02} = 7.54$) to 5.70 in 2008 ($e^{1.74} = 5.70$). The latter implied value for 2008 is no longer especially high relative to what prevails in other countries. The micro-class trend in Germany may be understood, then, as a convergence-generating one, as it has the effect of pushing an outlier country closer to the international mean.

The Swedish case is distinctive, by contrast, for its quite striking decline in the gradational term. We suggested earlier that gradational reproduction rests fundamentally on "loading up" desirable occupations with all sorts of assets that then facilitate reproduction. If the most desirable occupations are, for example, loaded up with high income, then parents in such occupations can use their income to assist their children in securing desirable occupations. The distinctive feature of Swedish egalitarianism, as it played out during the latter part of the twentieth century, is that it had the effect of distributing assets more uniformly across occupations and thereby prevented privileged parents from always being able to assist their children.

The standard account that fluidity is everywhere increasing thus conceals the manifold ways in which this increase is generated. If Sweden's distinctive form of egalitarianism dismantled gradational inequality (and preserved big-class inequality), the U.S. variant focused mainly on big-class inequality (and preserved gradational inequality), while the German decline has played out entirely at the micro-class level. It is a strength of our approach to reveal how these fundamental differences in the weakening of the origin-by-destination association comes about.

Conclusions

The purpose of this chapter has been to take seriously the sociological view that occupations are the "backbone" of the stratification system. We have advanced a new multidimensional model of mobility that incorporates the three main ways in which occupational reproduction is generated (gradational, big-class, micro-class). We then used this model to examine cross-nationally common features of mobility, cross-national differences in mobility, and the pattern of trends in mobility.

We find that all three forms of reproduction are in evidence in Sweden, the United States, Japan, and Germany. Although the importance of big-class and gradational reproduction has long been appreciated by mobility analysts, our results indicate that micro-class reproduction is also a prominent feature of contemporary mobility regimes. If this type of reproduction is ignored, as it conventionally is, it artificially inflates big-class reproduction and thus misleads us about the way in which opportunities are unequally distributed. This conclusion holds in all of the countries we examined, even in those, such as Japan, that are not typically understood as ones with deeply institutionalized occupations.

We also replicate here the increasingly accepted finding that social reproduction is declining in most industrial countries. However, conventional "black-box" models of trends cannot identify the sources of such decline, whereas our multidimensional mobility model reveals that the decline is achieved in country-specific ways. Although standard postmodernist accounts have long stressed the generic decline of the big-class form, we find that, contrary to such accounts, the big-class form is declining only in those non-European countries that were never all that hospitable to the big-class form. In Sweden and Germany, the big-class form remains as strong as ever, and the decline in reproduction is instead generated in other ways. We have suggested that U.S. egalitarianism takes the form of an attack on big-class inequality, Swedish egalitarianism takes the form of an attack on gradational inequality, and German institutional developments have rendered the micro-class form especially vulnerable.

Although micro-class reproduction is weakening in Germany, it remains, of course, exceedingly strong there, as well as in all of the other countries studied here. Should we be troubled by this especially strong form of reproduction? The skeptic might suggest that only an academic would worry that the child of a construction worker, for example, has a particularly high propensity to become a construction worker. We find such an argument unconvincing. The micro-class form cannot be dismissed in this fashion precisely because it is generating much of the big-class reproduction that is observed in a mobility table. We *should* care about the immobility of construction workers because micro-class immobility of this sort is a principal mechanism ensuring that the working class reproduces itself across generations. The results from our earlier analyses (see Jonsson et al. 2009) show that big-class reproduction arises largely because offspring frequently remain within their micro-class of origin.

Does this imply that policy should be redirected to rooting out such micro-class reproduction? We think not. Indeed, because there is still net big-class and gradational reproduction that is *not* occupationally generated, we are surely well advised to continue attacking those residual forms with the usual policy tools (such as equalizing access to education). Given the prominence of micro-class reproduction, we cannot pretend that such tools will ever achieve full equalization, but at this point it is likely that they purchase the most equalization at the lowest cost.

Appendix

Occupational Changes in a Generation (OCG I & II)
Peter M. Blau, Otis Dudley Duncan, David L. Featherman, Robert M. Hauser. 1962/1973. *Occupational Changes in a Generation (OCG I & II)*. Ann Arbor: University of Michigan, Inter-University Consortium for Social and Political Research. Available at: http://www.icpsr.umich.edu/icpsrweb/ICPSR/studies/06162 (accessed May 23, 2011).

General Social Survey (GSS)
Smith, Tom W, Peter Marsden, Michael Hout, and Jibum Kim. 2011. *General Social Surveys, 1972–2010* [machine-readable data file]. Principal Investigator, Tom W. Smith; Co-Principal Investigator, Peter V. Marsden; Co-Principal Investigator, Michael Hout; Sponsored by National Science Foundation. Chicago: National Opinion Research Center [producer]; Storrs, Conn.: The Roper Center for Public Opinion Research, University of Connecticut [distributor]. Available at: http://www.norc.org/GSS+Website/ (accessed May 23, 2011).

Survey of Social Stratification & Mobility (SSM)
Survey of Social Stratification and Mobility (SSM). n.d. Social Science Japan Data Archive, Center for Social Research and Data Archives, Institute of Social Science, University of Tokyo. Available at: http://ssjda.iss.u-tokyo.=ac.jp/en/ (accessed May 23, 2011).

Japan General Social Survey (JGSS)
Tanioka, Ichiro, Noriko Iwai, Michio Nitta, and Hiroki Sato. n.d. *Japanese General Social Survey (JGSS)*. Available at: http://jgss.daishodai.ac.jp/english/ (accessed May 23, 2011).

German Social Survey (ALLBUS)
GESIS—Leibniz-Institute for the Social Sciences. 2009. *ALLBUS 2008—German General Social Survey*. GESIS Data Archive, Cologne, Germany, ZA4600 Data File vers. 1.0.0., doi:10.4232/1.4600. For more information

go to: http://www.gesis.org/en/allbus/general-information/or https://
social-survey.gesis.org/index.php3 (both accessed May 23, 2011).

German Socioeconomic Panel (GSOEP)
Research Data Center of the SOEP. n.d. *German Socioeconomic Panel*
(GSOEP). Information available at: http://www.diw.de/en/diw_02.c.
221178.en/about_soep.html and http://www.diw.de/en/diw_02.c.222518.
en/research_data_center_of_the_soep.html (accessed May 23, 2011).

German Life History Study (GLHS) LV I-III
Center for Research on Inequalities and the Life Course. n.d. *German Life
History Study* (GLHS). Available at: http://www.yale.edu/ciqle/GLHS/
index.html (accessed May 23, 2011).

ZUMA-Standard Demographic Survey
GESI—Leibniz-Institute for the Social Sciences. 2010. *ZUMA Standard
Demographic Survey, 1976–1982.* Version 1.0.0, 13.04.2010, doi:10.4232/
1.1233. Available at: http://info1.gesis.org/dbksearch18/SDESC2.asp?
no=1233&search=&search2=&DB=E&tab=0&notabs=&nf=1&af=&ll=10
(accessed May 23, 2011).

International Social Justice Project (ISJP)
Wegener, Bernd, and David S. Mason (principal investigators). 1991/1996.
International Social Justice Project, 1991 and 1996. Version 1.0.0, 13.04.2010,
doi:10.4232/1.3522. Universität Heidelberg und Humboldt Universität
Berlin; Butler University, Indianapolis; International Social Justice Project.
Available at: http://www.sowi.hu-berlin.de/lehrbereiche/empisoz/fors
chung/isjp; data from 2000 available upon request (accessed May 23, 2011).

Swedish Census, 1970, 1975, 1980, 1985, and 1990
Statistics Sweden. Various years. *Swedish Census,* 1970, 1975, 1980, 1985, and
1990 (linked to 1960 & 1970 Censuses). Available at: http://www.scb.se/
Statistik/BE/BE0205/_dokument/BE0205_BS_2000.pdf (accessed May 23,
2011).

Table 5A.1   Fit Statistics for Selected Models

Model	L^2	df	Δ	BIC
1. Cross-nationally constant reproduction (figure 5.3)	137,234	24,880	11.18	−211,892
2. Cross-nationally variable reproduction (table 5.3 and figure 5.4)	136,520	24,865	11.13	−212,396
3. Linear trend in the United States (table 5.4)	20,816	25,026	20.61	−248,229
3. Linear trend in Japan (table 5.4)	8,385	19,592	26.71	−172,951
3. Linear trend in Germany (table 5.4)	11,579	17,403	29.29	−155,499
3. Linear trend in Sweden (table 5.4)	141,380	31,900	11.54	−306,328

Source: Authors' calculations based on original research. See appendix text for
data sources.

Notes

1. This line of reasoning implies that countries with high rates of income mobility may not necessarily have high rates of gradational mobility (as measured here). Although there are many reasons why such differences might emerge across types of mobility (see Erikson and Goldthorpe 2010), one important source is cross-national differences in the occupation-income correlation (and hence the extent to which desirable occupations are laden with reproduction-ensuring income).
2. The fit statistics for our model contrasts remain correct even when data are sparse.
3. We calculated the eighty-two micro-class scores by assigning them to detailed occupations within the U.S. samples and then aggregating these detailed occupations up to the micro-class level.
4. When applied to our eighty-two-category scheme, the Nakao-Treas prestige scale correlates 0.87 with the international ISEI scale (Ganzeboom, de Graaf, and Treiman 1992) and 0.79 with the scale values derived by Goodman's RC model (Goodman 1979).
5. Some class analysts treat gradational effects as part and parcel of big-class effects. In deference to such analysts, we have also fitted models without the gradational term (Jonsson et al. 2009), and in so doing the class effects, of course, increase. We separate gradational and class effects here to cast light on whether intergenerational processes take on a continuous or lumpy form.
6. In estimating this model, we have reweighted each of the national samples to ten thousand cases, as doing so ensures that our pooled estimates are not unduly affected by large-sample countries. The gradational term is also omitted from figure 5.3 because we wish to cast in the sharpest possible relief the relative sizes of the immobility terms. The fit statistics for the model of figure 5.3 are presented in appendix table 5A.1.
7. We could instead constrain the inheritance effects to be the same within each class. Although one of our reviewers suggested that we do so, we are concerned that the resulting model error would distort the other parameters of interest.
8. For example, we report a "base" meso-class estimate for the United States of 0.21, which is simply the mean of the estimates for classic professions (0.28), managers and officials (0.11), other professions (0.10), sales (0.73), clerical (−0.18), craft (0.11), lower manual (0.25), and service workers (0.29).
9. The fit statistics for the models in table 5.4 are presented in appendix table 5A.1.

References

Bell, Daniel. 1973. *The Coming of Post-Industrial Society*. New York: Basic Books.
Beller, Emily, and Michael Hout. 2006. "Intergenerational Social Mobility: The United States in Comparative Perspective." *The Future of Children* 16(2): 19–36.

Björklund, Anders, and Markus Jäntti. 1997. "Intergenerational Income Mobility in Sweden Compared to the United States." *American Economic Review* 87(5): 1009–18.

Blau, Peter M., and Otis Dudley Duncan. 1967. *The American Occupational Structure*. New York: Wiley.

Breen, Richard, ed. 2004. *Social Mobility in Europe*. Oxford: Oxford University Press.

Breen, Richard, and Jan O. Jonsson. 2005. "Inequality of Opportunity in Comparative Perspective: Recent Research on Educational Attainment and Social Mobility." *Annual Review of Sociology* 31: 223–43.

———. 2007. "Explaining Change in Social Fluidity: Educational Equalization and Educational Expansion in Twentieth-Century Sweden." *American Journal of Sociology* 112(6): 1775–810.

Duncan, Otis Dudley. 1961. "A Socioeconomic Index for All Occupations." In *Social Structure and Mobility in Economic Development*, edited by Neil J. Smelser and Seymour Martin Lipset. London: Routledge.

Ebbinghaus, Bernhard, and Jelle Visser. 2000. *Trade Unions in Western Europe Since 1945*. London: Palgrave Macmillan.

Erikson, Robert, and John H. Goldthorpe. 1992. *The Constant Flux: A Study of Class Mobility in Industrial Societies*. Oxford: Clarendon Press.

———. 2010. "Has Social Mobility in Britain Decreased? Reconciling Divergent Findings on Income and Class Mobility." *British Journal of Sociology* 61(2): 211–30.

Erikson, Robert, and Jan O. Jonsson. 1993. *Ursprung och utbildning* (Origin and education). SOU (Official Reports of the Swedish Government) 1993: 81. Stockholm: Fritzes.

Esping-Andersen, Gøsta. 1990. *The Three Worlds of Welfare Capitalism*. Cambridge: Polity Press.

Featherman, David L., and Robert M. Hauser. 1978. *Opportunity and Change*. New York: Academic Press.

Ganzeboom, Harry B. G., Ruud Luijkx, and Donald J. Treiman. 1989. "Intergenerational Class Mobility in Comparative Perspective." In *Research in Social Stratification and Mobility*, vol. 8. Greenwich, Conn.: JAI Press.

Ganzeboom, Harry B. G., Paul de Graaf, and Donald J. Treiman. 1992. "A Standard International Socio-Economic Index of Occupational Status." *Social Science Research* 21(1): 1–56.

Goldthorpe, John H. 1980. *Social Mobility and Class Structure in Modern Britain*. Oxford: Clarendon Press.

———. 2002. "Globalization and Social Class." *West European Politics* 25(3): 1–28.

Goldthorpe, John H., and Keith Hope. 1974. *The Social Grading of Occupations: A New Approach and Scale*. Oxford: Clarendon Press.

Goodman, Leo A. 1979. "Multiplicative Models for the Analysis of Occupational Mobility Tables and Other Kinds of Cross-Classification Tables." *American Journal of Sociology* 84(4): 804–19.

Grusky, David B. 2005. "Foundations of a Neo-Durkheimian Class Analysis." In *Approaches to Class Analysis*, edited by Erik Olin Wright. Cambridge: Cambridge University Press.

Harding, David J., Christopher Jencks, Leonard M. Lopoo, and Susan E. Mayer. 2005. "The Changing Effect of Family Background on the Incomes of American Adults." In *Unequal Chances: Family Background and Economic Success*, edited by Samuel Bowles, Herbert Gintis, and Melissa Osborne. New York: Russell Sage Foundation.

Hauser, Robert M., and John R. Warren. 1997. "Socioeconomic Indexes for Occupations: A Review, Update, and Critique." *Sociological Methodology* 27(1): 177–298.

Herting, Jerald R., David B. Grusky, and Stephen E. van Rompaey. 1997. "The Social Geography of Interstate Mobility and Persistence." *American Sociological Review* 62(2): 267–87.

Hodge, Robert W. 1981. "The Measurement of Occupational Status." *Social Science Research* 10: 396–415.

Hout, Michael. 1988. "More Universalism, Less Structural Mobility: The American Occupational Structure in the 1980s." *American Journal of Sociology* 93(6): 1358–400.

Ishida, Hiroshi. 1993. *Social Mobility in Contemporary Japan.* Stanford, Calif.: Stanford University Press.

———. 2010. "Does Class Matter in Japan? Demographics of Class Structure and Class Mobility from a Comparative Perspective." In *Social Class in Contemporary Japan,* edited by Hiroshi Ishida and David H. Slater. London: Routledge.

Jencks, Christopher, Lauri Perman, and Lee Rainwater. 1988. "What Is a Good Job? A New Measure of Labor Market Success." *American Journal of Sociology* 93(6): 1322–57.

Jonsson, Jan O., David B. Grusky, Matthew Di Carlo, Reinhard Pollak, and Mary C. Brinton. 2009. "Micro-Class Mobility: Social Reproduction in Four Countries." *American Journal of Sociology* 114(5): 1475–521.

Kocka, Jürgen. 1981. *Die Angestellten in der deutschen Geschichte 1850–1980: Vom Privatbeamten zum angestellten Arbeitnehmer* (White-collar employees in Germany 1850–1980: From private civil servants to salaried employees). Göttingen: Anderhoeck & Ruprecht.

Korpi, Walter. 1983. *The Democratic Class Struggle.* London: Routledge.

Müller, Walter, and Markus Gangl. 2003. *Transitions from Education to Work in Europe: The Integration of Youth into EU Labor Markets.* Oxford: Oxford University Press.

Nakane, Chie. 1970. *Japanese Society.* Berkeley: University of California Press.

Nakao, Keiko, and Judith Treas. 1992. "The 1989 Socioeconomic Index of Occupations: Construction from the 1989 Occupational Prestige Scores." General Social Survey (GSS) methodological report 74. Chicago: National Opinion Research Center (NORC).

Nicoletti, Cheti, and John F. Ermisch. 2007. "Intergenerational Earnings Mobility: Changes Across Cohorts in Britain." *B.E. Journal of Economic Analysis and Policy* 7(2, Contributions): article 9.

Pakulski, Jan. 2005. "Foundations of a Post-Class Analysis." In *Approaches to Class Analysis,* edited by Erik Olin Wright. Cambridge: Cambridge University Press.

Parkin, Frank. 1971. *Class Inequality and Political Order: Social Stratification in Capitalist and Communist Societies.* New York: Praeger.

Siegel, Paul M. 1971. "Prestige in the American Occupational Structure." Ph.D. diss., University of Chicago.

Sombart, Werner. 1906. *Warum gibt es in den Vereinigten Staaten keinen Sozialismus?* (Why is there no socialism in the United States?). Tübingen, Germany: Mohr.

Treiman, Donald J. 1970. "Industrialization and Social Stratification." In *Social Stratification: Research and Theory for the 1970s,* edited by E. O. Laumann. Indianapolis, Indiana: Bobbs Merrill.

———. 1977. *Occupational Prestige in Comparative Perspective.* New York: Academic Press.

Weeden, Kim A., and David B. Grusky. 2005. "The Case for a New Class Map." *American Journal of Sociology* 111(1): 141–212.

Wright, Erik Olin. 1997. *Class Counts.* Cambridge: Cambridge University Press.

Xie, Yie. 1992. "The Log-Multiplicative Layer Effect Model for Comparing Mobility Tables." *American Sociological Review* 57(3): 380–95.

PART II

EARLY CHILDHOOD AND PRESCHOOL EFFECTS

Chapter 6

Income-Related Gaps in School Readiness in the United States and the United Kingdom

JANE WALDFOGEL AND ELIZABETH WASHBROOK

A LARGE BODY of work has documented substantial gaps in cognitive and behavioral outcomes between low- and higher-income children at the start of school (see, for example, Duncan and Brooks-Gunn 1997; Taylor, Dearing, and McCartney 2004). There is mounting evidence from fields as diverse as neuroscience, economics, and psychology that these early skill gaps have long-term consequences for children's educational performance and their economic and social well-being in adulthood (Knudsen et al. 2006; Rouse, Brooks-Gunn, and McLanahan 2005). Particularly in today's labor market, which increasingly rewards skills and penalizes those with low levels of education, gaps in early skills and subsequent school achievement have important implications for the future well-being of individuals and society (Autor, Katz, and Kearney 2006; Belfield and Levin 2007; Danziger 2007). A further reason for concern about such income-related differentials is that they are a marker for a lack of intergenerational mobility.

In the United States, concern about inequality of educational outcomes has sparked numerous state and local school reform efforts, as well as the landmark federal Elementary and Secondary Education Act of 2001 (the "No Child Left Behind" law). Inequality in school readiness is an important contributor to inequality of later achievement, as evidence shows that half or more of gaps in educational outcomes are already present at school entry (Phillips, Crouse, and Ralph 1998). In the United Kingdom, too, there is evidence that sizable gaps are present in early childhood and widen during the school years (Feinstein 2003). Addressing inequality of educational achievement has been an important component of the U.K. government's decade-long antipoverty initiative, which has included an array of programs, including generous

175

in-work and out-of-work benefits for low-income families with children and the provision of free part-time nursery school places for all three- and four-year-olds (Brewer and Gregg 2001; Hills and Waldfogel 2004; Waldfogel 2010).

This chapter compares the magnitudes of the income-related gaps in school readiness for two contemporary cohorts of British and American children. We show that substantial income-related differences in cognitive ability and smaller gaps in behavioral outcomes are apparent in early childhood in both countries, even among cohorts born in the twenty-first century. If policy is to work to close these gaps, it is vital that we identify the reasons why low-income children fall behind and the areas in which interventions may be most fruitful. Low-income children differ from their more affluent counterparts along many dimensions: demographic characteristics like parental education, race-ethnicity, and family structure; the warmth and stimulation of their home environment; housing conditions and the local environment; health-related factors like birth weight and maternal mental and physical health; and their exposure to high-quality child care and preschool education. Each of these factors differs in both its association with family income and the extent to which it is consequential for cognitive and behavioral development. To be effective in closing gaps in outcomes, policy must target areas in which the joint effect of these associations is strong.

In this chapter, we conduct decompositions of the income-related gaps in school readiness in the two countries. Our explanatory groupings distinguish between basic demographic characteristics, which we can be reasonably confident measure common constructs across the two countries, and a richer set of policy-relevant factors, which are more likely to be subject to measurement differences across the two countries' surveys.

Using data from the two countries to carry out parallel analyses of the income-related gaps in school readiness offers two main advantages over a single-country study. First, any single birth cohort survey conflates national-specific differences in the associations between key variables with study-specific differences in the measurement of particular constructs. Measurement problems may be less acute for variables with objective scales, such as birth weight and educational qualifications, but are likely to be problematic in the construction of early cognitive and socio-emotional outcomes or parenting behaviors, for which there is no widely agreed metric. Individual studies also have strengths and weaknesses in different areas. For example, the U.S. data set has rich observational data on the quality of parenting from videotapes that are taken of parents interacting with their children; the coding of these interactions by expert raters yields information on an important dimension of early experience not captured well in the U.K. data set. Conversely, the U.K. data set contains detailed measures of financial hardship and community-level deprivation, potentially important factors not measured in the U.S. data set. Given these data differences, any findings of regularities across the two studies—of which there are many—strengthen our conclusions about the underlying constructs that are truly predictive of child development.

Second, the cross-country comparison is informative given the very different public policy environments in the United States and the United Kingdom. When seen from an international vantage point, the United States and the United Kingdom are often thought of as being very similar welfare states (see, for example, Esping-Andersen 1990). Both are Anglo-American countries whose welfare state has its origins in the English Poor Laws. However, there are some notable differences in the policies in place in the two countries, particularly when it comes to early childhood.

The United States remains one of the few advanced industrialized countries without a national policy providing a period of paid maternity leave (Waldfogel 2006). Under the Family and Medical Leave Act of 1993, qualifying employees may take up to twelve weeks of leave following a birth, but only about half of new parents are covered and eligible, the period of leave is quite short by international standards, and the leave is unpaid. The United States also differs from other advanced industrialized countries in having a system of early childhood care and education that relies very heavily on the private market (Kamerman and Waldfogel 2005). Subsidies are provided to low-income working families, but funding is insufficient to support all eligible families. The federal Head Start program provides preschool education to disadvantaged three- and four-year-olds, but again, it does not serve all eligible children. Public prekindergarten programs serve only a small share (roughly one-sixth) of the nation's four-year-olds. Thus, children's experience of preschool in the United States remains very strongly correlated with their parents' resources, with the most advantaged children the most likely to participate (Meyers et al. 2004).

In the United Kingdom, in contrast, parents of children born at the start of the twenty-first century had the right to take up to three months of unpaid parental leave, and mothers benefited from twenty-nine weeks of job-protected maternity leave, with eighteen weeks paid. (This policy has since been extended to twelve months of job-protected leave, with nine months paid.) These children came of age under the New Labour government of Tony Blair and Gordon Brown, who came into office in 1997 and implemented a host of initiatives aimed at ending child poverty (Hills and Waldfogel 2004; Waldfogel 2010). Low-income families with young children in this cohort benefited from sizable increases in means-tested benefits as well as in the universal child allowance program. Those living in the lowest-income communities would also have been able to benefit from home visiting and child care services provided by the Sure Start program to children younger than three years. And this cohort of children was entitled to free universal preschool at ages three and four, although only on a part-time basis and in a range of programs of varying quality. Another point of contrast with the United States is that all U.K. children would have been covered by the National Health Service. To the extent that the broader array of U.K. policies were effective in narrowing income-related gaps in school readiness, these policy differences might lead us to expect income-related gaps in outcomes to be smaller in the United Kingdom than in the United States *if all else were equal.* However, since the characteristics of families and the ways in which they vary across income groups may differ across countries, this assumption may not hold. In particular, if, in the absence of New Labor policies, the United Kingdom would have had larger income-related gaps in child outcomes than the United States, our comparison of contemporary cohorts might uncover relatively similar gaps—or indeed even greater gaps in the United Kingdom than in the United States.

Our data come from two nationally representative birth cohort studies of children born at the start of the twenty-first century. For the United States, we use data from the Early Childhood Longitudinal Study–Birth Cohort (ECLS-B), which gathered data on more than ten thousand children born in 2001, with interviews at roughly nine months, two years, and four years post-birth. For the United Kingdom, we use data from the Millennium Cohort Study (MCS), which collected data on more than nineteen thousand children born in 2000 and 2001, with interviews at nine months, three years, and five years post-birth. Both surveys oversampled some populations of interest, but when properly weighted, the data are nationally representative of all families with newborns in each country. The two surveys contain several cognitive test scores, maternal ratings of behavioral problems, information on family income at each wave, and data on a wealth of potential explanatory factors that we organize into basic demographic characteristics, parenting behaviors, neighborhood and material possessions, family health and well-being, and preschool care arrangements.

Data

We turn now to our data, including sample selection, income measures, and scoring methods.

Sample Selection

The ECLS-B contains data on 10,700 children.[1] We retain only families who participated in all three waves (at nine months, two years, and four years)—a sample of 8,900 children—and use this sample to define the income quintile boundaries. Missing data for the cognitive and behavioral assessments at the third wave lead to a final working sample size of 7,250. The MCS contains data on 19,474 children. Imposing the same restrictions on participation reduces the income sample to 12,874, and the working sample falls further to 8,864 because of missing data on at least one outcome measure. All estimates are weighted using the sampling weights provided, and standard errors are adjusted for clustering and complex survey design.

The two problems of survey attrition and item nonresponse on the child outcome measures raise the possibility that our working samples are not representative of all children and, more seriously, that this nonrandom selection is different across countries. The first issue of attrition is handled by the use of survey weights in all analyses (including the definition of the income quintile boundaries), which adjust for nonrandom dropout at the third wave on the basis of a rich set of characteristics observed in previous waves. Survey weights, however, cannot adjust for differentially missing outcome data among the remaining third-wave sample.[2] We find evidence that in both surveys low-income children were more likely to have missing outcome measures, conditional on having participated in the third wave of the survey. To the extent that missing outcome data are correlated with underlying child abilities within income groups, this implies that our estimates understate the true socioeconomic gaps in both countries. There is some evidence that the social grading of missing data is more pronounced in the U.K. data than in the U.S. data, but without outcome data we cannot test whether this is also true within income groups, which is what matters for cross-country comparability.

Income Measures

We use three reports of household income from each survey: one at nine months for both countries, ones at three years and five years for the United Kingdom, and ones at two years and four years for the United States.[3] We deflate these (so that they are in constant units) and also equivalize them (to adjust them for family size and composition). We then take an average of the three deflated and equivalized measures and divide the sample into quintiles on the basis of the resulting variable, using survey weights to ensure that the quintiles correspond to the relevant national distribution.

Both surveys collected banded information on total annual household income at each date, but they differed in that the U.S. survey requested gross income and the U.K. survey requested net income. To convert the discrete survey measures into comparable continuous gross income scales, we impute the median gross household income for each band using data from the Family Resources Survey (FRS) in the United Kingdom and the March Current Population Survey (CPS) in the United States.[4] We use samples of all households containing a child under age six over the relevant period, and we allow the median imputed value to depend on headship status and year and month of survey as well as the specified income band. Figures are deflated using the All Items Retail Price Index (RPI) (the United Kingdom) and the Consumer Price Index (CPI) (the United States) and equivalized using the square root of household size as a denominator. Finally, we convert the U.K. income figures into U.S. dollars using the Organization for Economic Co-operation and Development (OECD) 2005 purchasing power parity (PPP) rate of 0.636.[5] We note that our categorization of families relies only on rankings rather than absolute amounts, but there remains a risk that income position is measured with differential precision in the two surveys. We have tried to guard against this as far as possible, but the size of the income-related gaps in the country with the poorer income measure will be relatively underestimated.

Cognitive Outcome Scores

Following Leon Feinstein (2003), we combine multiple cognitive outcome measures into a single index using principal components analysis (PCA). The first principal component, by definition, accounts for as much of the variability in the data as possible and is theoretically the optimum transform for given data in least square terms. The technique allows us to reduce the dimensionality of the data and to extract the maximum possible "signal" from a number of potentially noisy measures.

The MCS cognitive outcome measure is constructed from five subscales: the Bracken School Readiness Assessment (BSRA) at age three, which measures abilities with respect to colors, letters, numbers and counting, sizes, comparisons, and shapes; the British Ability Scales Naming Vocabulary (BAS-NV) scale at both ages three and five, which measures verbal ability and spoken vocabulary; the BAS Picture Similarities (BAS-PS) scale at age five, which measures nonverbal problem-solving skills; and the BAS Pattern Construction (BAS-PC) scale at age five, which measures visual and spatial ability.

The ECLS-B cognitive outcome measure is constructed from six subscales, all assessed at the third wave (age four). Three of these—the assessments of literacy, mathematics, and receptive language abilities—were developed specifically for the study and employ scoring techniques based on item response theory (IRT). The literacy measure taps abilities such as letter recognition, letter sounds, recognition of simple words, and phonological awareness; the mathematics assessment captures number sense, geometry, counting, operations, and patterns; and the receptive language assessment, like the BAS-NV, assesses verbal ability and spoken vocabulary. The other three subscales measure expressive language, color knowledge, and fine motor copying ability.

For both the U.S. and U.K. measures, we adjust each subscale for child age at assessment by fitting the subdata to a cubic trend in age in months (conducted separately for girls and boys). PCA is then applied to the residuals, and the first extracted component is standardized to mean zero, standard deviation one, using the survey weights to approximate the underlying population distribution.

Calculation of Cronbach's alpha suggests that the reliability of the two scales is very similar across the countries ($\alpha = 0.75$ for the U.K. index and 0.79 for the U.S.). In both cases, the first principal component accounts for 49 percent of the variation in the underlying data and is the only component with an eigenvalue greater than one (the standard criteria for selecting the number of components to retain to adequately represent the data). The scoring coefficients on each of the subscales and their correlations are given in tables 6A.2 and 6A.3 of the online appendix (see note 2).

The three subscales with the highest loadings in the U.S. measure are the mathematics, literacy, and receptive vocabulary subscales, which all have scoring coefficients of around 0.5. The scales that load most strongly on the U.K. index (and with similar weights as the top three U.S. scales) are conceptually the most similar to these—the naming vocabulary scales at ages three and five and the Bracken School Readiness Assessment. The other scales, which largely measure nonverbal skills such as copying ability and problem-solving skills, have slightly lower loadings of around 0.3 to 0.4.

Behavioral Outcome Scores

Unlike the cognitive test scores, behavioral outcomes are measured by maternal responses at wave 3 to a series of statements about the child's behavior rather than by objective assessments. There are twenty-five items in the U.K. MCS instrument, which together form the five subscales of the Strengths and Difficulties Questionnaire (SDQ; Goodman 1997): conduct problems, hyperactivity and inattention, emotional symptoms, peer problems, and prosocial behaviors (reversed). The U.S. ECLS-B contains twenty-four individual items. These do not form any one recognized behavioral scale, although many of the items are taken from the Preschool and Kindergarten Behavioral Scales, second edition (PKBS-2), and are highly similar to the SDQ items. We select twenty-one of the twenty-four ECLS-B items as covering the same domains as the SDQ subscales (see table 6A.4 of the online appendix for details).

Again we use PCA to combine the individual items into a single behavioral index. The results of the behavior PCA differ in a number of ways from those of the cognitive PCA. Behavior is multidimensional in nature and can be classified by a range of typologies: the five SDQ subscales are one example; the common distinction between "externalizing" and "internalizing" behavior is another. We would not expect all the observed measures to be driven by a single latent construct, and indeed the eigenvalues from the PCA suggest that four (U.K.) or five (U.S.) independent components are needed to fully capture the variation in the data. Nevertheless, all the items in each scale are positively correlated with one another, and Cronbach's alpha is high for the two indices at 0.82 for the United Kingdom and 0.85 for the United States. Our aim in this analysis is to provide a summary measure of socio-emotional well-being that can be compared across countries and contrasted with cognitive development. We do not aim to distinguish particular psychological or clinical constructs.

The first extracted component explains 19 percent of the variation in the U.K. data and 25 percent in the U.S. data. The loadings on each of the items (shown in the online appendix) are modest but fairly equal in size. Seventeen of the twenty-one U.S. items have scoring coefficients between 0.2 and 0.3, as do twelve of the twenty-five U.K. items. Hence, in both cases the indices are weighted averages of the full range of items and do not load heavily onto a small number of specific items differentially across countries. The component extracted from the data, like the cognitive index, is standardized to mean zero, standard deviation one. Note that it is an index of behavioral *problems,* such that higher scores indicate more adverse outcomes.

Explanatory Variables

One aim of this study is to make as full use as possible of the extensive data collected in the birth cohort studies. We hence employ a very large number of variables taken from all three waves of both surveys. Table 6.1 gives a summary of all variables used in our analysis. We are able to define most basic demographic variables in a common way across surveys. Exceptions are the coding of race-ethnicity, which reflects the differential composition of the two populations, the inclusion of controls for country within the United Kingdom, and maternal education, which depends on the system of national qualifications.

We then define four groups of policy-relevant factors that capture potential mechanisms linking income and outcomes. Definitions of these variables are study-specific, but we attempt to group them into categories that broadly capture the same underlying construct. Parenting behavior covers maternal warmth and sensitivity, reading to the child, out-of-home-activities, parenting style, and miscellaneous other variables. Neighborhood and material possessions includes durables like cars and computers, savings and wealth, neighborhood conditions, and housing conditions. Family health and well-being covers the child's health at birth, maternal physical health, maternal mental well-being, and prenatal smoking and breast-feeding. And finally, child care arrangements cover maternal labor market participation and primary mode of care from birth to age four or five. Models also include indicator variables for missing data and a child gender dummy.

Table 6.1   Summary of Explanatory Variables

Variable Grouping	ECLS-B (United States)	MCS (United Kingdom)
Maternal education	Less than high school; high school graduate; some college; degree (wave 1)	Less than GCSE[b] A–C; GCSE A–C; A level; degree (wave 1)
Number of children	Number of younger/ same-age children in household (zero, one, or two or more) (wave 3) Number of older children (younger than eighteen) in household (zero, one, two, or three or more) (wave 3)	As with ECLS-B
Race/ethnicity/ country of origin	White non-Hispanic (omitted); black non-Hispanic; Hispanic; Asian; mixed; other Mother born outside the United States Other language spoken in home (wave 1)	White; black/black British; Indian; Pakistani/ Bangladeshi; mixed; other Mother born outside the United Kingdom Other language spoken in home (wave 1) Country of residence (England, Scotland, Wales, Northern Ireland) (wave 1)
Family structure	Always co-resident married biological parents; always cohabiting biological parents; always single mother (no resident father); some single mother (resident father at waves 1 or 2); other (all waves)	As with ECLS-B
Mother's age at birth	Younger than twenty; twenty to twenty-four; twenty-five to twenty-nine; thirty to thirty-four; thirty-five and older	As with ECLS-B
Parenting Warmth and sensitivity	Interviewer observations of mother-child relationship (wave 2) Ratings of maternal responsiveness and sensitivity from videotaped interactions: NCATS (wave 1); Two Bags (waves 2 and 3)[a]	Interviewer observations of mother-child relationship (wave 2)

(Table continues on p. 184.)

Table 6.1   *Continued*

Variable Grouping	ECLS-B (United States)	MCS (United Kingdom)
Reading	Frequency with which parent reads to child (waves 2 and 3)	Frequency with which mother reads to child (waves 2 and 3)
Out-of-home activities	Visited zoo or art gallery in last month (wave 2)	Number of places of interest visited in last year (wave 3)
	Visited library with child in last month (waves 2 and 3)	Frequency with which child is taken to library (waves 2 and 3)
	Number of lessons ever participated in (sports, drama, dance, music, art, performing arts, crafts) (wave 3)	Number days per week child attends sport or exercise class (wave 3)
Parenting style	Expresses affection with hugs and kisses; easygoing and relaxed with child (wave 3)	Family has lots of rules; rules strictly enforced (wave 2)
	Has trouble sticking to rules; lacks energy to make child behave (wave 3)	Proportion of times parent makes sure child obeys instruction or request (wave 3)
	Rules and routines about bedtime (waves 2 and 3)	Rules and routines about bedtime (waves 2 and 3)
	Spanked child or used time-out in last week (waves 2 and 3)	Spanks child or uses time-out at least once a month (waves 2 and 3)
Other	How far expect child to go in school—for example, less than high school diploma to complete a Ph.D. (wave 3)	Home is really disorganized; can't hear self think; has calm atmosphere (waves 2 and 3)
	Knowledge of Infant Development Inventory (wave 1)	Mother's beliefs about good parenting practices (wave 1)
Neighborhood and material possessions		
Material possessions	Computer (wave 3)	Computer (wave 1)
	Car (all waves)	Car (waves 1 and 2)
	Number of books (wave 3)	Working telephone (waves 1 and 2)
	Household food-insecure, with or without hunger (all waves)	

Table 6.1   *Continued*

Variable Grouping	ECLS-B (United States)	MCS (United Kingdom)
Savings and wealth	Has savings account (all waves) Owns any stocks (all waves)	Saves regularly (waves 2 and 3) Number of bills behind with (waves 2 and 3)
Neighborhood conditions	Public housing–rent subsidy (all waves) Neighborhood good place to raise children; safe from crime; most families lived there long time (wave 2)	Home rented from council or housing association (all waves) Satisfaction with neighborhood; problems with noise; litter; vandalism (wave 1) Interviewer assessment of local area, for example, condition of buildings, vandalism, dog mess, feeling of safety (wave 2) Index of Multiple Deprivation rank decile (wave 1)
Housing conditions	House or building a good place to raise children (wave 2)	Average persons per room (all waves) Problem with dampness (all waves) Access to garden (all waves)
Family health and well-being		
Health at birth	Birth weight Gestation less than thirty-seven weeks Special care unit at birth	As with ECLS-B
Mother's physical health	General self-rated health (all waves) Mother's BMI overweight; obese (wave 3)	Limiting ill health index (wave 3) Mother's BMI overweight; obese (wave 3)
Mother's mental well-being	CES-D[c] depression scale (waves 1 and 3)	Malaise scale (wave 1) Kessler 6 depression scale (wave 3) Locus of control (wave 1) Social support scale (wave 1)
Smoking and breastfeeding	Breast-fed (never, less than three months, three to six months, more than six months) Mother smoked during pregnancy	As with ECLS-B

(Table continues on p. 186.)

Table 6.1   *Continued*

Variable Grouping	ECLS-B (United States)	MCS (United Kingdom)
Care arrangements		
Pregnancy and first year	Mother worked in year before birth Mother worked in first three months Mother employed (not at all, less than thirty hours a week, thirty hours or more) (wave 1) Main child care arrangement (parent only, other relative, nonrelative, center) (wave 1, working mothers only)	As with ECLS-B
Two to three years	Mother employed (not at all, less than thirty hours a week, thirty hours or more) (wave 2) Main child care arrangement (parent only, other relative, nonrelative, center) (wave 2, working mothers only)	As with ECLS-B
Four to five years	Mother employed (not at all, less than thirty hours a week, thirty hours or more) (wave 3) Type of center-based care (preschool, pre–kindergarten, child care center, other center, none) (wave 3)	Mother employed (not at all, less than thirty hours a week, thirty hours or more) (wave 3) Type of center-based care (nursery class–school, day nursery, preschool, play group, none) (wave 3)

Source: Authors' compilation based on data from Early Childhood Longitudinal Study–Birth Cohort (National Center for Education Statistics 2007) and Millennium Cohort Study (University of London 2010a, 2010b, 2010c).
Note: All specifications also include a full set of indicators for missing items and a control for child gender.
[a] NCATS = Nursing Child Assessment Teaching Scale. The Two Bags task, like NCATS, is an instrument in which parent and child cue videotaped engaging in semi-structured activities, and is designed to assess the parent-child relationships. It is a modification of the Three Bags task, which was used in the Early Head Start Research and Evaluation Project and in the NICHD Study of Early Child Care.
[b] General Certificate of Secondary Education.
[c] Center for Epidemiological Studies Depression Scale.

Figure 6.1   Mean Gross Equivalized Annual Household Income by Income Quintile Group

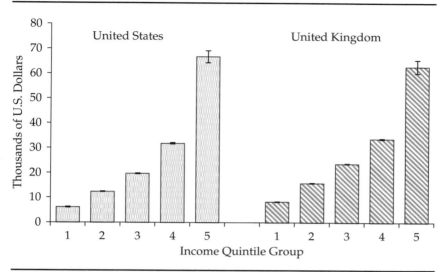

Source: Authors' calculations based on data from Early Childhood Longitudinal Study–Birth Cohort (National Center for Education Statistics 2007) and Millennium Cohort Study (University of London 2010a, 2010b, 2010c).
Notes: Incomes are in March 2005 U.S. dollars. Incomes are averaged over three survey waves. Estimates and confidence intervals are weighted to adjust for complex survey design. U.S. sample: 7,250 observations; U.K. sample: 8,864 observations. Quintile 1 is the lowest-income quintile group, quintile 2 the second lowest, and so on. The vertical lines at the end of each bar represent 95 percent confidence intervals around the estimates.

Income and School Readiness in the United States and the United Kingdom

Average incomes of this cohort of parents are slightly lower in the United States ($28,300) than in the United Kingdom ($30,600), although this in part reflects the younger age of parents in the United States. On average, U.S. mothers were 27.3 years of age at the birth of the cohort child, compared with 29.7 for U.K. mothers.[6] Figure 6.1 provides a graphic illustration of representative income levels in each income quintile group (see table 6.A5 of the online appendix for exact figures). The distributions of gross household income among families with children under age six are similar in the United States and the United Kingdom, but with some notable differences. The average income of the poorest quintile is higher in the United Kingdom—by 35 percent—than in the United States, and this difference persists, although less sharply, right up to the fourth income

Figure 6.2   Mean Cognitive Ability Standardized Score by Income Quintile Group

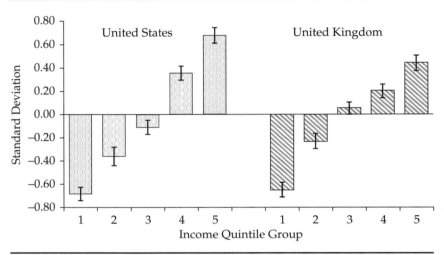

Source: Authors' calculations based on data from Early Childhood Longitudinal Study–Birth Cohort (National Center for Education Statistics 2007) and Millennium Cohort Study (University of London 2010a, 2010b, 2010c).

Notes: Composite score is constructed by principal components analysis (PCA) and standarized to mean zero, one standard deviation. Estimates and confidence intervals are weighted to adjust for complex survey design. U.S. sample: 7,250 observations; U.K. sample: 8,864 observations. The vertical lines at the end of each bar represent 95 percent confidence intervals around the estimates.

quintile. It is only for the richest income quintile that the confidence intervals around the mean overlap for the two countries. Figure 6.1 illustrates the dramatic degree of income inequality in the United States, where the incomes of the richest quintile are, on average, over ten times those of the poorest quintile and over three times those of the median quintile; in the United Kingdom, the comparable multipliers are around seven and a half and two and a half.

The mean cognitive standardized scores for each quintile group are shown in figure 6.2 (and online appendix table 6A.6). Again, there are similarities and differences across the two countries. The gap in average test scores between the poorest and richest quintiles is over a standard deviation in both countries: 1.36 in the United States and 1.09 in the United Kingdom. In contrast to the pattern for income, the gaps in cognitive development increase linearly, rather than exponentially, from quintile to quintile. Children in the lowest income quintile score around two-thirds

Figure 6.3   Mean Behavior Problems Standardized Score by Income Quintile Group

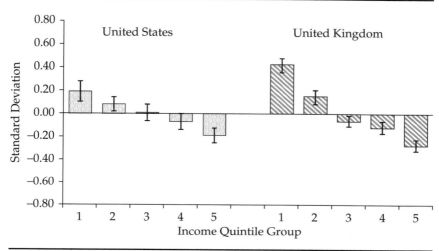

Source: Authors' calculations based on data from Early Childhood Longitudinal Study–Birth Cohort (National Center for Education Statistics 2007) and Millennium Cohort Study (University of London 2010a, 2010b, 2010c).
Notes: Higher scores indicate greater behavioral problems. Composite score is constructed by PCA and standarized to mean zero, one standard deviation. Estimates and confidence intervals are weighted to adjust for complex survey design. U.S. sample: 7,250 observations; U.K. sample: 8,864 observations. The vertical lines at the end of each bar represent 95 percent confidence intervals around the estimates.

of a standard deviation below the mean in both the United States and the United Kingdom, and the confidence intervals provide no evidence of systematic differences in the relative performance of the lowest-income children in the two countries.

The relative cognitive outcomes of children in the second-lowest and middle-income quintiles appear relatively better in the United Kingdom than the United States, while the reverse is true for the outcomes of children in the second-highest- and highest-income quintiles. The aim of our analysis is not to compare standardized scores directly across countries, but rather to focus on the gaps for different groups relative to the country-specific mean outcome of the middle-income quintile group. It is therefore notable that the average outcomes of this reference group are relatively negative in the United States compared with the United Kingdom.

The mean behavior problems standardized scores for each income quintile group are shown in figure 6.3 (and online appendix table 6A.7). The patterns are reversed because higher scores on this measure indicate more adverse outcomes. It is immediately noticeable that the income gradients in behavioral development are smaller than the gradients in cognitive outcomes. The standard deviation gap between the highest and lowest income groups is –0.38 in the United States and –0.69 in the United Kingdom. Greater income-related inequality in behavior in the United Kingdom largely reflects the particularly high scores of the lowest-income quintile group. In contrast to the pattern for cognitive outcomes, there is no evidence of greater inequality at the top of the income distribution in the United States than in the United Kingdom. The middle-income quintile group again appears slightly negatively selected in the United States and positively selected in the United Kingdom, but these differences are marginal, and they are smaller than those associated with cognitive development.

Explaining the Income-Related Gaps in School Readiness

As noted earlier, we use the median-income quintile (Q3) as the omitted reference category when analyzing income-related gaps in school readiness. Formally, we estimate ordinary least squares models (weighted for sampling design) of the baseline model:

$$C_i = \sum_{q=1,2,4,5} \gamma_q (1 | INC\_Q_i = q) + \mu_i \tag{6.1}$$

C_i is the ith child's standardized outcome score, $(1 | INC\_Q_i = q)$ is an indicator variable equal to one if family income is in the qth quintile, and μ_i is an orthogonal error term. Without controls, the γ coefficients in equation 6.1 are simply the gap in mean outcome scores between children in the qth quintile and those in the omitted middle-income quintile.

When controls are added to equation 6.1, the γ coefficients are the income-related outcome gaps holding constant the included covariates—what can be thought of as "within-group" income differences. The essence of our approach is to try to "explain" the raw γ coefficients by the inclusion of various sets of controls. If we can drive them to zero, then the income-related outcome gaps can be fully accounted for by differences in observed factors.

Figure 6.4 focuses on the cognitive outcome gaps (see also online appendix table 6A.8). The unconditional results in the top panel show that income-related gaps are significantly different from zero in all cases—for both countries and for all quintile groups. In our multivariate analysis in the following section, we focus on the gap between quintiles 1 and 3— the middle-income reference group—a gap we refer to as the "low-income penalty," and the gap between quintiles 3 and 5, which we refer to as the "high-income advantage."

Figure 6.4   Cognitive Outcome Gaps: Alternative Specifications

No Controls

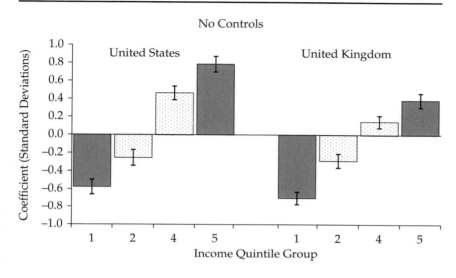

Common Demographic Controls Added

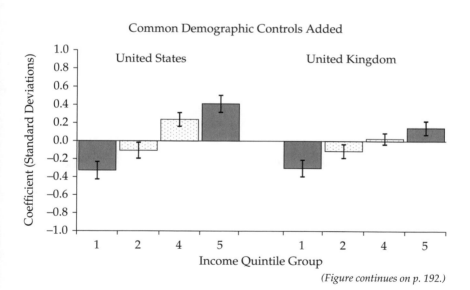

(Figure continues on p. 192.)

Figure 6.4   *Continued*

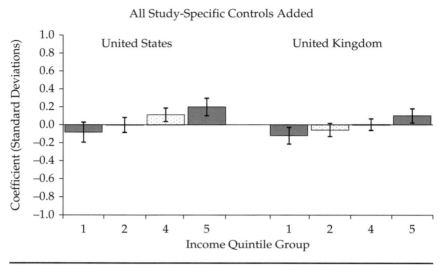

All Study-Specific Controls Added

Source: Authors' calculations based on data from Early Childhood Longitudinal Study–Birth Cohort (National Center for Education Statistics 2007) and Millennium Cohort Study (University of London 2010a, 2010b, 2010c).
Notes: Graphs show coefficients on income quintile group dummies, relative to the omitted middle-income quintile group (quintile 3). Shaded bars highlight the "low-income penalty" and the "high-income advantage" (the coefficients on the lowest and highest quintile groups, respectively) that are the focus of the subsequent more detailed analyses. The vertical lines at the end of each bar represent 95 percent confidence intervals around the estimates.

The middle panel shows that conditioning on a common set of basic demographic characteristics—broadly, maternal education; race, ethnicity, and country of origin; and household composition—reduces the income-related gaps substantially, by about half in the United States and more in the United Kingdom. This makes clear that low-income families are much more likely than their middle- and higher-income peers to have attributes that are independently associated with lower cognitive scores, and this is even more true in the United Kingdom than in the United States. Nevertheless, all the income-related differences remain significantly different from zero, with the exception of the fourth income quintile in the United States.

The bottom panel of figure 6.4 shows the result of conditioning on the full array of explanatory variables in both data sets. The measures included in this stage are not fully comparable across countries, but it is clear that both sets of measures have power in explaining the income-related cognitive gaps, even after controlling for demographic characteristics. The extent to which the gaps are explained differs across countries. The lower scores of U.S. children in the lowest two income groups are fully accounted for by the observed measures, but there remains a small unexplained advantage in the higher-income groups. For the United Kingdom, the gaps for the income groups immediately above and below the median are no longer significant, but both the low-income penalty and the high-income advantage remain significant (if small).

Figure 6.5 shows the same statistics for behavioral outcomes. The patterns here are very different. For the United States, only the lowest- and highest-income quintile gaps are significantly different from zero, and even these differences become insignificant when we condition on a basic set of demographic characteristics (middle panel). For the United Kingdom, the "near-poor" second income quintile also exhibits significantly more behavior problems than the median quintile, and all the gaps remain significant—although reduced by half or more—when we adjust for demographic composition. The addition of full sets of study-specific controls in the bottom panel not only eliminates any remaining income-related differences but flips the sign of the income coefficients. This implies that low-income children exhibit marginally *fewer* behavior problems than their more affluent counterparts with equivalent characteristics. The wide confidence intervals around these estimates, however, indicate that we should interpret these remaining income-related differences as essentially zero.

The Role of Specific Policy-Relevant Factors

The results in figures 6.4 and 6.5 show that, in total, we observe sufficient data on the study children to explain virtually all of the income-related gaps in developmental outcomes. They do not tell us, however, which factors are relatively more important in accounting for the gaps. This issue is crucial for thinking about where policy interventions may be most effective.

To explore this we employ a two-step method that allows us to divide up the reduction in the income coefficient into the contribution of particular factors. In the first step, we add all the control variables to the baseline model 1.

$$C_i = \sum_{q=1,2,4,5} \gamma_q(1|INC\_Q_i = q) + \sum_j X_{ij}\beta_j + \mu_i \tag{6.2}$$

X_{ij} is the value of the jth covariate for child i, and β_j is the predicted difference in the outcome associated with that characteristic, holding all else constant.

Figure 6.5   Behavioral Outcome Gaps: Alternative Specifications

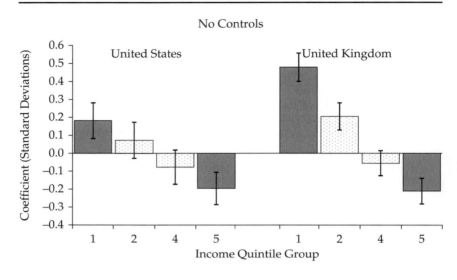

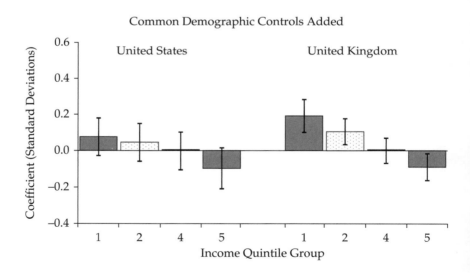

Figure 6.5   *Continued*

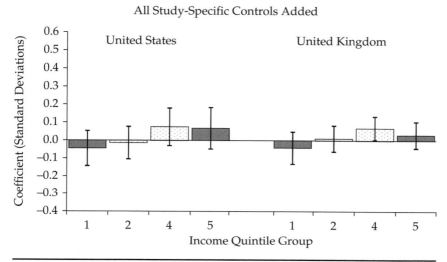

Source: Authors' calculations based on data from Early Childhood Longitudinal Study–Birth Cohort (National Center for Education Statistics 2007) and Millennium Cohort Study (University of London 2010a, 2010b, 2010c).
Notes: Graphs show coefficients on income quintile group dummies, relative to the omitted middle-income quintile group (quintile 3). Shaded bars highlight the "low-income penalty" and the "high-income advantage" (the coefficients on the lowest and highest quintile groups, respectively) that are the focus of the subsequent more detailed analyses. The vertical lines at the end of each bar represent 95 percent confidence intervals around the estimates.

In the second step, each covariate is regressed individually on the set of income quintile dummies:

$$X_{ij} = \sum_{q=1,2,4,5} \lambda_{qj}(1|INC\_Q_i = q) + v_{ij} \qquad (6.3)$$

The coefficient λ_{qj} gives the income-related gap in the value of the jth covariate between children in quintile q and those in the omitted quintile 3. Substituting equation 6.3 into equation 6.2 gives:

$$C_i = \sum_{q=1,2,4,5} \left\{ \left(\sum_j \lambda_{qj}\beta_j \right) + \gamma_q \right\}(1|INC\_Q_i = q) + \left\{ \left(\sum_j \beta_j v_{ij} \right) + \mu_i \right\} \qquad (6.4)$$

Equation 6.4 is simply a regression of C_i on the income quintile dummies and hence is equivalent to equation 6.1. The first term in curly brackets shows that the raw income coefficient on quintile q can be broken down into a sum of terms. The term $\lambda_{qj}\beta_j$ reflects both the degree of income grading in X_{ij} (λ_{qj}) and the extent to which X_{ij} "matters" for the outcome in question (β_j). A factor makes a contribution to the income-related gap only if *both* of these are not zero. The residual unexplained component (γ_q) is the remaining income coefficient in equation 6.2 and the one graphed in figures 6.6 through 6.9.

Figure 6.6 shows the results of one breakdown for the cognitive outcome gaps—the model conditioning on basic demographic characteristics shown in the middle panel of figure 6.4. The common definition of these covariates across the two studies allows us to make direct comparisons between the United States and the United Kingdom. There are certain similarities across countries; for example, the lack of educational qualifications among low-income mothers is the biggest single demographic factor accounting for the income-related gaps in cognitive development in both countries. Greater rates of single parenthood and larger family sizes among low-income families make modest contributions to the gradients. The fact that low-income children are more likely to be from immigrant families or from racial or ethnic minority groups also explains a small fraction of their cognitive gaps in both countries. However, this factor contributes to the high-income advantage only in the United States. In the United Kingdom, families in the top income quintile are more likely than those in the median income quintile to use another language in the home at nine months, a factor associated with small reductions in cognitive scores.

The most noticeable difference between the two countries in figure 6.6 is the penalty to early motherhood in the United Kingdom. Results of the first step (available on request) show that, compared to children of mothers age twenty-five to twenty-nine at the time of the birth, children of teen mothers in the United Kingdom score 0.35 of a standard deviation lower on the cognitive measure, conditional on the other controls, and children of those age twenty to twenty-four score 0.20 of a standard deviation lower. The equivalent cognitive penalties in the United States are minute and not significantly different from zero.

This difference may reflect greater negative selection into early motherhood in the United Kingdom. Some evidence in favor of this explanation is provided by the fact that early motherhood is much more common in the United States overall. In the U.S. sample, 11 percent of births were to teen mothers, and a further 25 percent were births to women age twenty to twenty-four. In the United Kingdom, the equivalent figures are just 5 percent and 12 percent, respectively.[7]

Figure 6.7 shows the results for specifications that add controls for a number of policy-relevant mechanisms. Comparison with figure 6.6

Figure 6.6   Breakdown of Cognitive Outcome Gaps, Conditional on Basic Demographic Characteristics Only

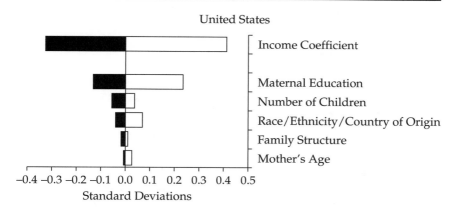

United States

Income Coefficient

Maternal Education

Number of Children

Race/Ethnicity/Country of Origin

Family Structure

Mother's Age

−0.4 −0.3 −0.2 −0.1 0.0 0.1 0.2 0.3 0.4 0.5
Standard Deviations

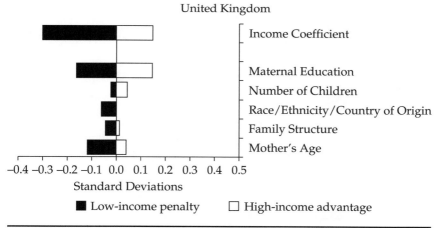

United Kingdom

Income Coefficient

Maternal Education

Number of Children

Race/Ethnicity/Country of Origin

Family Structure

Mother's Age

−0.4 −0.3 −0.2 −0.1 0.0 0.1 0.2 0.3 0.4 0.5
Standard Deviations

■ Low-income penalty   □ High-income advantage

Source: Authors' calculations based on data from Early Childhood Longitudinal Study–Birth Cohort (National Center for Education Statistics 2007) and Millennium Cohort Study (University of London 2010a, 2010b, 2010c).
Notes: "Low-income penalty" refers to the gap in outcomes between quintile 1 (the lowest-income quintile group) and quintile 3 (the middle-income reference group). "High-income advantage" refers to the gap in outcomes between quintile 5 (the highest-income group) and quintile 3.

gives an indication of the extent to which these mechanisms displace the effect of income group and other demographic characteristics. In general, these policy-relevant factors are most strongly associated with the unexplained within-group influence of income, which drops substantially. The role of maternal education is also noticeably reduced in both countries.

Figure 6.7 Breakdown of Cognitive Outcome Gaps, Conditional on All Study-Specific Controls

United States

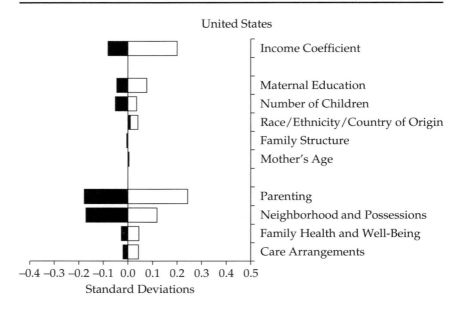

Income Coefficient

Maternal Education
Number of Children
Race/Ethnicity/Country of Origin
Family Structure
Mother's Age

Parenting
Neighborhood and Possessions
Family Health and Well-Being
Care Arrangements

−0.4 −0.3 −0.2 −0.1 0.0 0.1 0.2 0.3 0.4 0.5
Standard Deviations

United Kingdom

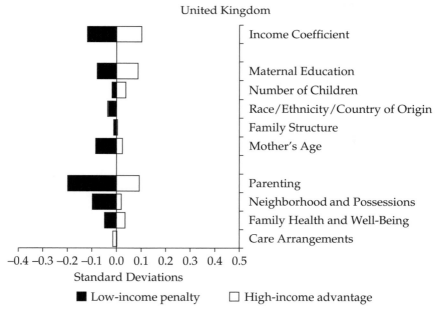

Income Coefficient

Maternal Education
Number of Children
Race/Ethnicity/Country of Origin
Family Structure
Mother's Age

Parenting
Neighborhood and Possessions
Family Health and Well-Being
Care Arrangements

−0.4 −0.3 −0.2 −0.1 0.0 0.1 0.2 0.3 0.4 0.5
Standard Deviations

■ Low-income penalty   □ High-income advantage

Source: Authors' calculations based on data from Early Childhood Longitudinal Study–Birth Cohort (National Center for Education Statistics 2007) and Millennium Cohort Study (University of London 2010a, 2010b, 2010c).

Measurement differences across the two surveys prevent us from making direct comparisons about the relative importance of, for example, income-related differences in parenting in the United States and the United Kingdom. Rather, the results provide two different pieces of evidence about which factors may be important in explaining the gaps.

In both countries, differential parenting behaviors between low- and higher-income parents account for a large fraction of the cognitive gaps. Tables 6A.10 and 6A.11 in the online appendix provide a little more detail on the factors driving these results (online appendix available at http://www.russellsage.org/smeeding_jantti_erikson_online_appendix.pdf). In the U.S. survey, direct videotaped observations of the warmth and sensitivity of mother-child interactions are particularly important, as are the frequency with which the child is read to and engagement in out-of-home activities like clubs and classes. In the United Kingdom, the same types of parenting behavior emerge as important, although in differing proportions, which may be due to measurement differences.

The factors that we group together under neighborhood and material possessions are also conditionally associated with the observed cognitive gaps. Possessions (such as a computer, books, a car, a phone, and food security) make the single largest contribution in this group in both surveys. Poor neighborhood conditions (such as local deprivation indicators and maternal ratings of neighborhood safety) also make small contributions in both studies. Indicators of savings and wealth are important in the U.S. survey, but not in the U.K one, while measures of poor housing conditions have some predictive power in the U.K. survey but not the U.S. one.

Income-related differences in family health and well-being appear to play a secondary role in generating cognitive outcome gaps. In particular, maternal mental well-being (captured, for example, by self-completed depression scales) is strongly correlated with income in both countries, but has virtually no predictive power for children's cognitive outcomes. Where there are differences that matter, they relate more to differences in the child's birth weight and the mother's physical health.

Finally, we find only a very small role for differential child care arrangements between low- and higher-income families in explaining cognitive outcome differences. We include in this section maternal employment status—as a proxy for nonmaternal care arrangements in general—as well as type of care used at each survey wave. The only factor with any predictive power is the greater attendance at preschools and prekindergartens of higher-income U.S. children, which is associated with modest boosts to cognitive scores. Several caveats are important here. First, we do not capture dimensions of child care quality or consistency of arrangements, both of which are likely to differ with income and may matter for cognitive development. Second, the relationship between income and care arrangement is likely to be complicated: for example, stay-at-home mothers are drawn from both the very disadvantaged and the very advantaged, and some low-income children may be eligible for government programs such as Head Start and child care subsidies. And third, even if differential care experiences are not the driver of early cognitive inequalities among current cohorts of children, they may nevertheless be an important policy mechanism that could be used to compensate for the large income-related differences in parenting and the home environment, given what prior research has shown about the greater benefits of good-quality child care for disadvantaged children (see, for example, Magnuson and Waldfogel 2005).

Switching the focus to behavioral outcomes, figure 6.8 shows the results of conditioning on basic demographic factors alone. Again, outcome differences between children of mothers with different levels of educational attainment are a key driver of the income-related gaps. Differences associated with family structure are noticeably more important drivers of the gaps in behavioral outcomes than they are for cognitive outcomes, particularly in the United Kingdom. Online appendix tables 6A.12 and 6A.13 show that the greater prevalence of single-mother households (those with no resident father figure in one or two waves and those with no resident father in all three waves) among low-income households has implications for the inequalities in behavioral development in both countries.

Behavioral differences associated with maternal age and race, ethnicity, or country of origin, however, operate in different directions in the two countries. In the United Kingdom, early motherhood and non-native, non-white status are associated with both low income and greater behavioral problems. These same factors, while also associated with low income in the United States, are there associated with *fewer* behavioral problems, conditional on other demographic characteristics. Since behavioral problems are reported by mothers, it is possible that these differences reflect not just "real" differences in children's behavior but also systematic differences in reporting by different groups. If these differences in behavioral problems do reflect reporting differences, that might help explain why income-related gaps in behavior are smaller in the United States than in the United Kingdom.

Figure 6.9 shows the results of adding all the controls to the behavior models. The switch in sign on the residual income coefficient implies that, if anything, adverse parenting behaviors and family well-being measures are more strongly associated with behavior problems in higher- than in lower-income households. Note that the sign of the maternal education contribution changes from negative to positive in the U.S. case, indicating marginally greater behavioral problems among the children of the highly educated, when all else is held equal. Again, this may be suggestive of differences in how more- and less-educated mothers view and report on their children's behavior.

Figure 6.8   Breakdown of Behavioral Outcome Gaps, Conditional on Basic Demographic Characteristics Only

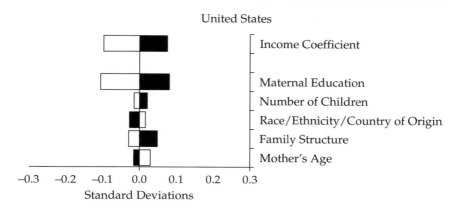

United States

Income Coefficient

Maternal Education
Number of Children
Race/Ethnicity/Country of Origin
Family Structure
Mother's Age

−0.3   −0.2   −0.1   0.0   0.1   0.2   0.3
Standard Deviations

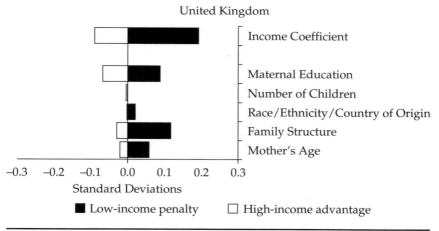

United Kingdom

Income Coefficient

Maternal Education
Number of Children
Race/Ethnicity/Country of Origin
Family Structure
Mother's Age

−0.3   −0.2   −0.1   0.0   0.1   0.2   0.3
Standard Deviations

■ Low-income penalty   □ High-income advantage

Source: Authors' calculations based on data from Early Childhood Longitudinal Study–Birth Cohort (National Center for Education Statistics 2007) and Millennium Cohort Study (University of London 2010a, 2010b, 2010c).

Differential parenting behaviors between low- and higher-income families are clearly key predictors of the behavioral, as well as the cognitive, outcome gaps in both countries. Parenting style emerges as a particularly important dimension here. Harsh discipline, a noisy and chaotic home environment, and inconsistent enforcement of rules are all more common in low-income families and are associated strongly with more behavioral problems, although the possibility of reverse causation must be recognized here (if children with more difficult behavior evoke harsher parenting on the part of their caregivers).

Figure 6.9

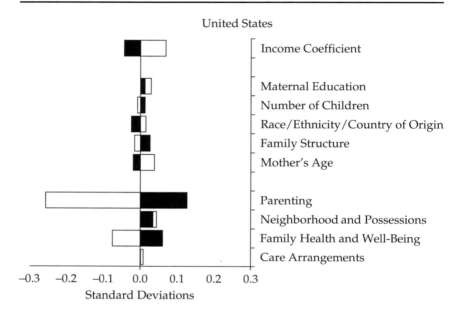

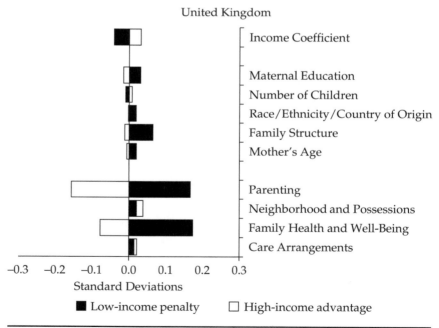

Source: Authors' calculations based on data from Early Childhood Longitudinal Study–Birth Cohort (National Center for Education Statistics 2007) and Millennium Cohort Study (University of London 2010a, 2010b, 2010c).

In contrast to our findings for the cognitive outcome gaps, family health and well-being are more strongly associated with income-related differences in behavior problems than are differences in neighborhood and material possessions. Mother's mental well-being is in particular a substantial predictor, whereas it plays virtually no role at all in explaining the cognitive gaps. (Although, again, we may be concerned that this reflects differential reporting of children's behavior or reverse causation.) Differences in material possessions and savings and wealth, however, have little association with behavior problems, and in some cases (for example, savings and wealth in the United States) the correlation is between the characteristics of the more affluent and adverse behavioral outcomes.

Conclusions

Our analyses of contemporary birth cohort data confirm that income-related gaps in school readiness—of concern because of what they presage in terms of future inequality as well as intergenerational immobility—exist in both the United States and the United Kingdom. In addition, our analyses shed some light on the policy-relevant mechanisms that underlie these disparities.

Although some of our findings mostly confirm what we have known for some time about the sources of income-related differences in school readiness between low- and higher-income children, others are more novel. Thus, the fact that we find a substantial role for differences in maternal education as well as some differences related to family size and composition is not surprising. However, it is striking how large a role differences in parenting behavior play, even after controlling for a rich set of demographic characteristics and other policy-relevant mechanisms. The finding that parenting is important confirms results from an earlier study that focused mainly on the U.S. data (Waldfogel and Washbrook 2008), as well as analyses of the U.K. data (see, for example, Ermisch 2008), but given that the present study included more extensive controls than prior analyses, this result is particularly striking. Moreover, the consistency of this finding across two such disparate policy contexts is also striking, increasing our confidence that these parenting measures are tapping into something that may be important for child development across contexts. Why do we find larger effects of parenting than some prior studies? In part, our findings probably reflect the richness of the measures available in our data sets. It is also important to note that we are focusing on preschool-age children, for whom parenting is likely to be a particularly important influence.

Our results have some implications for policy. As discussed earlier, to be policy-relevant a factor (such as parenting behavior) must meet two criteria: it must differ between low- and higher-income families, and it must influence child development. But before drawing policy conclusions, we must take one further criterion into account—we must have evidence that effective and feasible programs exist to address that factor, whether by closing gaps between low- and higher-income families or by mitigating the effect of that factor on child development. Thus, in the parenting area, our results point clearly to the potentially important role that programs to improve parenting in low-income families could play, but policymakers must also consider whether such programs exist and are feasible to implement. Many scholars have noted that the evidence on parenting programs has been mixed at best: many programs show little or no evidence of effectiveness in improving child outcomes. However, a few programs have been shown in rigorous studies to improve parenting in low-income families *and* to improve associated child outcomes. One such program, the Nurse-Family Partnership, is now being expanded to more sites in the United States and is also being piloted in the United Kingdom. (Other promising parenting programs are discussed in Waldfogel and Washbrook 2008.)

Our results may also have some implications for child care policy. We found little evidence in the U.K. data that differential attendance in child care programs was affecting gaps in school readiness, but this is perhaps to be expected given that all children in this cohort had access to part-time free nursery provision. However, that provision is not of very high quality, and current policy reforms are focused on attempting to raise the quality through measures such as raising staff qualifications. There is also interest in the United Kingdom in expanding access to preschool for disadvantaged children by offering them free slots at age two and/or longer hours at ages three and four. Prior research on the beneficial effects of high-quality child care programs for disadvantaged children suggests that such measures could help close gaps, particularly in the cognitive domain. In the U.S. context, promising initiatives include recent expansions in Early Head Start and Head Start, as well as plans to increase federal funding for state prekindergarten programs.

Despite some differences in results across countries, the overall impression is one of similarity. It is striking how much the development of low-income children lags behind their more affluent peers, as is the similarity between the United States and the United Kingdom in this respect. A natural question arises: can similar disparities and patterns be found in other advanced industrialized countries? In ongoing research, we are extending these analyses to two other Anglo-American countries—Canada and Australia (see Bradbury, Corak, Waldfogel, and Washbrook, forthcoming).

Another useful focus for further research would be to analyze these income-related gaps as children age. We can do so with the U.K. data, but regrettably, the U.S. data (the ECLS-B) do not follow children beyond school entry. Nevertheless, even without following these children further into school, these analyses point to large income-related gaps that we know from other research are likely to be associated with later gaps in life outcomes. As such, they provide serious grounds for concern about the social consequences of income inequality as well as about the extent of intergenerational mobility (or immobility) in these two countries.

Prepared for the conference "Intergenerational Mobility (IGM) Within and Across Nations: The Promise of Cross-National Research to Explain and Isolate the Factors That Enhance or Impede Mobility," held at the University of Wisconsin–Madison, September 20 through 22, 2009. The authors are grateful to the Russell Sage Foundation, the European Commission, FP 6, and the Pew Charitable Trusts for supporting the conference, and to the Sutton Trust, the Leverhulme Trust, the Economic and Social Research Council, and the National Institute of Child Health and Human Development (NICHD) for additional research support.

Notes

1. All unweighted frequencies from the ECLS-B data are reported rounded to the nearest 50, in accordance with National Center for Education Statistics (NCES) rounding rules.
2. This issue is explored in more detail in section 1 of the online appendix (available at http://www.russellsage.org/smeeding_jantti_erikson_online_appendix.pdf).
3. The three household income measures were completed between 2001 and 2006 in both the U.S. and U.K. surveys.
4. The fact that the U.K. respondents reported net income implies that the imputation of gross income for this sample may lead to greater measurement error, and therefore greater attenuation bias, than in the U.S. estimates. Set against this possibility, however, is the fact that U.K. income was reported as one of thirty-eight bands (nineteen each for single and couple households), while U.S. income was reported as one of only thirteen bands and so is measured less precisely in this regard. Because we use income quintiles in the main analysis, families are distinguished only by their rankings in terms of gross income and results do not rely on estimates of the actual dollar amounts.
5. With regard to missing data, we use the imputed income measures provided in the ECLS-B data to include households with missing income data in the calculation of the quintile boundaries. The MCS does not provide imputed income data, so we predict missing values using income in other waves, household composition, and parental education, occupation, and employment status.
6. If we fit a quadratic in maternal age to the income data and calculate the expected income of a mother age thirty at the birth of the cohort child, the U.S. figure is slightly higher ($30,400) than the U.K. figure ($30,000).

7. Early motherhood is also much less strongly socially graded in the United States. Twenty-one percent of British mothers in the lowest income quintile were younger than twenty at the time of the birth, and a further 28 percent were between ages twenty and twenty-four. Equivalent figures for the United States are not wildly different, at 24 percent and 36 percent, respectively. However, early motherhood is much rarer among middle-income-quintile families in the United Kingdom. While 14 percent and 30 percent of middle-income U.S. mothers gave birth under age twenty and between ages twenty and twenty-four, respectively, in the United Kingdom only 2 percent and 11 percent of middle-income mothers did so.

References

Autor, David, Lawrence Katz, and Melissa Kearney. 2006. "The Polarization of the U.S. Labor Market." *American Economic Review Papers and Proceedings* 96(2): 189–94.

Belfield, Clive R., and Henry M. Levin. 2007. *The Price We Pay: Economic And Social Consequences Of Inadequate Education.* Washington, D.C.: Brookings Institution Press.

Bradbury, Bruce, Miles Corak, Jane Waldfogel, and Elizabeth Washbrook. In Press. "Inequality During The Early Years: Child Outcomes And Readiness To Learn In Australia, Canada, United Kingdom, and United States." In *Inequality from Childhood to Adulthood: A Cross-National Perspective on the Transmission of Advantage,* edited by John Ermisch, Markus Jantti, and Tim Smeeding. New York: Russell Sage Foundation.

Brewer, Mike, and Paul Gregg. 2001. "Eradicating Child Poverty in Britain: Welfare Reform and Children Since 1997." Working paper WP01/08. London: Institute of Fiscal Studies.

Danziger, Sheldon. 2007. "Fighting Poverty Revisited: What Did Researchers Know Forty Years Ago? What Do We Know Today?" *Focus* 25(1): 3–11.

Duncan, Greg, and Jeanne Brooks-Gunn, eds. 1997. *Consequences of Growing Up Poor.* New York: Russell Sage Foundation.

Ermisch, John. 2008. "Origins of Social Immobility and Inequality: Parenting and Early Child Development." *National Institute Economic Review* 205(1): 62–71.

Esping-Andersen, Gøsta. 1990. *Three Worlds of Welfare Capitalism.* Princeton, N.J.: Princeton University Press.

Feinstein, Leon. 2003. "Inequality in the Early Cognitive Development of British Children in the 1970 Cohort." *Economica* 70(277): 73–97.

Goodman, Robert. 1997. "The Strengths and Difficulties Questionnaire: A Research Note." *Journal of Child Psychology and Psychiatry* 38(5): 581–86.

Hills, John, and Jane Waldfogel. 2004. "A 'Third Way' in Welfare Reform: What Are the Lessons for the United States?" *Journal of Policy Analysis and Management* 23(4): 765–88.

Kamerman, Sheila, and Jane Waldfogel. 2005. "Market and Non-Market Institutions in Early Childhood Education and Care." In *Market and Non-Market Institutions,* edited by Richard Nelson. New York: Russell Sage Foundation.

Knudsen, Eric, James Heckman, Judy Cameron, and Jack Shonkoff. 2006. "Economic, Neurobiological, and Behavioral Perspectives on Building America's Future Workforce." *Proceedings of the National Academy of Sciences* 103(27): 10155–62.

Magnuson, Katherine, and Jane Waldfogel. 2005. "Child Care, Early Education, and Racial/Ethnic Test Score Gaps at the Beginning of School." *The Future of Children* 15(1): 169–96.

Meyers, Marcia, Dan Rosenbaum, Christopher Ruhm, and Jane Waldfogel. 2004. "Inequality in Early Childhood Education and Care: What Do We Know?" In *Social Inequality,* edited by Kathryn Neckerman. New York: Russell Sage Foundation.

National Center for Education Statistics. 2007. *Early Childhood Longitudinal Study, Birth Cohort* (ECLS-B) [9-Month—Preschool Restricted-Use Data File and Electronic Codebook (CD-ROM)]. NCES 2008-034. Washington, D.C.: NCES.

Phillips, Meredith, James Crouse, and John Ralph. 1998. "Does the Black-White Test Score Gap Widen After Children Enter School?" In *The Black-White Test Score Gap,* edited by Christopher Jencks and Meredith Phillips. Washington, D.C.: Brookings Institution Press.

Rouse, Cecilia, Jeanne Brooks-Gunn, and Sara McLanahan. 2005. "School Readiness, Closing Racial and Ethnic Gaps: Introducing the Issue." *The Future of Children* 15(1): 5–14.

Taylor, Beck, Eric Dearing, and Kathleen McCartney. 2004. "Incomes and Outcomes in Early Childhood." *Journal of Human Resources* 39(4): 980–1007.

University of London. Institute of Education. Centre for Longitudinal Studies. 2010a. *Millennium Cohort Study: First Survey, 2001–2003* [computer file]. 9th Edition. Colchester, Essex: UK Data Archive [distributor], April 2010. SN: 4683.

———. 2010b. *Millennium Cohort Study: Second Survey, 2003–2005* [computer file]. 6th Edition. Colchester, Essex: UK Data Archive [distributor], April 2010. SN: 5350.

———. 2010c. *Millennium Cohort Study: Third Survey, 2006* [computer file]. 4th Edition. Colchester, Essex: UK Data Archive [distributor], April 2010. SN: 5795.

Waldfogel, Jane. 2006. "Early Childhood Policy: A Comparative Perspective." In *The Handbook of Early Childhood Development,* edited by Kathleen McCartney and Deborah Phillips. London: Blackwell.

———. 2010. *Britain's War on Poverty.* New York: Russell Sage Foundation.

Waldfogel, Jane, and Elizabeth Washbrook. Forthcoming. "Early Years Policy." *Child Development Research.*

Chapter 7

Economic Deprivation in Early Childhood and Adult Attainment: Comparative Evidence from Norwegian Registry Data and the U.S. Panel Study of Income Dynamics

GREG J. DUNCAN, KJETIL TELLE,
KATHLEEN M. ZIOL-GUEST, AND ARIEL KALIL

F AMILY INFLUENCES early in life play an important role in children's development. It is well documented in studies from Europe and the United States that the family environments of young children are important predictors of cognitive and behavioral skills, as well as of outcomes later in life, such as education, labor market participation, earnings, health, and crime (d'Addio 2007). In particular, the literature shows that children of families with low income and education have substantially worse prospects for success in life than other children (Duncan, Ziol-Guest, and Kalil 2010; Holzer et al. 2007).

The early childhood period may be especially sensitive to environmental influences. Low income and its attendant stressors have the potential to shape the neurobiology of the developing child in powerful ways that may lead directly to poorer outcomes later in life (Knudsen et al. 2006). Poverty in early childhood can also affect adult attainment, behavior, and health indirectly through parents' material and emotional investments in their children's learning and development.

The detrimental effects of early low family income may be less severe in stronger welfare states such as those in Scandinavia, possibly because high-quality basic services (like health care and child care) and educational opportunities are publicly provided and utilized by low- and high-income families alike. We explore this question with a comparative look at a country with a weak safety net and extensive childhood poverty (the United States) and a country with a strong welfare state that secures adequate income, basic needs, and education for all residents (Norway).

Specifically, we use comparable methods and data to investigate the adult attainment consequences of low childhood income in the United States and Norway. We describe child low-income dynamics in the two countries and estimate associations between low income between a child's prenatal year and fifteenth birthday and adult achievement outcomes, measured as late as age thirty-seven. Outcomes include completed schooling, adult earnings, and adult unemployment. Our particular focus is on low income early in childhood.

Previous Literature

Although parent-child correlations in labor market earnings are positive in the Scandinavian countries, intergenerational mobility is somewhat higher there than in the United Kingdom and the United States (Björklund and Jäntti 1997, 2000; Bratberg, Nilsen, and Vaage 2007). This may result from the ability of the Scandinavian egalitarian welfare model to mitigate the effects of family background and the possible economic constraints imposed by low income on the family of origin. There is some indication, however, that intergenerational mobility is not homogeneous across the income distribution (Bratberg, Nilsen, and Vaage 2007; Bratsberg et al. 2007).

Espen Bratberg, Øivind Anti Nilsen, and Kjell Vaage (2007) point out that family background factors, such as low market skills and weak preferences for education, could be more detrimental to the mobility of adult children in the lower part of the earnings distribution than at the top, and they discount the possible role of financial constraints. At the same time, these authors report, mobility has increased over time and the role of parental income has decreased more for children at the lower end of the distribution than at the top. These patterns match the intentions of the expansion of public programs in Norway during the 1970s and 1980s.

Nonetheless, the Norwegian intergenerational earnings elasticity for adult earnings in the bottom of the distribution (0.32 for those born in 1960) is not that much less than the figure of 0.40 often cited for U.S. men. Indeed, despite its welfare system, Norway's gaps between children of advantaged and disadvantaged families are substantial. Synnve Schjølberg and her colleagues (2008) find that, by age three, children of parents with a university education have substantially better language development than other children. And large gaps in grades are found between children of parents with high and low education in Norwegian public schools

(Haegeland et al. 2005). Skill differences persist through adolescence and into adulthood. Children of parents with low income are more likely to become low-income earners as adults (Bratberg, Nilsen, and Vaage 2008), and children of social assistance claimants are more likely to claim social assistance as adults (Lorentzen and Nilsen 2008). Finally, low childhood socioeconomic position is associated with increased mortality for most causes of death during young adulthood (age twenty-five to thirty-five) among Norwegians (Strand and Kunst 2007).

Causal Effects of Childhood Income

Greg Duncan and Jeanne Brooks-Gunn (1997) were the first to take a broad look at the possible longer-run consequences of early childhood poverty in the United States. Twelve groups of researchers working with ten different non-experimental but longitudinal data sets estimated longitudinal models of early childhood income effects on later attainment, behavior, and health. On the whole, the results suggest that family income has substantial, albeit selective, associations with children's subsequent attainments. First, family income has consistently larger associations with measures of children's cognitive ability and achievement than with measures of behavior, mental health, and physical health. Second, family economic conditions in early childhood appear to be more important for shaping ability and achievement than family economic conditions during adolescence. And third, the association between parental income and children's achievement appears to be nonlinear, with the biggest impacts at the lowest levels of income.

More recently, we used long-run U.S. data from the Panel Study of Income Dynamics (PSID) to investigate the consequences of poverty between a child's prenatal year and fifth birthday for a host of adult achievement, health, and behavior outcomes, measured as late as age thirty-seven (Duncan et al. 2010). Controlling for economic conditions in middle childhood and adolescence, as well as demographic conditions at the time of the birth, we find statistically significant and, in some cases, quantitatively large detrimental effects of early poverty on a number of attainment-related outcomes (adult earnings and work hours) and some health outcomes (adult body mass; see Ziol-Guest, Duncan, and Kalil 2009), but not on such behavioral outcomes as out-of-wedlock childbearing and arrests. Most of the adult earnings effects appear to operate through early poverty's association with adult work hours. This chapter replicates some of these analyses using Norwegian Registry (NR) data.

The economics literature has typically ignored the idea that the effects on children's development of economic conditions depend on childhood stage, and instead it focuses on the role of "permanent" income, assuming that families anticipate bumps in their life-cycle paths and can save and borrow freely to smooth their consumption across these bumps (Blau 1999).

However, there are several reasons to think that family income during early childhood is critical for children's long-term attainments. Flavio Cunha and his colleagues (2005) propose an economic model of development in which preschool cognitive and socio-emotional capacities are key ingredients of human capital acquisition during the school years. In their model, "skill begets skill," with early capacities boosting the productivity of school-age human capital investments. To the extent that cognitively enriching early home environments lays the groundwork for success in preschool and beyond, parents' ability to purchase books, toys, and enriching activities during this stage of development is paramount (Yeung, Linver, and Brooks-Gunn 2002).

Income and economic insecurity can also affect parental abilities by influencing parents' mental health. Parental psychological stress or harsh parenting behaviors can be especially detrimental during early childhood (Bronfenbrenner and Morris 1998; Godfrey and Barker 2000; Shonkoff and Phillips 2000), given the primacy of sensitive mother-child interactions for the development of young children's emotion regulation (Waters and Sroufe 1983). For example, children's mastery in early childhood of the developmental task of regulating their emotions can have long-run impacts on their achievement, behavior, and health (Fox 1994). Finally, early childhood stressors related to low income could interfere with critical periods in biological development—for example, by altering or dysregulating biological systems, with adverse implications for future health (Godfrey and Barker 2000).

A recent series of studies have used Scandinavian registry data to estimate various intergenerational economic models associations (Aakvik, Salvanes, and Vaage 2005; Björklund and Jäntti 2000; Bratberg, Nilsen, and Vaage 2008; Bratsberg et al. 2007; Humlum 2008; Jäntti et al. 2006). In an approach similar to the one we take here, Arild Aakvik, Kjell Salvanes, and Kjell Vaage (2005) find that family income when children are zero to six years of age is a significant predictor of children's educational attainment, and that the effect of early childhood income on children's eventual years of schooling is about twice as big as the effect of income during the years sixteen to eighteen, even when permanent income is controlled. Although statistically significant, the size of the effects in this study is quite small.

Other recent studies using administrative registers from Statistics Norway have used displacement of fathers due to plant closings to examine the intergenerational consequences of income shocks. In one study, Mari Rege, Kjetil Telle, and Mark Votruba (forthcoming) find that fathers' job losses occurring as a result of plant closures have an adverse effect on adolescents' school grades when graduating from secondary school (though the effect does not seem to be driven by income losses, suggesting that this effect may be due to the social distress of unemployed fathers). Bratberg and his colleagues (2008), using similar data, analyze the effects of worker displacement in 1982 to 1985 on their children's earnings in 1999 to 2001, when the children were twenty-five to thirty years old. They find that, although displacement appears to have a negative effect on the earnings and employment of those affected, there are no significant effects on offspring's earnings. Their study does not, however, distinguish income losses in different childhood periods, nor does it capture income losses that might have occurred during the early childhood period.

Researchers generally do not dispute simple correlations between income and child developmental outcomes, but there is much controversy about whether these correlations can be given causal interpretations. Unobservable determinants of children's adult outcomes that are correlated with early childhood family income—such as parental abilities or mental health problems or frequent moves—are of key concern in assessing the causal impact of early family income on children's adult outcomes. Studies using more sophisticated methods to address this omitted-variable problem have recently emerged. For example, Kevin Milligan and Mark Stabile (2008) and Gordon Dahl and Lance Lochner (2008) utilize reforms in child transfer programs and tax rules in Canada and the United States to generate exogenous changes in family income. Both studies find effects of early childhood family income on children's achievement-related outcomes.

The approach we pursue here is to use children born in Norway and the United States between 1968 and 1975 to estimate the association between early childhood family income and outcomes of the child measured from age twenty-four to age thirty-seven (until 2005). Our work extends that of Aakvik, Salvanes, and Vaage (2005) by including more cohorts; adopting a longer time horizon and a broader array of outcomes; allowing for differential effects of increments to low versus high family income; using a more comprehensive measure of childhood income; and, most importantly, comparing Norwegian and U.S. results. To avoid attributing to income what should be attributed to correlated determinants of both childhood income and adult outcomes, we include a number of key control variables that were available around the time of birth of the child. In addition, our estimates of the association between early childhood income and adult outcomes include controls for income in middle childhood and adolescence. It is difficult to think of omitted-variable bias stories involving early income that would not be controlled in large measure with the inclusion of income later in childhood.[1]

Data

We use administrative register data compiled by Statistics Norway, which includes every individual in the entire resident population of Norway, on average comprising more than fifty thousand children born each year. We are able to link information on parents to children around the time of birth and throughout childhood. Additionally, a host of measures of the child's adult outcomes are generally available from 1992 until 2005. We focus on three: completed schooling, earnings, and unemployment. The target study sample consists of the roughly 500,000 males and females born between 1968 and 1975, with register data beginning in the prenatal year and extending to 2005, when these individuals were between ages thirty and thirty-seven. The very large case counts in the Norwegian data produce narrow confidence intervals for regression coefficients, which prompts us to pay special attention to the magnitude, not just the statistical significance, of estimated coefficients.

Comparative data, also spanning 1968 to 2005, are drawn from the U.S. Panel Study of Income Dynamics. The PSID has followed a nationally representative sample of families and their children since 1968. Our analysis sample consists of 1,589 respondents who participated in the PSID in adulthood and had nonmissing data on at least one outcome. While the Norwegian data cover every resident of Norway, the U.S. data suffer from possible bias owing to differential nonresponse, which is highest among the poorest households. We adjust for differential nonresponse by using the PSID's attrition-adjusted weights in all of our analyses.

Childhood Income

We have created a measure of household income in each year of the child's life starting in the prenatal year.[2] Norwegian total household income in kroner is based on tax files, which include net income that is subject to taxation (earnings from labor, unemployment money, sick leave money, pensions, income from self-employment, and income from capital including interest and dividends). To this income measure we add cash transfers like child allowances. These values are calculated for the child's mother and added to the amount reported for the mother's cohabitant (generally her husband).[3] For the U.S. comparison, we use the PSID's high-quality edited measure of annual total family income, which includes taxable income and cash transfers to all household members. For the analyses, Norwegian and U.S. incomes are inflated to 2005 levels using the Norwegian and U.S. consumer price indexes (CPIs). To establish comparability between the two data sets, we convert the 2005 Norwegian krone to U.S. dollars using the exchange rate for 2005—6.4 Norwegian kroner per U.S. dollar—obtained from the Organization for Economic Co-operation and Development (OECD). We average these annual income measures across three periods: the prenatal year through the calendar year in which the child turned five, ages six to ten, and ages eleven to fifteen.

Although income is measured in similar ways in the two data sets, some issues may be important to keep in mind when interpreting our findings.

Using exchange rates or purchasing power parities (PPP) to adjust for differences in actual purchasing power is problematic, particularly for individuals at different portions of the income distribution. There are considerable discrepancies between PPP and exchange rates—in 2005 the PPP was 8.90 while the exchange rate was 6.44. The exchange rate has also been volatile, but the PPP has been fairly stable over recent years. Although this might argue for using the PPP relative to the exchange rate, the latter provides a more comparable set of income distributions for our descriptive comparisons. The qualitative regression results are the same regardless of whether we convert the measures of family income in fixed 2005 prices by using the PPP of 8.90 or the exchange rate of 6.44. Our adult attainment measures—years of completed schooling, log earnings, and percentage of adult years of unemployment—are unaffected by currency conversion issues.

We use pretax income measures in both countries. The public provision of health services, education, and social insurance (sick leave and unemployment, for example) in Norway and country differences in tax schedules and in-kind transfer programs introduce noncomparabilities in both pre- and post-tax income. In addition, some of the sources of income included in the PSID, like pecuniary support from friends and relatives and alimony, are not included in the Norwegian measure. There are also some public transfers—in particular generous public loans for education and housing, scholarships, and access to highly subsidized child care (both center-based and preschool)—that are not included in the Norwegian measure.

Adult Outcomes

Dependent variables in our analyses span educational and employment domains. Years of completed schooling are based on reports around age twenty-four.[4] Data on the child's adult earnings are gleaned from all available annual survey or register reports of earned income, beginning when the child was age twenty-four. As with childhood income, we use country CPIs to adjust for inflation and the exchange rate to convert from 2005 kroner to 2005 U.S. dollars. To adjust earnings for age and calendar year, we regress all of our yearly earnings observations on sets of dummy variables measuring the age of the respondent in the given year and the calendar year of measurement. We then generate residuals from this regression for each sample individual's earnings observations and average these residuals across all of the yearly earnings observations that a given individual generates. We center these average residuals on the sample mean by adding them to the overall sample mean earnings. As a final step, we take the natural logarithm. This adjusted earnings measure is used in all of the regression analyses presented here.

Unemployment experiences are captured with the percentage of years after age twenty-four that the individual received any unemployment compensation (in Norway) or reported any time spent unemployed (in the PSID).

Control Variables and Regression Procedures

To avoid attributing to income what should be attributed to correlated determinants of both childhood income and our outcomes of interest, we include a number of control variables in all of our regressions.[5] The controls used in the regressions for both data sets are birth year dummies, child sex (female = 1), whether the child is the firstborn of his or her mother, the number of siblings, the age of the mother at the time of the birth, whether the child's mother was married at the time of the birth, years of completed schooling of the parent in the birth year (both mother and father in the NR and head of household in the PSID), and fixed effects for geographic location around the time of birth (mother's municipality of residence—430 in all—in Norway and region of the United States in the PSID). The PSID regressions also include controls for race. All of our OLS regressions are run in Stata 10.0 SE and are adjusted for family-of-origin clustering on the mother using Huber-White methods.

Results: A Comparative Look at Childhood Income

Table 7.1 presents descriptive statistics on the Norwegian and PSID samples. The 496,110 Norwegian children resided within 338,738 families. Forty-two percent of the children in both samples are firstborn; PSID children have more siblings on average than do Norwegian children. Parental schooling levels around the time of the child's birth are slightly higher in the PSID than in Norway. Norwegian mothers average twenty-six years of age when the child was born, which is roughly one and a half years older than PSID mothers (see chapter 3, this volume). At the time of the child's birth, the vast majority of these mothers were married.

On average, the Norwegian cohorts had completed 12.9 years of schooling by age twenty-four; the comparable PSID sample average is 13.4 years. The Norwegian birth cohort experienced unemployment in almost 12 percent of their adulthood (since age twenty-four); the counterpart figure for the PSID sample is just below 10 percent. Finally, mean earnings are slightly lower in Norway than in the United States. In figure 7.1, we focus on distributional differences by converting kroner into dollars using the ratio of the medians in the two data sets. We observe that Norway

**Table 7.1   Descriptive Statistics: Norwegian Registry and
U.S. Panel Study of Income Dynamics**

	NR		PSID	
	Mean or Proportion	Standard Deviation	Mean or Proportion	Standard Deviation
Childhood income				
Prenatal to age five	34,846 [26,722]	16,829	47,842	28,341
Age six to age ten	45,779 [33,538]	20,336	54,226	39,013
Age eleven to age fifteen	46,732 [37,007]	22,788	59,068	45,369
Demographics				
Female	49%	—	47%	—
Firstborn	42%	—	42%	—
Number of siblings	1.97	1.29	2.21	1.79
Mother's education	10.87	2.03	—	—
Father's education	11.46	2.7	12.09	2.94
Age of mother at birth	26.22	5.37	24.84	5.76
Mother married at birth	92%	—	84%	—
Outcomes				
Completed schooling (years)	12.89	2.21	13.39	2.14
Average annual earnings	30,245 [24,230]	18,593	34,564	30,932
Percentage of years spent any time unemployed	11.88	18.34	9.92	18.00
N	496,110		1,589	

Source: Authors' calculations based on the Panel Study of Income Dynamics (2010) and administrative data compiled by Statistics Norway (Akselsen, Lien, and Sivertstøl 2007).
Note: Norwegian childhood income is in kroner converted annually to U.S. dollars using exchange rates (PPP-adjusted income is shown in brackets), and then to fixed 2005 dollars using the U.S. CPI. PSID is weighted using the attrition-adjusted weights provided in the data set.

has more zero earners than the United States, but that, apart from the zeroes, the United States has more low earners.

Comparing Income Distributions

Both of our data sets provide annual income measures between children's prenatal years and late adolescence. As shown in table 7.1, average household income increases across childhood in both countries, but more

Figure 7.1   Distribution of Median-Equated Adult Earnings

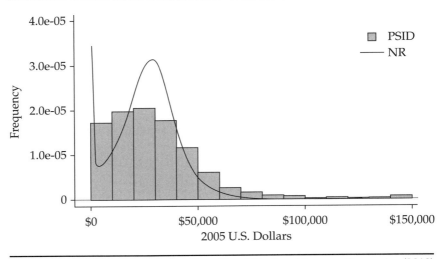

Source: Authors' calculations based on Panel Study of Income Dynamics (2010) and administrative data compiled by Statistics Norway (Akselsen, Lien, and Sivertstøl 2007).

rapidly in Norway (by 38 percent between the birth-to-age-five and age-eleven-to-fifteen periods) than in the United States (where the comparable increase is 23 percent).[6] This difference is presumably related to the higher economic growth in Norway compared with the United States over the period. As expected, there are lower within-period variances in the Norwegian data.

Childhood income distributions for the two countries are shown for early childhood (prenatal to age five) in figure 7.2 and for the entire childhood period (prenatal to age fifteen) in figure 7.3. To focus exclusively on distributional differences, we convert kroner into dollars using the ratio of the medians in the two data sets. Compared with the U.S. income distribution, the Norwegian distribution is compressed, with relatively small right and left tails. Though it is well documented that these differences largely reflect important and actual differences in the income distribution between the two countries (see, for example, Aaberge et al. 2002), we cannot rule out the possibility that some of the differences in the distributions can be attributed to minor differences in how income is measured in the two data sets.

Although we can see that average income rises more quickly across childhood for Norwegian children than for U.S. children, table 7.2 presents a more complete picture of income mobility between early and late

Figure 7.2   Distribution of Median-Equated Early Childhood Family Income

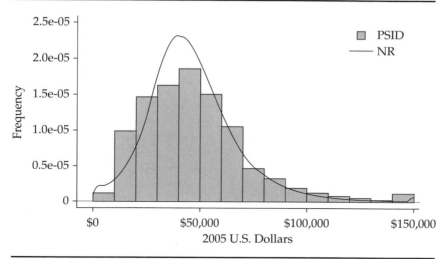

Source: Authors' calculations based on Panel Study of Income Dynamics (2010) and administrative data compiled by Statistics Norway (Akselsen, Lien, and Sivertstøl 2007).

Figure 7.3   Distribution of Median-Equated Childhood Family Income

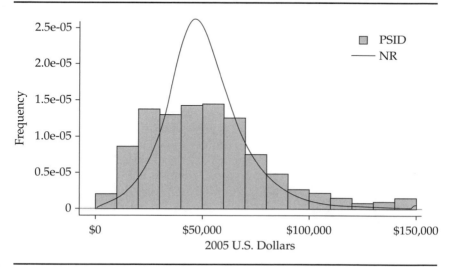

Source: Authors' calculations based on Panel Study of Income Dynamics (2010) and administrative data compiled by Statistics Norway (Akselsen, Lien, and Sivertstøl 2007).

Table 7.2   Family Income Mobility Across Childhood

Average Family Income Between the Prenatal Year and Age Five	Average Family Income Between Age Eleven and Fifteen						Ratio of Median Income (Prenatal to Age Five) to Quintile Break Point (Prenatal to Age Five)
	(Lowest) Quintile 1	Quintile 2	Quintile 3	Quintile 4	(Highest) Quintile 5		
Norway (NR)							
Quintile 1	46%	26%	15%	9%	5%	100%	0.76
Quintile 2	22	30	25	16	6	100	
Quintile 3	15	23	27	24	11	100	
Quintile 4	11	14	22	30	24	100	
Quintile 5	7	7	11	21	54	100	1.18
United States (PSID)							
Quintile 1	56	30	10	3	1	100	0.76
Quintile 2	29	32	22	12	5	100	
Quintile 3	9	21	33	25	12	100	
Quintile 4	4	11	23	38	24	100	
Quintile 5	1	6	12	23	58	100	1.22

Source: Authors' calculations based on Panel Study of Income Dynamics (2010) and administrative data compiled by Statistics Norway (Akselsen, Lien, and Sivertstol 2007).

Note: Table entries show proportion of the prenatal-to-age-five income group in the later-period income group. Rows add up to 100 percent.

childhood. In this table, each child is sorted into his or her respective family income quintile for income averaged across early (the prenatal year to age five) and late (age eleven to fifteen) childhood. Each row shows the proportion of the early income group's movement into later income groups. For example, 46 percent of Norwegian children who were in the lowest income quintile in early childhood were also in the lowest income quintile in adolescence, whereas 5 percent moved from the lowest into the highest income quintile. Corresponding U.S. figures are 56 percent and 1 percent, respectively—indicating less mobility out of the bottom in the United States. By and large, table 7.2 shows somewhat greater income mobility among Norwegian than American children.[7]

Results: Childhood Income and Adult Attainments

To preview the results from our full regression analysis, table 7.3 presents results from a series of descriptive regressions for both the NR and PSID samples. Across the columns of the first row, each of our three outcomes is regressed only on a measure of the seventeen-year average childhood income (prenatal through age fifteen). All coefficient estimates are standardized, so first-row entries amount to simple correlations between income and each of the outcomes. As expected, all of the correlations are positive, although correlations for schooling and, especially, earnings are much smaller in the Norwegian data than the U.S. data.

In the second row (model 2), the simple correlations shown in the first row are adjusted for the extensive set of background control variables noted earlier, all of which are measured around the time of birth. In the U.S. data, all of the correlations become considerably smaller; in the case of unemployment, the adjusted correlation is no longer statistically significant. Thus, a substantial portion of the simple correlation between U.S. childhood income and these three adult outcomes can be accounted for by the disadvantageous conditions associated with birth into a low-income household. In the Norwegian data, adjustments for correlated background conditions drop the completed schooling correlation by more than half and the unemployment correlation by nearly half, but do not change the earnings correlation at all.

To assess whether increments to low income matter more than increments to the incomes of children growing up in middle-class or affluent families, model 3 regresses the adult outcomes on the natural logarithm of the seventeen-year average childhood income, plus background controls. Whereas our first two models assume that an incremental dollar increase to a poor family's income has the same beneficial effect on a child's adult outcomes as the same increase to an affluent family's income, the logarithmic transformation assumes equal *percentage* effects. Higher standardized

Table 7.3   Standardized Regression Coefficients from Various Models of Childhood Income and Adult Outcomes

Model	Period	Years of Schooling Completed		Annual Earnings (ln)		Percentage of Years Spent Any Time Unemployed	
		NR	PSID	NR	PSID	NR	PSID
Model 1: No controls; seventeen-year average childhood income	Prenatal to age fifteen	.20**	.34**	.08**	.27**	–.13**	–.12**
Model 2: Background controls; seventeen-year average childhood income	Prenatal to age fifteen	.08**	.18**	.08**	.18**	–.07**	–.04
Model 3: Background controls; natural logarithm of seventeen-year average childhood income	Prenatal to age fifteen	.10**	.28**	.11**	.27**	–.07**	–.09*
Model 4: Background controls; natural logarithm of average stage-specific childhood income	Prenatal to age five	.01*	.15**	.09**	.21**	–.04**	–.04
	Age six to age ten	.01**	–.04	.00	.07	.00	.04
	Age eleven to age fifteen	.10**	.20**	.06**	.02	–.04**	–.10

Source: Authors' calculations based on Panel Study of Income Dynamics (2010) and administrative data compiled by Statistics Norway (Akselsen, Lien, and Sivertstøl 2007).
*p < .05; **p < .01

coefficients (in absolute value) in logarithmic as opposed to linear models would suggest that money matters more for the outcomes of children reared in lower-income households than for those in higher-income households.

As shown in the third row of table 7.3 (model 3), the standardized coefficients for the logarithmic models are at least as large as the coefficients for the linear models (model 2) for both the Norwegian and U.S. samples, although the jumps are much higher in the PSID. That is, the adjusted correlation with unemployment time becomes statistically significant again. Thus, these adult measures appear to be more sensitive to low childhood incomes in the United States relative to Norway.

To address the issue of the childhood stage-specificity income associations, the final regressions in table 7.3 (model 4) replace the single seventeen-year average log childhood income measure with three childhood stage-specific measures of log income. These models thus allow the association to be different for family income at three specific stages of childhood. All background controls are included in these models. With each childhood stage accounting for approximately one-third of childhood, we would expect that the three coefficients should (approximately) sum to the all-childhood coefficient presented in model 3. If childhood income matters equally across all three stages, the three coefficients should be roughly the same size and about one-third the magnitude of the model 3 coefficients.

In the case of completed schooling, adolescent income has larger associations than earlier incomes for both countries, with the correlation being almost twice as large in the United States than in Norway. Early income also has a statistically significant coefficient ($p < .05$) in both countries.

The largest stage-specific correlation is in the PSID between adult earnings and early childhood income. Indeed, for U.S. children there appears to be little role for income beyond age five. In the case of adult earnings in the Norwegian data, early childhood and adolescent income have similarly modest but statistically significant coefficients. The size and patterns of statistical significance in the case of unemployment suggest little role for income in any stage of childhood.

Taken together, the descriptive regression results shown in table 7.3 suggest that childhood stage matters in understanding links between childhood income and adult success, although not as much in the Norwegian data compared with the U.S. data. Moreover, many of the adult outcomes appear to be more sensitive to increments to low as opposed to middle-class or higher family incomes.

A more detailed look at childhood-specific income effects is provided in the regression models shown in table 7.4. For each childhood stage's income, two spline coefficients are estimated. The first reflects the estimated effect of an additional $10,000 annual income in the given stage for

Table 7.4   OLS Spline Regression Models of Childhood Income and Years of Completed Schooling, Adult Earnings, and Percentage of Years Spent Any Time Unemployed

| | | Years of Completed Schooling | | | |
| | | NR | | PSID | |
		Coefficient (SE)	Different Slopes	Coefficient (SE)	Different Slopes
Average annual income, prenatal to age five	Less than $25,000	.17** (.01)	**	.30 (.33)	n.s.
	More than $25,000	.00 (.00)		.05 (.04)	
Average annual income, age six to age ten	Less than $25,000	.13** (.02)	**	.78** (.25)	**
	More than $25,000	−.01** (.00)		−.06 (.04)	
Average annual income, age eleven to age fifteen	Less than $25,000	.29** (.02)	**	−.26 (.20)	*
	More than $25,000	.08** (.00)		.10** (.03)	
Test of equality of three "less than $25,000" coefficients		**		*	

Source: Authors' calculations based on Panel Study of Income Dynamics (2010) and administrative data compiled by Statistics Norway (Akselsen, Lien, and Sivertstøl 2007). *Notes:* Regressions include controls for birth year fixed effects, child sex (female = 1), whether the child was the firstborn of his or her mother, the total number of siblings, the age of the mother at the time of the birth, and whether the child's mother was married at the time of the birth (and whether the child's mother was cohabiting at the time of the birth in NR). To account for parental schooling, both mother's and father's education at birth were included in the NR regressions, and head-of-household schooling was included in the PSID regressions. Finally, about 430 fixed effects for mother's municipality of residence around the time of birth were included in the NR regressions, and PSID regressions included controls for region of residence in the year of the child's birth. PSID regressions are weighted. In both sets of analyses standard errors (SE) are corrected to account for the presence of siblings by clustering on the mother's ID. The columns labelled "Different Slopes" provide the significance of the test that the low-income (less than $25,000) and higher-income (more than $25,000) slopes are different.
$^{+}p < .10$; $^{*}p < .05$; $^{**}p < .01$

	Annual Earnings (ln)				Percentage of Years Spent Any Time Unemployed			
	NR		PSID		NR		PSID	
	Coefficient (SE)	Different Slopes	Coefficient (SE)	Different Slopes	Coefficient (SE)	Different Slopes	Coefficient (SE)	Different Slopes
	.23** (.01) .02** (.01)	**	.56* (.24) .04* (.02)	*	−.62** (.11) −.07 (.05)	**	−4.89 (4.31) −.08 (.27)	n.s.
	.06** (.01) −.01** (.01)	**	.13 (.17) .01 (.02)	n.s.	−.41** (.11) −.10+ (.05)	**	1.78 (3.54) .31 (.28)	n.s.
	.16** (.01) .02** (.01)	**	−.09 (.13) .00 (.02)	n.s.	−.14 (.16) −.31** (.10)		.83 (2.36) −.32 (.26)	n.s.
		**		*		**		n.s.

children whose income in that stage averaged less than $25,000. All three sets of income variables, plus the background controls, are included in all regressions. The columns labeled "Different Slopes" report results from a statistical test of the null hypothesis of equal within-period slopes. The final row shows results for a test of equality of all three lower-income segment (less than $25,000) slopes.

In contrast to table 7.3, coefficients in table 7.4 are unstandardized and therefore show changes in the originally scaled dependent variables associated with $10,000 increments to average childhood stage-specific income. The "less than $25,000" results are termed the "lower-income" segment; the other results relate to what we term the "higher-income" segment.

The most striking result in table 7.3—that early childhood income is important for adult earnings in the PSID—persists in table 7.4. The "0.56" coefficient means that, adjusting for income later in childhood and the other control variables, an additional $10,000 per year of family income between the prenatal year and the child's fifth birthday is associated with an increase in the natural logarithm of adult earnings of 0.56 (75 percent). In contrast, $10,000 increments to early childhood income for higher-income U.S. children are associated with a 0.04 (4 percent) increase in log earnings. The p-value reported in the "Different Slopes" columns indicates that the slope for the lower-income early childhood group is significantly different from the slope for those with higher income. More modest coefficient differences show up in the Norwegian earnings data—a $10,000 increment in low income early in childhood is associated with a 0.23 (26 percent) increase in adult log earnings; a comparable increment for higher-income children is associated with a 0.02 (2 percent) adult log earnings increase. In both countries' adult earnings regressions, early childhood income appears to matter more than income later in childhood.

Other results presented in table 7.4 produce fewer cross-country similarities. Focusing on coefficient size rather than significance level, income in adolescence appears to matter the most for Norwegian children but has an insignificant (and negative) coefficient estimate in the United States. In the case of unemployment, the scaling of the dependent variable (as the percentage of years in which any unemployment is reported) produces larger coefficients, but only in the case of the PSID are the estimates larger than one (that is, a $10,000 income increase is associated with at least a one-percentage-point increase in the percentage of years unemployed).

Discussion

It has been suggested that the high mobility observed in the Scandinavian countries compared with the United States is a function of a variety of policies aimed at reducing inequality. The Norwegian welfare state, with its high-quality and universally available public programs, ranks low in terms of economic inequality (Bratberg et al. 2007). Nevertheless, we find a regression-adjusted correlation between low income experienced in early childhood in Norway and the chances of later-life economic success. These correlations are substantially lower, however, than in the U.S. data.

One potential puzzle is determining how early income can be linked (positively) to earnings but not (negatively) to unemployment. In our earlier PSID-based work (Duncan, Ziol-Guest, and Kalil 2010), we found that variation in adult work hours accounts for the bulk of the link between early childhood income and annual adult earnings and that childhood income has an insignificant effect on hourly earnings in adulthood. We investigated the work hours effects further by estimating whether early childhood income appears to operate by reducing unemployment or time out of the labor force altogether as opposed to full- versus part-time work. For both men and women, the income effects are strongest for full-time versus less-than-full-time work. Lacking adequate measures of work hours in the Norwegian Registry, we are unable to replicate these analyses, but at least for the U.S. data they suggest that the margin on which early childhood income has its biggest effect is in sustaining full-time work as opposed to part-time work rather than avoiding unemployment.

Comparisons of intergenerational mobility across countries raise important questions about cross-national differences in whether countries offer fair opportunities for their citizens. As Bratberg and his colleagues (2007) discuss, poor children may grow up to be poor adults because of inherited preferences for market work, inherited differences in market ability, or constraints on their ability to secure and invest in opportunities, such as in education and skill development. Although some moral philosophers have argued that the state should not attempt to reduce inequalities originating from inborn traits (Nozick 1974), others have maintained that a person deserves only to benefit by virtue of his freely chosen effort. In the latter tradition, it would follow from John Roemer (1998) that childhood circumstances over which the child has no control—like family income, education, or structure—are not legitimate sources for inequality. But inequality of outcomes that is due to different amounts of effort are acceptable (see also Roemer 2004 and Björklund, Jäntti and Roemer, forthcoming). Along similar lines, Adam Swift (2005) regards it as unfair that a child's future prospects depend on his or her parents' capabilities.

The Norwegian welfare state has attempted in many ways to "level the playing field" with respect to the circumstances that are beyond children's control, including parental earnings.[8] This has been especially true for publicly subsidized center-based child care, as well as for higher education, which is publicly financed and for which there are no fees. Expansions of child care and educational opportunities in Norway have increased attainment over time for the most disadvantaged, as intended (Aakvik, Salvanes, and Vaage 2005; Havnes and Mogstad, forthcoming). As such, Norway, to a greater extent than the United States, has sought to reduce the importance of family background in securing opportunities typically associated with successful human capital development.

Nonetheless, we find continuity over time in the economic success of parents and offspring, even in a country as generous as Norway. An important task that remains is to identify the mechanisms that account for the intergenerational persistence of economic status and to decide, as a society, the state's role in blocking or preventing these mechanisms. Few people believe that there should be complete independence between parents' and children's economic success. In the name of fairness, one may reasonably ask whether the state should play a role in mitigating the circumstances of disadvantaged children who are unable to realize their potential because their parents lack not simply the economic means but also the abilities, mental health, or knowledge to help them maximize their chances for success. After all, as Swift (2005, 267) argues, from the child's perspective, "what one's parents are like is entirely a matter of luck." From a normative perspective, it may make no difference for the child whether he or she inherits genes or a supportive environment or money. This is a potentially more radical notion of equality, but it forces us to ask the question: what does it mean to "level the playing field"?

Swift (2005) offers one framework for thinking about which of the mechanisms that produce intergenerational correlations in outcomes are "morally suspect," thereby warranting prevention or intervention, and which, in contrast, reflect the "essence" of the family and therefore should be respected, valued, and protected by society as private interactions. In the morally suspect group, he argues, belong bequests of property, the purchasing of expensive education or advantaged neighborhoods, and access to superior health care. The essence of the family group, in contrast, includes all manner of "spontaneous and informal parent-child interaction" (274) that constitute children as the people they are or will become. (Swift offers as examples such parental activities as reading bedtime stories, transmitting positive attitudes toward work, and talking about things at mealtimes.) A key tenet in Swift's framework is that direct activities that allow parents to marshal their own resources to (unfairly) maximize their children's future economic well-being are the least worthy of respect. Although some private family interactions may in fact account for the intergenerational persistence of economic success, Swift views this as an "accidental by-product" of such interactions (275).

Three interrelated goals can help to guide our thinking on this issue. From an empirical perspective, the relative importance of different mechanisms in generating persistence across generations in economic status must be better understood. From a philosophical perspective, the lines between freedom of familial association and state intervention in the pursuit of equality of opportunity must continue to be debated. And from a policy perspective, the plausibility and practicability of different modes of state intervention must be assessed.

Empirical social scientists can contribute to these efforts by working to establish the channels that link early childhood poverty to later life outcomes. In the Norwegian case, we can rule out with greater certainty that such channels include reduced access to health care, education, and the like. (Indeed, recent evidence from a variety of countries suggests that "the cultural capital" of families plays a key role in accounting for inter-generational correlations in economic status; see Esping-Andersen 2004).

Unfortunately, the administrative data we rely on here provide little insight into plausible mechanisms. One mechanism linking early childhood poverty to adult earnings identified in our previous work with the U.S. data (Duncan, Ziol-Guest, and Kalil 2010) is adult work hours—early childhood poverty predicts adult differences in individuals who are and are not successful in sustaining full-time working careers. But the factors that influence adult work hours are not entirely clear—individuals' preferences for long work hours and ability to maintain work are plausible "noncognitive" skills that could be important, that might be influenced by the attitudes and preferences that prevailed in the family of origin, and that might not necessarily be related to the economic investments that parents made (or did not make) in raising their children. But this uncertainty about influences on adult work hours does not rule out the potential importance of trying to shore up those skills with the same degree of effort that has been mounted to increase public supports to disadvantaged children via channels that operate largely outside of their families. As Gøsta Esping-Andersen (2004) notes, such efforts are most likely to succeed when mounted in tandem with financial investments in disadvantaged families. Indeed, the analysis of Bratberg and his colleagues (2007) suggests, importantly, that although constraints in the form of influence of family on offspring's preferences play an important role for those children who end up in the bottom of the Norwegian income distribution as adults, these constraints have weakened over time, in particular for this population, along with expansions in the Norwegian welfare state. These trends suggest that public-sector investments (such as in education or in other socioeconomic arenas) can affect the long-run influence of family background in the more private spheres of family preferences and aspirations.

This comparison of the relative magnitude of the impact of early childhood poverty on the long-run outcomes in the two countries makes it tempting to conclude that if the United States adopted some of the generous child-focused programs provided in Norway, it could reduce the deleterious effects of early childhood poverty that stem from constraints on adequate access to health care, higher education, and the like. But this is a difficult conclusion to draw given the relative homogeneity and small size of Norway versus the vast and heterogeneous landscape of the United States and the nature of behavioral responses to the policy changes. Nevertheless, evidence from studies such as the one conducted by Gordon Dahl and Lance Lochner (2008) have shown that expansions in U.S. social welfare programs like the earned income tax credit (EITC) can make meaningful improvements in the lives of poor children. That evidence, in concert with this chapter's findings, suggests that it may be possible to dampen the influence of early childhood poverty with some of the more comprehensive programs and services provided by a generous welfare state.

Transfer policies directed toward children in the United States rarely take into account the age of the child. If indeed a child's development in early childhood is more sensitive to economic deprivation than it is later, then perhaps child age should figure more prominently into setting benefit levels. This could take the form of adding to the existing child tax credits or benefit levels for such families. Targeting these transfers, or similar programs, to families with the youngest children may offer the largest benefit for later-life attainment and achievement.

Notes

1. Another common way of handling omitted-variable bias is with family fixed-effects (sibling difference) models. We estimated such models with our PSID data and found qualitatively similar results but very large standard errors. Precision is not an issue with large-N Norwegian registries, and we intend to explore such models in future work.

2. With income reported for calendar years and conceptions occurring continuously, there is some imprecision in matching income to the prenatal year. If a child was born prior to July 1, we take the prenatal year to be the prior calendar year. If the birth was after July 1, then the prenatal year is considered to be the year in which the birth occurred. Similarly, we define "under age six" as the last calendar year before the child's sixth birthday. Thus defined, our "early childhood" period consists of seven calendar years.

3. The registries provide us with unique identifiers for spouses, and we mainly rely on two assumptions to form households. First, we assume that married couples live together. Second, we assume that the two parents live together if they had an additional child together or if they got married after the birth of the child (and that they were neither married to someone else nor having a child with anyone else in between).

4. There may be a tendency to complete schooling at older ages in Norway than in the United States. Experimentation with regressions where years of completed schooling are measured at age thirty in Norway provide estimates of different magnitudes, but the main qualitative picture remains similar.

5. In an effort to make the analyses as comparable as possible, we include control variables that are relatively identical in both countries. Our findings are robust to inclusion of early childhood measures of wealth in the Norwegian regressions, as well as a list of parental attitudes, expectations, and test scores available around the time of birth in the PSID regressions.
6. To facilitate comparability across the two countries in the 1970s, in table 7.1 we have converted income in kroner to U.S. dollars *annually* using exchange rates (PPPs in brackets) and then to fixed 2005 U.S. dollars using the U.S. consumer price index. Elsewhere in the chapter, we maintain comparability over time by following the conversion approach outlined in the data section.
7. Although one potential reason for greater mobility out of low income might be that Norwegian children have incomes that are closer to the first-quintile threshold, the final column of table 7.2 shows that this was not the case— children in the lowest income quintile in both countries had income that averaged 76 percent of the first-quintile cutoff. High-income children in the United States were 22 percent above the fifth-quintile cutoff compared with 18 percent of Norwegian children.
8. It is important to keep in mind that our analyses of the effects of early childhood income use data from the 1970s, when the Norwegian welfare state was considerably less generous than it is today. To see if there are any trends in effects *within* our 1968 to 1975 birth cohorts, we reran our earnings models with a dummy variable for the 1968 to 1971 subset of this cohort interacted with the two prenatal-to-age-five spline segments. Small (but statistically significant) positive coefficients indicate that the first spline segment is indeed more steeply sloped (coefficient of 0.25 versus 0.20) for the earlier cohorts, as are the coefficients on the second spline segment (roughly 0.04 versus 0.02).

References

Aaberge, Rolf, Anders Björklund, Markus Jäntti, Mårten Palme, Peder J. Pedersen, Nina Smith, and Tom Wennemo. 2002. "Income Inequality and Income Mobility in the Scandinavian Countries Compared to the United States." *Review of Income and Wealth* 48(4): 443–69.

Aakvik, Arild, Kjell G. Salvanes, and Kjell Vaage. 2005. "Educational Attainment and Family Background." *German Economic Review* 6(3): 377–94.

Akselsen, Anders, Sandra Lien, and Øyvind Sivertstøl. 2007. FD-trygd. Variabelliste. (FD-trygd. List of variables.) Notater 17, Statistics Norway. Oslo.

Björklund, Anders, and Markus Jäntti. 1997. "Intergenerational Mobility in Sweden Compared to the United States." *American Economic Review* 87(5): 1009–18.

———. 2000. "Intergenerational Mobility of Socioeconomic Status in Comparative Perspective." *Nordic Journal of Political Economy* 26(1): 3–33.

Björklund, Anders, Markus Jäntti, and John E. Roemer. Forthcoming. "Equality of Opportunity and the Distribution of Long-Run Income in Sweden." *Social Choice and Welfare.*

Blau, David M. 1999. "The Effect of Income on Child Development." *Review of Economics and Statistics* 81(2): 261–76.

Bratberg, Espen, Øivind Anti Nilsen, and Kjell Vaage. 2007. "Trends in Intergenerational Mobility Across Offspring's Earnings Distribution in Norway." *Industrial Relations: A Journal of Economy and Society* 46(1): 112–29.

———. 2008. "Job Losses and Child Outcomes." *Labor Economics* 15(4): 591–603.

Bratsberg, Bernt, Knut Røed, Oddbjørn Raaum, Robin Naylor, Markus Jäntti, Tor Eriksson, and Eva Österbacka. 2007. "Nonlinearities in Intergenerational Earnings Mobility: Consequences for Cross-Country Comparisons." *Economic Journal* 117(519): C72–92.

Bronfenbrenner, Urie, and Pamela A. Morris. 1998. "The Ecology of Developmental Processes." In *Handbook of Child Psychology,* vol. 1, *Theoretical Models of Human Development,* 5th ed., edited by Richard M. Lerner. New York: Wiley.

Cunha, Flavio, James J. Heckman, Lance Lochner, and Dimitriy V. Masterov. 2005. "Interpreting the Evidence on Life Cycle Skill Formation." In *Handbook of the Economics of Education,* edited by Erik A. Hanushek and Finis Welch. Amsterdam: North Holland.

d'Addio, Anna Cristina. 2007. "Intergenerational Transmission of Disadvantage: Mobility or Immobility Across Generations? A Review of the Evidence for OECD Countries." Social Employment and Migration working paper 52. Paris: Organization for Economic Co-operation and Development.

Dahl, Gordon, and Lance Lochner. 2008. "The Impact of Family Income on Child Achievement: Evidence from the Earned Income Tax Credit." Working paper 14599. Cambridge, Mass.: National Bureau of Economic Research.

Duncan, Greg J., and Jeanne Brooks-Gunn, eds. 1997. *The Consequences of Growing Up Poor.* New York: Russell Sage Foundation.

Duncan, Greg J., Kathleen M. Ziol-Guest, and Ariel Kalil. 2010. "Early Childhood Poverty and Adult Attainment, Behavior, and Health." *Child Development* 81(1): 306–25.

Esping-Andersen, Gøsta. 2004. "Unequal Opportunities and the Mechanisms of Social Inheritance." In *Generational Income Mobility in North America and Europe,* edited by Miles Corak. Cambridge: Cambridge University Press.

Fox, Nathan 1994. "The Development of Emotion Regulation: Biological and Behavioral Considerations." In *Monographs of the Society for Research in Child Development,* vol. 59. Chicago: University of Chicago Press.

Godfrey, Keith M., and David J. P. Barker. 2000. "Fetal Nutrition and Adult Disease." *American Journal of Clinical Nutrition* 71(5): 1344S–52S.

Haegeland, Torbjørn, Lars J. Kirkebøen, Oddbjørn Raaum, and Kjell Gunnar Salvanes. 2005. "Family Background, School Resources, and Marks at Graduation in Norwegian Primary Education." In *Education 2005: Attendance and Qualifications.* Oslo: Statistics Norway.

Havnes, Tarjei, and Magne Mogstad. Forthcoming. "No Child Left Behind. Subsidized Child Care and Children's Long-Run Outcomes." *American Economic Journal: Economic Policy.*

Holzer, Harry, Diane Whitmore Schanzenbach, Greg J. Duncan, and Jens Ludwig. 2007. "The Economic Costs of Poverty in the United States: Subsequent Effects of Children Growing Up Poor." Paper prepared for the Poverty Task Force of the Center for American Progress. Washington (January 24).

Humlum, Maria Knoth. 2008. "Timing of Family Income, Borrowing Constraints, and Child Achievement." Working paper 2008-12. Aarhus, Denmark: University of Aarhus, Economics Department.

Jäntti, Markus, Bernt Bratsberg, Knut Røed, Oddbjørn Raaum, Robin Naylor, Eva Österbacka, Anders Björklund, and Tor Eriksson. 2006. "American Exceptionalism in a New Light: A Comparison of Intergenerational Earnings Mobility in the Nordic Countries, the United Kingdom, and the United States." Discussion paper 1938. Bonn, Germany: Institute for the Study of Labor (IZA).

Knudsen, Eric I., James J. Heckman, Judy L. Cameron, and Jack P. Shonkoff. 2006. "Economic, Neurobiological, and Behavioral Perspectives on Building America's Future Workforce." Proceedings of the National Academy of Sciences 103(27): 10155–62.

Lorentzen, Thomas, and Roy Nilsen. 2008. "Is Poverty Inherited? Long-Run Effects of Growing Up in Families That Receive Social Assistance Benefits." Fafo-rapport 2008(14).

Milligan, Kevin, and Mark Stabile. 2008. "Do Child Tax Benefits Affect the Well-being of Children? Evidence from Canadian Child Benefit Expansions." Working paper 14624. Cambridge, Mass.: National Bureau of Economic Research.

Nozick, Robert. 1974. Anarchy, State, Utopia. New York: Basic Books.

Panel Study on Income Dynamics. 2010. Panel Study on Income Dynamics, 1968–2006 [public-use dataset]. Produced and distributed by the Institute for Social Research, Survey Research Center, University of Michigan, Ann Arbor, Mich. Available at: http://psidonline.isr.umich.edu/ (accessed May 15, 2011).

Rege, Mari, Kjetil Telle, and Mark Votruba. Forthcoming. "Parental Job Loss and Children's School Performance." Review of Economic Studies.

Roemer, John E. 1998. Equality of Opportunity. Cambridge, Mass.: Harvard University Press.

———. 2004. "Equal Opportunity and Intergenerational Mobility: Going Beyond Intergenerational Income Transition Matrices." In Generational Income Mobility in North America and Europe, edited by Miles Corak. Cambridge: Cambridge University Press.

Schjølberg, Synnve, Ratib Lekhal, Mari Vaage Wang, Imac Maria Zambrana, Kristin S. Mathiesen, Per Magnus, and Christine Roth. 2008. "Forsinket Språkutvikling: En Foreløpig Oversikt Basert På Data fra Den Norske Mor Og Barn Undersøkelsen" ("Delayed Language Development: A Preliminary Overview Based on Data from the Norwegian Mother and Child Survey"). Report 2008:10. Oslo: Nasjonalt Folkehelseinstitutt.

Shonkoff, Jack, and Deborah A. Phillips, eds. 2000. From Neurons to Neighborhoods: The Science of Early Childhood Development. Washington, D.C.: National Academy Press.

Strand, Bjørn Heine, and Anton Kunst. 2007. "Childhood Socioeconomic Position and Cause-Specific Mortality in Early Adulthood." *American Journal of Epidemiology* 165(1): 85–93.

Swift, Adam. 2005. "Justice, Luck, and the Family." In *Unequal Chances: Family Background and Economic Success,* edited by Samuel Bowles, Herbert Gintis, and Melissa Osborne Groves. Princeton, N.J.: Princeton University Press.

Waters, Everett, and L. Alan Sroufe. 1983. "Social Competence as a Developmental Construct." *Developmental Review* 3(1): 79–97.

Yeung, W. Jean, Miriam Linver, and Jeanne Brooks-Gunn. 2002. "How Money Matters for Young Children's Development: Parental Investment and Family Processes." *Child Development* 73(6): 1861–79.

Ziol-Guest, Kathleen M., Greg J. Duncan, and Ariel Kalil. 2009. "Early Childhood Poverty and Adult Body Mass Index." *American Journal of Public Health* 99(3): 527–32.

PART III

EDUCATION

Chapter 8

Causal Effects of Parents' Education on Children's Education

JOHN ERMISCH AND CHIARA PRONZATO

T HE ASSOCIATION between the educational attainments of parents and those of their children has been one of the measures featured in the study of intergenerational mobility. It has been either the focus itself or part of the exploration of the reasons for earnings, income, or social class persistence—the opposite of mobility (see, for example, chapter 2, this volume). Parental education is, of course, just one aspect of family background that influences children's subsequent achievements as adults, but it is an important one. For instance, parents' educational attainments may have a large impact on their earnings, alter the productivity of their time investments in their children (such as reading to them), or affect their children's aspirations.

Another motivation for this study is the substantial rise in educational attainments across generations, with women's qualifications having increased more than men's in nearly all Organization for Economic Co-operation and Development (OECD) countries (Buchman and DiPrete 2006). An important question is whether an increase in parents' education increases the educational attainments of their children, with attendant impacts on their children's health, productivity, lifetime income, and life chances more generally. Because of the different trends by gender, we also would like to know whether the mother's education and the father's education have different causal impacts on their children's education.

In this study, we aim to estimate the causal impacts of parents' education. We focus on a comparison between the United States and Norway, although we compare Norway with some other countries to a more limited extent. Table 8.1, taken from a recent study (Hertz et al. 2007), puts the two countries in the context of other developed countries. It reports the average correlation (across nine to ten five-year birth cohorts) between the average

Table 8.1   Average Parent-Child Years of Education Correlation

Country	Correlation
Italy	0.54
United States	0.46
Switzerland	0.46
Ireland	0.46
Poland	0.43
Belgium (Flanders)	0.40
Sweden	0.40
Czech Republic	0.37
Netherlands	0.36
Norway	0.35
New Zealand	0.33
Finland	0.33
United Kingdom	0.31
Denmark	0.30

Source: Authors' adaptation of Hertz et al. (2007).
Note: Average of mother's and father's education, ages twenty to sixty-nine, surveyed 1994 to 2004.

of parents' years of education and those of their children.[1] With the Norwegian Registry (NR) data that we use in this chapter (described further later in the chapter), the corresponding correlation is 0.38.[2] The correlation for the United States is clearly much higher.

Such a correlation, or a corresponding coefficient from a regression of children's education against that of their parents, is unlikely to reflect solely a true causal effect of parents' education on their children's education.[3] For instance, if people's abilities affect their educational attainment and parents' and children's abilities are correlated, then the regression coefficient also reflects this correlation. Recent studies of the correlations in cognitive test results between parents and their children indicate substantial correlations, on the order of 0.4 (Anger and Heineck 2009; Björklund, Eriksson, and Jäntti 2010; Black, Devereux, and Salvanes 2008). Ability may reflect not only genes but also skills acquired during childhood. Aspects of the family environment that promote the acquisition of such skills may also be correlated with parents' educational attainments and their abilities, further undermining a causal interpretation of the intergenerational correlation.[4] The results of the twins analyses reported later in the chapter indicate that, at least for Norway, the United States, and Sweden, the correlations reported in table 8.1 overstate the causal impact of parents' education on children's education, and we suspect that this is also the case for other countries.

We use the theoretical framework provided here to structure empirical analyses that may allow us to identify the causal impact of mother's

Table 8.2   Sibling Correlations in Years of Education: Norway, 2001

	Correlation	N
Twins		
All	0.53	2,807
Pair of brothers	0.59	932
Pair of sisters	0.62	1,027
One brother, one sister	0.35	848
Siblings with at most five years' difference in age		
All	0.37	68,957
Pair of brothers	0.38	18,225
Pair of sisters	0.41	16,256
One brother, one sister	0.32	34,476
Siblings with nine to thirteen months' difference in age		
All	0.42	2,798
Pair of brothers	0.46	714
Pair of sisters	0.42	656
One brother, one sister	0.39	1,428

Source: Authors' calculations based on data from the Norwegian Registry (not publicly available).

and father's education on their children's education. Before doing that, however, it is helpful to put parents' education in the general context of family background.

Sibling Correlations

The correlation between siblings in some outcomes such as educational attainment is a broader measure of family background and community effects on that outcome than the parent-child correlation (Björklund, Eriksson, and Jäntti 2010; Björklund, Lindahl, and Lindquist 2010). The Norwegian Registry data described in detail later in the chapter allows us to compute correlations in years of education between siblings born in the years 1973 to 1978 (age twenty-three to twenty-eight in 2001, when we observe their educational attainment). Table 8.2 shows these correlations for twins, combining monozygotic (MZ) and dizygotic (DZ) twins, nontwin siblings, and siblings born close together (between nine and thirteen months' difference in age) and distinguishing between brothers and sisters.

Focusing on same-sex correlations, the correlations are about 0.6 for twins and 0.4 for nontwins, with the nontwin sibling correlation being slightly higher if the birth interval between siblings is small. How can we interpret these correlations? Let

$$E_{ij} = bE_{pj} + f_j + \varepsilon_{ij} \qquad (8.1)$$

where E_{pj} is the average of the two parents' education; f_j is a family/community effect assumed to be uncorrelated with E_{pj} and the individual effect ε_{ij}, and b is the intergenerational correlation coefficient. Measuring child and parent education in standard deviation units and taking the correlation between siblings, it follows directly from equation 8.1 that the sibling correlation indicates the fraction of the total variance in years of education that is attributable to shared family and community. Further, the relationship between the sibling correlation and the parent-child (intergenerational) correlation is as follows: sibling correlation = b^2 + other shared factors that are uncorrelated with parents' education. In the samples in the middle panel of table 8.2, the parent-child education correlation (using average parents' education) is 0.38, implying that only 0.14 (35 percent) of the 0.4 nontwin sibling correlation in education arises because of the educational attainment of their common parents. The rest is due to other common family and community factors.

A similar sibling correlation in years of education is obtained for a relatively small sample (229 families, 487 people) of British young people, born between 1972 and 1984 (born in 1979 on average) and observed when age twenty-two or older (the mean age was twenty-six), who can be matched to their brother or sister: the sibling correlation in this sample is 0.35.[5] The correlation between the average parental years of education and the child's years of education in this sample is 0.36, and so it accounts for 37 percent of the sibling correlation.[6]

In order to explore further how parents' education and other attributes reduce the variance attributed to family and community effects and the correlation between siblings, we estimate the parameters of a family random effects model.[7] More specifically, we generalize equation 8.1: years of education for individual i in family j (E_{ij}) is assumed to be given by

$$E_{ij} = X_{ij}\beta + f_j + \varepsilon_{ij} \qquad (8.2)$$

where X_{ij} is a set of individual (for example, age, sex) and family (for example, parents' education) variables, and f_j is a family/community effect assumed to be uncorrelated with X_{ij} and the individual effect ε_{ij}. We estimate the parameters β and the variances of the family/community and individual effects—the so-called between- and within-family variances—respectively. The sibling correlation net of covariates is the between-family variance divided by the sum of the between- and within-family variances. It indicates the importance of other shared family factors that are uncorrelated with the variables in X_{ij}.

Table 8.3   Decomposition of Family Variance

	Age Only	Age and Parents' Education Only	All Covariates
Sisters[a]			
Sibling correlation	0.397	0.286	0.256
Between-family variance	2.226	1.355	1.160
Percentage reduction in family variance relative to first column		39.1%	47.9%
Brothers[b]			
Sibling correlation	0.373	0.261	0.240
Between-family variance	1.871	1.111	0.996
Percentage reduction in variance relative to first column		40.6%	46.7%

Source: Authors' calculations based on data from the Norwegian Registry (not publicly available).
Notes: In addition to age, mother's and father's education, parental covariates are father's earnings, mother's earnings, mother's years of work, father's years of work, mother's transfer income, father's transfer income, number of children, and whether separated or not, all measured as of 1993 (that is, history variables are as of 1993).
[a] N of families = 27,736; N of children = 13,655.
[b] N of families = 31,166; N of children = 15,349.

The first row of table 8.3 shows the sibling correlation, and the second row shows the between-family variance net of covariates (that is, the variance of f_j). In the first column, we control only for the child's age (in X_{ij}); in the second we also control for parents' education, and in the third we control for a number of other parental attributes (measured in 1993) as well, including their incomes, work experience, family size, and whether or not they were separated. The third row shows the percentage reduction of between-family variance that occurs when we control the family covariates. Controlling for parents' education reduces the between-family variance by 40 percent, and adding the other covariates reduces it by an additional 6 to 9 percent. The sibling correlation also falls from about 0.4 to about 0.25. That is, about one-half of the between-family variance is attributable to factors that are common to brothers and sisters but not correlated with the parental attributes that we are able to measure from the Norwegian Registry data.

A similar exercise can be performed with the small British sample of siblings described earlier, but we can compare only the equivalent of the first two columns in table 8.3 (where we also control for gender in the first column). Adding parents' education to the regression reduces the sibling correlation from 0.36 to 0.24 and reduces the between-family variance by 43 percent (from 1.547 to 0.881). The similarities with the Norwegian results are striking. Again, parents' education is an important part of the shared family background of siblings, but far from the only important aspect of the shared environment.

We wish, however, to go beyond description of family background influences on educational attainments and estimate the causal impacts of mother's and father's education on their children's education. The following theoretical framework for structuring empirical analyses may allow us to identify these causal impacts.

The Theoretical Framework

Investments in children that affect their educational attainment require both parental time and money. Parents' time spent with their children transmits abilities, aspirations, and values that affect how well the children do in education, and there are many goods bought by parents—from early child care to home computers to direct tuition and private education—that affect the level of education children achieve. Parents' education affects the amount and productivity of these inputs. Our aim is to estimate the effect of a woman's (man's) education on her (his) children's education while controlling for her (his) partner's education. A reasonable interpretation of such an estimate is that the woman matches with a man with the same education despite her higher education, which would only occur if all women's education increased by the same amount. Thus, our analysis approximates the answer to the following thought-experiment and policy question: what would happen to the mean educational attainment of children if the educational attainments of all women (men) were increased for the same distribution of available partners? There are alternative questions—for example, how does an increase in a woman's education affect her child's education, inclusive of the effects on the person she marries?—but in light of a general increase in parents' education, we focus on the former question.

A Child's Education Equation

We follow Jere Behrman and Mark Rosenzweig (2002) and assume that a child's educational attainment depends linearly on the educational attainment of each parent (Ed_{mother} and Ed_{father}), plus some unobserved *pre-education* endowments. Although it is hard to be specific about the constituents of these endowments, thinking about them is important because they are likely to be correlated with parents' education. The first of these endowments is the *earnings* endowment of each parent ($Endow_{mother}$ and $Endow_{father}$), which affects their hourly earnings, and hourly earnings, in turn, have income, time allocation, and bargaining effects on their children's education, as described in the discussion of the effects of parents' education. It is because of these effects that we single out earnings endowments. As defined here, earnings endowments reflect genetic inheritance and pre-education environmental influences. We also assume that there is an endowment of the mother expressing her child-rearing skill ($ParSk_{mother}$) and a child-specific attribute (e^c):

$$Ed_{child} = \delta_1 Ed_{mother} + \delta_2 Ed_{father} + \Gamma_1 Endow_{mother}$$

$$+ \Gamma_2 Endow_{father} + ParkSK_{mother} + e^c \tag{8.3}$$

Such a reduced-form equation is consistent with many models of family resource allocation in which human capital investments in the next generation (or the fruits of them) are valued by parents. Although the father's skill in child-rearing could also appear in this equation, it is plausible that the mother's time is more important in child-rearing, and so we take that into account in this stark manner.

The coefficient on each parent's education measures the effect of his or her education net of the effects of his or her endowments, which are likely to be correlated with educational attainments. In the context of economic models of the family, the parental education coefficients should reflect three separate effects of a parent's education on the education of his or her child (see, for example, Ermisch 2003, 86–90). First, there is an *income effect*, which is positive because higher education increases the capacity to earn income in the market and more income is spent on everything that parents value. Second, there is a *substitution* or *time allocation effect*, which depends on the impact of a parent's education on the cost of human capital investment in his or her children. How costs vary with a parent's education depends on how much education increases the parent's earning capacity, how much of the parent's time is spent on child education–enhancing activities, and how much the parent's education increases the productivity of his or her time in such activities. A parent's marginal cost of investment could, for example, decrease with higher education because education enhances productivity sufficiently relative to the parent's earning capacity ("market productivity"), or there may be no effect on the marginal cost of a parent's education because that parent contributes little time to human capital investment in children. Third, there may be a *bargaining effect*; for example, if mothers value children's education more than fathers do and higher education increases her bargaining power, higher mother's education relative to the father's would increase children's education through this channel. In addition, an analysis of American parents' time use (Guryan, Hurst, and Kearney 2008) suggests that time spent with children is valued more by better-educated parents.[8] The coefficients associated with the parents' earnings endowments also reflect income, time allocation, and bargaining effects, but in addition they reflect the association between parents' endowments and their children's endowments—heritability.

Least squares estimation of the parameters of the child's education equation is unlikely to identify the effects of parents' education on children's because the parents' unobserved endowments are omitted from the regression. Their earnings endowments are likely to be correlated with their educational attainments, both because each parent's education is correlated with his or her own endowment and because each parent's endowment is correlated with that of the other parent and the other parent's education through matching in the marriage market.

Twin-Mothers

How might data on twin-mothers help address this problem? The assumption that we make to identify the effects of parents' education is that $ParSk_{mother}$ and $Endow_{mother}$ depend entirely on either genes or their common childhood environment, making them common to identical (MZ) twins. Then taking the difference between the offspring's education equations of identical twin sisters eliminates the sisters' endowments, leaving only differences in the twins' and their spouses' educational attainments and differences in their spouses' earnings endowments on the right-hand side of the equation. More formally, if Δ indicates a difference, the differenced children's (cousins') education equation is:

$$\Delta Ed_{child} = \delta_1 \Delta Ed_{mother} + \delta_2 \Delta Ed_{father} + \Gamma_2 \Delta Endow_{father} + \Delta e^c \quad (8.4)$$

But why do twins who are supposed to have identical values of $ParSk_{mother}$ and $Endow_{mother}$ end up with different levels of education? There are clearly other aspects of their individual experiences that influence their educational attainments. In order for estimation of the differenced equation to identify the effects of parents' education, these other aspects must not have a *direct* effect on the education of their children. That is another way of stating our identifying assumption.

Omission of the difference in the fathers' endowments ($\Delta Endow_{father}$) from the differenced equation could still cause a problem because it may be correlated with the difference in the twin-mothers' education and the difference in their spouses' education. For example, if fathers' endowments are positively correlated with their education, omission of the difference in fathers' endowments would tend to bias upward the estimated impact of fathers' education (δ_2). We need a measure of the difference in the spouses' earnings endowments.

Earning Capacity Equation

Assume that each person's observed earnings per hour (*Earnings*) depend on their educational attainment (*Ed*), their work experience (*Exper*), their *pre-education* earnings endowment (*Endow*), and luck, measurement error, and so on (*v*):

$$Earnings = \beta Ed + \beta_x Exper + Endow + v \quad (8.5)$$

From a sample of identical twins we can eliminate the earnings endowments by taking the difference between them, thereby obtaining estimates of the effects of education and work experience on earnings (β and β_x) that are not contaminated by correlation between a person's endowment and his or her education and work experience. With the estimates of β and β_x, we can obtain an estimate of the person's endowment plus the luck term, $Endow + v$. If v mainly reflects measurement error or earnings shocks, then we have an error-ridden measure of endowments, thereby imparting errors-in-variables bias to our estimates if true endowments and education are correlated. Alternatively, if v mainly reflects post-education persistent factors and people sort themselves into couples partly on the basis of v, then it is appropriate to control for $Endow + v$. Given the uncertainty about the correct assumption, we present estimates of the parameters of the differenced children's (cousins') education equation with and without the measure of $\Delta Endow_{father}$. In our empirical application, most of the twins have nine years of data, which are averaged, to estimate β and β_x. This makes it more likely that v reflects persistent factors.

Twin-Fathers

What can we learn from twin-fathers? If $Endow_{father}$ is the same for each twin,

$$\Delta Ed_{child} = \delta_1 \Delta Ed_{mother} + \delta_2 \Delta Ed_{father} + \Gamma_1 \Delta Endow_{mother}$$
$$+ \Delta ParSk_{mother} + \Delta e^c \tag{8.6}$$

Although we can use the same method to measure the difference in the mothers' earnings endowments as used for fathers, using differences between twin-fathers does not remove the impact of the mother's parenting skills from the picture, and if these are correlated with the mother's earnings endowment or the father's education, estimates of the effects of parents' education would be biased. Of course, the implication of a larger chance of omitted variable bias with twin-fathers is a consequence of our assumption that it is mainly the mother's parenting skills that are important. If the father's parenting skills also played an important role in shaping the child's educational attainments, then the estimates based on twin-mothers would suffer from a similar problem.

In general, if it is the case that the mother's child-rearing skills are more important than the father's, then the omission of the parenting skills endowment from the twin-difference education equations would have more of an impact on the estimates of the effects of parents' education based on twin-fathers than those based on twin-mothers. If the mother's parenting skills endowment is positively correlated with the education of the father through matching in the marriage market, then we expect that estimates of the effect of the father's education obtained from twin-fathers will be larger than those obtained from twin-mothers. Similarly, the estimated effect of the mother's education obtained from twin-fathers would also be larger than those obtained from twin-mothers if the mother's parenting skills endowment is correlated positively with her education. We do in fact find this pattern in our baseline results for both Norway and the United States.

The Norwegian Data

The foundation of the samples used in our empirical analysis is a register-based panel data set covering the entire resident population of Norway for the years 1993 to 2001. Information on household size and composition, as well as individual information such as place of residence, date of birth, educational attainment, and work status, is obtained from these data. Here twins are defined as people of the same sex, born in the same calendar year and month from the same parents. About half are likely to be MZ (identical) twins, while the other half are DZ (fraternal), who are the same in terms of inheritance of genes as other siblings and who differ from other siblings in being born on the same day. Both twin-parents and their children needed to be alive in 1993 to be observed in our data, and to be in our analytical samples both twins had to have at least one child over the age of twenty-two in 2001. Education levels are measured in 1993 for twins (parents) and in 2001 for their children. The levels of education are transformed into years of education according to the maximum level of education attained. The sample of twin-mothers consists of 2,914 children (older than age twenty-two) from 787 families, and the twin-father sample consists of 3,020 children from 790 families. Appendix table 8A.1 provides descriptive statistics comparing our twins' samples with the general population.

Baseline Results: Norway and the United States

All specifications of the twins' regressions include, in addition to the other parent's education, the gender and age of the child and whether or not the parents were living together in 1993.[9] Female children remain in education for about half a year longer, and parental separation tends to reduce the child's years of education in all estimated models. In each case, we compare two specifications: without and with an estimate of the other parent's earnings endowment estimated according to our theoretical framework.[10]

The results for Norway in the top panel of table 8.4 indicate similar effects of each parent's education using either twins' sample: the estimated effect of mother's education is never statistically different from father's education, either between the mothers' and fathers' twins-estimators or within each twin-type estimator. The corresponding ordinary least squares (OLS) estimates for mother's and father's education effects are 0.249 and 0.213, respectively, from the twin-mothers' sample and 0.220 and 0.218 from the twin-fathers' sample, neither being statistically different from the other. Using twin-fathers produces larger estimated effects for both parents' edu-

Table 8.4   Twins Estimates of Parents' Education on Child's Education

Method	Twin-Mothers		Twin-Fathers	
	No Endowment Control	Endowment Control	No Endowment Control	Endowment Control
Norwegian data[a]				
Mother's	0.104	0.101	0.157	0.156
education	(0.040)	(0.040)	(0.030)	(0.030)
Father's	0.118	0.119	0.159	0.157
education	(0.025)	(0.025)	(0.033)	(0.033)
U.S. data[b]				
Mother's	−0.274	−0.263	0.043	0.016
education	(0.145)	(0.145)	(0.139)	(0.145)
Father's	0.133	0.141	0.344	0.350
education	(0.071)	(0.072)	(0.162)	(0.162)

Source: For Norwegian data, Pronzato (2010); for U.S. data, Behrman and Rosenzweig (2002, tables 4 and 5).
Notes: All specifications include the gender and age of the child and an indicator of parents' not living together in 1993. Standard errors in parentheses.
[a] $N = 1{,}575$ twin-mothers, 1,582 twin-fathers.
[b] $N = 424$ twin-mothers, 244 twin-fathers.

cation than estimates based on twin-mothers, and with these estimates mother and father effects are nearly identical. The coefficient of the earnings endowment (not shown) is positive (and larger in the twin-fathers' estimate) but has only a small effect on the estimates of the effects of parents' education. We also tested whether effects of parental education differ by the sex of the child and found no evidence of significant differences using the twins' samples.[11]

The bottom panel of table 8.4 shows analogous estimates for U.S. twins from Behrman and Rosenzweig (2002), using a sample of MZ twins from the Minnesota Twin Register, with information obtained from a mail survey. Children of twins from both countries' samples were born around the same time—the early 1970s. The estimated effect of father's education from the U.S. sample is significantly larger than that of mother's education.[12] The effect of mother's education is estimated to be small, if not negative. These results are strikingly different from the Norwegian estimates, although the small U.S. samples, particularly for twin-fathers, produce fairly imprecise estimates of the effects, even when the estimates differ significantly from zero.

For both countries, the larger estimated impacts of both parents' education found with the twin-fathers' sample are consistent with the unobserved mother's parenting skills endowment being correlated positively with her education and her partner's education, as predicted in the discussion of our theoretical framework. This is because the twin-fathers' estimates do not difference-out her parenting skills endowment.

An issue that has not, to our knowledge, been raised with a twins- (or sibling-) difference strategy to identify effects is the fact that the cousin offspring are part of the same extended family.[13] To the extent that this generates similarities between cousins because of social influence within the extended family, offspring differences in education may be compressed, which may reduce the estimated impacts of parents' education.[14] Furthermore, sisters may interact more within the extended family than brothers, thereby reducing estimated parental education effects from the twin-mothers' sample relative to those using the twin-fathers' sample. If so, that may also account for the larger effects estimated from twin-fathers' samples.

Estimates for MZ twins from the Norwegian data can be obtained by using information on siblings, who are comparable in terms of shared genes to DZ twins. The average effect of the twin-parents' education for the mixture of MZ and DZ twins is $\delta_A = 0.5\delta_{MZ} + 0.5\delta_{DZ}$, because about half of the twins are identical. To make the sibling estimates as comparable as possible to DZ twins, we focus on same-sex siblings born between nine and thirteen months of one another—this sample provides our estimate of δ_{DZ}.[15] To illustrate, in the case of endowment controls, the shared-mother sibling estimate of the effect of mother's education is 0.136, and the shared-father sibling estimate of the effect of father's education is 0.124.[16] In conjunction with the corresponding twins' estimates in the top panel of table 8.4, these estimates imply that for Norwegian MZ twins the estimated effect of mother's education is 0.066 (standard error = 0.089) and the effect of father's education is 0.190 (standard error = 0.072). At first sight, these estimates for MZ twins appear to be more comparable to the U.S. estimates in the sense that the estimated effect of father's education is larger than that of mother's education and the latter is not statistically significantly different from zero. But the point estimate of the effect of father's education is smaller in Norway than in the United States, and the estimated effect of mother's education is larger than in the United States, and indeed, owing to their imprecision, the Norwegian estimated effects do not differ statistically between fathers and mothers.

To summarize, from table 8.4 it appears that in Norway each parent's education has a similar effect on their children's educational attainments, while in the United States it is only father's education that has an impact on the education of his offspring. The relatively low precision of the U.S. estimates makes it difficult, however, to come to strong conclusions—for instance, the twin-fathers' estimates of the effect of father's education for MZ twins do not differ significantly between the two countries despite a difference in the point estimate of 0.16 (the standard error of the difference is 0.18). There is some indication, however, from the MZ twins' point estimates that the effect of the mother's education may be smaller than that of the father's education, both in Norway and the United States. Furthermore, MZ twins' estimates for Sweden (Holmlund, Lindahl, and Plug 2008, 32) indicate a marginally significant positive effect of father's education (0.111; standard error = 0.063) using a twin-fathers' sample, but a virtually zero effect of mother's education (−0.014; standard error = 0.055) using a twin-mothers' sample.[17] Because of the imprecision of the estimates, the difference in parental effects is not statistically significant.

Behrman and Rosenzweig (2002) argue that mother's education may have had a smaller effect because a mother's time in the home is critical to the development of her children's skills that pay off in terms of educational attainments, and since better-educated mothers work more in paid employment, they spend less time at home with their children during childhood. We investigate this in the case of Norway in the next section.

The Impact of Mother's Employment History on Children's Education

First, using Norwegian twin-mothers, we find that an additional year of mother's education does indeed increase her work experience (as measured by her years of pension contributions as of 1993; mean = 14.6 years) by about six months (standard error = 1.4 months). The father's education has an insignificant negative effect on the mother's work experience.

To investigate whether or not the educational attainments of Norwegian children are sensitive to the time spent at home by their mothers, we use a different method—one that compares similar women rather than twins. We select a sample of mothers who had at least one child over the age of twenty-two in 2001, who have had their children with only one partner, and for whom we have data on pension points (related to the level of their earnings) in 1993. We form clusters of mothers, all of whom have the same level of education and age, the same number of children, the same age of oldest child, and the same level of education for the father. Thus, each cluster is homogeneous with respect to these variables. There are 34,365 such clusters, with an average of 13.2 women per cluster (454,943 observations in total). We then estimate a fixed-effects regression in which the average years of education of a woman's children (age over twenty-two) is the dependent variable, the cluster to which she belongs is a fixed effect, and the explanatory variables are the years she spent in employment (as measured by her pension contributions), her average pension points, the father's years in employment and his average pension points, whether the parents are separated, and the percentage of her children who are daughters. Thus, we use only *within-cluster variation* to estimate the effect of the explanatory variables; by construction, variation within a cluster in the

**Table 8.5   Fixed-Effects (by Cluster) Estimates of Impacts of Parents'
Employment Experience on the Average Years of
Children's Education**

	Parameter Estimate	Standard Error
Percentage daughters	0.349	0.007
Parents separated	−0.537	0.008
Mother's pension years	0.014	0.001
Mother's average pension points	0.043	0.004
Father's pension years	0.011	0.001
Father's average pension points	0.143	0.003
Constant	11.812	0.023

Source: Authors' calculations based on data from the Norwegian Registry (not publicly available).
Note: Cluster is defined so that all mothers in the cluster have the same level of education and age, the same number of children, the same age of oldest child, and the same level of education for the father.
N observations = 454,943; N clusters = 34,365

mother's experience in paid employment is not correlated with the variables that define the cluster. Data from 1997 on hours and wages indicate that pension points are significantly correlated with wages and hours and so represent a proxy for them.

Theoretically, an additional year in employment has potentially opposing impacts on children's education: it reduces parents' time spent at home with their children, but it increases family income (that is, less time inputs to children but more goods inputs). The results reported in table 8.5 indicate that more employment experience increases children's years of education, contrary to the hypothesis put forward by Behrman and Rosenzweig (2002) to explain the small effect of mother's education estimated with their data. It appears that the income effect dominates or that the actual reduction in time spent with children is small, with other nonmarket time being reduced in response to more employment time (as suggested by Guryan, Hurst, and Kearney 2008).

One way in which children of mothers who spent more time in paid employment have higher educational attainments is by doing better in school, thus increasing their chances of pursuing higher education. We have data on grades obtained by children at the end of lower secondary school for the 1986 cohort of children, who finished lower secondary school in 2002. For this group of children, we form clusters based on the same criteria as earlier and perform a fixed-effects regression that exploits within-cluster variation to estimate the impact of parents' years of employment on the child's grades. We focus on grades in three subjects, Norwegian, mathematics, and English, and results for math grades are reported in table 8.6.

The explanatory variables are the same as in table 8.5, with two exceptions: (1) because the unit of observation is the child, not the mother, per-

Table 8.6   **Fixed-Effects (by Cluster) Estimates of Impacts of Parents' Employment Experience on the Math Grade of Their Children at Age Sixteen**

	Parameter Estimate	Standard Error
Female	0.138	0.011
Parents separated	−0.255	0.016
Mother's pension years, up to age four of child	0.003	0.002
Mother's average pension points, up to age four of child	0.044	0.008
Father's pension years, up to age four of child	−0.001	0.002
Father's average pension points, up to age four of child	0.021	0.006
Mother's pension years, ages four to seven of child	0.018	0.007
Mother's average pension points, ages four to seven of child	−0.007	0.006
Father's pension years, ages four to seven of child	0.000	0.012
Father's average pension points, ages four to seven of child	0.023	0.005
Constant	3.151	0.035

Source: Authors' calculations based on data from the Norwegian Registry (not publicly available).
Note: Cluster is defined so that all children in the cluster have the same mother's level of education and age, the same number of siblings, the same age of oldest sibling, and the same level of education for the father.
N observations = 1, 057; N clusters = 5,886

centage of daughters is replaced by a dummy variable for being female; and (2) we split parents' work experience and average pension points into two segments of childhood: (a) up to the child's fourth birthday, and (b) the next three years of childhood (from the child's fourth to seventh birthdays). While the later segment refers precisely to a phase in the development of the child whose outcome is observed, the earlier segment summarizes the whole career of the parent, from its beginning to the fourth birthday of the child. Therefore, the effects of pension years and pension points may not seem easy to interpret since they depend on how mothers distribute their time at work between the years prior to the child-birth and the four years following it. However, by clustering for the age of the oldest child and the number of older children, the comparison is among women who are most likely experiencing a first career interruption at the same time (given by the same age of the oldest child) and the same number of interruptions due to maternity (given by the same number of older children). These two variables, used for the clustering, should help to compare women with potentially similar careers.

The results indicate that mother's employment experience up to age four of the child is not statistically significant, with the exception of English grades, for which it has a positive effect. Mother's work experience between the ages of four and seven of the child has a significant positive effect on grades in all three subjects. The pattern of coefficients for math grade results shown in table 8.6 is representative of the two other subjects.

These exercises strongly suggest that, at least in Norway, even if the effect of mother's education is smaller than that of the father's education, this is not because her greater employment experience reduces her child's performance in school or her child's years of completed education. Indeed, it appears to be an advantage to spend time in contexts other than that of the home. Of course, the conclusion may be different for the United States because of, for example, differences in child care arrangements for working mothers, which are likely to be more accessible, cheaper, and of better quality in Norway than the child care options on which a large section of the U.S. population must rely.

The analyses in tables 8.5 and 8.6 are also relevant to a policy change in Norway in August 1998. A cash-benefit is now offered to families with a child between one and three years old (maternity leave is one year) who make no or very limited use of state-subsidized child care facilities. The amount of the benefit is up to 400 euros a month, it is not taxable, and it is not tested against parents' income or labor market participation. Ghazala Naz (2004) finds that women, particularly highly educated women, did less paid work after the reform, while husbands' working hours did not change. Our results suggest that children are unlikely to benefit from the reform in terms of better educational outcomes, although there may of course be other benefits.

Heterogeneous Effects

Do the effects of parents' education differ according to their level of education? In addition to the intrinsic interest of this question, splitting the sample by parents' education level approximates two alternative ways of identifying the causal effects of parents' education: studying adopted children, and the consequences of a reform in the education system. The former exploits the lack of a genetic link between parents and adopted children, while the latter generates an exogenous change in educational attainment for some cohorts or regions, a common example being an increase in compulsory schooling age. Usually the parents who adopt are not representative of the population—they are on average older and better educated.[18] In contrast, reforms of compulsory schooling affect only education at the bottom of the distribution because that is where the reform produces the exogenous change in parents' education (for example, raising the minimum school-leaving age from fifteen to sixteen). A common finding in the adoption studies (see, for example, Björklund, Lindahl, and Plug 2006; Plug 2004) is that the effect of father's education is positive and statistically significant

Table 8.7   Twins' Estimates of Effects of Parents' Education on Child's Education, Norwegian Data, by Parents' Education Level

	Twin-Mothers		Twin-Fathers	
Method	Eleven or Fewer Years of Education	More Than Eleven Years of Education	Eleven or Fewer Years of Education	More Than Eleven Years of Education
Mother's education	0.121 (0.083)	0.102 (0.118)	0.192 (0.048)	0.180 (0.056)
Father's education	0.124 (0.031)	0.064 (0.076)	0.096 (0.099)	0.287 (0.079)
N children	2,187	270	1,529	602
N families	573	79	389	173

Source: Authors' adaptation of Pronzato (2010).
Notes: All specifications include the gender and age of the child and an indicator of parents not living together in 1993. Standard errors in parentheses.

while mother's education does not have a significant causal impact. In contrast, studies of reforms of compulsory schooling (for example, Black, Devereux, and Salvanes 2005) find a significant positive effect of mother's education, but a negligible effect of father's education.[19] This pattern is replicated in a study that uses both of these ways of identifying causal effects with the same source of Swedish register data (Holmlund, Lindahl, and Plug 2008). The larger effect of father's education for those with higher levels of education may reflect more father-child interaction among higher-educated fathers, in both intact and separated-parent families. Here we exploit the data on Norwegian twins to estimate the effects of parents' education for two groups: one in which both parents have eleven or fewer years of education, and one in which both have more than eleven years of education. The results are shown in table 8.7.

From the twin-fathers' samples, the pattern from previous studies is replicated in the following sense: in the low-education sample, mother's education has a relatively large and statistically significant effect, in contrast to father's education, while in the high-education sample, the effect of father's education is larger than that of mother's, although both are statistically significant. The patterns are less consistent with previous studies when using the twin-mothers' samples, from which it appears that each parent's education has similar effects, if any. From this evidence, it is difficult to come to clear conclusions about which part of the parental education distribution has larger effects, if any.

Another aspect of heterogeneity is different effects of parental education for daughters and sons. Claudia Buchman and Thomas DiPrete's (2006) analysis suggests that this could be important, and gender-specific effects may differ according to the level of the parent's education. Because of relatively small sample sizes, it is difficult to investigate this issue with samples of twins. To explore the issue further, we use large samples of parent-siblings born thirteen to sixty months apart. We opt to trade some bias for much better precision. Compared to the Norwegian twins' estimates in table 8.4, the estimated impacts of mother's education are slightly larger. For example, for the specifications with endowment control, the effects of mother's and father's education from the sister-mothers' estimates are 0.126 and 0.162, respectively (compared with 0.096 and 0.124 from the mother-twins' estimates); from the brother-fathers' estimates, the corresponding estimates are 0.192 and 0.132, respectively (compared with 0.161 and 0.158 in table 8.4). The likely direction of bias from using siblings rather than twins is less clear for the impact of father's education because the brother-fathers' estimate for the effect of father's education is actually smaller than the corresponding twins' estimate.

Table 8.8 shows that using the full sample of sister-mothers, an additional year of mother's education raises a son's education by 0.096 years, but raises a daughter's education by 0.159 years. An additional year of father's education raises his offspring's education by 0.162 years, irrespective of the gender of the child. Estimates using brother-fathers show a similar pattern by gender of the child, with the effects of mother's education being generally higher and those of father's education being lower than estimated from sisters.

The gender pattern is repeated when focusing on samples in which both parents have eleven years of education or less. A Danish study (Bingley, Jensen, and Romani 2009, table 8.2), using a schooling reform that mainly affects less-educated parents, comes to different conclusions: the effect on sons' education is larger than for daughters irrespective of the gender of the parent. Also, a similar Norwegian study (Black, Devereux, and Salvanes 2005), using a reform in compulsory schooling, finds only a significant positive effect of mother's education on son's education (in the low-education [less than ten years] sample). For better-educated parents in our study, the gender pattern is less clear because the results differ between the sisters' and brothers' samples. For the former, father's education has a much larger effect than that of the mother, and the father's education has larger effects for sons than daughters. With the sample of brother-fathers, the effect of mother's education is larger than that of father's education, and the mother's effect is even larger for daughters.

It appears, then, that the differential effect of mother's education always favors daughters, while the gender interaction with father's education is less clear in direction and often statistically insignificant, even with our large samples. Although mothers may favor girls over boys in their child investments—say, through more interaction with them—the larger effect of their education on daughters also suggests that another mechanism is behind this effect: in short, the effect of mothers on their daughters' aspirations and motivation may be a "role model" effect.

Table 8.8   Siblings' Estimates of Effects of Parents' Education on Child's Education, Norwegian Data

	Overall	Eleven or Fewer Years of Education	More Than Eleven Years of Education
Sisters born thirteen to sixty months apart			
Mother's education	0.096	0.113	0.046
	(0.007)	(0.015)	(0.025)
Mother's education × daughter	0.063	0.115	0.045
	(0.008)	(0.017)	(0.030)
Father's education	0.162	0.162	0.170
	(0.006)	(0.007)	(0.016)
Father's education × daughter	−0.005	0.016	−0.055
	(0.007)	(0.009)	(0.019)
N families	29,029	18,679	2,677
N children	101,396	72,753	8,922
Brothers born thirteen to sixty months apart			
Mother's education	0.162	0.173	0.157
	(0.006)	(0.009)	(0.012)
Mother's education × daughter	0.064	0.094	0.030
	(0.007)	(0.012)	(0.015)
Father's education	0.133	0.159	0.121
	(0.006)	(0.016)	(0.014)
Father's education × daughter	−0.007	0.029	−0.025
	(0.006)	(0.018)	(0.016)
N families	30,491,	14,566	5,840
N children	121,413	62,025	20,728

Source: Authors' calculations based on data from the Norwegian Registry (not publicly available).
Notes: All specifications include the gender and age of the child, an indicator of parents' not living together in 1993 and the earnings endowment of partner. Standard errors in parentheses.

Conclusions

We have shown that parents' education is an important, but hardly exclusive, part of the common family background that generates positive correlation between the educational attainments of siblings from the same family. But the correlation between the educational attainments of parents and those of their children overstates considerably the causal effect of parents' education on the education of their children. Our estimates based on Norwegian twin-mothers indicate that an additional year of either mother's or father's education increases their children's education by as little as about one-tenth of a year (the twins' estimates may be downward-biased). Although estimates of the effects based on twin-fathers are about 50 percent higher for both parents, we have reason to believe that these estimates are biased upward. There is some evidence that the mother's effect is larger among less-educated parents, while the father's effect is larger among better-educated parents. We also find that the effect of mother's education is larger for daughters than for sons.

Comparing indirect estimates for monozygotic twins in Norway and Sweden with identical twins' estimates from the United States, it appears that father's education has a larger effect than that of mother's education in all three countries, but the parental effects differ significantly only in the U.S. analysis. One explanation for a smaller maternal effect is that better-educated mothers work more in paid employment and spend less time interacting with their children. We test this hypothesis for Norway using a matching estimator and find no evidence to support it; indeed, children of otherwise identical mothers (on a number of criteria, including both parents' education) who worked more in paid employment complete *more* years of education. Of course, the relationship may differ in the United States, say, because child care arrangements are generally not as cheap or high-quality as in Norway. Also, in light of the imprecision of our point estimates for the United States, it may be that the difference in parental effects is not really that much larger in the United States than in Norway or Sweden.

Comparison of the twins' estimates with conventional regression estimates for Norway suggests that about half of the correlation between parent and child education reflects the correlation of activities and attitudes of parents that improve their children's educational achievements with the parents' own education rather than a causal impact. In recent research, one of the authors (Ermisch 2008) tries to quantify the impact of educational activities and parenting style on a child's preschool development. Ermisch suggests that even though these parental inputs to child development have significant effects on child development and are strongly correlated with parents' education, a large part of the differences in early cognitive and behavioral development by parents' education or income group remains unaccounted for by these inputs. Thus, there remains much to discover about the aspects of "what parents do" that enhance their children's educational attainments and how these aspects are correlated with the parents' education.

We are grateful to Taryn Galloway for valuable advice on the Norwegian education system and use of the registry data; to Tom DiPrete, Anders Björklund, and the editors for comments on early versions of this chapter; and to the Economic and Social Research Council, the European Research Council, and the European Centre for Analysis in the Social Sciences for financial support for this research.

Appendix

Table 8A.1   **Descriptive Statistics on Norwegian Parents and Children (Twins and Overall Population)**

	Mothers		Fathers	
	Twins	Population	Twins	Population
Parent's level				
Age (1993)	44.3	47.1	47.5	50.8
	(6.1)	(8.6)	(6.9)	(9.4)
Number of siblings (1993)	3.45	3.72	3.42	3.89
	(3.42)	(4.99)	(3.87)	(5.37)
Years of schooling (1993)	10.9	11.2	11.5	11.6
	(2.1)	(2.2)	(2.6)	(2.6)
Earnings (1993) (in euros)	13,342	12,382	23,216	20,423
	(10,287)	(10,312)	(17,750)	(19,381)
Transfers (1993) (in euros)	3,067	3,210	2,281	3,437
	(4,329)	(4,275)	(4,900)	(6,025)
Self-employed (1993)	0.103	0.097	0.224	0.260
Number of children (1993)	2.45	2.42	2.44	2.51
	(0.94)	(1.02)	(0.94)	(1.07)
N parents	1,575	278,390	1,582	303,703
Child's level				
Age (2001)	27.0	29.4	27.8	29.7
	(7.0)	(8.8)	(7.2)	(9.3)
Years of schooling (2001)	12.9	12.9	12.9	12.9
	(2.4)	(2.4)	(2.4)	(2.4)
Other parent's schooling	11.6	11.5	11.1	11.0
(1993)	(2.6)	(2.6)	(2.2)	(2.2)
Divorce (1993)	0.205	0.176	0.187	0.159
Earnings (2001) (in euros)	25,111	25,540	25,488	25,740
	(17,999)	(19,289)	(17,571)	(19,360)
Transfers (2001) (in euros)	3,235	3,393	3,177	3,365
	(5,520)	(5,673)	(5,339)	(5,655)
Self-employed (2001)	0.076	0.097	0.083	0.105
N children	3,857	674,507	3,853	764,256
N children over twenty-two	2,914	545,523	3,020	618,550

Source: Authors' adaptation of Pronzato (2010).
Notes: Average values with standard deviations in parentheses; "self-employed" is a dummy variable indicating whether part of the income is from self-employment work; "number of children" comprises children of any age; "age" at the child's level is measured for all children, whereas the other variables at the child's level are summarized only for children over age twenty-two.

Notes

1. On average, Tom Hertz and his colleagues (2007) find no trend in these correlations over the birth cohorts of 1930 to 1985, although for the United States and the United Kingdom there is evidence of a modest upward trend for more recent cohorts. In broad terms, however, the average should be comparable to the birth cohorts represented in this study.

2. That correlation is calculated from a sample of people born in the years 1973 to 1978 with at least one sibling, corresponding to the sample used in the middle panel of table 8.2 and the bottom panel of table 8.3. The parents' education was measured in 1993. The correlations with the mother's and father's education are virtually the same.

3. Recall that the correlation coefficient is the product of the regression coefficient and the ratio of the standard deviation in parents' years of education to the standard deviation in children's years of education.

4. For instance, John Ermisch (2009) shows that better-educated mothers tend to score higher on educational activities and to have better child-mother interactions with their young children. Such behavior is associated with better cognitive development during the preschool years. Supportive behavior toward older children is also more evident among better-educated mothers, and this behavior is associated with better educational attainments for their children.

5. These are respondents in the British Household Panel Survey (BHPS) who can be matched to their parents because we observed them living together at least once during the survey from 1991 to 2006.

6. The parent-child correlation is lower—0.26 for children age twenty-two and older—when we do not confine the sample to matched siblings.

7. This exercise is inspired by the one undertaken by Björklund, Lindahl, and Lindquist (2010) to account for the sibling correlation in income.

8. Positive education gradients in time spent with children contrast with negative ones for typical leisure and home production activities, thereby suggesting this "different preferences" interpretation.

9. The regressions take the form $E_{ij} = X_{ij}\beta + f_j + \varepsilon_{ij}$, where f_j is now a fixed effect that may be correlated with the variables in X_{ij}. We use the usual fixed-effects estimation procedure, which eliminates f_j by subtracting the within-family mean of each variable from that variable.

10. Ideally, the earnings variable in the twins' earning capacity regressions should be hourly earnings, but the register data do not contain hours; the estimate of the endowment is based on average annual earnings, using nine years to compute the averages in most cases.

11. In a much larger sample of all same-sex siblings, mother's education has a larger effect on daughters than on sons, but the effect of father's education is the same irrespective of the child's sex.

12. The corresponding OLS estimates for mother's and father's education effects are 0.137 and 0.286, respectively, from the twin-mothers' sample and 0.254

and 0.325 from the twin-fathers' sample, the difference in parental effects being statistically different in the twin-mothers' sample.

13. We are grateful to Tom DiPrete for pointing out this possibility.
14. As is well known, measurement errors in parents' education also operate to reduce the estimated impact, particularly in fixed-effects estimation.
15. In fact, the effects of mother's and father's education estimated from samples of siblings change very little when the birth interval between siblings is widened; see Pronzato (2010).
16. Neither of these estimates is significantly different from the estimate from the corresponding twins-estimator. In the mother-sibling estimates, the estimated effect of the father's education (standard error in parentheses) is 0.136 (0.027), and the estimated effect of the mother's education from the father-sibling estimator is 0.187 (0.031).
17. These estimates are based on samples of 5,886 children of twin-mothers and 4,061 children of twin-fathers selected from Swedish register data from among parents born between 1945 and 1955. The estimates control for estimates of the other parent's education in each sample (not presented here). These Swedish estimates of parents' education effects based on pooled MZ and DZ twins are not significantly different from the corresponding estimates in table 8.4 for Norway.
18. Also, children are not randomly assigned—adoption authorities may try to match children to adoptive couples who are similar to their natural parents.
19. But Paul Bingley, Vibeke Jensen, and Annette Romani (2009) find positive and nearly equal effects of mother's and father's education on children's education (0.114 and 0.123, respectively, and not significantly different from one another), using a 1958 reform in Denmark that affects children in the eighth and ninth grades. Thus, their estimated effects of parents' education are very similar to our overall Norwegian estimates based on twins (table 8.4), in both their size and the absence of a significant difference between the parents.

References

Anger, Silke, and Guido Heineck. 2009. "Do Smart Parents Raise Smart Children? The Intergenerational Transmission of Cognitive Abilities." Socio-Economic Panel (SOEP) paper no. 156. Berlin: German Institute for Economic Research (DIW Berlin).

Behrman, Jere R., and Mark R. Rosenzweig. 2002. "Does Increasing Women's Schooling Raise the Schooling of the Next Generation?" *American Economic Review* 92(1): 323–34.

Bingley, Paul, Vibeke Myrup Jensen, and Annette Quinto Romani. 2009. "Intergenerational Transmission of Human Capital: Reform-Based Evidence from Denmark." Paper presented to the annual conference of the European Society for Population Economics. Seville (June 12).

Björklund, Anders, Karin Hederos Eriksson, and Marcus Jäntti. 2010. "IQ and Family Background: Are Associations Strong or Weak?" *B.E. Journal of Economic Analysis and Policy* 10(1, Contributions): article 2.

Björklund, Anders, Lena Lindahl, and Matthew J. Lindquist. 2010. "What More Than Parental Income? An Exploration of What Swedish Siblings Get from Their Parents." *B.E. Journal of Economic Analysis and Policy* 10(1, Contributions): article 102.

Björklund, Anders, Mikael Lindahl, and Erik Plug. 2006. "The Origins of Intergenerational Associations: Lessons from Swedish Adoption Data." *Quarterly Journal of Economics* 121(3): 999–1028.

Black, Sandra E., Paul J. Devereux, and Kjell G. Salvanes. 2005. "Why the Apple Doesn't Fall Far: Understanding Intergenerational Transmission of Human Capital." *American Economic Review* 95(1): 437–49.

———. 2008. "Like Father, Like Son? A Note on the Intergenerational Transmission of IQ Scores." Discussion paper no. 3651. Bonn, Germany: Institute for the Study of Labor (IZA).

Buchman, Claudia, and Thomas A. DiPrete. 2006. "The Growing Female Advantage in College Completion: The Role of Family Background and Academic Achievement." *American Sociological Review* 71(4): 515–41.

Ermisch, John. 2003. *An Economic Analysis of the Family*. Princeton, N.J.: Princeton University Press.

———. 2008. "Origins of Social Immobility and Inequality: Parenting and Early Child Development." *National Institute Economic Review* 205(1): 62–71.

———. 2009. "Young Child-Parent Relationships." In *Changing Relationships*, edited by Malcolm Brynin and John Ermisch. New York: Routledge.

Guryan, Jonathan, Erik Hurst, and Melissa Kearney. 2008. "Parental Education and Parental Time with Children." *Journal of Economic Perspectives* 22(3): 23–46.

Hertz, Tom, Tamara Jayasundera, Patrizio Piraino, Sibel Selcuk, Nicole Smith, and Alina Veraschchagina. 2007. "The Inheritance of Educational Inequality: International Comparisons and Fifty-Year Trends." *B.E. Journal of Economic Analysis and Policy* 7(2, Advances): article 10.

Holmlund, Helena, Mikael Lindahl, and Erik Plug. 2008. "Estimating the Intergenerational Schooling Effect: A Comparison of Methods." Discussion paper 3630. Bonn, Germany: Institute for the Study of Labor (IZA).

Naz, Ghazala. 2004. "The Impact of Cash-Benefit Reform on Parents' Labor Force Participation." *Journal of Population Economics* 17(2): 369–83.

Plug, Erik. 2004. "Estimating the Effect of Mother's Schooling on Children's Education Using a Sample of Adoptees." *American Economic Review* 94(1): 358–68.

Pronzato, Chiara. 2010. "An Examination of Paternal and Maternal Intergenerational Transmission of Schooling." *Journal of Population Economics*. Available at: doi: 10.1007/s00148-010-0311-2.

Chapter 9

Children's Cognitive Ability and Parents' Education: Distinguishing the Impact of Mothers and Fathers

JOHN JERRIM AND JOHN MICKLEWRIGHT

D ISCUSSION OF transmission of socioeconomic status from parents to children needs to consider gender differences in both generations. Parents pass on a measure of their advantage or disadvantage to their children, and it is clearly of interest whether fathers pass on more than mothers, and whether it is sons or daughters who gain or lose more from the transmission. A number of authors have produced important insights into the different strengths of the gender-specific parent-child links. Their studies have been motivated in particular by the desire to distinguish the role of mothers. Notable examples include Jere Behrman (1997) from economics and Sylvia Korupp, Harry Ganzeboom, and Tanja van der Lippe (2002) from sociology. Our main value added is to show how these links differ across a large pool of rich industrialized nations, using a data source that is specifically intended to allow cross-country comparison. We investigate whether there are common patterns across countries and whether some countries are outliers to these patterns.

The child outcome that we consider is an educational one, reflecting the role accorded to education in explaining intergenerational mobility in income by economists and in social class by sociologists (Blanden, Gregg, and Macmillan 2007; Erickson and Goldthorpe 2002). We analyze children's cognitive ability as recorded in standardized tests of math, science, and reading skills at age fifteen. We relate this analysis to the years of education of mothers and of fathers. We use data for thirty countries from the 2003 round of the Programme for International Student Assessment (PISA), coordinated by the Organization for Economic Co-operation and Development (OECD).

Before describing our data and presenting our results, we begin by discussing the impact of parental education on children's learning, consider why the links might vary with gender in either generation, and review some existing empirical evidence.

Motivation and Literature

It is well known that children's educational outcomes vary sharply with their parents' socioeconomic background. Differences in outcomes with parental background emerge early at the preschool level and are reinforced in childhood and the teenage years through to tertiary education. There is plenty of evidence for different countries, and summaries can be found in OECD (2008) and Stephen Machin (2009).

Child outcomes can be usefully conceptualized within the simple framework proposed by Robert Haveman and Barbara Wolfe (1995), who drew on Arleen Leibowitz (1974). This framework has three outcome variables—ability, final schooling level, and adult income. These outcomes are linked in a recursive structure: ability helps determine final schooling level, and both help determine income in adulthood. In this chapter, we are concerned just with ability, as measured by test scores toward the end of compulsory schooling at age fifteen. Ability, within the Haveman and Wolfe framework, has two proximate determinants: home investments, represented by the quantity and quality of time and goods inputs in the child, and heredity (see figure 9.1, which also shows the determinants of final schooling level). Home investments are in turn determined by parents' education and abilities, both directly and indirectly through family income. Parents' abilities are passed on in part through genetic inheritance.

Within this framework, the correlation of children's ability and parents' education reflects a number of factors: a direct effect through home investment, discussed later; an indirect effect through family income; and assuming parental education and ability are correlated, the impact of that ability coming through both home investments and genetic inheritance.[1]

The framework also serves as a reminder that the total correlation of parental education with the child's education is not revealed in an analysis of children's ability alone. The child's final schooling level is a function of home investments and family income as well as his or her ability, and hence it reflects additional impacts through those pathways from parental education. We illustrate this using data for the United States drawn from the National Educational Longitudinal Survey (NELS) cohort. We regress completed years of the child's education on years of father's and mother's education. We then add to the equation variables measuring child test scores for math, science, and reading skills at age fourteen. The estimated coefficients for parental education are reduced by only one-third, illus-

Figure 9.1   The Determination of Children's Ability and Final Schooling Levels

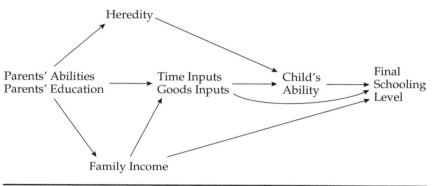

Source: Authors' adaptation of Haveman and Wolfe (1995, figure 1).

trating that a substantial part of the association of final schooling with parental education does not come through the child's ability in the early teenage years.[2]

How might the impact of mother's and father's education differ within this framework? Much of the interest to date in distinguishing the separate contributions of each parent to intergenerational transmission of socioeconomic status has been motivated by a desire to give due recognition to the role of women (see, for example, Behrman 1997; Beller 2009; Johnston, Ganzeboom, and Treiman 2005; Korupp, Ganzeboom, and van der Lippe 2002). More-educated mothers, it is argued, are more likely than fathers with the same level of education to make higher investments in the production function of their children's cognitive achievement, in terms of quantity and quality of both time and goods. The more educated the mother, the more efficient her use of the time she spends with her child. Education may also increase women's bargaining power within the household, giving them more control over family income—again increasing home investments in the child. And the impact of each parent may differ for sons and daughters, it is reasoned, owing to differences in aspirations and expectations. A well-educated mother may act as a stronger role model for her daughters than for her sons, for example. Finally, the importance to children of each parent may vary over their childhood. If the mother's schooling has a greater association than the father's with the ability scores of their high school–age children, this could reflect the particular advantage to those children (if that is the case) of having a more-educated mother in their early childhood—for example, in the time she spent reading to them, the books in the home, the use made of preschool, or the choice of elementary school.[3]

The relative importance of fathers and mothers could be similar across countries. To continue with the example of early childhood, any special significance of educated mothers at this age may hold across different cultures and institutions. Or there may be differences, associated, for example, with variation across countries in the position of women in society. Part of any differences in the importance of each parent is played out in outcome variables that are not the concern of this chapter—final schooling level and adult income in the Haveman and Wolfe (1995) framework, including in the case of income through occupational choice.

Most existing evidence relates to the child's final level of schooling rather than the child's ability during high school. The child's years of education are regressed on years of education of the mother and years of the father's education and, typically, some variables chosen to control for other factors. Ideally, evidence would exhibit the following features, although this ideal is rarely found:

1. Results shown without any control variables as well as with them
2. Allowance for the impact of unobserved parental ability
3. Recognition of the distinction between natural, step-, and single parents
4. Education entered flexibly as levels achieved rather than just as years
5. Models estimated separately for boys and girls
6. Large sample size

Results with no controls (1) allow the full association of children's and parents' education to be revealed, including indirect as well as direct channels—for example, through family income. This is the approach we take in our analysis. Moreover, comparing different studies, we see that there is often a "distressingly small overlap in the explanatory variables included in the models" (Haveman and Wolfe 1995, 1855), and this makes comparisons of results that include controls (which also vary in definition) difficult. Results without controls reflect the correlation of parental education with unobserved ability unless the latter is controlled for in some way (2), which usually it is not. Many children do not live with both of their natural parents (3). The education of a "parent figure" that is reported during high school may not correspond to the education of a parent present during early childhood. Inherited ability is only proxied by parental education for natural parents. The specification of education, whether of parents or children, as a continuous variable measured in years risks hiding nonlinearities (4). Interest in gender differences sometimes extends only to the parents without allowing for differences in the children's generation (5). Large sample sizes (6) increase the chance of identifying gender differences among both parents and children and differences between natural, step-, and single parents.

Haveman and Wolfe (1995, 1855) conclude from their survey of the U.S. evidence that "the human capital of the mother is usually more closely related to the [educational] attainment of the child than is that of the father." Behrman (1997) takes a more detailed look at this question, focusing on studies from the United States and a range of developing countries, where a priori the importance of mother's education is expected to be greater. He also finds that mother's education tends to be somewhat more important than father's education, but emphasizes that the margin is not as large as suggested by what he sees as conventional wisdom and that there is a considerable degree of variation across studies. Mother-daughter associations in general appear to be stronger than those for mothers and sons. Likewise, the father-son links appear stronger on average than the father-daughter links, but Behrman concludes that the pattern here is less clear. He also notes that the evidence is more wide-spread for children's schooling level than for cognitive ability, the focus of this chapter.

Recent contributions to the literature provide some evidence for rich industrialized countries other than the United States—for example, Jennifer Baxter (2002) for Australia, Guido Heineck and Regina Riphahn (2007) for Germany, John Ermisch and Marco Francesconi (2001) for the United Kingdom, and Anders Björkland, Markus Jäntti, and Gary Solon (2007) for Sweden.[4] All of these authors focus on the child's final schooling level, whether measured in years of education, measured in categories, or prox-ied by qualifications obtained. They all include results that either have no controls or control only for immigrant status (either by including indica-tors of this or by selecting natives only) and number of siblings (which may already reflect some of the impact of parental education, since more-educated women tend to have fewer children). Data sets often combine cohorts from a wide range of years. Heineck and Riphahn (2007, 17) con-clude that "maternal education has weaker effects for sons' than for daugh-ters' outcomes." Baxter's (2002) results defy easy summary given the flexibility in the way both children's and parents' levels of education are entered in her models, but they appear to show father's education having a greater association with sons than does mother's education, while the reverse is true for daughters. Ermisch and Francesconi (2001, table A1) cannot reject the hypothesis of no differences by gender within either generation in the United Kingdom, but with a different U.K. data set, Lorraine Dearden, Stephen Machin, and Howard Reed (1997, 57) find the same pattern that Baxter does for Australia—"Father's education is more important for sons, mother's education is more important for daugh-ters"—although the differences are not strongly significant.

The analysis of Sweden by Björkland, Jäntti, and Solon (2007) is notable for satisfying most of the features of an ideal study listed ear-lier. A large sample of some sixty-five thousand individuals provides a realistic opportunity to analyze separately different combinations of natural parent and stepparent—for example, natural mother and stepfather, or stepmother and natural father. It even yields over one thousand children with adoptive parents. This in turn permits conclusions about the impact of unobserved parental ability transmitted through genetic inheritance, because a striking feature of the data is that a child can be linked to a natural parent even when he or she is not the rearing parent. Among children raised by both natural parents, the results show father-son links to be some 30 percent larger than father-daughter links ($t = 6.9$), but reveal no statistical difference in mother-son and mother-daughter links ($t = 0.84$).[5]

The background for our own analysis is therefore one of rather mixed evidence that is more abundant for the United States than for other countries and focused on schooling levels rather than ability.

Data

The Programme for International Student Assessment (PISA) is a study of fifteen-year-olds' cognitive ability. Data are collected every three years. We use the 2003 data and analyze all OECD countries except Mexico and Japan.[6] In each country, a minimum of 150 schools are included in the sample, selected with probability proportional to size. Students are then randomly selected from within these schools. Average response rates of both schools and pupils are high (90 percent in both cases), although this varies moderately between countries.[7] The achieved sample size in 2003 across the countries we consider was 189,404 observations.

In 2003, PISA tested children's ability in one "major" (math) and two "minor" (reading and science) domains.[8] We focus in particular on the results for math. However, mothers and fathers may have different roles in developing their children's cognitive ability in each of the three subjects. Recall the framework given in figure 9.1. For example, if mothers spend more time reading to their children than fathers do, maternal education might be more important for the development of children's reading skills. Likewise, if fathers spend more time helping children with math, paternal education may be particularly associated with scores in this subject. We therefore often provide results for all three domains.

Children's answers to the PISA test questions were summarized by the survey organizers into a score for each of the three domains, using an item-response model. The intuition is that true ability in each subject is unobserved and must be estimated from the answers to the test. The item-response model is used to generate five "plausible values" for ability in each subject for each individual, each value estimating the individual's true proficiency in the subject concerned and being equally plausible. These scores were scaled by the survey organizers to have a mean (across all participating PISA countries) of five hundred points and standard deviation of one hundred. We follow the organizers' recommended use of the data by running our regression models for each plausible value and then averaging the estimated coefficients and standard errors. We also use the survey weights.

Children were asked two questions about their parents' education: what level they completed at school, and what type of tertiary qualifications they held. Responses were recorded into International Standard Classification of Education (ISCED) levels. Although these are designed to be internationally comparable, variation in definitions across countries may remain (Steedman and McIntosh 2001). We convert ISCED levels into years of education, using country-specific conversion coefficients provided by the PISA organizers (OECD 2004, 308). We have already noted that parental education may have a nonlinear influence on children's ability. However, we have chosen to use years of education for its simplicity in interpretation and ease in presentation of results across a number of countries.

We drop children who are first- or second-generation immigrants. Their parents' education cannot necessarily be interpreted in the same way as that of parents of native children. This reduces the sample size by over one-fifth. The reduction is particularly prominent in New Zealand, Australia, Luxembourg, and Switzerland, where over 40 percent of observations are dropped. We also exclude children not living with both their natural mother and natural father, since in this case it is unclear to whom the information collected on parental education refers.[9] For children living with their natural parents, we can be reasonably certain that the association of parental education and children's ability reflects all the various pathways described in figure 9.1, including genetic inheritance. Again, there is a large reduction in the sample size, especially in the United States and, perhaps surprisingly, in Turkey; an additional 40 percent of children are excluded from the analysis. A further 2 percent of observations are excluded where information is missing for both mother's and father's education. In seven out of thirty countries (Australia, New Zealand, England, Scotland, the United States, Luxembourg, and Switzerland), half the original sample has been excluded following these selection criteria. The overall sample size has been reduced by over 40 percent, to 106,873 observations.

Table 9.1 shows a moderate association between mother's and father's years of education. The correlation coefficient is between 0.4 and 0.6 for most countries. Mother's education and father's education are reported as the same for typically about half the sample in each country. This association is not surprising given the degree of assortative mating—individuals selecting partners with similar characteristics (for a survey of the literature, see Blossfeld 2009.) Yet, although the correlation between mother's and father's education is strong, it is not so large as to prevent us from trying to identify their separate associations with children's cognitive ability.

Table 9.1   Mother's and Father's Years of Education

Country	Label	Sample Size	Correlation Between Mother's and Father's Values	Mother's Education = Father's Education	One Parent's Education Is Missing
Iceland	ISL	2,108	0.36	42%	1%
England	ENG	1,891	0.40	43	5
Australia	AUS	4,745	0.41	46	2
Norway	NOR	2,116	0.41	51	2
New Zealand	NZL	1,540	0.41	43	7
Northern Ireland	NI	1,745	0.41	42	4
Finland	FIN	3,789	0.42	52	1
France	FRA	2,086	0.42	51	3
Sweden	SWE	2,345	0.43	53	2
Belgium	BEL	4,656	0.44	53	3
United States	USA	2,158	0.44	64	0
Canada	CAN	14,418	0.45	51	1
Scotland	SCOT	1,219	0.45	42	4
Austria	AUT	2,801	0.46	50	1
Germany	DEU	2,365	0.46	51	3
Netherlands	NLD	2,484	0.47	52	3
Denmark	DNK	2,276	0.48	46	2
Ireland	IRL	2,522	0.48	46	1
Switzerland	CHE	3,612	0.50	54	2
Luxembourg	LUX	1,226	0.51	54	9
Czech Republic	CZE	4,243	0.53	54	1
Greece	GRC	2,506	0.53	48	0
Italy	ITA	8,329	0.53	49	1
Slovakia	SVK	5,473	0.54	78	1
Spain	ESP	7,885	0.57	51	3
Poland	POL	3,682	0.58	59	0
Turkey	TUR	2,752	0.58	43	1
Hungary	HUN	3,135	0.62	53	2
Korea	KOR	3,861	0.68	61	1
Portugal	PRT	2,905	0.76	60	1
Total		106,873	0.61	54	2

Source: Authors' calculations based on data from Programme for International Student Assessment 2003 (see OECD 2004).
Notes: Based on data after sample selection rules have been applied (no migrants, children living with natural parents only, at least one parent's education coded).

Measurement error in the education variables, from children acting as proxy respondents, may be a concern. Wolfram Schulz (2006) investigates this problem using a convenience sample collected as part of the PISA 2006 field trial. Parents and children were asked separately to report the mother's and father's education level, with a choice of five categories. They gave the same category in 63 percent of cases for father's education and 66 percent for mother's education. However, the figure varied substantially between education levels. For example, when children reported "university" as their father's education level, 86 percent of fathers also gave this answer. Yet when children reported "non-university tertiary education," only 39 percent of fathers agreed. Comparisons can also be made using data for ten countries in the actual 2006 PISA sweep.[10] Our investigation of these data shows results not dissimilar to those in the field trial, including much lower agreement between parental and child reports for non-university tertiary education. We also find some substantial variation across countries in these figures—with, for example, notable differences in Italy in the numbers reporting secondary education to be the highest qualification obtained by mothers (18 percent of children but 44 percent of mothers).

One way to test the influence of measurement error in parents' education is to estimate two sets of regressions with the 2006 data, one using the parents' responses and the other using the children's, and then to compare the results.[11] We exclude immigrants and cases with incomplete information on mother's and father's education in either the parental or child questionnaire. We cannot exclude children not living with their natural parents, since the 2006 data contain no information on family structure. We estimate the regressions separately for the ten countries and then take the unweighted average of the parameter estimates. Using children's reports of education, a child whose father is university-educated scores forty-one points higher on average in the PISA reading test than if the father had less than secondary schooling. (The standard deviation of scores is about one hundred points.) When using fathers' reports of education, the same regression yields a forty-five-point difference. The corresponding estimates for maternal university education are thirty-eight points with the child's reports and forty-nine points with the mother's reports. This indicates some notable attenuation in estimates when using the children's reports. Attenuation, at least for university education, is the general pattern in individual countries, but there is some substantial variation from country to country. We do not feel that we have enough evidence on which to base any adjustment of our estimates using the child reports for the full set of thirty countries. But the need for further research on the quality of the parental education measures in PISA is clear.

We can illustrate the variation across countries in the links between the generations shown in our subsample of 2003 PISA data when we do not distinguish fathers from mothers. We regress the child's math score on years of parental schooling, taking whichever is the higher, father's or mother's, although in about half of the cases there is no difference, as already seen in table 9.1. In presenting the results in figure 9.2, we multiply the estimated regression coefficient by four, the number of years a university degree course takes in many countries, and then divide by the standard deviation of children's test scores in the pooled (all country, all children) sample, which is equal to one hundred. This produces a standardized coefficient.[12] We can interpret this coefficient as the number of "international" standard deviations of test scores associated on average with a four-year increase in parental education. We also adopt this practice in the next section.

The variation across countries is marked, the standardized estimate varying from less than 0.2 of a test score standard deviation to about 0.8. Note the particularly strong relationship between parental schooling and children's ability in the United States and England and in the four central European countries, where the Czech Republic and Hungary stand out.[13] It is also interesting to make pairwise comparisons between certain countries. The figure for the United States is twice that for Canada (0.56 compared to 0.27). Likewise, parental education has greater association with children's math ability in England compared to Scotland, and in Denmark compared to Sweden.[14]

Results

We now test the association between each parent's education and the child's cognitive skills at age fifteen, using regression models in which each parent's years of education enters separately. To be clear, although we use the terms "effect" and "impact" at times for convenience, we are not presuming a causal relationship in any of the models we estimate. We intend these models as "catch all" regressions, with the parental variables reflecting all direct and indirect influences of the parents' education.

Fathers' Education Versus Mothers' Education

In the first model, we allow for gender differences in the parents' generation only, restricting the effect of each parent's education to be the same for boys and girls (individuals are denoted by the subscript i). Missing value dummies for each parent's education are included in this and all subsequent regressions.

$$A_i = \alpha + \gamma \, \text{gBOY}_i + \lambda_1 \, \text{gPA}_i + \lambda_2 \, \text{gMA}_i + \xi_i, \qquad (9.1)$$

where A is the child's test score; BOY equals one if the child is a boy and is zero otherwise; PA is father's years of schooling; MA is mother's years of schooling; and ξ is the error term.

Figure 9.2   Children's Math Score and Highest Parental Education

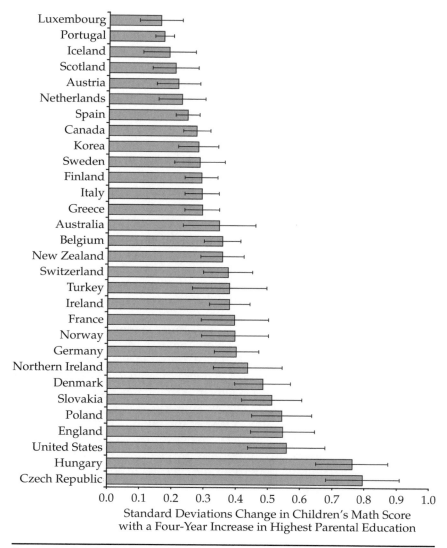

Standard Deviations Change in Children's Math Score
with a Four-Year Increase in Highest Parental Education

Source: Authors' calculations based on data from Programme for International Student Assessment 2003 (OECD 2004).
Note: The horizontal lines at the end of each bar represent 95 percent confidence intervals around the estimates.

We test the following hypothesis for each country:

H1: Mothers and fathers have the same effect on children's ability ($\lambda_1 = \lambda_2$).[15]

Figure 9.3 plots the estimated values of the regression coefficients, λ_1 and λ_2, which we have scaled in the way described in the previous section—multiplying by four and dividing by one hundred. As before, we see the estimated impact of four additional years of a parent's education, measured in "international" standard deviations of test scores. So a figure of 0.5 means that a rise in mother's or father's education of four years is associated on average with a rise in test score equal to one-half of an international standard deviation.

Countries that sit in the top right of the diagram have the greatest association between parental education and child ability—that is, the least educational mobility. The farther the country lies away from the forty-five-degree line, the greater the difference between the effects of mother's education and father's education. A circle around the country name shows that the difference is significant—that is, we reject H1—at the 5 percent level. A square shows that it is significant at the 10 percent level.

Out of the thirty countries, fourteen have circles or squares. These countries are somewhat more frequently found above the line, implying a greater effect of fathers. In several, the differences are large in percentage terms—in the Netherlands, Switzerland, Germany, and Australia, the father's effect is at least twice the mother's, and in the United States it is some 50 percent larger.[16] Differences of a similar magnitude are found in the countries that are significantly below the line. It is difficult to detect clear general patterns, whether in terms of groups of countries or in terms of the overall level of parental effect. It does not appear to be the case that where family background is especially important, this is associated with one parent in particular. All the Nordic countries are below the line, but none significantly so. The same is true of the poorer countries, Greece, Portugal, and Turkey, in line with the view of Behrman (1997) that mother's education may be especially important lower down the development scale. There is no common pattern for the central European countries. In several northern European countries, such as Sweden, Belgium, England, and Denmark, the difference between the effect of mothers' education and fathers' education is small.

This variation about the forty-five-degree line shows that there are substantial cross-country differences in the relative importance of mothers and fathers. But at the same time, half the countries have no circles or squares: we cannot reject the null hypothesis of no difference in father's and mother's impact in half of the countries, even at the 10 percent level. Table 9.2 reports results from the regression model when we combine the data for all countries so as to vastly increase the sample size (we include

Figure 9.3   H1: Mother's and Father's Education and Child's Math Score

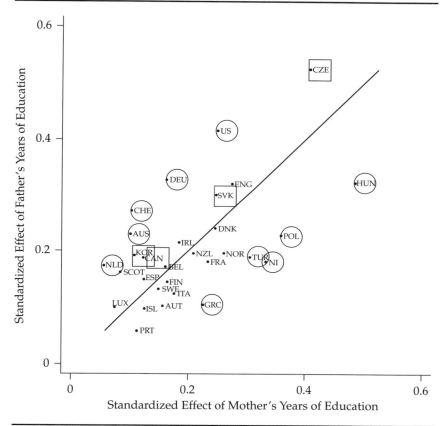

Source: Authors' calculations based on data from Programme for International Student Assessment 2003 (OECD 2004).
Notes: The forty-five-degree line represents where mother's and father's education have equal influence on their children's math score. Circles (squares) indicate countries where the effect of mother's and father's education is statistically different at the 5 percent (10 percent) significance level. The x and y axes show the standardized effect of mother's and father's education—that is, by how many (international) standard deviations a child's test score changes with a four-year increase in the parent's education.

country dummies). Of course, this has the disadvantage of restricting the impact for fathers and mothers to be the same in each country—in effect, we are averaging across both the vertical and horizontal dimensions in the graph. The *p*-values reported in table 9.2 show that we reject the null of no difference in this pooled sample at the 5 percent level (but never at the 1 percent level) for all three subjects (math, science, and reading). And

Table 9.2   Tests of Hypotheses for the Three PISA Domains, Pooled Sample of Thirty Countries (p-values)

Hypothesis		Math	Reading	Science
H1	Mother → Child = Father → Child	0.04	0.03	0.02
H2	Mother → Daughter = Father → Daughter	0.24	0.42	0.31
H3	Mother → Son = Father → Son	0.00	0.02	0.02
H4	Father → Son = Father → Daughter	0.04	0.13	0.21
H5	Mother → Son = Mother → Daughter	0.03	0.31	0.25
H6	Mother ↔ Father Interaction = 0	0.00	0.00	0.00

Source: Authors' calculations based on data from Programme for International Student Assessment 2003 (OECD 2004).
Notes: Figures in the table refer to p-values; estimation of standard errors allows for clustering of children within schools.

in this pooled sample, fathers on average have more effect (not shown). For example, for math, the standardized coefficient estimates are 0.238 for fathers and 0.208 for mothers.

Distinguishing Between Sons and Daughters

Our review of the literature suggested that parents may be more effective at transferring their human capital to children of the same gender. The next model takes this into account by introducing interactions between each parent's education and the child's gender:

$$A_i = \alpha + \gamma \text{ gBOY}_i + \beta_1 \text{ gPA}_i + \beta_2 \text{ gMA}_i + \beta_3 \text{ gBOY}_i \text{ gPA}_i$$

$$+ \beta_4 \text{ gBOY}_i \text{ gMA}_i + \xi_i \qquad (9.2)$$

We begin by comparing the effect of mothers and fathers separately for sons and daughter; hence, we test two hypotheses.

H2: Mothers and fathers have the same effect on daughters ($\beta_1 = \beta_2$).
H3: Mothers and fathers have the same effect on sons ($\beta_1 + \beta_3 = \beta_2 + \beta_4$).[17]

Figures 9.4 and 9.5 show the results of testing these hypotheses for each country for math, and tables 9.2 and 9.3 give the results for each subject for the pooled sample of all countries. The pooled sample results show a clear difference between sons and daughters. For daughters, we always fail to reject the null hypothesis, while for sons we always reject it. Father's education is more important than mother's for sons. For example, table 9.3 shows that four additional years of mothers' education is estimated to increase their sons' math score by 0.163 (= 0.202 − 0.039) of an international standard deviation. The same addition in fathers' education leads to an increase of 0.232 (= 0.198 + 0.034), about 40 percent more.

Figure 9.4   H2: Mother's and Father's Education and Daughter's Math Score

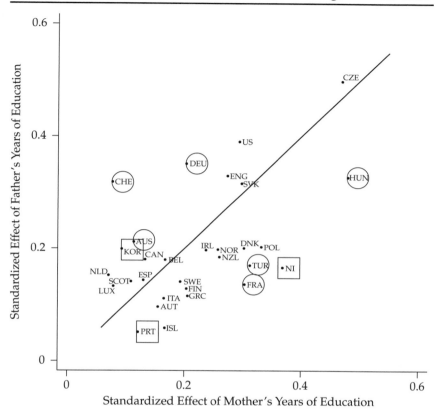

Source: Authors' calculations based on data from Programme for International Student Assessment 2003 (OECD 2004).
Notes: The forty-five-degree line represents where mother's and father's education have equal influence on their children's math score. Circles (squares) indicate countries where the effect of mother's and father's education is statistically different at the 5 percent (10 percent) significance level. The x and y axes show the standardized effect of mother's and father's education—that is, by how many (international) standard deviations a child's test score changes with a four-year increase in the parent's education.

The picture for individual countries in part reflects these results—there are fourteen countries above the forty-five-degree line in figure 9.4 for daughters, signifying that fathers are more important, but twenty countries in figure 9.5 for sons. (The Nordic countries are all below the line in figure 9.4, but not in figure 9.5.) In most countries, however, the null cannot be rejected, whether for sons or for daughters. Germany and Australia

Figure 9.5   H3: Mother's and Father's Education and Son's Math Score

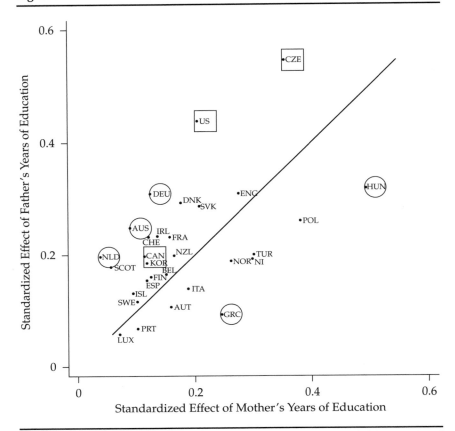

Source: Authors' calculations based on data from Programme for International Student Assessment 2003 (OECD 2004).
Notes: The forty-five-degree line represents where mother's and father's education have equal influence on their children's math score. Circles (squares) indicate countries where the effect of mother's and father's education is statistically different at the 5 percent (10 percent) significance level. The x and y axes show the standardized effect of mother's and father's education—that is, by how many (international) standard deviations a child's test score changes with a four-year increase in the parent's education.

are the only countries significantly above the line for both sons and daughters.

We now test two further hypotheses based on the same model:

H4: Fathers have the same effect on sons as on daughters ($\beta_3 = 0$).
H5: Mothers have the same effect on sons as on daughters ($\beta_4 = 0$).

Table 9.3   Standardized Regression Coefficients for the Three PISA Domains, Pooled Sample of Thirty Countries

	Math	Reading	Science
Boy (γ)	0.114 (0.046)	−0.372 (0.046)	0.039 (0.048)
Father's years of education (β_1)	0.198 (0.011)	0.186 (0.011)	0.218 (0.012)
Boy × father's years of education (β_3)	0.034 (0.016)	0.025 (0.017)	0.022 (0.018)
Mother's years of education (β_2)	0.202 (0.013)	0.173 (0.012)	0.198 (0.014)
Boy × mother's years of education (β_4)	−0.039 (0.016)	−0.015 (0.016)	−0.018 (0.017)

Source: Authors' calculations based on data from Programme for International Student Assessment 2003 (OECD 2004).
Notes: Standard errors in parentheses. Their estimation allows for clustering of children within schools. The models include a dummy variable for each country, although the coefficients are not reported. The β coefficients represent the standardized effect of that variable: by how many (international) standard deviations a child's test score changes with a four-year increase in mother's or father's education. The γ coefficient shows the difference between boys and girls using the same metric; for example, boys are estimated to have reading scores that on average are 0.372 of an international standard deviation lower than those of girls, holding other factors constant.

Note the difference between H2 and H3 on the one hand and H4 and H5 on the other. The first pair of hypotheses focuses on the differences in effects of mothers and fathers for children of a specified gender. Now we consider one parent at a time, but compare their effect on sons and daughters.

Figure 9.6 suggests that there is little evidence against H4 and not much variation from country to country. Countries sit quite tightly round the forty-five-degree line. The null hypothesis is rejected nowhere, although it is just barely rejected for math at the 5 percent level in the pooled sample (tables 9.2 and 9.3), with fathers having somewhat more effect for sons. Figure 9.7 for girls also shows less scatter than the earlier graphs, but the obvious change from figure 9.6 for boys is that most countries are now to the right of the forty-five-degree line (twenty-three out of thirty). Mothers appear to have more influence on girls' ability in math than on boys' ability, although only in France and Denmark is the difference statistically significant. The broad pattern in figure 9.7 is reflected in the results for math in tables 9.2 and 9.3. An increase of mother's education of four years is associated with an increase in a daughter's math score of 0.202 of a standard deviation, compared to a 0.163 increase for sons (= 0.202 − 0.039), a modest difference. However, for reading and science we cannot reject the null of no difference in effect.

Figure 9.6   H4: Father's Education and Son's and Daughter's Math Scores

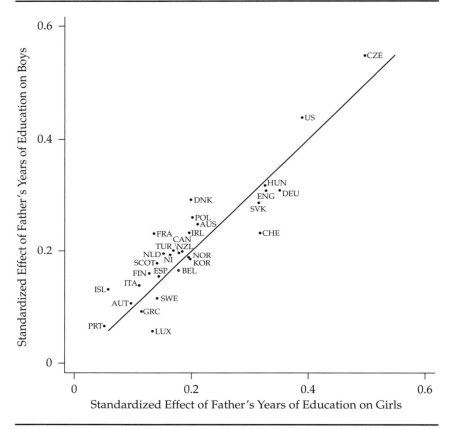

Source: Authors' calculations based on data from Programme for International Student Assessment 2003 (OECD 2004).
Notes: The forty-five-degree line represents where father's education has equal influence on boys' and girls' math scores. See also figure 9.3.

Complementarities Between Parents

The preceding models have constrained mother's and father's education to have independent effects on children's cognitive ability. However, the influence of one may depend on the other. There could be substitution possibilities between mother's and father's schooling, as described by Behrman (1997). This would mean that the effect of having a highly educated mother is smaller if the father is also highly educated. On the other hand, mother's and father's education could be complementary. In this case, better-educated mothers are more effective at passing on

Figure 9.7   H5: Mother's Education and Son's and Daughter's Math Scores

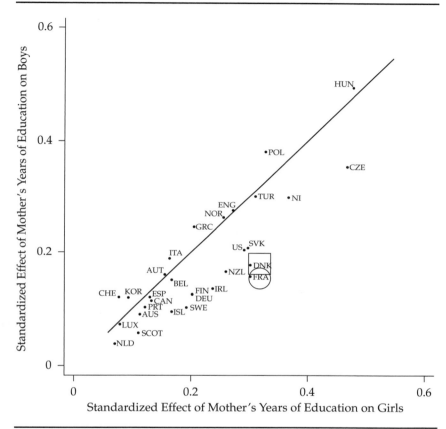

Source: Authors' calculations based on data from Programme for International Student Assessment 2003 (OECD 2004).
Notes: The forty-five-degree line represents where mother's education has equal influence on boys' and girls' math scores. See also figure 9.3. There is a statistically significant difference at the 10 percent level in Finland, though this is not clearly illustrated in the graph owing to the overlapping country labels.

their human capital to children if the father is also better educated. There seems only a scant existing literature on this issue.[18]

We test for these effects by including an interaction between mother's and father's education in our first model (which restricts the parental effects to be the same for sons and daughters). (As before, by "effect" we mean "association.") The model is now specified:

$$A_i = \alpha + \gamma \text{ ɢBOY}_i + \psi_1 \text{ ɢPA}_i + \psi_2 \text{ ɢMA}_i + \psi_3 \text{ ɢPA}_i \text{ ɢMA}_i + \xi_i \quad (9.3)$$

We test the hypothesis:

H6: Mothers' and fathers' influences do not interact with each other ($\psi_3 = 0$).

Results for the pooled sample show a positive coefficient on the inter-action term for all three subjects, implying complementarity, and one that is well determined ($t = 5.9$ for math, for example).[19] When estimating the model for each individual country, we find the interaction to be positive in twenty-two countries and significant at the 5 percent level in nine countries. The latter group includes three of the four central European countries and all three countries from the United Kingdom present in the data— England, Scotland, and Northern Ireland. A statistically significant nega-tive impact at the 5 percent level is found in three countries: Italy, Portugal, and Switzerland.

The typical pattern of complementarity suggests that assortative mating may strengthen the intergenerational transmission of human capital, at least as far as the outcome we have considered in this chapter is concerned—children's cognitive ability in their early to mid-teens. Educational "homogamy"—that is, marriage to a person of the same edu-cational level—leads to "advantageous (and disadvantageous) economic and sociocultural resources of two individuals [being] . . . pooled and cumulated" (Blossfeld 2009, 515). Complementarity implies that the impact of this pooling and cumulation on children's learning is not addi-tive. However, our results here are best seen as suggestive; they require further elaboration in the light of possible measurement error and better theoretical underpinning.

Conclusions

To our knowledge, existing studies have not considered the separate associations of mothers' and fathers' education with their sons' and daughters' cognitive ability for a large number of countries using data designed with cross-national comparison in mind. We therefore have made here a contribution to the literature on how educational advantage and disadvantage are transferred between generations by exploring these gender differences for thirty rich industrialized nations, restricting atten-tion to children living with both natural parents. This complements a small body of work that has investigated the links usually for a single country, focusing in the main on children's final level of schooling rather than cognitive ability.

It is not easy to make broad generalizations from our results. The picture often differs substantially across countries; mothers are more important in some, fathers in others. This cross-national variation supports the mixed evidence in our review of the literature. It also serves as a reminder that we should be cautious about making general statements on the basis of evidence drawn from a single country—for example, the United States—for which the earlier evidence seems more abundant than elsewhere.

That said, we attempt a summary of the general picture, focusing on the results for ability in math. First, it is more common for father's education to have a greater effect than mother's education. Remember, we use "effect" without implying causality. Second, this appears to be particularly true of sons, although there are plenty of countries that are counterexamples. Third, there seems to be more variation across countries in the gender differences in the parents' generation than the children's. Fourth, there is some suggestion that mothers' education has more effect on their daughters' ability than on their sons', yet the difference is often small. Fifth, it seems that we should consider not only the relative importance of each parent's education but also how they combine. Our results suggest that they may typically combine positively; mother's and father's education appear complementary in their association with the child's ability.

This last observation leads to the first avenue for further work. We have not distinguished between couples where the father is more educated than the mother and those where the opposite is the case. The type of combination of father's and mother's education may matter for the child's learning, although selection bias can be expected—women who "marry up" (hypergamy) may differ from those who "marry down" (hypogamy) in unobserved ways that influence their child's learning.

A second avenue is to enrich the measurement of each parent's socioeconomic status, moving beyond education alone. An obvious possibility is occupation, following the lead of, for example, Korupp, Ganzeboom, and van der Lippe (2002). Each parent's occupation is recorded in PISA, although, again, it is reported by the child. Our preliminary exploration of these data, adding measures of father's and mother's occupation to our regressions, tended to produce a clearer pattern that mothers "matter" more for girls, while fathers are more important for boys. Inter alia, further work in this direction would require a conceptual framework to complement that in figure 9.1 for parental education.

The third avenue is to try to relate the cross-national patterns we have found to country-specific policies or institutions. This is a challenge. There seems to be no easy explanation for fathers having more influence than mothers in countries like Australia and Germany, for the opposite to be true in Hungary and Turkey, and for there to be no significant differences in, for example, England and Belgium. One possibility that we cannot yet entirely rule out is that the differences we observe across countries in the PISA data are often due to variations in data quality; our measure of family background is reliant upon fifteen-year-old children knowing and accurately reporting their mother's and father's levels of education, and we have drawn attention to evidence that questions whether this is the case.

Despite the limitations and the avenues still to explore, we have at least highlighted the role that gender may play in the transfer of human capital between generations. In this respect, the spirit of the chapter contrasts with a reasonable amount of existing work on economic and social mobility. We advocate investigation of gender differences in other aspects of intergenerational mobility, accompanying further work on the role that these differences play in children's cognitive abilities.

John Micklewright thanks the Institute for Research on Poverty (IRP) at the University of Wisconsin–Madison for hospitality during a visit when this chapter was begun. We thank seminar and conference participants at IRP, the Central European University, and the University of Bamberg for comments. The work was partly financed by the Russell Sage Foundation.

Notes

1. There is no explicit role for schools in the model. We can think of parents' choice of schools, subject to various constraints, also being determined by their education and abilities. If schools have a positive impact, the simple correlation of parental education and child ability partly reflects this pathway.
2. Members of the NELS cohort were first interviewed in 1988 at age fourteen. We imputed completed years of education for both cohort members and parents from variables for highest qualification achieved.
3. On the channels by which educated mothers influence early childhood learning and the evidence for this, see, for example, Coneus and Sprietsma (2009).
4. For further evidence on the United States, see, for example, Behrman and Rosenzweig (2002) and Farré, Klein, and Vella (2009). Korupp, Ganzeboom, and van der Lippe (2002) compare the United States with (West) Germany and the Netherlands, but they include parental occupation as well as education in their models.
5. The father-son link is stronger than the mother-son link ($t = 3.5$), and the mother-daughter link is stronger than the father-daughter link, although the difference in this case is not well determined ($t = 2.05$). We calculate T-statistics from the reported standard errors for each regression coefficient (Björkland, Jäntti, and Solon 2007, table 2, column 1) and have thus ignored covariances when estimating the standard error of the difference in coefficients.
6. Japan is excluded because data are missing for all observations on some key variables, including whether the child lives with his or her biological parents or step-parents.
7. Question marks over response patterns in England are analyzed in Micklewright, Schnepf, and Skinner (2010).

8. The PISA assessment focuses on children's functional skills—whether they can apply what they have learned to real-life situations. It is argued that this assists the cross-national validity of the study, allowing measurement of achievement against a standard in a culture-free way.

9. Children are told, "Some of the following questions are about your mother and father or those person(s) who are like a mother or father to you, for example, guardians, step-parents, foster parents, et cetera. If you share your time with more than one set of parents or guardians, please answer the following questions for those parents/guardians you spend the most time with."

10. Among OECD countries, parents are questioned as well as children in Germany, Denmark, Iceland, Italy, Korea, Luxembourg, New Zealand, Poland, Portugal, and Turkey.

11. We assume that any measurement error lies only in the child's reports, although this may not be the case. See also Lien, Friestad, and Klepp (2001).

12. Four years is also roughly the international standard deviation of both mother's and father's years of education. The international standard deviations for both test scores and years of education tend to be higher than most national standard deviations because they reflect both within- and between-country differences.

13. The position of the central European countries is consistent with large differences in education attainment by family background during the Communist period, as well as with any differences that have emerged since then (Shavit and Blossfeld 1993; UNICEF 1998).

14. Comparison with results in Schütz, Ursprung, and Wössmann (2008, table 3), drawn on by Machin (2009), is a reminder that the detailed cross-country picture of intergenerational mobility may depend on the measure of socioeconomic status that is selected and the data set that is used: these authors use data from the Trends in Maths and Science Study and books in the home to proxy family background. We find a correlation of only 0.43 for our family background associations in figure 9.2 with theirs for the same countries. See Brown et al. (2007) on the comparability of surveys.

15. In the terminology of Korupp, Ganzeboom, and van der Lippe (2002), $\lambda_2 = 0$ implies what they refer to as the "conventional" model that only fathers "matter." Our H1 reflects their "joint" model, and rejection of H1, together with nonzero λ_2, is analogous to their "individual" model. Note, however, that our outcome variable differs.

16. A similar pattern is found in the NELS data for the United States when we regress age fourteen scores on parental education (see note 2).

17. Rejection of H2 and H3 is in line with the "sex role" model of Korupp, Ganzeboom, and van der Lippe (2002).

18. For example, Behrman cites Ricardo Barros and David Lam (1996), who find evidence of a positive interaction suggesting complementarity.

19. Not surprisingly, the inclusion of the interaction term reduces the precision of the estimated main effects of each parent's education. They remain strongly

significant individually, but, for example, in the math equation the effect of mother's education is not statistically different from the effect of father's education.

References

Barros, Ricardo, and David Lam. 1996. "Income and Educational Inequality in Children's Schooling Attainment." In *Opportunity Foregone: Education in Brazil,* edited by Nancy Birdsall and Richard Sabot. Baltimore: Johns Hopkins University Press.

Baxter, Jennifer. 2002. "How Much Does Parental Education Explain Educational Attainment of Males and Females in Australia?" Negotiating the Life Course discussion paper DP-015. Canberra: Australian National University.

Beller, Emily. 2009. "Bringing Intergenerational Social Mobility Research into the Twenty-First Century: Why Mothers Matter." *American Sociological Review* 74(4): 507–28.

Behrman, Jere. 1997. "Mother's Schooling and Child Education: A Survey." Working paper 97-025. Philadelphia: University of Pennsylvania, Penn Institute for Economic Research (PIER).

Behrman, Jere, and Mark Rosenzweig. 2002. "Does Increasing Women's Schooling Raise the Schooling of the Next Generation?" *American Economic Review* 92(1): 323–34.

Blanden, Jo, Paul Gregg, and Lindsey Macmillan. 2007. "Accounting for Intergenerational Income Persistence: Noncognitive Skills, Ability, and Education." Discussion paper 2554. Bonn, Germany: Institute for the Study of Labor (IZA).

Blossfeld, Hans-Peter. 2009. "Educational Assortative Marriage in Comparative Perspective." *Annual Review of Sociology* 35: 513–30.

Björklund, Anders, Markus Jäntti, and Gary Solon. 2007. "Nature and Nurture in the Intergenerational Transmission of Socioeconomic Status: Evidence from Swedish Children and Their Biological and Rearing Parents." *B.E. Journal of Economic Analysis and Policy* 7(2, Advances): article 4.

Brown, Giorgina, John Micklewright, Sylke Schnepf, and Robert Waldmann. 2007. "International Surveys of Educational Achievement: How Robust Are the Findings?" *Journal of the Royal Statistical Society* series A 170(3): 623–46.

Coneus, Katja, and Maresa Sprietsma. 2009. "Intergenerational Transmission of Human Capital in Early Childhood." Discussion paper 09-038. Mannheim, Germany: Centre for European Economic Research (ZEW).

Dearden, Lorraine, Stephen Machin, and Howard Reed. 1997. "Intergenerational Mobility in Britain." *Economic Journal* 107(440): 47–66.

Erikson, Robert, and John Goldthorpe. 2002. "Intergenerational Inequality: A Sociological Perspective." *Journal of Economic Perspectives* 16(3): 31–44.

Ermisch, John, and Marco Francesconi. 2001. "Family Matters: Impacts of Family Background on Educational Attainments." *Economica* 68(270): 137–56.

Farré, Lídia, Roger Klein, and Francis Vella. 2009. "Does Increasing Parents' Schooling Raise the Schooling of the Next Generation? Evidence Based on Conditional Second Moments." Discussion paper 3967. Bonn, Germany: Institute for the Study of Labor (IZA).

Haveman, Robert, and Barbara Wolfe. 1995. "The Determinants of Children's Attainments: A Review of Methods and Findings." *Journal of Economic Literature* 33(4): 1829–78.

Heineck, Guido, and Regina Riphahn. 2007. "Intergenerational Transmission of Educational Attainment in Germany: The Last Five Decades." Discussion paper 2985. Bonn, Germany: Institute for the Study of Labor (IZA).

Johnston, Aaron, Harry Ganzeboom, and Douglas Treiman. 2005. "Mothers' and Fathers' Influences on Educational Attainment." Paper presented to International Sociological Association RC28 conference. Oslo (May 6–8).

Korupp, Sylvia, Harry Ganzeboom, and Tanja van der Lippe. 2002. "Do Mothers Matter? A Comparison of Models of the Influence of Mothers' and Fathers' Educational and Occupational Status on Children's Educational Attainment." *Quality and Quantity* 36(1): 17–42.

Leibowitz, Arleen. 1974. "Home Investments in Children." *Journal of Political Economy* 82(2): S111–31.

Lien, Nanna, Christine Friestad, and Knut-Inge Klepp. 2001. "Adolescents' Proxy Reports of Parents' Socioeconomic Status: How Valid Are They?" *Journal of Epidemiological Community Health* 55(10): 731–37.

Machin, Stephen. 2009. "Inequality and Education." In *The Oxford Handbook of Economic Inequality*, edited by Wiemer Salverda, Brian Nolan, and Timothy Smeeding. Oxford: Oxford University Press.

Micklewright John, Sylke Schnepf, and Chris Skinner. 2010. "Nonresponse Biases in Surveys of School Children: The Case of the English PISA Samples." Discussion paper no. 4789. Bonn, Germany: Institute for the Study of Labor (IZA).

Organization for Economic Co-operation and Development (OECD). 2004. *Learning for Tomorrow's World—First Results from PISA 2003*. Paris: OECD.

———. 2008. *Education at a Glance*. Paris: OECD.

Schulz, Wolfram. 2006. "Measuring the Socioeconomic Background of Students and Its Effect on Achievement in PISA 2000 and PISA 2003." Paper presented to the annual meeting of the American Educational Research Association. San Francisco (April 7–11).

Schütz, Gabriela, Heinrich Ursprung, and Ludger Wössmann. 2008. "Education Policy and Equality of Opportunity." *Kyklos* 61(2): 279–308.

Shavit, Yossi, and Hans-Peter Blossfeld. 1993. *Persistent Inequality: Changing Educational Attainment in Thirteen Countries*. Boulder, Colo.: Westview Press.

Steedman, Hilary, and Steven McIntosh. 2001. "Measuring Low Skills in Europe: How Useful Is the ISCED Framework?" *Oxford Economic Papers* 53(3): 564–81.

UNICEF. 1998. *Education for All?* MONEE project regional monitoring report 5. Florence, Italy: UNICEF International Child Development Centre.

PART IV

DIRECT MONETARY TRANSFERS

Chapter 10

Unequal Giving: Monetary Gifts to Children Across Countries and over Time

JULIE M. ZISSIMOPOULOS AND JAMES P. SMITH

T HERE IS a long history and a sizable body of research that cuts across disciplinary fields on how families, parents in particular, affect the outcomes of their children over a child's lifetime. Early influential studies on status attainment motivated research that shed light on how parents' educational and occupational attainment influenced that of their children. A related vein of research focuses on the importance of family support at a particular time in a child's life, the transition to adulthood (see, for example, Marini 1978; Sandefur, Eggerling-Boeck, and Park 2005; Schoeni and Ross 2005). As Robert Schoeni and Karen Ross (2005) point out, one way parents can influence the outcomes of their children in the transitional stage from ages eighteen to thirty-four is through monetary transfers for housing, food, assistance with educational expenses, and direct cash transfers, and they quantify these transfers at approximately $38,000.

Although parents transfer an enormous amount of resources to their children when the children are living in the parental home, during their adulthood, and past the transition to adulthood, some children continue to receive direct monetary gifts and loans from their parents. Indeed, monetary gifts may help children finance the purchase of a first home (Guiso and Jappelli 2002), relax credit constraints (Cox and Jappelli 1990), finance higher education (Brown et al. 2006), and smooth consumption in response to a transitory wealth or income shock such as job loss. These monetary gifts may also be an important mechanism within families to equalize economic outcomes among children (Becker 1981). Empirical evidence reveals that wealthy families transfer considerable resources to their children, while middle-class and poor households do not (Hurd, Smith, and Zissimopoulos 2007; Schoeni and Ross 2005), and thus, although they may equalize outcomes among children in a given family, transfers may also extend inequalities across generations.

How important direct financial transfers from parents to children are to the outcomes of children depends in part on the institutional environment and the interaction of public and private transfers. For example, if family members are altruistically linked, their private transfers will undo government redistribution. Prior empirical study of this "crowd-out" phenomenon has often depended on testing the parents' motive for making the transfer to infer the extent of crowd-out. However, the literature is inconclusive about what motive, if any, dominates. For example, studies that find support for altruistically motivated parental transfers imply that private transfers neutralize the effects of public transfers (Cox, Eser, and Jimenez 1998; Lillard and Willis 1997; McGarry and Schoeni 1995; Pezzin and Schone 1997; Schoeni 1997). At the same time, studies that find support for exchange-motivated parental transfers imply less or no crowd-out (Bernheim, Shleifer, and Summers 1985; Cox 1987; Cox and Rank 1992). Moreover, in the United States, children within a family commonly receive unequal amounts of money from their parents while the parents are alive, consistent with motivations to equalize outcomes among children, but receive mostly equal amounts upon their parents' death (Hurd and Smith 2002), fueling debate as to why inter vivos giving and bequest patterns differ and the motivation for transfers more generally.

In the United States and much of Europe, about one-fifth to one-quarter of parents give some money to their adult children in a typical year. Even in countries with strong welfare states, parents provide monetary support to their adult children (Albertini, Kohli, and Vogel 2007; Attias-Donfut and Ogg 2005). To shed light on the role of direct financial transfers from parents to adult children in the intergenerational transmission of wealth, we ask: How much money do children receive at a single point in time and over time? What is the role of parental economic status and social insurance programs in determining the magnitude of financial gifts to adult children?

We first examine annual inter vivos transfers of money from parents to children in the United States and ten European countries using the 2004 waves of the Health and Retirement Study (HRS) and the Survey of Health, Ageing, and Retirement in Europe (SHARE) to establish the size of the transfer and the distribution within and across countries. We then study how much of the cross-national variation in transfers is explained by public expenditure on social programs and individual factors. We discuss other factors that may explain the remaining cross-country variation in the magnitude of monetary transfers to children, including the role of shared housing and tax regimes. Our methodology provides some direct evidence on the interplay of private and public transfers by utilizing cross-national variation in policies and transfers. Harmonized data across countries facilitate the use of these methods, which usually cannot be applied within a single country where there is no or limited variation across households in public transfers policies.

Second, utilizing the long panel of the HRS, we calculate up to sixteen years of inter vivos financial transfers to children in the United States to study the long-run behavior of parental monetary giving to children across families and within a family. Importantly, most of what we currently understand about parental financial transfers to children is based on single-period estimates. The long-run magnitudes of parental monetary gifts to adult children and the persistence of giving over time shed light on their relevance for the intergenerational transmission of wealth.

We find in all countries that some parents give money to children and many do not. The average annual amount of money that parents gave all their children in 2004 was about €1,000 ($1,226) in countries represented in SHARE (about €420, or $515, per child) and just over €1,800 ($2,208, about €580, or $711, per child) in the United States. The distribution of amounts, however, reveals a lot of heterogeneity. Five percent of U.S. parents gave about €9,000 ($11,038) or more annually to all their children. Among the countries in SHARE, the top 5 percent gave €5,000 ($6,132) or more to children each year. The difference in the average amount given is explained in part by differences in parental socioeconomic status and the variation in social public expenditures. The estimates of the amount of money that parents gave children, however, are based on a single point in time; total wealth transfers to children through the mechanism of direct financial giving depends in part on how persistent transfers are over time.

In the United States, over sixteen years, parents on average gave $37,765 to all their children. Each child received $11,122, while a child receiving in the top 5 percent of the distribution received $54,602. The distribution of sixteen-year transfers was more equal than the distribution of two-year transfers across families. Moreover, over time children in the same family were more likely to receive the same amount, particularly children with very wealthy parents, challenging the view that inter vivos giving and bequest giving are fundamentally different.

Multivariate model results reveal that a short-term view of the money given to children by parents suggests that giving is primarily compensatory (for example, given to low-earning children) or based on some immediate need (for a new house or to recover from the loss of a house, to finance education, for grandchildren). Over a long-term horizon, however, a child's education is one of the few remaining sources of difference in the money given to children. The timing and level of financial transfers to fund education (or housing) may have a significant impact on the welfare of a child and on intergenerational mobility if the financing is essential in the schooling decision. The magnitude of inter vivos transfers over time, however, is simply not large enough to affect the distribution of resources within or between families in the next generation.

Data Description

Our research for the United States relies on longitudinal data from the Health and Retirement Study, a set of biennial surveys first fielded in 1992 and 1993 by the University of Michigan with the objective of monitoring economic transitions in work, income, and wealth, as well as changes in many dimensions of health status among those over fifty years old.[1] We use data from survey waves 1992, 1993, 1994, 1995, and 1996, then biennially thereafter to 2006.[2] The measures of inter vivos transfers are based on questions asked of respondents about financial help provided to children in this basic form: "Including help with education but not shared housing or shared food (or any deed to a house), in the last two years did you or your spouse give financial help totaling $500 or more to any of your children (or grandchildren)?" They include follow-up questions about the amount of money and to whom the money was given.[3]

Our research for Europe is based on the 2.3.0 release of the first wave (2004) of the Survey of Health, Ageing and Retirement in Europe.[4] Data from the first wave of SHARE are representative of the population of individuals age fifty and over from eleven European countries: Austria, Belgium, Denmark, France, Germany, Greece, Italy, the Netherlands, Spain, Sweden, and Switzerland.[5] SHARE is modeled on the HRS and designed for cross-national research such as this. In SHARE data, financial transfers from parents to children are measured over a twelve-month period prior to the interview in this basic form: "Not counting any shared housing or shared food, have you or your husband/wife/partner given any financial or material gifts to anyone inside or outside this household amounting to €250 or more?" Follow-up questions are included about the amount of money and to whom the money was given for up to three children.[6] Additionally, the interviewer is instructed to clarify that "financial or material gift" means giving money or covering specific costs such as medical care, insurance, schooling, or a down payment for a home, and that it does not include loans.

The wording of the questions about money given by parents to children is similar across the two surveys but not exact. Respondents in the United States are asked to include loans, while SHARE respondents are asked to exclude loans. For comparability across countries, we divide by two amounts given to children over a two-year period in the United States for an annual transfer amount. In addition, we use gifts of $500 or more as the lower censor point. That is, we set to zero all amounts in the SHARE data below €407.68 (equal to $500 in 2004).

Results

Cross-Country Variation in Annual Gifts of Money from Parents to All Children

We examine the total sum of money that parents give to all their children for all European countries represented in the first wave of SHARE (2004)—with the exception of Switzerland, because of the low response rate, and the United States from the 2004 wave of HRS. Table 10.1 shows the percentage of parents who made financial gifts to their children, the mean amount that parents gave to all children in the ninetieth and ninety-fifth percentiles, and the mean and median amounts that parents gave, conditional on having given money to children, for the twelve countries. A few households in Belgium report giving extremely high amounts, so table 10.1 also lists amounts based on observations censored above the ninety-eighth percentile.

Thirty-nine percent of parents gave $500 (€408) or more to all their children in the United States over a two-year period from 2002 to 2004. We calculate an annual percentage, taking into account the persistence of giving by some households, to be 25.2 percent, a higher fraction than the average of the SHARE countries (19.7 percent).[7]

Average amounts given to all children are higher in the United States (€1,862) than in the countries represented in SHARE (€1,012). Parents in SHARE countries that give to children give them €5,127 each year. Although this amount is higher than the conditional amount (€4,795) given by parents in the United States, it is primarily driven by a few high values; when outliers are excluded, the average amount given to all children, conditional on giving, is slightly higher in the United States than in the SHARE countries.

With the exception of Spain, the percentage of parents in the SHARE countries giving money to children is variable, ranging between 16 percent (Italy) and 27 percent (Sweden). Only 8 percent of parents in Spain report giving money to children over a twelve-month period, although those parents who do give their children money give generously—on average about €5,500. Only in Belgium do parents give on average more money (unconditional amounts) to their children than in the United States, although trimming the top 2 percent of values reveals that average amounts are highest in the United States. Conditional on giving, parents in three of the ten countries in Europe give higher amounts of money to children (conditional, trimmed values—last column of table 10.1) compared to the United States: Belgium, Denmark, and France. Parents in the Netherlands and Greece give amounts to all children, conditional on giving, that are similar to what parents in the United States give (based on trimmed values).

Table 10.1   Money Given by Parents to All Their Children in 2004, by Country (in 2004 Euros)

| | | Unconditional | | | | Conditional | | Trimmed at 98th Percentile | | | |
| | | | | | | | | Unconditional | | | Conditional |
	N	Percentage	Mean	90th	95th	Mean	Median	Mean	90th	95th	Mean
Austria	1,161	26.4	€1,062	€2,000	€4,057	€4,021	€1,500	€476	€2,000	€3,000	€1,941
Belgium	2,186	19.1	2,688	3,000	7,500	14,109	3,114	723	2,000	5,000	4,237
Denmark	1,027	25.2	1,219	3,125	7,125	4,838	2,561	708	2,689	4,033	3,037
France	1,801	18.7	1,439	2,400	6,000	7,716	2,602	577	1,587	4,000	3,429
Germany	1,676	26.9	968	2,600	5,000	3,603	2,000	603	2,000	4,000	2,380
Greece	1,712	24.8	1,174	3,000	6,000	4,738	2,000	636	2,000	4,000	2,740
Italy	1,530	16.1	841	1,038	4,000	5,233	1,695	307	1,000	2,000	2,169
Netherlands	1,708	19.1	1,037	2,000	5,000	5,427	2,500	507	1,545	3,840	2,897
Spain	1,492	8.4	467	0	1,803	5,549	3,000	139	0	744	2,256
Sweden	1,936	27.4	660	2,179	3,268	2,410	1,307	450	1,634	2,723	1,737
U.S.	11,861	38.9[a]	1,862	4,484	8,969	4,795	1,794	1,098	4,077	6,523	2,939
All SHARE countries	16,229	19.7	1,012	2,000	5,000	5,127	2,000	463	1,500	3,000	2,579

Source: Authors' calculations based on data from SHARE Project (2004) and 2004 HRS (University of Michigan 2004).
Note: Weighted results.
[a] U.S. percentage giving based on average over two years. Estimated one-year giving is 25.2 percent.

Within countries, giving by parents across households is very unequal. For example, conditional mean amounts given are at least two times median amounts. Five percent of U.S. parents give about €9,000 or more annually to their children (about €2,800 annually per child). Among the SHARE countries, the top 5 percent give €5,000 or more to their children annually (about €2,100 annually per child).

Observable differences across households explain some of the variation in giving behavior within countries and across countries. Table 10.2 shows the mean values of the characteristics of our sample of parents by country. Some notable differences across countries include a low rate of respondents with a college education in Italy and Spain (less than 10 percent) compared to about 20 percent or more in the other SHARE countries and the United States, and a higher average number of children in the United States (3.2) than in the European countries represented in the SHARE data (average across all is 2.4). On average, the SHARE countries have lower income and wealth than the United States. Household gross income in wave 1 is measured with error due to substantial nonresponse; thus, we also report in table 10.1 average net income from the second wave of SHARE.

We next describe how money given to children varies with the age and wealth of the parent across a given country. To document mean age and wealth patterns in transfer amounts that are not primarily the result of high outlier amounts, we report the values of money gifts to all children trimmed at the ninety-eighth percentile. Figure 10.1 shows that in both the United States and the SHARE countries the amount of money given to children declines with age. The amount given at age eighty-one or older is half what is given at age fifty to fifty-five in the European countries represented in SHARE. The decline is even more pronounced in the United States. Because the age of the respondent parents is correlated with the age of their children, the patterns reflect both. Both age and cohort effects are present in these cross-sectional patterns, although longitudinal analysis based on the HRS also reveals declining amounts of money with age (Hurd, Smith, and Zissimopoulos 2007). In all SHARE countries and in the United States, the amount of money that parents give to all their children increases with wealth. Wealth in both surveys includes housing and nonhousing (financial) assets such as real estate, transportation, business wealth, stocks and bonds, checking and savings accounts, and other retirement savings accounts, but it does not include future claims on public or employer-provided pensions. Parents in the top 25 percent of the wealth distribution give over four times as much to their children as those in the bottom quarter of the wealth distribution. In the United States, the average amount of money given to all children by high-wealth parents is almost €2,000 annually, compared to only €400 for low-wealth parents. High-wealth families across countries give vastly different amounts (see

Table 10.2 Characteristics of Parents by Country, 2004

Country	N	Percentage Married	Percentage College	Mean Children	2004 Wealth[a]	2004 Income[b]	2006 Income[c]
Austria	1,161	56%	21%	2.26	€167,037	€26,356	€31,306
Belgium	2,186	65	25	2.43	305,576	28,193	36,051
Denmark	1,027	56	30	2.45	279,279	43,714	55,695
France	1,801	59	18	2.53	299,710	36,284	29,337
Germany	1,676	59	24	2.22	165,006	28,816	26,920
Greece	1,712	62	12	2.16	191,152	14,222	36,444
Italy	1,530	66	6	2.35	220,543	16,332	24,741
Netherlands	1,708	65	17	2.71	221,017	31,507	35,718
Spain	1,492	66	9	2.75	307,708	32,451	31,879
Sweden	1,936	58	20	2.50	245,206	33,025	43,842
United States	11,861	54	22	3.22	330,404	48,589	n.a.
All SHARE countries	16,229	62	16	2.42	234,242	28,007	30,115

Source: Authors' calculations based on data from SHARE Project (2004) and 2004 HRS (University of Michigan 2004).

Note: Weighted results.

[a]Net wealth is sum of stocks, bonds, IRAs, checking and savings accounts, business, house, and "other," less debt and mortgage.

[b]Income is sum of household income from earnings, pensions, transfers, assets, and "other"; it includes only regular payments (for example, no lump sums or support by family members). Income in SHARE wave 1 had substantial nonresponse. Although imputations were computed with a conditional hot deck for responses bracketed into income categories, there was also substantial nonresponse to the brackets; thus, the mean values reported for wave 1 should be interpreted with caution.

[c]Because of income nonresponse in wave 1, we also report 2006 *net* income for 81 percent of the SHARE sample for which it is available in wave 2 release 2.3.0 (weighted).

Figure 10.1   Amount of Money Given to Children, by Parent Age for the United States and the European SHARE Countries, in 2004

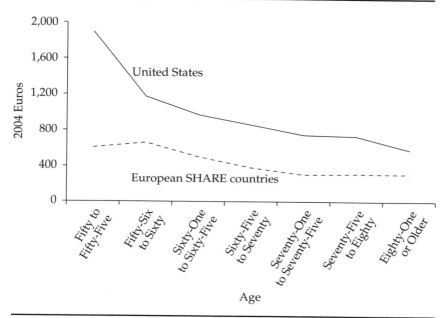

Source: Authors' calculations based on data from SHARE Project (2004) and 2004 HRS (University of Michigan 2004).
Notes: Amounts in 2004 euros trimmed above the ninety-eigth percentile. Weighted results.

figure 10.2). High-wealth parents in Belgium and Denmark give just under €1,500 annually, high-wealth parents in Italy give €400, and in Spain they give only €162 annually.

Cultural values, social institutions, and, more generally, the strength of the welfare state may explain some of the cross-country differences in parental monetary transfers to adult children (Albertini, Kohli, and Vogel 2007; Attias-Donfut and Ogg 2005). The relationship between the welfare state and family transfers is inconclusive and depends on the motives for giving. On the one hand, services offered by the state may "crowd out" or substitute for giving by families if families are altruistically linked. For example, state-financed higher education may crowd out financing of higher education by parents. On the other hand, families and institutions may complement each other by providing services or income simultaneously, or the existence of public support may be neutral on parental giving.

The United States and the SHARE countries vary considerably with respect to social expenditures. Table 10.3 reports social expenditures as

Figure 10.2   Amount of Money Given to Children, by Parent Wealth Quartile for Twelve Countries, in 2004

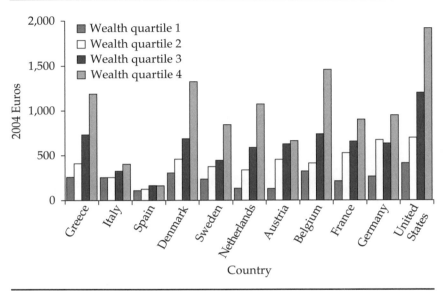

Source: Authors' calculations based on data from SHARE Project (2004) and 2004 HRS (University of Michigan 2004).
Notes: Amounts in 2004 euros trimmed above the ninety-eigth percentile. Weighted results.

a percentage of GDP, by country and purpose: old age, health, unemployment, tertiary education, and family. Old age and tertiary education expenditure (−0.83) are highly (and negatively) correlated. Social expenditure on old age, unemployment, and family is lower in the United States than in the ten European countries we study. The United States spends slightly more on tertiary education as a percentage of GDP. There is variation across the European countries in social expenditure. Public expenditure on old age support as a percentage of GDP is high in Austria, Germany, and Italy; the Netherlands and the United States spend about half of what these three countries spend. Belgium and Denmark spend more than the other countries on unemployment, and the United States and Greece spend the least (0.40). Public expenditure on tertiary education as a percentage of GDP is the highest in Austria (3.6 percent) and the lowest in Italy (0.8 percent). The United States spends 1.3 percent of GDP on tertiary education. Public expenditure on family is much higher in Denmark (3.5 percent) and Sweden (3.2 percent) than in the United States, which spends less than 1 percent of GDP for these purposes (0.65 percent). If transfers are earmarked for assisting with homeownership, then the size of the mortgage market may be correlated with cross-country

Table 10.3   Country-Level Social Expenditure and Population-Level Statistics, 2004

Country	As a Percentage of GDP						For Population Ages Twenty-Five to Thirty-Four		
	Old Age	Health	Unemployment	Tertiary Education[a]	Family	Mortgage Debt[b]	Unemployed	Attained Tertiary Education	Fertility Rate
Austria	12.7%	6.7%	1.2%	3.6%	2.9%	19.0%	5.5%	20.3%	1.42
Belgium	7.1	7.5	3.4	1.3	2.6	27.9	10.0	40.7	1.72
Denmark	7.1	5.9	3.3	2.4	3.5	74.3	5.8	37.6	1.78
France	10.7	7.8	1.8	1.2	3.0	22.8	9.7	38.4	1.90
Germany	11.2	7.6	1.7	1.1	1.9	54.0	11.5	22.9	1.36
Greece	10.4	5.1	0.4	1.4	1.2	13.9	12.4	25.3	1.31
Italy	11.5	6.6	0.5	0.8	1.3	11.4	10.3	14.8	1.33
Netherlands	5.6	5.8	1.6	1.4	1.6	78.8	4.6	34.5	1.73
Spain	7.9	5.8	2.2	0.9	2.1	32.3	9.6	38.1	1.33
Sweden	9.8	6.8	1.3	1.9	3.2	40.4	8.7	42.3	1.75
United States	5.4	6.9	0.4	1.3	0.7	58.0	5.1	39.0	2.05
All SHARE countries	10.2	6.9	1.5	1.2	2.1	34.5	10.0	28.3	1.50

Sources: Authors' calculations based on data from OECD Social Expenditure Database—social and welfare statistics, Employment, Labour, and Social Affairs pensions, labor force statistics, and general statistics (OECD 2008b); *OECD Education at a Glance 2008* (OECD 2008a); residential mortgage debt from *OECD Economic Outlook 2004* (OECD 2004); Austria data from *IMF World Economic Outlook* (IMF 2008).

Notes: The OECD Social Expenditure Database groups benefits with a social purpose into the following areas: "old age"—pensions, early retirement pensions, and home help and residential services for the elderly; "health"—spending on in- and outpatient care, medical goods, and prevention; "family"—child allowances and credits, child care support, income support during leave, and single-parent payments; "unemployment"—unemployment compensation, severance pay, and early retirement for labor market reasons; and "housing"—housing allowances and rent subsidies. "Tertiary education" is defined here as direct public expenditure on educational institutions plus public subsidies to households (which include subsidies for living costs) and other private entities. The fertility rate is the number of children born to women ages fifteen to forty-nine.

[a]For 2005.

[b]For 2002.

variation in the amounts of money given to children. Residential mortgage debt as a percentage of GDP (column 6 of table 10.3) measures the size of the market or the availability of mortgage finance. It may also, however, reflect ownership preferences and tax incentives. Table 10.3 shows that Italy and Greece have the lowest levels of mortgage debt (11.4 percent and 13.9 percent, respectively), and they also have low average transfers compared to the other countries, while Denmark and the Netherlands have the highest levels of mortgage debt (74.3 percent and 78.8 percent, respectively), followed by the United States (58.0 percent). Table 10.3 also reports other average country-level differences that may help explain cross-country differences in the amount of money that parents give to adult children: the percentage of the population age twenty-five to thirty-four who are unemployed, the percentage of this age group who have attained tertiary education, and the fertility rate. Unemployment rates are low and tertiary education attainment and fertility are high in the United States. All of the European countries have lower fertility rates than the United States, while unemployment rates are generally higher in the European countries than in the United States. The percentage of the population age twenty-five to thirty-four with a tertiary education varies in Europe: the highest rates are in Sweden (42 percent) and Belgium (41 percent), and the lowest rate is in Italy (15 percent).

We employ multivariate methods to study how parental socioeconomic status, demographics, country-level social expenditures (percentage of GDP), the residential mortgage market, and characteristics of the population explain the amount of money that parents give to all their children, annually pooling the 2004 data from SHARE and HRS. The first model estimates the amount of money that parents give children (€2004 trimmed at the ninety-eighth percentile), annually adjusting for age, marital status, education level, number of children, income, and wealth and including country indicators. Ordinary least squares (OLS) results are given in the first column of table 10.4. The second model includes, instead of country fixed effects, country-level measures of the social expenditures and characteristics described in table 10.3. Because the distribution of the amount given is highly unequal, with most children not receiving any money in a given year, we also estimate quantile regression models at the ninetieth percentile (model 3).

Estimates of model 1 confirm that income, wealth, and education of parents are important predictors of the amount of money that children receive. A high-wealth (or high-income) parent (top 25 percent of the respective distribution) transfers €635 (€580) more annually to all children than a low-wealth (or low-income) parent. College-educated parents transfer €492 more annually to children than parents without a college degree. The effects of income and wealth are about three times larger at the ninetieth

Table 10.4   Linear Regression Model of Amount of Money That Parents Give to All Children (2004 Euros)

Model	Mean (1)	Mean (2)	Ninetieth Percentile (3)
Constant	2,630.4**	91.4	3,398.6**
Male	27.2	27.8	63.3*
Age	−57.8**	−57.9**	−146.0**
Age-squared	0.337**	0.338**	0.889**
Married	−83.1**	−82.4**	−116.9**
College	491.9**	491.9**	1,565.5**
[One child]			
Two children	106.9**	106.9**	135.3**
Three or more children	120.5**	120.0**	54.6
[Income quartile 1]			
Income quartile 2	88.5**	88.4**	183.5**
Income quartile 3	180.1**	179.7**	564.7**
Income quartile 4	580.3**	579.7**	1,886.1**
[Wealth quartile 1]			
Wealth quartile 2	130.9**	130.8**	189.3**
Wealth quartile 3	310.4**	310.2**	743.2**
Wealth quartile 4	635.2**	634.9**	1,985.9**
[United States]			
Austria	−475.3**		
Belgium	−226.2**		
Denmark	−319.9**		
France	−330.9**		
Germany	−308.7**		
Greece	−211.1**		
Italy	−520.7**		
Netherlands	−365.5**		
Spain	−726.1**		
Sweden	−458.2**		
Social expenditures (as percentage of GDP)			
Old age		−13.7	15.1
Health		−10.5	−2.1
Tertiary education		261.7**	358.5**
Family		−217.3*	−358.3**
Unemployment		71.4	41.7
Population ages twenty-five to thirty-four			
Percentage unemployed		94.9**	105.9**
Percentage attained tertiary education		−10.2	3.4
Fertility rate		1,086.4**	925.4**
Mortgage debt (as percentage of GDP)		2.6*	4.4**

(Table continues on p. 302.)

Table 10.4   *Continued*

Model	Mean (1)	Mean (2)	Ninetieth Percentile (3)
N	27,472	27,472	27,472
R-squared	0.086	0.086	0.15
Value of dependent variable	690.78	690.78	2178.65

Source: Authors' calculations based on data from SHARE Project (2004) and 2004 HRS (University of Michigan 2004).
Notes: Dependent variable "amount of money" trimmed at the ninety-eighth percentile. See table 10.3 note for definitions of social expenditures.
*significant at 5 percent; **significant at 1 percent.

percentile, confirming that the largest amounts of giving are concentrated among high-income and high-wealth parents (model 3).[8]

Parents in all European countries represented in the SHARE data give less to children than do parents in the United States. Comparing the model estimates of country effects to the mean values in table 10.1 (unconditional trimmed values), the difference in transfer amount between the United States and the European countries in the SHARE data is reduced by between 20 and 50 percent. Thus, the difference in giving to children between the United States and the SHARE countries is explained in part by cross-country differences in parents' socioeconomic and demographic characteristics.

Estimates of social policy expenditures (table 10.4, models 2 and 3) show some relationship to transfer amount, but do not provide strong evidence in favor of a "crowd-out" of family transfers by government expenditures. Spending on tertiary education is positively related to parental monetary gifts to children, although the amounts are small relative to these social expenditures. For example, a 1 percent increase in GDP spending on tertiary education increases transfers by €262 (on a base of €691). Public spending on family policies has a negative effect on giving by parents (–€217) that is higher at the ninetieth percentile (–€358), but is again overall a small effect. The percentage of the population ages twenty-five to thirty-four who are unemployed is associated with an increase in transfers, although again, the magnitude is small. The fertility rate is positively associated with money given to all children: an additional child increases the amount of money given to children by €1,000 at the mean and just under that amount at the ninetieth percentile. The size of the mortgage market has a very small, positive effect on the money given to children and thus, as measured here, does not appear to be an important source for generating differences in giving across countries.

In sum, there is much heterogeneity across households and countries in the amount of money given by parents to all of their children. In all countries, some households give money to children and many do not. In part, the unequal distribution of money given to children across households is only partially explained by differences in parental socio-economic status and demographics. The amount given to children is higher in the United States than in Europe, and within the European countries in the SHARE data, amounts are high in Denmark and Belgium and low in Spain. Some of the differences in the amounts that parents give their children across countries are explained by social public expenditure.

Another type of transfer, shared housing, may explain some of the cross-country differences. Marco Albertini, Martin Kohli, and Claudia Vogel (2007) document co-residency rates for the countries in the SHARE data, revealing high rates for Spain, Italy, and Greece. Although high co-residency rates in Spain may explain the low probability of parental monetary transfers in that country relative to other European countries, co-residency is approximately as high in Greece and Italy, but compared to these countries the likelihood that parents will give money to their children is at least twice as high as in Spain. Estate, bequest, inheritance, and inter vivos gift taxes ("transfer taxes") may also affect the decision about whether to make transfers, and when. Katarina Nordblom and Henry Ohlsson (2006) show that transfer taxes vary across countries in multiple dimensions: what is taxed (for example, estates in the United States compared to inheritances in many European countries), when they are taxed (for example, inter vivos gifts and inheritances are taxed at the time of transfer), how much is exempt from taxation, and the tax rate. In general, tax design is similar in many European countries and thus unlikely to explain most of the cross-country variation in Europe (Nordblom and Ohlsson 2006). Although tax-exempt amounts are lower in Europe than in the United States, most households transfer amounts significantly below what is permitted by the tax law (McGarry 2001; Poterba 1998). Finally, the permanent and transitory attributes of each child (data not included in these models) probably explain some of the remaining heterogeneity.

On average, the amounts of money that older parents give to all their children annually in any country does not appear to be large enough to transmit meaningful wealth inequalities across generations. For example, in the United States annual transfers to all children are €1,862, about €580 per child. Mean transfers to all children are highest in Belgium (€2,688) and lowest in Spain (€467). The distribution of amounts, however, reveals a lot of heterogeneity in the amounts of money. Five percent of U.S. parents give about €9,000 or more annually to their children. Among the SHARE countries, the top 5 percent give €5,000 or more to their children each year. Even these sums of money, however, would not play a significant role in financial wealth disparities across countries. The estimates of the amount of money that parents give their children are based on a single point in time, and total wealth transfers to children through the mechanism of direct financial giving depend in part on how persistent transfers are over time. We examine the long panel of the HRS to shed light on this issue.

Parents' Monetary Gifts to Children over Time in the United States

How large is the amount of money that parents give children over time? Is the unequal giving at a point in time of households in the United States and Europe mimicked when we look over time? That is, if some households give a lot to children and persistently give a lot over time, then the implication is that the intergenerational transmission of wealth inequality for these households may be larger. Moreover, within a household, how unequal are transfers given to all children at a point in time and over time? The answer to this second question may shed light on the long-standing debate in the United States on how to reconcile the unequal inter vivos monetary transfer to children within a family with the equal giving of bequests. To answer both questions, we turn to the long panel of data from the HRS.

How Much Money Do Parents Give Adult Children?   We use up to eight waves of data from the HRS, 1992 to 2006, to measure how much money parents give to children over a period of up to sixteen years. Tables 10.5 and 10.6 show the distribution of the amount of money that parents give to children for various lengths of time. Table 10.5 shows the money that parents give to *all* their children (average number of children is 3.3) and table 10.6 reports the per child amount. On average, over two years parents give $5,102, and over sixteen years $37,765, to all their children (table 10.5). Each child receives on average $1,559 and over sixteen years $11,122—or about $780 per year if he or she receives money each year (table 10.6). Once again, mean amounts obscure the highly unequal nature of the distribution. Fifty percent of households give no money to their children over two years and give $12,368 or less over sixteen years (table 10.5).[9] Seventy-five percent of children receive no money over two years and receive $8,622 or less over sixteen years, or about $539 per year (table 10.6). In contrast, at the ninety-fifth percentile, households give $23,869 or more over two years to their children, and over sixteen years they give $141,636 or more. A child in the top fifth percentile receives $7,421 or more from parents over two years and $54,602 or more over sixteen years (table 10.6).

Table 10.5   Amount of Money That Parents Give to All Children over Time in the United States (2006 Dollars)

Percentile	Two Years	Four Years	Six Years	Eight Years	Ten Years	Twelve Years	Fourteen Years	Sixteen Years
Tenth	$0	$0	$0	$0	$0	$0	$0	$0
Twenty-fifth	0	0	0	0	0	0	560	1,575
Fiftieth	0	0	1,437	2,874	4,482	6,184	8,908	12,368
Seventy-fifth	2,474	6,614	11,266	16,337	22,187	27,426	33,635	40,630
Ninetieth	11,707	24,075	35,403	47,358	58,853	68,534	80,551	92,164
Ninety-fifth	23,869	45,091	62,119	80,817	96,367	110,385	126,097	141,636
Ninety-ninth	70,244	122,134	172,595	221,010	265,333	295,793	326,740	367,318
Mean	5,102	9,885	14,623	19,450	24,413	28,770	33,595	37,765
N	88,168	68,206	51,450	38,257	26,816	16,868	9,926	3,903

Source: Authors' calculations based on data from HRS waves 1992 to 2006 (University of Michigan 2006).

Table 10.6   Amount of Money That Parents Give to One Child over Time in the United States (2006 Dollars)

Percentile	Two Years	Four Years	Six Years	Eight Years	Ten Years	Twelve Years	Fourteen Years	Sixteen Years
Tenth	$0	$0	$0	$0	$0	$0	$0	$0
Twenty-fifth	0	0	0	0	0	0	0	0
Fiftieth	0	0	0	0	0	0	0	500
Seventy-fifth	0	585	1,437	2,597	3,927	5,215	6,614	8,622
Ninetieth	2,561	6,376	10,471	13,976	18,387	21,879	25,865	29,905
Ninety-fifth	7,421	15,019	22,454	29,134	35,379	40,863	47,411	54,602
Ninety-ninth	28,738	49,472	66,523	83,799	100,732	110,599	125,376	137,641
Mean	1,559	3,025	4,444	5,907	7,376	8,577	9,981	11,122
N	300,669	229,373	171,771	126,807	88,571	55,612	32,661	12,830

Source: Authors' calculations based on data from HRS waves 1992 to 2006 (University of Michigan 2006).

Table 10.7   **Amount of Money That Parents Give to a Seventeen- or Eighteen-Year-Old Child in School over the Next Six Years (2006 Dollars)**

Percentile	Two Years	Four Years	Six Years
Tenth	$0	$0	$0
Twenty-fifth	0	1,360	2,341
Fiftieth	2,474	8,392	11,336
Seventy-fifth	11,206	24,736	29,776
Ninetieth	27,206	48,681	54,973
Ninety-fifth	39,488	74,440	82,397
Ninety-ninth	84,047	136,841	140,439
Mean	9,216	18,374	21,651
N	2,000	1,523	1,144

Source: Authors' calculations based on data from HRS waves 1992 to 2006 (University of Michigan 2006).

Is the Amount of Money Given to Children Large?   On average, the amount of money a child receives each year is small, about $780. The average age of children in the HRS is thirty-two, and average income is $45,000. In terms of life-cycle events, the average child is not in school, is married, and has a child, and just under half of them do not yet own a home. (Appendix table 10A.2 shows mean characteristics for the children of HRS respondents.) Thus, many children in the HRS have aged past the life-cycle events that might generate parental giving, particularly college and higher education. Table 10.7 shows the amount of money received by a child in school and between the ages of seventeen and eighteen over the next six years. Within this age group, the average amount that a child receives is about $9,000 over two years, $18,374 over four years, and slightly more ($21,651) over six years, or about $4,600 per year. This is about 50 percent more than all children in this age group receive (that is, including those not in school). Annual parental transfers for college-age children of $4,600 are 50 percent of average college tuition costs in 2005 ($9,144) and 30 percent of average tuition plus room and board expenses of $16,048 (College Board 2005). Many students receive some form of financial aid, which thereby reduces tuition and room and board expenses to an average of $11,286. Thus, parental financial transfers represent 40 percent of annual college expenses after financial aid. A child in the highest 5 percent receives $39,488 or more over two years. The annual tuition for a private, four-year college is approximately $20,000. Appendix table 10A.3 provides a summary of average public and private college costs for 2005. For children in college, the level of parental transfers is significant; however, the question remains of how essential parental financing is in the school decision.

Table 10.8 shows the average income and wealth for households based on their position in the distribution of giving to children. As

Table 10.8 Average Income and Wealth of Parents Who Make Positive Transfers, Based on Position in Transfer Distribution (2006 Dollars)

Transfer Percentile	Two Years	Four Years	Six Years	Eight Years	Ten Years	Twelve Years	Fourteen Years	Sixteen Years
Average income								
Tenth								
Twenty-fifth							$53,918	$57,742
Fiftieth			$63,456	$65,371	$65,783	$66,352	69,351	73,930
Seventy-fifth	$79,963	$85,833	84,920	88,082	89,861	91,159	91,088	93,228
Ninetieth	129,328	103,399	107,299	109,144	107,403	97,645	106,830	115,898
Ninety-fifth	134,160	149,612	144,170	153,037	142,747	149,762	148,081	146,638
Ninety-ninth	207,954	203,318	244,447	263,879	266,910	249,607	269,637	245,059
N	88,168	68,206	51,450	38,257	26,816	16,868	9,926	3,903
Average wealth								
Tenth								
Twenty-fifth							230,276	239,125
Fiftieth			323,373	323,120	322,224	314,206	302,363	310,426
Seventy-fifth	483,665	508,441	500,075	524,088	501,630	492,904	497,107	468,133
Ninetieth	738,121	679,024	694,924	668,382	663,007	640,974	585,190	590,030
Ninety-fifth	968,004	1,023,683	1,070,261	1,051,883	982,176	935,639	867,894	856,740
Ninety-ninth	2,349,257	2,339,929	1,930,942	2,110,465	2,114,367	1,980,913	1,963,744	2,071,066
N	88,168	68,206	51,450	38,257	26,816	16,868	9,926	3,903

Source: Authors' calculations based on data from HRS waves 1992 to 2006 (University of Michigan 2006).
Notes: Income and wealth of parents that make positive transfers. See table 10.5.

Table 10.9   Persistence of Monetary Giving by High-Giving Households

Parents Who Gave in at Least:	Sixteen-Year Transfers at Seventy-Fifth Percentile and Above	Sixteen-Year Transfers at Ninetieth Percentile and Above
Eight waves	14.8%	24.2%
Seven waves	33.3	49.6
Six waves	54.3	73.2
Five waves	73.5	87.5
Four waves	85.1	93.9
Three waves	94.4	99.0
Two waves	98.3	99.7
One wave	100.0	100.0
N	937	351

Source: Authors' calculations based on data from HRS waves 1992 to 2006 (University of Michigan 2006).

expected, households that give to children have higher income and wealth than those that do not. For example, households at the ninety-fifth percentile have $134,160 annual income and $968,004 in wealth. Households that give substantially to children give more as a percentage of their income and wealth. At the seventy-fifth percentile of the transfer distribution, annual household giving represents 1.5 percent of household annual income, and total household giving over sixteen years is 8.7 percent of average household wealth. At the ninety-fifth percentile of the transfer distribution, annual household giving represents 8.9 percent of household annual income, and total household giving over sixteen years is 16.5 percent of average household wealth.

Are Transfers Persistent Over Time?   Table 10.5 shows that after sixteen years fewer households give no money to children than after two years, which suggests that giving by households is not persistent over time. This is not true for households that give large amounts of money to children. Table 10.9 shows, for the parental households in the seventy-fifth and ninetieth percentiles of the sixteen-year transfer distribution, the percentage giving in at least one wave, at least two waves, and through eight waves. Almost three-quarters (73.5 percent) of households at the seventy-fifth percentile or higher of sixteen-year giving gave in at least five waves of data (sixteen years). Households further up in the distribution gave more persistently. Eighty-eight percent of households at the ninetieth percentile or higher of sixteen-year transfer amounts gave in at least five waves, while 94 percent gave in at least half of the eight waves.

Figure 10.3   Money Given to All Children in the United States: Ratio of Nineteeth and Seventy-Fifth Percentiles to Median and Nineteeth to Seventy-Fifth

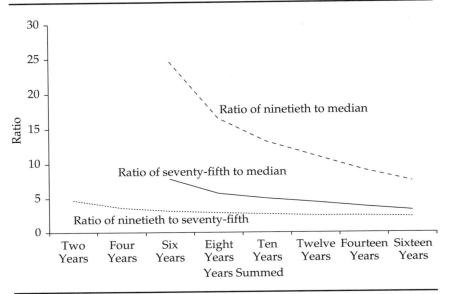

Source: Authors' calculations based on data from SHARE Project (2004) and 2004 HRS (University of Michigan 2004).
Note: Unconditional transfer amounts based on table 10.5.

To illustrate how the distribution of money given to all children changes over time, we plot in figure 10.3 the ratio of the seventy-fifth percentile to the median, the ninetieth percentile to the median, and the ninetieth to the seventy-fifth percentile. Transfer amounts across households become substantially more equal over time. Six-year amounts of money given to all children at the seventy-fifth percentile are almost eight times the median amount, while the ratio of sixteen-year amounts reduces to just over three. Six-year amounts of money given to children at the ninetieth percentile are over twenty-four times the median amount, while the ratio of the ninetieth percentile to the median of sixteen-year amounts reduces to seven and a half times. Even at the top quarter of the distribution, there are large differences in the amount of money given to all children over two years that reduces when the time horizon is sixteen years. The ratio of the ninetieth percentile to the seventy-fifth is 4.7, but it declines to 2.3 after sixteen years. We find that over time the amount of money that parents give to all children becomes more equal across households. After sixteen years, however, 25 percent of children do not receive any money and 50 percent receive $500 or less, while 5 percent receive almost $55,000.

The Equality of U.S. Parents' Monetary Gifts to Children Within the Family

How do parents divide monetary gifts among their children? A consistent empirical finding in the literature is that parents divide assets among children equally at death but give unequally while alive. These established facts, however, have been based on inter vivos giving over a short period of time, usually one or two years. We turn our analysis now to how parents divide money among children, using information provided by HRS respondents on the amounts of money given to each child and linking children across multiple waves of data—up to eight waves or sixteen years of recorded giving to children.

Do All Children in a Family Receive Parental Financial Transfers?   Table 10.10 shows the percentage of households giving money to all their children, none of their children, or only some of their children over various lengths of time, from two years to sixteen years. The sample is based on households that give at least one time to one child over sixteen years. We show results for all households and by number of children. Among all households, only 11.6 percent of parents give money to all their children (among households with two or more children) over a two-year time period. This steadily increases with time, and by sixteen years 43 percent of parents have given money to all their children and the remaining 57 percent have given to some but not all their children. Households that give money to none of their children drop quickly over eight years, from 51 percent to 16 percent. Although the actual percentages vary, the pattern is consistent across all household sizes.

Do All Children in a Family Receive the Same Amount of Money?   We calculate how much money parents of more than one child give each child, summing across different lengths of time (for example, two years, four years, and up to sixteen years). We calculate the difference in amount between what each child receives and the average amount that children in that family receive (the absolute value thereof), divided by the average amount. Thus, if all children receive the same amount, the ratio is zero. A ratio of one may be interpreted as a 100 percent difference between child i in family j and the average of children in family j. We plot the mean of this ratio by number of children in figure 10.4

Table 10.10   Multi-Child Households Giving Money to All Children in the Household

Time	All Households			Two-Child Households			Three-Child Households			Households with Four or More Children		
	All Children	No Children	Some Children	All Children	No Children	Some Children	All Children	No Children	Some Children	All Children	No Children	Some Children
Two years	11.6%	51.4%	37.0%	22.5%	48.3%	29.1%	9.6%	52.7%	37.7%	3.6%	53.0%	43.3%
Four years	19.3	33.6	47.1	36.1	30.9	33.0	16.7	35.0	48.3	6.6	35.0	58.3
Six years	25.4	23.1	51.5	46.2	20.6	33.2	22.6	24.4	53.0	9.7	24.3	66.1
Eight years	30.1	16.1	53.8	53.6	14.2	32.2	27.1	17.2	55.7	12.3	16.8	70.8
Ten years	33.8	11.0	55.2	59.1	9.8	31.1	30.9	11.7	57.4	14.6	11.5	73.9
Twelve years	37.2	6.6	56.2	63.9	5.8	30.3	34.4	7.1	58.5	16.8	7.0	76.2
Fourteen years	39.8	3.0	57.3	67.3	2.1	30.6	36.9	3.4	59.7	18.9	3.4	77.8
Sixteen years	42.8	0.0	57.2	70.6	0.0	29.4	40.3	0.0	59.7	21.5	0.0	78.5

Source: Authors' calculation based on data from HRS waves 1992 to 2006 (University of Michigan 2006).
Note: The sample comprises those born in the years from 1931 to 1941 who entered the HRS in 1992 and had given money to children at some time over the eight waves. The pattern is the same for other cohorts.

Figure 10.4   Within-Household Equality of Money Given to Children over Time in the United States

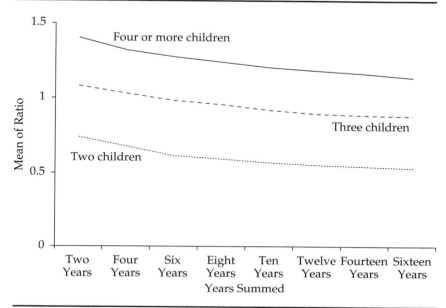

Source: Authors' calculations based on data from 2004 HRS (University of Michigan 2004).
Note: Mean of ratio: absolute value of difference in amount of money given to child *i* in family *j* and average amount given to all children in family *j*, divided by average amount given to all children.

and for low and high wealth and income in figures 10.5 and 10.6, respectively. Two distinct patterns emerge. First, as the number of children in a family increases, so does inequality in transfer amount (level differences by number of children across all time periods). For example, for a two-year time period, the mean ratio for a two-child family is 0.74, and for a family with four or more children it is 1.43. The increasing ratio by family size is driven in part by the greater opportunity for more than one child in the family to receive no transfers as the number of children increases.

Second, for all family sizes, the amount of money that children receive becomes more equal over time. For example, over a two-year period, child *i* in family *j* receives 75 percent more (less) than her sibling, but after sixteen years she receives only 50 percent more (less). Thus, the level of inequality in inter vivos giving to children is to an extent an artifact of the time period over which transfers are observed. High-wealth or high-income parents give more equally to their children than low-wealth and

Figure 10.5   Within-Household Equality of Money Given to Children over Time in the United States, by Household Wealth

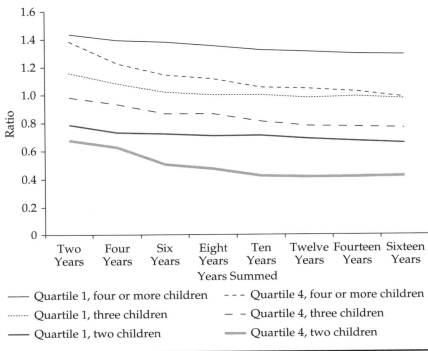

— Quartile 1, four or more children   - - - Quartile 4, four or more children

...... Quartile 1, three children   — - Quartile 4, three children

— Quartile 1, two children   ═══ Quartile 4, two children

Source: Authors' calculations based on data from 2004 HRS (University of Michigan 2004).
Note: Mean of ratio: absolute value of difference in amount of money given to child i in family j and average amount given to all children in family j, divided by average amount given to all children.

low-income parents (figures 10.5 and 10.6), and more so over time (see the steeper slope of the high-wealth and high-income lines in figures 10.5 and 10.6). In sum, the child who is most likely to be receiving the same amount of money as his or her siblings has only one sibling and has high-income and high-wealth parents.

Multivariate Model Results for Short- and Long-Term Money Transfers to Children in the United States

Next, we study the factors associated with receipt of money from a parent over different lengths of time. We model the probability that a child will get money from her parents and the amount of money she actually

Figure 10.6   Within-Household Equality of Money Given to Children over Time in the United States, by Household Income

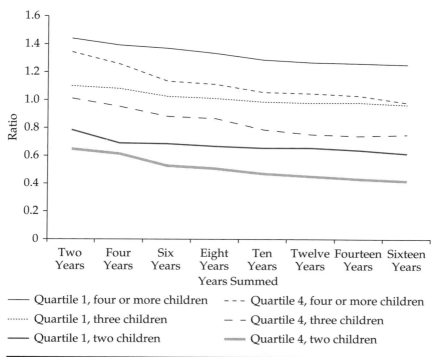

Quartile 1, four or more children   – – – Quartile 4, four or more children

······· Quartile 1, three children   — – Quartile 4, three children

Quartile 1, two children   Quartile 4, two children

Source: Authors' calculations based on data from 2004 HRS (University of Michigan 2004).
Note: Mean of ratio: absolute value of difference in amount of money given to child i in family j and average amount given to all children in family j, divided by average amount given to all children.

gets, conditional on receiving, for a sample of children who were present in seven waves, for a total of 32,661 child-year observations.[10] We estimate three models for the probability that a child receives money (and three additional models for the amount of money received), one for each of three time periods: two years, eight years, and fourteen years; we report marginal effects of covariates in table 10.11. All covariates are measured at the initial wave. In order to interpret our findings in the context of increasing average probabilities of giving and amount given with time, we describe results in terms of percentage change from the baseline probability or amount as well as in terms of overall level. Estimates of the marginal effects for key covariates are provided in table 10.11 and for all in appendix table 10A.1.

Table 10.11 Linear Regression Model Results for Money That Parents Give a Child over Two, Eight, and Fourteen Years

	Probability Child Receives Money			Amount of Money		
	Two Years	Eight Years	Fourteen Years	Two Years	Eight Years	Fourteen Years
Parent covariate						
Parent wealth quartiles						
1	-0.052**	-0.127**	-0.138**	-2,196**	-2,925**	-3,367*
2	-0.023**	-0.049**	-0.051**	-1,445*	-1,411*	-1,381
[3 omitted]						
4	0.037**	0.081**	0.097**	2,171**	7,879**	14,600**
Parent income quartiles						
1	-0.079**	-0.129**	-0.147**	-165	-3,201**	-6,488**
2	-0.041**	-0.062**	-0.060**	-998	-1,373*	-3,073*
[3 omitted]						
4	0.055**	0.059**	0.054**	2,578**	5,687**	11,657**
Child covariate						
In school	0.069**	0.058**	0.058**	-1,744	4,200*	2,980
Education at baseline						
Less than high school	-0.012	-0.014	-0.022*	-1,462	-453	455
Some college	0.008	0.021**	0.024**	139	531	-386
College	0.010	0.003	-0.000	1,583*	1,463*	3,005*
In school × high education						
In school × less than high school	-0.034	0.006	-0.006	3,253	-2,799	-3,190
In school × some college	0.123**	0.070**	0.026	6,176**	4,033*	8,307**
In school × college	0.077**	0.037	0.003	3,729*	-657	1,367

Homeownership						
Own home	-0.021**	-0.060**	-0.055**	2,331**	1,367	1,360
New home	0.018	0.041*	0.023	157	-894	-2,408
Same home	-0.029**	-0.020	-0.027*	-1,105	43	-2,540
Lose home	0.005	0.022	0.025	4,362*	1,373	2,765
Number of children						
One to three	0.022**	0.055**	0.067**	-862	468	2,616
Four or more	0.049**	0.072**	0.075**	318	501	2,267
Coresides with parent	0.006	0.068**	0.085**	1,405*	2,192**	3,180
Lives close to parent	0.017**	0.035**	0.048**	539	1,613**	1,455
Earnings quartiles [1 omitted]						
2	-0.024**	-0.016*	-0.002	-343	-957	-526
3	-0.079**	-0.064**	-0.037**	-256	-2,378**	-2,849
4	-0.101**	-0.099**	-0.073**	-189	-1,619	-1,168
N	32,661	32,661	32,661	5,300	11,768	14,409
R-squared	0.152	0.213	0.234	0.087	0.124	0.069
Mean dependent variable	0.162	0.36	0.441	9,368	14,455	19,858

Source: Authors' calculations based on data from HRS 1992 to 2006, sample of respondents present in seven waves (University of Michigan 2006).

Notes: All covariates measured at baseline. Model also includes other parent and child characteristics; see appendix table 10A.1. All amounts CPI-adjusted (transfers, income, wealth, earnings).

*significant at 5 percent; **significant at 1 percent

Parents' Income and Wealth

We find that receipt of money over two years is highly dependent on a parent's current ability to give, as measured by income, but over a greater time period—fourteen years—a long-run measure of socioeconomic status, wealth, is more important than income. For example, a child with a parent in the top twenty-fifth percent of the income distribution is 34 percent (5.5 percentage points on a baseline of 0.16) more likely to get money over two years than a child with a parent in the third income quartile, but only 12 percent more likely to get money over fourteen years. In contrast, the likelihood that a child with a high-wealth parent will get money is equal (about 22 percent more likely relative to a child with parents in the third wealth quartile) over two, eight, and fourteen years. Conditional on receiving money, the amount that a child with high-income and high-wealth parents receives relative to a child with low-income and low-wealth parents becomes larger over time. For example, a child with a parent in the top twenty-fifth percentile of the wealth distribution receives $2,171 more over two years than a child with a parent in the third quartile of the wealth distribution, or 23 percent more than the two-year average, and that child gets over $14,600 more over fourteen years, or 74 percent of the fourteen-year average amount. Over fourteen years, there is a difference of about $18,000 between what a child with a low-wealth parent receives and what a child with a high-wealth parent receives.

Children's Education   In the short term (over two years), children get money from their parents in response to their immediate needs—for example, to finance their higher education, to compensate for their low earnings or loss of a house, or to meet the needs of their own children. The greater amounts received by college-educated children relative to high school–educated children appear to be related to parents paying for college: being in school increases the baseline probability of receiving money over two years by 43 percent relative to not attending school. Over fourteen years, however, being in school at baseline increases the baseline probability of receiving money by only 13 percent. Children attending college ("in school" and the highest degree is "some college" at baseline) receive $4,571 more than children not in school and whose highest degree is high school over two years. Over fourteen years, the differences in the money received by children attending college at baseline ("some college") and those who do not attend college persist, with those children attending college at baseline receiving $10,901 more than those who are not in school and have completed high school at baseline. Although we do not know whether the money received is for educational expenses, the findings are consistent with this interpretation.

Children's Income   Low-income children are more likely to receive money in the short term, but over time income differences are much less predictive of receipt of money. For example, a child in the top twenty-fifth percentile of the earnings distribution is ten percentage points less likely to get money from a parent than a child in the lowest earnings quartile, which represents a 62 percent decline from the baseline probability. Over fourteen years, a child in the top twenty-fifth percentile of the earnings distribution at baseline is seven percentage points less likely to get money from a parent than a child in the lowest earnings quartile, which represents only a 17 percent decline from the baseline probability. Conditional on receiving a transfer, there is no difference between a high-income child and a low-income child in the amount of money each receives.

Children's Housing and Children   Children who are homeowners are less likely to receive money from parents, although the effect of being a new homeowner is no different from not being a homeowner. Conditional on receiving money from parents, children who become homeowners over two years or were homeowners and lost a home received $2,488 and $6,693 more, respectively, than children who were never homeowners over two years, but there is no difference in the amount of money received after fourteen years. The magnitude of these numbers suggests that, on average, assisting with homeownership is not an important factor driving parental transfers. Finally, the likelihood of giving to children increases with the number of grandchildren, particularly in the short run. For example, a child with four or more children is five percentage points more likely to receive money from parents over two years than a child with no children (a 30 percent increase from the baseline probability), and the differences between children with and without children diminishes over time.

In sum, a short-term view of the money given to children by their parents suggests that giving is compensatory (low earnings) to an extent and based on immediate need (to purchase a new house or recover from the loss of a house, to finance education, or for grandchildren) and that the amount given for any of these needs is not large. Over a long time horizon, a child's education is one of the remaining sources of difference in money given to children. Children in college or in school with a college degree received more money over the next fourteen years than those who are not in school and have a high school degree, although, again, the difference in amount is not large.

Conclusions

Although the likelihood that parents will give money to their children each year and the amount they give varies across the United States and the ten European countries we studied, the average amounts they give annually are not enough to affect wealth inequalities across generations in any country, even if given persistently over time. Data on monetary gifts to children over time in the United States reveal that giving is most persistent among households that give high amounts to children over two years. Children receive money in response to immediate needs in the short term (low income, housing, school). The average two-year amount a child receives from his or her parents is about $1,560, and $11,120 over sixteen years; thus, the magnitude of inter vivos transfers over time is simply not large enough to affect the distribution of resources within or between families in the next generation. However, the timing and level of financial transfers—for example, to smooth consumption after an income shock or to finance higher education—may have a significant impact on the welfare of a child. Annual parental transfers for college-age children in the United States were 50 percent of average college tuition costs in 2005, and 30 percent of average tuition plus room and board expenses. The effect of parental transfers to finance higher education on intergenerational mobility in the United States depends in part on whether the financing is essential in the schooling decision.

Moreover, parental monetary transfers for college and higher education are just one of many factors generating intergenerational transmission of human capital accumulation and may not be the most important. For example, in Spain only 15 percent of individuals age fifty-five to sixty-four have a college degree, but 39 percent of individuals age twenty-five to thirty-four have a college degree, and direct monetary transfers to children are the lowest of all the countries we studied—an average of €470 annually (although co-residency is high). In contrast, in Italy 9 percent of individuals age fifty-five to sixty-four have a college degree and only 16 percent of individuals age twenty-five to thirty-four have a college degree. Parental monetary transfers to children in Italy, while higher than in Spain (€873 annually), are still low. In both countries, public expenditure on tertiary education is high, and much higher than in the United States. Additional study is needed to better understand how parental financial investment in higher education affects intergenerational mobility through education and is affected by public provision of higher education financing. Panel microdata on parental transfers for children's education and methods utilizing cross-country and over-time variation in public expenditure on education offer a promising avenue for this research.

Appendix

Table 10A.1   Model Results for Money That Parents Give a Child over Two, Eight, and Fourteen Years in the United States

	Probability Child Receives Money			Amount of Money		
	Two Years	Eight Years	Fourteen Years	Two Years	Eight Years	Fourteen Years
Intercept	0.720**	0.909**	1.201**	23,337	19,533	−36,675
Parent Characteristic						
Married	0.254**	0.267*	0.315**	−9,390	−4,034	59,592**
Male	−0.000	0.013*	0.015**	−1,208**	−444	−1,474
Respondent age	−0.004	−0.008*	−0.010**	77	351	2,606**
Respondent age-squared	0.000	0.000**	0.000**	0	−2	−24**
Spouse age	−0.009**	−0.010**	−0.011**	321	−21	−2,536**
Spouse age-squared	0.000**	0.000**	0.000**	−3	1	25**
Respondent less than high school	−0.017**	−0.045**	−0.066**	−508	−1,377	−1,996
Respondent some college	0.020**	0.053**	0.052**	−149	−1,576*	−4,000**
Respondent college	0.044**	0.064**	0.050**	394	2,050**	690
Spouse less than high school	−0.013*	−0.039**	−0.047**	2,049**	717	320
Spouse some college	−0.007	0.002	0.003	148	59	273
Spouse college	0.027**	0.026**	0.022*	1,522*	3,523**	9,534**
Two to four children	−0.159**	−0.197**	−0.196**	−1,381	−8,773**	−9,823**
Five or more children	−0.226**	−0.321**	−0.338**	−2,327**	−11,767**	−14,879**
Wealth lowest quartile	−0.052**	−0.127**	−0.138**	−2,196**	−2,925**	−3,367*
Wealth second quartile	−0.023**	−0.049**	−0.051**	−1,445*	−1,411*	−1,381
Wealth top quartile	0.037**	0.081**	0.097**	2,171**	7,879**	14,600**
Income lowest quartile	−0.079**	−0.129**	−0.147**	−165	−3,201**	−6,488**
Income second quartile	−0.041**	−0.062**	−0.060**	−998	−1,373*	−3,073*
Income top quartile	0.055**	0.059**	0.054**	2,578**	5,687**	11,657**

(Table continues on p. 322.)

Table 10A.1 *Continued*

Child characteristic	Probability Child Receives Money			Amount of Money		
	Two Years	Eight Years	Fourteen Years	Two Years	Eight Years	Fourteen Years
Child is stepchild	−0.060**	−0.131**	−0.146**	−1,528	−3,146**	−8,544**
Child age	−0.004	0.011*	−0.002	−1,455*	−688	570
Child age-squared	−0.000	−0.001**	−0.000	36	10	−53
Male	0.001	−0.005	−0.006	−65	5	−772
Coupled	−0.016**	−0.040**	−0.045**	529	−189	−426
Work part-time	0.042**	0.049**	0.038**	−93	509	979
Work full-time	−0.006	−0.002	−0.003	−1,890**	−1,549*	−1,384
In school	0.069**	0.058**	0.058**	−1,744	4,200*	2,980
Less than high school	−0.012	−0.014	−0.022*	−1,462	−453	455
Some college	0.008	0.021**	0.024**	139	531	−386
College	0.010	0.003	−0.000	1,583*	1,463*	3,005*
In school × less than high school	−0.034	0.006	−0.006	3,253	−2,799	−3,190

In school × some college	0.123**	0.070**	0.026	6,176**	4,033*	8,307*
In school × college	0.077**	0.037	0.003	3,729*	-657	1,367
Own home	-0.021**	-0.060**	-0.055**	2,331**	1,367	1,360
New home	0.018	0.041*	0.023	157	-894	-2,408
Same home	-0.029**	-0.020	-0.027*	-1,105	43	-2,540
Lose home	0.005	0.022	0.025	4,362*	1,373	2,765
One to three children	0.022**	0.055**	0.067**	-862	468	2,616
Four or more children	0.049**	0.072**	0.075**	318	501	2,267
Coresides with parent	0.006	0.068**	0.085**	1,405*	2,192**	3,180
Lives close to parent	0.017**	0.035**	0.048**	539	1,613**	1,455
Income second quartile	-0.024**	-0.016*	-0.002	-343	-957	-526
Income third quartile	-0.079**	-0.064**	-0.037**	-256	-2,378**	-2,849
Income top quartile	-0.101**	-0.099**	-0.073**	-189	-1,619	-1,168

Source: Authors' calculations based on data from HRS 1992 to 2006, sample of respondents present in seven waves (University of Michigan 2006).
Notes: All covariates measured at baseline. Model includes missing and cohort indicators. All amounts CPI-adjusted (transfers, income, wealth, earnings).
*significant at 5 percent; **significant at 1 percent.

Table 10A.2   Descriptive Statistics of U.S. Sample for Regression Model

Variable	Mean
Parent covariates	
Married	0.75
Male	0.41
Respondent age	59.33
Spouse age	44.00
Respondent less than high school	0.34
Respondent some college	0.18
Respondent college	0.14
Spouse less than high school	0.22
Spouse some college	0.13
Spouse college	0.12
Two to four children	0.55
Five or more children	0.42
Household income (mean)	$61,169
Household wealth(mean)	$284,124
Child covariates	
Child is stepchild	0.11
Child age	32.28
Male	0.51
Married	0.55
Work part-time	0.10
Work full-time	0.68
In school	0.09
Less than high school	0.12
Some college	0.21
College	0.24
In school × less than high school	0.005
In school × some college	0.04
In school × college	0.02
Own home	0.44
New home	0.03
Same home	0.14
Lose home	0.01
One to three children	0.53
Four or more children	0.06
Coresides with parent	0.15
Lives close to parent	0.27
Earnings or income	$44,287

Source: Authors' calculations based on data from HRS waves 1992 to 2006 (University of Michigan 2006).

Table 10A.3   College Costs in 2005

	Private	Public	Both
Percentage of enrolled population[a]	0.232	0.768	1.00
Tuition	$21,235	$5,491	$9,144
Tuition plus room and board	29,026	12,127	16,048
Financial aid	9,600	3,300	4,762
Tuition plus room and board, less aid	19,426	8,827	11,286
Parental annual transfer			4,608

Source: Authors' compilation based on data from College Board (2005) and U.S. Bureau of the Census (2007).
[a]U.S. Bureau of the Census (2007).

Notes

1. The first survey, the Health and Retirement Study (HRS), began as a national sample of about 7,600 households (12,654 individuals) with at least one person in the birth cohorts of 1931 through 1941 (about fifty-one to sixty-one years old at the wave 1 interview in 1992). The second, the Assets and Health Dynamics of the Oldest Old (AHEAD), began in 1993 and included 6,052 households (8,222 individuals) with at least one person born in 1923 or earlier (age seventy years or older in 1993). In 1998, HRS was augmented with baseline interviews from at least one household member from the two birth cohorts 1924 through 1930 and 1942 through 1947 and was representative of all birth cohorts born in 1947 or earlier. In 2004 the HRS was again augmented with interviews from the birth cohort 1948 through 1953.

2. For the original HRS respondents from the 1992 survey wave, we use a total of eight waves of transfer data from 1992 to 2006, which accounts for money given to children over sixteen years. For the original AHEAD respondents from 1993, we have seven waves of data for a total of fourteen years of transfers. For respondents added in 1998, we have five survey waves from 1998 to 2006, or ten years of transfer data, and for the most recent cohort added, the early baby boomers, we have two waves of data from 2004 and 2006 (four years of transfer data).

3. In the 1992 and 1994 survey waves of the original HRS, the transfer questions varied slightly from the more recent waves. In 1992, HRS asked about financial help of $500 or more over *one* year, and in 1994 the threshold was $100. To make transfers over waves comparable, we make the simplistic assumption that two-year transfer amounts are two times the annual giving amount in 1992 and censor to zero amounts less than $500 for the survey year 1994.

4. The SHARE data collection has been primarily funded by the European Commission. Additional funding came from the U.S. National Institute on Aging. Data collection for wave 1 was nationally funded in Austria, Belgium, France, and Switzerland.

5. The overall household response rate is 55.4 percent. The response rate is lowest in Switzerland (37.4 percent) and highest in France (69.4 percent).

6. Although only three transfers are reported, this captures about 99 percent of all transfers. Only 13 percent of households have four or more children, and 96 percent of these households report two transfers or less. That is, only 115 households with four or more children use all available placeholders for reporting transfers and may possibly have made an additional transfer that was not recorded.

7. Giving to children is persistent over time (Hurd, Smith, and Zissimopoulos 2007). The probability of giving over two years conditional on having given the previous two years is 0.30. Under the assumption that biennial persistence approximates annual persistence, then about 25.2 percent of parents give annually.

8. We check the sensitivity of the income results to the wave 1 income measure by comparing model estimates obtained using wave 2 income, compared to using wave 1 income for the same sample, and find the estimates to be unchanged.

9. The median amount for households is $12,368, while the per child amount is just $500, reflecting that many children are receiving no money.

10. The sample constrained to be in all seven waves is about two and a half years younger than the full sample, with the same education level and about $5,000 more income on average.

References

Albertini, Marco, Martin Kohli, and Claudia Vogel. 2007. "Intergenerational Transfers of Time and Money in European Families: Common Patterns—Different Regimes?" *Journal of European Social Policy* 17(4): 319–34.

Attias-Donfut, Claudine, and Jim Ogg. 2005. "European Patterns of Intergenerational Financial and Time Transfers." *European Journal on Aging* 2(3): 161–73.

Becker, Gary S. 1981. *A Treatise on the Family.* Cambridge, Mass.: Harvard University Press.

Bernheim, B. Douglas, Andrei Shleifer, and Lawrence H. Summers. 1985. "The Strategic Bequest Motive." *Journal of Political Economy* 93(6): 1045–76.

Brown, Meta, Maurizio Mazzocco, John Karl Scholz, and Ananth Seshadri. 2006. "Tied Transfers." Working paper. Madison: University of Wisconsin.

College Board. 2005. "Trends in College Pricing." Trends in Higher Education Series. New York: College Board Publications.

Cox, Donald. 1987. "Motives for Private Income Transfers." *Journal of Political Economy* 95(3): 508–46.

Cox, Donald, and Tullio Jappelli. 1990. "Credit Rationing and Private Transfers: Evidence from Survey Data." *Review of Economics and Statistics* 72(3): 445–54.

Cox, Donald, and Mark Rank. 1992. "Inter-Vivos Transfers and Intergenerational Exchange." *Review of Economics and Statistics* 74(2): 305–14.

Cox, Donald, Zekerizy Eser, and Emmanuel Jimenez. 1998. "Motives for Private Transfers over the Life Cycle: An Analytical Framework and Evidence for Peru." *Journal of Development Economics* 55(1): 57–80.

Guiso, Luigi, and Tullio Jappelli. 2002. "Private Transfers, Borrowing Constraints, and the Timing of Home Ownership." *Journal of Money, Credit, and Banking* 34: 315–39.

Hurd, Michael, and James P. Smith. 2002. "Expected Bequests and Their Distribution." Working paper W9142. Cambridge, Mass.: National Bureau of Economic Research (NBER).

Hurd, Michael, James P. Smith, and Julie Zissimopoulos. 2007. "Intervivos Giving over the Life Cycle." RAND WR 524. Santa Monica, Calif.: RAND Corporation.

International Monetary Fund (IMF). 2008. *IMF World Economic Outlook* (April). Available at: http://www.imf.org/external/pubs/ft/weo/2008/01/index.htm (accessed May 15, 2011).

Lillard, Lee A., and Robert Willis. 1997. "Motives for Intergenerational Transfers: Evidence from Malaysia." *Demography* 34(1): 115–34.

Marini, Margaret Mooney. 1978. "The Transition to Adulthood: Sex Differences in Educational Attainment and Age at Marriage." *American Sociological Review* 4(4): 484–507.

McGarry, Kathleen. 2001. "The Cost of Equality: Unequal Bequests and Tax Avoidance." *Journal of Public Economics* 79(1): 179–204.

McGarry, Kathleen, and Robert F. Schoeni. 1995. "Transfer Behavior in the Health and Retirement Study: Measurement and the Redistribution of Resources Within the Family." *Journal of Human Resources* 30(S): 184–225.

Nordblom, Katarina, and Henry Ohlsson. 2006. "Tax Avoidance and Intra-Family Transfers." *Journal of Public Economics* 90: 1669–80.

Organization for Economic Co-operation and Development (OECD). 2004. *Economic Outlook 2004.* Paris: Organization for Economic Co-operation and Development.

———. 2008a. *Education at a Glance 2008.* Paris: Organization for Economic Co-operation and Development.

———. 2008b. Family Database. Available at: http://www.oecd.org/els/social/family/database (accessed May 16, 2011).

Pezzin, Liliana E., and Barbara Steinberg Schone. 1997. "The Allocation of Resources in Intergenerational Households: Adult Children and Their Elderly Parents." *American Economic Review* 87(2): 460–64.

Poterba, James. 1998. "Estate and Gift Taxes and Incentive for Inter Vivos Giving in the United States." Working paper 6842. Cambridge, Mass.: National Bureau of Economic Research (NBER).

Sandefur, Gary, Jennifer Eggerling-Boeck, and Hyunjoon Park. 2005. "Off to a Good Start? Postsecondary Education and Early Adult Life." In *On the Frontier of Adulthood: Theory, Research, and Public Policy*, edited by Richard A. Settersten Jr., Frank F. Furstenberg Jr., and Rubén G. Rumbaut. Chicago: University of Chicago Press.

Schoeni, Robert F. 1997. "Private Interhousehold Transfers of Money and Time: New Empirical Evidence." *Review of Income and Wealth* 43(4): 423–48.

Schoeni, Robert F., and Karen Ross. 2005. "Material Assistance Received from Families During the Transition to Adulthood." In *On the Frontier of Adulthood: Theory, Research, and Public Policy,* edited by Richard A. Settersten Jr., Frank F. Furstenberg Jr., and Rubén G. Rumbaut. Chicago: University of Chicago Press.

SHARE Project. 2004. *Survey of Health, Ageing, and Retirement in Europe,* release 2.3.0. Available at: http://www.share-project.org (accessed May 17, 2011).

University of Michigan. 2004. *Health and Retirement Study 2004.* Ann Arbor: Institute for Social Research, University of Michigan. Available at: http://hrsonline.isr.umich.edu (accessed May 17, 2011).

———. 2006. *Health and Retirement Study 2006.* Ann Arbor: Institute for Social Research, University of Michigan. Available at: http://hrsonline.isr.umich.edu (accessed May 17, 2011).

U.S. Bureau of the Census. 2007. *American Community Survey, 2005–2007.* Washington: U.S. Bureau of the Census.

PART V

SOCIAL AND LABOR MARKET INSTITUTIONS

Chapter 11

The Role of Social Institutions in Intergenerational Mobility

BRIAN NOLAN, GØSTA ESPING-ANDERSEN,
CHRISTOPHER T. WHELAN, BERTRAND MÂITRE,
AND SANDER WAGNER

T HE PRIMARY goal of intergenerational mobility (IGM) research has always been to explain how and why social origins influence people's life chances. This focus has naturally placed family attributes at center stage. But the role of social institutions—most notably education systems—as a mediating factor has also been central to IGM theory. Indeed, generations of stratification research were premised on the core assumption that equalizing access to education would weaken the impact of social origins. In theory, policies and institutions, as well as macroeconomic and historical contexts, have been identified as crucial in shaping patterns of social mobility (d'Addio 2007). But apart from education, empirical research has contributed little concrete evidence on how this occurs.

Since institutions are said to mediate the link between origins and destination, we first need to be clear about what precisely they are supposed to mediate. In other words, we need to begin with a firm identification of the most salient social origin mechanisms. Here we can benefit from two major advances in recent empirical research: first, the effort to identify the relative importance of genes, and second, the identification of early childhood conditions as fundamental for subsequent achievements.

We are beginning to understand that a sharp distinction between nature and nurture can be misleading, considering that there are clear interaction effects between the two. On the basis of Swedish register data, Anders Björklund, Markus Jäntti, and Gary Solon (2005) manage to tease out nature and nurture effects by examining children raised by biological parents, adoptive parents, or one biological parent with or without a stepparent; they also look at information on the biological parents even when they are not the rearing parents. Their results suggest that both pre-birth (including genetic) and post-birth environmental factors are important influences on subsequent socioeconomic status. Christopher Jencks and Laura Tach (2006) interpret these results as meaning that genes account for about two-fifths of the intergenerational correlation in earnings in Sweden, and they speculate that the figure might be about the same in the United States (though the data there are far less satisfactory). However, as they stress, "genes" include not only "ability" but also health, beauty, and skin color, and genetic makeup can affect one's environment in various ways: "Because our genes affect both the way others treat us and the choices we make for ourselves, we cannot estimate genes' impact 'holding the environment constant' " (Jencks and Tach 2006, 34). Haoming Liu and Jinli Zeng (2009) compare adopted and biological children in an attempt to identify the genetic effect with U.S. data from the Panel Study of Income Dynamics (PSID). Their findings give support to Jencks and Tach's view, suggesting that biological factors account for roughly half of the father-child earnings correlation.

Genetics aside, probably the most significant message from recent research has been the importance of early childhood conditions, whether for short-, medium- or long-run outcomes. Both cognitive skills and family finances matter for "getting ahead," but so do noncognitive abilities, social skills, cultural resources, motivation, and, more generally, the familial "learning milieu." It has become increasingly clear that cognitive and noncognitive skills depend hugely on family endowments that are not strictly financial or genetic. Some studies have tried to capture such endowments by including direct information on cultural assets such as books and cultural consumption, and these have been shown to be significantly associated with later outcomes. However, to our knowledge no one has been able to establish direct causal links in this regard. In any event, as we discuss later in the chapter, contemporary research has in this respect been quite successful in identifying key policies and institutions—in particular high-quality early childhood programs, which matter for both cognitive and noncognitive outcomes (Carneiro and Heckman 2003; Currie 2001; Karoly, Kilburn, and Cannon 2005; Waldfogel 2006).

We can now say with some certainty that one possible institutional influence—namely, the local neighborhood or community—matters far less to IGM than family attributes. Gary Solon, Marianne Page, and Greg Duncan (2000) use the cluster sampling design of the PSID to estimate both sibling and neighborhood correlations of years of schooling and find sibling correlations of around 0.5, whereas their neighborhood estimates are as low as 0.1. Oddbjørn Raaum, Kjell Salvanes, and Erik Sørensen (2003), using Norwegian census data, conclude likewise that neighborhood correlations are small compared to sibling correlations, be it for educational attainment or for long-run earnings. Without reviewing the wide range of studies involved (on which see, for example, Esping-Andersen 2004a, 2004b; d'Addio 2007), for our present purposes the key point is that they suggest that causal mechanisms related to the family are critical in IGM, and it is against that background that the role of social institutions must be considered.[1]

Over the past decade the role of institutions has undergone two major revisions. First, mounting evidence suggests that differences in the design of education systems seem to matter much less than had been thought. Second, researchers have begun to shift their focus to possible welfare state effects. If income inequalities affect how parents can invest in their children, welfare state redistribution ought to equalize children's life chances. We would, in particular, expect that effective poverty reduction should boost the mobility chances of the most disadvantaged. Differences in welfare state redistribution are well documented, but the extent to which they influence IGM—either directly or indirectly—is much less known. The key issue, of course, has to do with the salience of family income per se for child outcomes. Susan Mayer (1997), for example, argues persuasively that the income effect is less important than the parental characteristics (such as low skills, poor health, or deviance) that may also explain why they happen to be poor in the first place. From such a perspective, welfare state redistribution may not have much of an effect on mobility chances.

The findings of James Heckman and his colleagues regarding the centrality of early childhood stimulation not only provide clues as to why education systems matter less than was assumed but suggest an alternative source of potential welfare state effects (Heckman and Lochner 2000; Carneiro and Heckman 2003). Their "learning begets learning" model stresses the fundamental causal importance of conditions in the preschool years, especially those related to behavioral and cognitive development. Here disadvantage stems importantly from parental traits (such as poor cognitive and noncognitive skills). Their analyses suggest that high-quality preschool programs can be extraordinarily effective in closing the achievement gap for such disadvantaged children. This view finds additional support from the very few existing attempts to examine how the intensity of parenting (in terms of time spent with the children) influences later child outcomes (for a discussion, see Esping-Andersen 2009, chapter 4).

In this chapter, we aim to identify how welfare state institutions affect patterns of intergenerational mobility more broadly, emphasizing their role in alleviating the adverse effects of poverty and disadvantage.

Linking Institutions and Outcomes

Over the past decades, substantial advances have been made in understanding how differences in welfare state institutions, spanning education and training, the labor market, health care, taxation, and social protection, underpin the substantial variation across rich countries in, for example, income inequality and poverty levels and trends (illustrated, for example, by OECD 2008). Welfare state arrangements, whether analyzed on a country-by-country basis or in terms of distinctive welfare "regimes," have been shown to be central. This does not mean that societies can insulate themselves from external forces, nor that implications for policy can be easily drawn, but it does provide a more secure foundation for thinking about institutions and policies.

Deriving hypotheses about underlying causal processes and testing them empirically in a particular national setting has yielded important insights. But in order to tease out welfare state effects we need, almost by definition, to pursue research that compares across countries and time. Research in this vein, for instance, has now firmly established that income inequality is greater in the United States than in the United Kingdom, and greater in both these countries than in the Scandinavian countries. Such findings have stimulated intensive research on the impact of government redistribution and labor market institutions, as well as on the role of demographic characteristics such as household structures. We also know that income inequality in the United States and the United Kingdom has risen more sharply over the past decades than in other Organization for Economic Co-operation and Development (OECD) countries and that these increases were concentrated in specific subperiods. This suggests, in turn, that rising inequality is not simply the inevitable consequence of skill-biased technological change. Hence, research has focused attention on how technological change actually influences earnings and household incomes in different institutional settings.

Also complicating efforts to identify welfare state effects on IGM is the multidimensional nature of social mobility. Different research traditions emphasize different kinds of mobility. Social mobility may be studied and assessed in terms of, inter alia, individual earnings, household income, poverty and disadvantage, wealth, social class, and education.

Some of these dimensions can be examined not only as final outcomes but also as critical intervening variables in the intergenerational transmission process. Education is an outcome in its own right, but also a predictor of earnings or occupational status, and individual earnings also influence household income and wealth. We should not expect a priori that institutions influence such outcomes in an identical fashion, or that settings that are more conducive to mobility in one domain (for example, education) necessarily carry over into another (such as income).

Intergenerational Mobility

Earnings

There have by now been extensive efforts to estimate intergenerational earnings elasticities between fathers and sons in a range of countries. Comparisons have been bedeviled by subtle differences in data and methods, but Björklund and Jäntti's (2009) "preferred" estimates for eleven countries may be taken as summarizing the current consensus. In their comparison, Denmark emerges as the most mobile nation (with a value below 0.2), followed by Sweden, Norway, Germany, and Australia (above 0.2), then Canada and the United Kingdom (slightly higher), and finally France, Italy, and the United States representing the least mobile cases (with values over 0.4). Strong father-son earnings correlations tend to be found in countries with greater income inequality, but the relationship is not straightforward considering that the elasticities for Germany, Australia, and Canada hardly differ from those for Sweden and Norway, and that France and Italy display elasticities that are nearly as high as in the United States. Here, as Björklund and Jäntti emphasize, we must note that the estimated confidence intervals around these estimates tend to be very wide, especially those based on survey data; thus, the figure for Australia is as low as the Nordic ones, but its confidence interval overlaps with those of Italy and the United States (see also Björklund and Jäntti 1997; Bonke, Hussain, and Munk 2006; Bratberg, Nilsen, and Vaage 2007; Corak 2004; Solon 2002). This ranking differs in some respects from that presented in Corak (2006) and OECD (2008), mainly because Björklund and Jäntti's lower elasticities for Germany and the United Kingdom derive from more recent studies. OECD (2008) also includes an estimate for Spain of about 0.3.

There are far fewer studies of intergenerational earnings transmission for women than for men. Elasticities with respect to father's earnings generally seem to be somewhat lower for daughters' than sons' earnings (see, for example, the discussion in Hirvonen 2006). Raaum and his colleagues (2007) find that the elasticity of own earnings with respect to (total) parental earnings is lower for women than men in Scandinavian countries, the United Kingdom, and the United States. However, they note a marked difference between married and single women in the United Kingdom and the United States, which they attribute to partners' joint labor supply decisions (an issue to which we return in discussing mobility in family income).

Such comparisons provide only a summary measure for all parent-offspring combinations, and this may yield a distorted view of reality if mobility patterns differ across the income distribution. This can have important implications from a welfare state perspective, in particular if (as some studies show) mobility from the bottom of the income distribution is significantly greater in countries with highly redistributive welfare states. Although some national studies report higher mobility in the middle of the distribution than in the tails, there is some inconsistency across studies. Ken Couch and Dean Lillard (2004) report lower mobility at the top and bottom of the earnings distribution for Germany and the United States. Bratberg and his colleagues (2007) show that in Denmark, Finland, and Norway the relationship between sons' and fathers' earnings is highly nonlinear, with sons who grow up in the poorest households having the same adult earnings prospects as those in moderately poor households, but with an increasingly positive effect of father's earnings in middle and upper segments. In the United States and the United Kingdom, on the other hand, the relationship is much closer to being linear. Cross-country comparisons of intergenerational earnings elasticities may thus be misleading with respect to transmission mechanisms in the central parts of the earnings distribution and uninformative in the tails. Jäntti and his colleagues (2006) present quintile transition matrices, which show quite substantial upward mobility from the bottom quintile in the Scandinavian countries, while, in contrast, the United Kingdom and, especially, the United States exhibit remarkably low mobility from the bottom. Another striking feature of their results is the very similar degree of retention within the top quintile across all countries. If these patterns are indeed related to welfare state redistribution, the upshot is that the Nordic welfare states concentrate their efforts at the bottom rather than across the entire income distribution.

The findings so far discussed tell us nothing about whether earnings mobility has increased or decreased over time. Estimating trends over time requires data that are very difficult to obtain. A few such dynamic studies have been attempted for individual countries, but they generally do not show any clear trends. Research focused on the United States has produced diverging conclusions. Susan Mayer and Leonard Lopoo (2005) find that social mobility rose for cohorts born during the 1950s and 1960s, though the rise was not statistically significant; Chul-In Lee and Gary Solon (2006), also using the PSID, find no major changes in mobility for the cohorts born between 1952 and 1975. Daniel Aaronson and Bhaskar Mazumder (2008) find a fall in intergenerational mobility among cohorts born after the mid-1950s. For the United Kingdom, analysis relating children's earnings to (total) parental income in the two cohort studies that started in 1958 and 1970 concludes that IGM has fallen over time (Blanden et al. 2004). But this has been questioned by Robert Erikson and John Goldthorpe (2010), who point to possible measurement error in parental income in one cohort versus the other. Using the British Household Panel Study (BHPS), Chetti Nicoletti and John Ermisch (2007) study intergenerational earnings mobility for two cohorts of sons born between 1950 and 1972 on the basis of predicted earnings for the fathers (using education, age, and occupation when the child was fourteen). Although they find no major changes across cohorts from 1950 to 1960, they do find a negative trend in mobility between 1961 and 1972—which would appear consistent with the conclusions of Jo Blanden and her colleagues (2004).

For France, Arnaud LeFranc and Alain Trannoy (2005) report that intergenerational mobility has been very stable across cohorts. Nicole Fortin and Sophie Lefebvre (1998) document similar stability for Canada from the mid-1980s to the mid-1990s, and Eva Österbacka (2001) reports no clear trend for Finland. Andrew Leigh (2007), using predicted father's earnings and data from four surveys back as far as 1965, finds no evidence that intergenerational earnings mobility has either risen or fallen over time in Australia. Espen Bratberg and his colleagues (2007), using quantile regressions, report that in Norway intergenerational earnings mobility increased from the early 1980s to the mid-1990s for both sons and daughters. For Finland, Tuomas Pekkarinen, Roope Uusitalo, and Sari Pekkala (2006) and Pekkala and Robert Lucas (2007) also find increasing mobility.

All in all, the evidence on intergenerational earnings mobility across nations and time would appear to be too ambiguous to support any strong hypotheses regarding welfare state effects. The results of the cross-section comparison conducted by Jäntti and his colleagues (2006) might be interpreted in terms of welfare state redistributive effects: it would appear that the Nordic countries have been comparatively effective in minimizing any mobility disadvantage associated with low-earning fathers (although they have done little to diminish the advantages of being rich). Yet the same findings could with equal plausibility be ascribed to the highly compressed wage structure within the Nordic countries—which in particular benefits low-wage workers (Esping-Andersen 2009).

Fathers' earnings is only one component, albeit often a dominant one, of families' total income. If mobility depends on how much parents can invest in their children's life chances, it would seem to be more relevant to focus on total family income. Only a small number of national studies have been able to examine family income across two generations. Laura Chadwick and Gary Solon (2002), using the PSID data, find that intergenerational elasticities based on total family income are higher (that is, there is less mobility) than those based solely on earnings. This could be the product of a number of factors: the effect on family income of capital income; variations in maternal labor supply and earnings potential, which clearly affect the distribution of family income; and assortative mating, which, being especially pronounced among high-educated couples, is also likely to augment income inequalities among families. John Ermisch, Marco Francesconi, and Thomas Siedler (2006), for example, find that in the United Kingdom, on average, 40 to 50 percent of the covariance between parents' income and one's own permanent family income can be attributed to the person to whom one is married (see also Harding et al. 2005; Hirvonen 2006; Holmlund 2006).

Comparative studies based on family income are even rarer, but Raaum and his colleagues (2007) find that the intergenerational transmission of family earnings, like individual earnings, is significantly stronger in the United States than in the Scandinavian countries, with the United Kingdom somewhere in between. Strikingly, they find that for married women in the United States and the United Kingdom, but not for married women in the

Scandinavian countries, the elasticity of their earnings with respect to parents' earnings is much lower than that of family earnings. This is because women marrying rich men respond by working fewer hours or by withdrawing from the labor market, and this cross–wage labor supply response outweighs the fact that these women also tend to have high earnings potential themselves.

There are few studies indeed that focus on mobility changes over time in terms of overall family income. One such study was conducted by Thomas Hertz (2007), who, using the PSID data, fails to find any meaningful trend in the intergenerational correlation of family income in the United States over the last twenty-five years. We can nonetheless point to trends that are likely to have had an impact, one of the most important being the increase in married women's labor force participation. The impact on intergenerational transmission of family income depends on whether the increase has been more pronounced for low-earning than high-earning women. If it has been greater among highly educated women (especially if accompanied by assortative mating), the outcome is likely to be less mobility in terms of family income. The extent to which this has actually occurred across countries is not yet clear.

The literature on intergenerational income mobility provides precious few clues as to any welfare state effects. Perhaps the most promising line of reasoning would be indirect—namely, how social policies and, in particular, parental leave and child care influence maternal labor supply. In the Nordic countries, mothers' labor supply varies relatively little across levels of education. In contrast, in many countries low-educated women are far less likely to work, as is also true of women married to rich husbands (Esping-Andersen 2009). The difficulty of pinning down any welfare state effects has much to do with the period-specific dual causality, which, by definition, must influence parent-child income correlations. The first chain of causality has to do with conditions in the period of childhood. To the extent that parental resources dictate child investments, much inequality in the childhood period should translate into stronger correlations and less mobility. The second chain of causality derives from the prevailing conditions in the period when the child has become an adult. It may be that the originally unequal distribution of child investments has minor consequences for mobility if there is great earnings compression in the adult period. Put differently, a very unequal start may not necessarily produce a similarly unequal end if, for example, institutions change.

That said, a promising avenue for future research would be to compare—in a quasi-experimental way—across sets of countries that share similar conditions (say, the shape of the income distribution) in the childhood period but also differ sharply in terms of the policy or institutional change that ought to affect earnings or income attainment in the later, adult period.

Poverty and Disadvantage

There is substantial evidence from country-specific studies that mobility is particularly limited toward the bottom of the socioeconomic hierarchy—that is, that poverty is inherited across generations. Examples from research in the United States include Wilson (1987), Gottschalk, McLanahan, and Sandefur (1994), Duncan and Brooks-Gunn (1997), Duncan and his colleagues (1998), and Corcoran (2001); for Canada, see Corak (2001). Recent U.K. studies include Sigle-Rushton (2004) and Blanden and Gibbons (2006). And similar studies that trace current poverty or disadvantage to conditions in childhood have been done for many other countries. However, this extensive literature does not provide a ready basis for assessing how the intergenerational transmission of poverty or disadvantage varies across countries. The same is true of welfare recipiency (see, for example, the results for Sweden and Canada in Corak 2004; for the United States, see Page 2004). But as OECD (2008) notes, available research does not allow us to compare directly the strength of this transmission across countries.

Similarly, the existing literature has little to say about whether there has been significant change over time in the probability of escaping from poverty from one generation to the next. Nevertheless, recent research on the consequences of growing up in poverty provides important pointers regarding the underlying mechanisms that shape mobility and, especially, the lack thereof. Studies that have focused on the United States (where, of course, child poverty is especially widespread) show that the inheritance of poverty is connected with substantially less schooling (poor children average two years less schooling than nonpoor children), poor health, and crime (Mayer 1997; Duncan and Brooks-Gunn 1997). Similar—if somewhat less dramatic—effects are documented for the United Kingdom (Gregg, Harkness, and Machin 1999) and for France (Maurin 2002; CERC 2004). But again, the key question is whether such adverse consequences can be ascribed to a low-income effect or whether responsibility lies with unobserved parent or child characteristics that may explain a family's poverty in the first place.

In this respect, the study by Paul Gregg and his colleagues (1999) is important, since they control for a child's abilities (through cognitive test scores at age seven) and still uncover strong poverty effects. In terms of parental characteristics, the impact of single motherhood has been subject to considerable scrutiny, especially in U.S. research. Most studies demonstrate strong negative effects of single motherhood on child outcomes, but they also suggest that the main reason has to do with poor economic conditions (McLanahan and Sandefur 1994; Biblarz and Raftery 1999; Gregg, Harkness, and Machin 1999).

As noted, comparative analyses of poverty effects on mobility are few and far between. Gøsta Esping-Andersen and Sander Wagner (2010) use the 2005 European Union Statistics on Income and Living Conditions (EU-SILC) intergenerational module to estimate the impact of economic hardship during childhood on both educational attainment and adult income (controlling also for sibling size, immigrant status, single motherhood, and parents' education) across a number of EU countries (Denmark, Norway, France, Italy, Spain, and the United Kingdom). The study concludes that the effects are indirect rather than direct. Economic hardship in childhood has no direct effects on adult income in any of the countries, but it has powerful indirect effects via the children's final educational attainment. For our purposes, the comparison across postwar cohorts (born, respectively, 1945 to 1957, 1958 to 1967, and 1968 to 1977) is of special interest. The main results are that the negative (indirect) effect of poverty disappears among the youngest cohorts in both Denmark and Norway, while it remains persistent (and even sharpens) in France, Italy, and Spain. In the United Kingdom, the effect persists, although it becomes slightly weaker within the youngest cohort. Since these findings line up nicely with the national contrasts found in the study by Jäntti and his colleagues (2006), the case in favor of welfare state effects is even clearer: the Scandinavian countries seem to be doing something that helps minimize the adverse consequences of economic want in childhood.

Wealth

Wealth is a key indicator of long-term command over resources and socioeconomic position, and the transfer of wealth across generations has been of long-standing interest because of its potential role in the intergenerational transmission of advantage and disadvantage. However, researching wealth transmission is very demanding in data terms, so available studies mostly focus on a single country. Robust comparisons of the distribution of wealth across countries or over time face severe difficulties in terms of harmonization of concepts and data; the data being assembled by the Luxembourg Wealth Study (LWS) represent a major step forward in terms of cross-sectional comparisons (see Jäntti, Sierminska, and Smeeding 2008; OECD 2008, chapter 10), but there is still considerable uncertainty about country rankings on wealth inequality.

However, capturing intergenerational persistence in wealth, and measuring direct transmission via inter vivos gifts and bequests, is particularly demanding in terms of data. Colin Harbury and David Hitchens (1979) report an intergenerational elasticity of inheritance between fathers of very rich children and their children in the United States of about 0.50; Paul Menchik (1979), using probate records for high-income persons in the United States to compare estates at death of parents and offspring, reports even higher elasticities. Kerwin Charles and Erik Hurst (2003) use special wealth modules in the PSID to compare wealth across generations and find an (age-adjusted) elasticity of 0.37, considerably lower than other studies, but this is before the offspring receive bequests. Anders Klevmarken (2004) analyzes Swedish Household Panel Survey data and finds that 34 percent of offspring inherited or received a gift, which accounts for less than 20 percent of current wealth. Most bequest recipients are middle-aged, and bequests and gifts do not appear to produce much mobility in wealth over time for offspring. U.S. studies using the Surveys of Consumer Finances (SCF) suggest that both inter vivos transfers and bequests account for a substantial proportion of total wealth, but that like total wealth, this is heavily concentrated toward the top; persistence in wealth across generations appears to be most pronounced there. Outside the top, wealth transfers may play a particularly important role in home-ownership. Once again, little robust evidence on cross-country differences in transmission patterns is available.

Clearly, the direct transfer of wealth in the form of gifts or inheritance is only one element in the association between the wealth levels of parents and their children, and it is not easy to say precisely how great a contribution it makes. Inherited wealth and earnings capacity can reinforce each other—wealth may underpin better education, health, and neighborhoods, as well as provide start-up capital for businesses (the family firm may be inherited directly). In the words of Samuel Bowles and Herbert Gintis (2002, 18), it "seems likely that the intergenerational persistence of wealth reflects, at least in part, parent-offspring similarities in traits influencing wealth accumulation." Bowles and Gintis suggest that the intergenerational transmission of wealth accounts for about 30 percent of the intergenerational correlation in income in the United States, but this has been contested. Although some studies have sought to capture how the distribution of wealth has been changing over time in particular countries (see, for example, Wolff 2004, 2007), we are not aware of any that are focused directly on measuring how the role of wealth in IGM has evolved.

Social Class

Sociologists have always shown a keen interest in intergenerational mobility; indeed, it is widely regarded as a core issue within the discipline. But rather than focus on incomes, mobility has primarily been analyzed in terms of social class, occupational status, and prestige. A comparative perspective has been central to this literature. For decades, postwar sociological mobility research was guided by the assumption that socioeconomic modernization should promote more social fluidity—that is, less social inheritance—as well as convergent patterns of IGM across countries. Robert Erikson and John Goldthorpe's (1992) hallmark study concludes that there are small differences across fifteen countries in the pattern and degree of social fluidity or relative mobility. They do, however, find greater mobility in Sweden, the only Scandinavian country included in their comparisons. They examine the impact of a number of "modernization" indicators, including level of industrial development, economic and educational inequality, and political attributes on social fluidity. But overall, they find no clear relationship between level of economic inequality and more open class structures.

The more recent comparative analyses in Breen (2004) and Breen and Jonsson (2005) report a trend toward convergence in class structures across countries and decreasing variation in rates of absolute mobility. In terms of relative mobility, they distinguish a group of more fluid countries (Israel, Sweden, Canada, Norway, Hungary, and Poland) and a group with rigid patterns (including Germany, Ireland, Italy, and France); the United States occupies an intermediate position. These findings seem to differ substantially from those of Erikson and Goldthorpe (1992). But the implications are somewhat muted by their conclusion that even quite substantial differences in fluidity have little impact on absolute mobility flows. They also find little evidence that variation in fluidity between countries is systematically related to overall levels of income inequality or to GDP.

To put a modernization thesis properly to the test we obviously want to know whether social inheritance is weakening over time. The thrust of Erikson and Goldthorpe's (1992) "constant flux" is that mobility has not increased (except in Sweden, the only Nordic country included in the study) when measured in terms of social class membership. Richard Breen (2004) and Breen and Jan Jonsson (2005), on the basis of data for a wider range of countries, suggest that while absolute mobility has been substantial in all industrialized countries, relative mobility rates have remained rather stable over time. This suggests that changes in mobility patterns are almost exclusively driven by social structural change in general, and by changes in the occupational structure in particular. In other words, as far as class mobility is concerned, the case for a potential welfare state effect would appear rather minimal. Still, the case of Swedish exceptionalism does merit closer scrutiny. Erikson and Jonsson (1996) suggest that the declining significance of class origin in Sweden is primarily the product of educational equalization that began in the 1960s.

Indeed, there has been considerable debate about trends in specific countries. For example, Goldthorpe and Colin Mills (2008) find a U-turn pattern in the United Kingdom: the middle decades of the twentieth century produced steadily rising rates of upward absolute class mobility, but this began to level off from the 1970s onward, with, if anything, a trend toward more downward mobility. For women, however, they find that total mobility rates changed less. This was due to two concomitant trends: on the one hand, women experienced increasing upward mobility, especially into the salariat; on the other hand, this occurred as overall downward mobility was increasing. Goldthorpe and Michelle

Jackson (2007), using the two British cohort studies, obtain similar results. Turning to relative rather than absolute mobility, they cannot reject the hypothesis that the pattern of social fluidity underlying the mobility experienced by members of the two cohorts is in fact the same from the earlier to the later cohort. Over Ireland's "Celtic Tiger" boom period, Christopher Whelan and Richard Layte (2006) find evidence for a substantial upgrading of the class structure, increased levels of absolute mobility, and also greater social fluidity.

It is evident that trends and cross-national differences in class mobility are difficult to connect directly to the welfare state. One major problem we confront is that Sweden is basically the only representative of the advanced Nordic countries that has been intensively investigated. Following the argument of Eriksson and Jonsson (1996), it may be that very egalitarian educational systems, like Sweden's, can help sponsor more class mobility. The most likely logic here is indirect: that educational equalization diminishes the importance of social class background for human capital attainment, which, in turn, implies a lower correlation between origins and occupational destiny.

Esping-Andersen and Wagner's (2010) analyses, based on the EU-SILC intergenerational module, include separate estimations of the impact of social class origins (adapting the Goldthorpe class scheme).[2] They find for both Denmark and Norway that the influence of class origins on adult (log) earnings disappears entirely for the two youngest cohorts of men *and* women (born, respectively, 1958 to 1967 and 1968 to 1977). But they also find that the impact of class origin in both countries remains quite stable as far as educational attainment is concerned. Unfortunately, the SILC data for Sweden do not permit comparable analyses. In contrast, the Esping-Andersen and Wagner analyses suggest that the class origin effect has remained stable and significant in France, Italy, and the United Kingdom— in terms of educational attainment and also in terms of adult (log) earnings.

Another potential but, to our knowledge, unexplored link is to the role of the welfare state as employer. Service-intensive welfare states, like the Nordic, employ almost one-third of the entire labor force and account, owing to their strong female bias, for almost half of all female employment. One potential indirect effect is therefore the welfare state's role in establishing the dual-earner family norm. Another indirect effect should be related to the occupational profile within public services. Although welfare state jobs undoubtedly provide greater job security, their expansion is not automatically synonymous with occupational upgrading. A very large proportion of social service jobs are low-skilled.

Education

Educational attainment is highly correlated across generations and has been recognized as a key mechanism in the transmission of socioeconomic status from parents to children in modern industrial societies. Parental education is a significant predictor of the level a child will attain, and education in turn is a key predictor of earnings and income, occupation and social class. The strength of intergenerational transmission of education also clearly varies across countries, as can be seen from studies comparing what survey respondents report to be their own and their parents' highest level of education attained. To be sure, despite the development of the ISCED classification for international comparisons, national differences in education systems can make it difficult to be sure one is comparing like with like. Results from the United States and the United Kingdom suggest intergenerational education elasticities between 0.20 and 0.45 (Dearden, Machin, and Reed 1997; Mulligan 1999). The estimates by Hertz and his colleagues (2007) of the intergenerational schooling correlation for the United States and twelve western European countries range from 0.30 in Denmark up to 0.54 in Italy, with the United States at 0.46 toward the high end of the spectrum, similar to Ireland and Switzerland. Finland, the Netherlands, and Sweden are toward the lower end of the range, but Great Britain and Northern Ireland (estimated separately) are even lower. Yossi Shavit and Hans-Peter Blossfeld's (1993) study of class effects on educational attainment conclude that Sweden deviates from other countries in terms of the constant flux.

Intergenerational influences can also be studied comparatively using the mathematics and literacy performance of fifteen-year-old students in various countries from the Program for International Student Assessment (PISA), organized by the OECD. Analyzing the impact of numerous background characteristics on mathematics scores, OECD (2008) concludes that parental education is by far the most important, although parental occupational status, household type, and migrant status and language all play a role. Based on simple bivariate comparisons, the negative impact of having a father with low education is strongest in the Czech Republic, Slovakia, Hungary, Germany, and Turkey; in contrast, the negative effect is smallest in Finland, Iceland, Italy, Norway, Portugal, and Sweden. (The patterns in terms of mother's education are similar.)

Esping-Andersen (2004a) uses International Adult Literacy Survey (IALS) data to analyze the impact of father's education on children's years of education in eight countries. Controlling for ability (that is, literacy test scores), he finds that the negative effect of low-educated fathers has diminished sharply in Scandinavia (especially for the very youngest cohorts, born around 1970), but that the effect remains strong and persistent in Germany, the United Kingdom, and the United States. In parallel analyses, Esping-Andersen (2009) finds that test score variations, both in mathematics and in literacy, are very strongly related to the familial learning milieu—that is, "cultural capital." As discussed in more detail later in the chapter, these findings point to the possible importance of a wholly different welfare state attribute—namely, the role of high-quality universal child care programs in equalizing early cognitive stimulation.

Much of the literature on education as a transmission mechanism has focused on the way the education system itself is structured and financed and on the barriers—financial and cultural—faced by students from poorer backgrounds in progressing from one level to the next. It is clear that institutions and structures do matter, and there appears to be a broad consensus that early tracking according to ability reduces educational mobility across generations (see, for example, Hanushek and Woessmann 2005). Gabriela Schütz, Heinrich Ursprung, and Ludger Woessmann (2005) estimate a "family background effect" and compare it across countries, finding that it increases with private expenditure and decreases with private enrollment and that these features of the education system can jointly account for 40 percent of the cross-country variation. To capture family background, they, like Esping-Andersen (2004a, 2009), use a variable for the quantity of books in the home as an indicator of the prevailing learning culture.

This example highlights the difficulties we face in our quest to identify the precise mechanisms that link family background to educational (and other) outcomes. The intergenerational transmission of educational success is undoubtedly the product of a complex mix of financial resources, knowledge, and parenting attitudes, values, and abilities. Some of these attributes are highly correlated, but some are not. We know that the intensity and content of parenting is highly correlated with parental education (McLanahan 2004; Esping-Andersen 2009). And yet there is virtually no correlation between family socioeconomic status and "number of books in the home." (Librarians earn little; the very rich have little time to read.)

Furthermore, we are beginning to realize that policies that promote the attainment of higher levels of education—central to strategies aimed at improving equality of opportunity—may not be adequate if our aim is to address the disadvantages that children from poorer backgrounds face from the outset. This point is very much emphasized in the recent literature that argues for an early childhood focus. Still, pervasive disillusionment with the apparent lack of major equalization flowing from the education-focused strategies adopted in many countries to date should not lead us to "throw out the baby with the bathwater." As we discuss later, the institutional design of the education system remains decisive.

Clear trends over time are difficult to ascertain, and it is even harder to link specific educational reforms to outcomes. Shavit and Blossfeld's (1993) seminal study of inequality in educational attainment summarizes its results in the title: *Persistent Inequality*. In spite of dramatic educational expansion during the twentieth century, most of the thirteen countries included in their study exhibited stability of inequalities. In the estimates that Hertz and his colleagues (2007) make of the intergenerational schooling correlation for the

United States and twelve western European countries, the United States and the United Kingdom are the only two countries to display a statistically significant increase over time in standardized persistence, whereas a downward trend is found in the Netherlands and Finland.

Breen and his colleagues (2009, 2010), focusing, respectively, on men and women, employ data sets with substantially larger samples over a longer period of time. Focusing on the familiar distinction between "primary" and "secondary" effects, they set out a number of reasons why a priori we might have expected educational inequalities to decline: economic growth and welfare state expansion, reinforced by changes within educational institutions, should have been to the advantage of working-class children; and the declining cost of education, increases in family income, and the lengthening of compulsory education should have had a significant impact on educational decisions. Their analyses for seven European countries indicate that social class advantages in education have become less acute. This decline has been most pronounced in Sweden, the Netherlands, Britain, Germany, and France, and less so in Italy, Ireland, and Poland.

Turning our attention to the role of specific changes in educational institutions, we note that the major school reform implemented in Sweden in the 1960s has been the subject of considerable study. It involved moving away from a traditional selective system to a mixed-ability, mass second-level system that abolished selection at age twelve, increased compulsory schooling, and imposed a national curriculum. As mentioned, Erikson and Jonsson (1996) see school reform as having played a major role in the marked reduction in inequalities in educational opportunities within Sweden. One important impact, conclude Costas Meghir and Martin Palme (2005), is that children with unskilled fathers are now both more likely to reach the new compulsory level of schooling and to go beyond it. This may account for increased intergenerational mobility (see also Holmlund 2006).

Pekkarinen and his colleagues (2006) also suggest that raising the age of tracking has been associated with a significant increase in intergenerational mobility in Finland. The study by Sandra Black, Paul Devereux, and Kjell Salvanes (2005) of the impact of an increase in the length of compulsory schooling, together with a reduction in tracking in Norway in the 1960s, finds that increasing the number of years that parents spend in school has a measurable impact on their children's education. (They conclude that this is for the most part not a causal relationship and that the high correlations between parents' and children's education are due primarily to family characteristics and inherited ability, not to education spillovers.) For the United States, Philip Oreopoulos, Marianne Page, and Ann Huff Stevens (2006) use variation across states in changes in compulsory school laws and conclude that an increase in the education of either parent reduces the probability that a child will repeat a grade and significantly lowers the likelihood that the child will drop out. By contrast, Guido

Heineck and Regina Riphahn (2007) find that, for Germany, in spite of major public policy interventions and education reforms, for the birth cohorts 1929 through 1978 there was no significant reduction in the role of parental background for child outcomes over the last decades.

The Welfare State and Intergenerational Mobility

As noted earlier, income redistribution would be one obvious route through which the welfare state could influence intergenerational mobility. In this case, we assume that mobility patterns are associated with levels of inequality or poverty. Is there a clear case for this link? The theoretical logic behind such a link is, as already noted, twofold. Inequalities in the period of childhood should translate into more unequal parental investment in offspring. Inequalities in the era of adulthood should, in contrast, reflect differential returns to human capital. Björklund and Jäntti (2009) plot intergenerational earnings elasticities against Gini coefficients for income inequality in the 1980s. In general, the countries with the most equal distributions of income at a given point in time also exhibit the greatest degree of income mobility. But the fit is far from perfect: Australia and Canada combine high mobility with moderately high inequality, and France displays less mobility than would be expected from its level of inequality.[3] Similarly, OECD (2008, 215) compares IGM elasticities with Gini coefficients around 2000 and argues that the evidence "is suggestive of a consistent cross-country pattern of low intergenerational mobility and high income inequality." But measuring inequality in 2000 means, of course, that it does not tap the conditions that prevailed during childhood. If inequality in one generation is passed on to subsequent generations, it would appear more relevant, from a welfare policy perspective, to focus on how childhood-era inequalities influence mobility opportunities.

Even if we observe a strong association between levels of inequality and IGM, this obviously does not imply causality. We clearly need to know much more about the mechanisms underlying the relationship. Solon (2004) offers one perspective in his argument that unequal earnings distributions and higher returns to education give better-off parents a greater incentive to invest in their children's human capital.[4] Following this line of reasoning, the unusually compressed wage structure in the Nordic countries may, then, account for their comparatively high mobility rates. And yet this kind of explanation is directly contradicted by other evidence. As discussed earlier, the patterns of mobility from the top parental income quintile are virtually identical in Scandinavia and in the United Kingdom and the United States (Jäntti et al. 2006). In fact, the higher Scandinavian mobility rates are almost exclusively due to much greater mobility opportunities than elsewhere for children who come from families in the *lowest* income quintile. To the extent that income matters at all, this suggests that the welfare policies of relevance are those that either directly (say, through income support) or indirectly (say, through low unemployment) reduce poverty and strengthen the financial resources of the worst-off.

The relationship between social class mobility and cross-sectional inequality has also received some attention. Erikson and Goldthorpe (1992, 396) argue that the advantaged and powerful classes seek to use their superior resources to preserve their own and their families' positions. If so, it follows that more equality of opportunity requires more equality of initial condition. Goldthorpe and Jackson (2007, 539) similarly note that, "insofar as widening inequality of condition, as, say, in incomes and wealth, of the kind that has characterized Britain in recent decades, tends to reduce social fluidity, it is on such long-range mobility that its first impact would appear most likely to show up." In relation to the United States, however, Stephen Morgan and Young-Mi Kim (2006, 186) argue that post-1980 trends in educational attainment "are less supportive of this classic proposition than one might have expected."

Michael Hout (2003, 2004) refers to the lack of correlation between social mobility and equality as the "Inequality-Mobility Paradox." There are two circumstances that may help explain this paradox. First, as Gregg and his colleagues (1999) suggest, rising income inequality (as experienced in the United Kingdom and the United States) affects families with children more dramatically than the rest of the population. Second, among families with children, rising inequality goes hand in hand with more income polarization, primarily because the gap between the bottom and the median widens—that is, low-income families fall behind (see also Blanden, Gregg, and Machin 2005). Such effects can be quite dramatic. Gregg and his colleagues (1999) show that, in the United Kingdom, the proportion of children living in poor families (less than half of average income) rose from 13 percent to 33 percent between 1979 and 1996.

The basic problem we face in terms of identifying the causal "smoking gun" is that it is very difficult to know whether lower inequality in and of itself helps to promote mobility, or whether it is the same institutions and policies that underpin lower inequality that also influence intergenerational mobility. In this scenario, low inequality and high IGM are the joint outcome of some underlying cause. The education, labor market, tax, and social protection policies that influence cross-sectional inequality might have—and may indeed be designed to have—a direct effect on mobility as well. Equalizing opportunities has always been an important element in policies to reduce inequality. And in most countries this has primarily been pursued by democratizing access to education.

We have strong evidence that the abolition of early tracking and the introduction of comprehensive school systems have helped promote IGM in Sweden, Finland, and Norway—primarily by boosting educational attainment among the least privileged social strata. Since these are also countries in which welfare state redistribution increased substantially over the same period, it is difficult to identify the extent to which higher mobility was the result of education reform or income equalization. In addressing this ambiguity, Blanden and her colleagues' (2005) analyses of the United Kingdom are interesting: they show that education reform, which delayed tracking, produced a substantial increase in intergenerational mobility, primarily to the benefit of children from low-income families. In this case, the increase in IGM cannot be ascribed to an increase in welfare state redistribution since, over the same period, income inequality actually grew. But these authors also show that less redistributive financing of British higher education helped strengthen the upper-class bias of the system.

So education policy undoubtedly plays a role in intergenerational mobility. Indeed, as Blanden's study suggests, it can both promote and repress mobility all at once. But it is also evident that even the most ambitiously egalitarian education policies cannot single-handedly cancel out social origin effects.

There are clearly other aspects of the welfare state, such as social security, labor market regulation, health care, housing, and family policies, that can influence mobility. What can we say with any degree of confidence about these elements of welfare state institutions and IGM? Since there are no clear correlations between aggregate levels of social spending and cross-sectional inequality or poverty, the size of the welfare state per se would appear to be irrelevant as far as mobility is concerned. In fact, we have almost no empirical research that addresses this question. In a comparison across U.S. states, however, Mayer and Lopoo (2008) find that high-spending states boast greater intergenerational mobility than the low spenders. The difference in mobility between advantaged and disadvantaged children is also smaller in high-spending compared to low-spending states, and expenditures aimed at low-income populations increase the future income of low-income children but not that of high-income children. These findings, however, simply beg the question: what, precisely, is it that connects spending with mobility? Are both perhaps driven by a common underlying factor? Or is greater mobility associated with spending on particular programs—such as income support to poor families?

How welfare states distribute cash transfers is likely to matter. There is some evidence that intergenerational transmission of welfare dependency may be related to program design. An empirical comparison of cash support schemes in the United States and Sweden suggests that passive programs are more likely to promote the transmission of welfare dependency than active ones (Corak 2004). More generally, benefit systems that rely heavily on means-testing are more likely to create poverty and un-employment traps. These, in turn, limit intragenerational mobility among those at the bottom and make it more likely that poverty and welfare dependency will persist into subsequent generations. Child poverty is undoubtedly associated with inferior life chances, and social policies that minimize child poverty are likely to also promote more intergenerational inequality. Income support is, in this regard, potentially effective. But so are policies that help reconcile motherhood and employment (see, for example, UNICEF 2007; Whiteford and Adema 2007). It has been calcu-lated that the risk of child poverty falls by a factor of four when mothers are employed (Esping-Andersen 2009).

Because differences in ability and education affect earnings, it would appear obvious that inequalities in the labor market—and more generally, labor market regulation—can influence IGM. It is not easy, however, to pin down the precise causal channels that link labor market institutions and behavior to intergenerational mobility. As discussed previously, the degree of wage dispersion should affect intergenerational earnings mobility and income mobility. OECD (2008) argues that less earnings dispersion, higher minimum wages, and broader bargaining coverage contribute to lower returns to education (and perhaps lower income inequality at any point in time), thus reducing the incentive for better-off parents to invest more in their children and, all else being equal, producing higher IGM (Solon 2004). However, if high minimum wages, earnings compression, and job pro-tection also promote more unemployment, the effect on IGM would be adverse. To begin with, unemployment tends to be strongly correlated with social origins; additionally, unemployment has negative consequences for lifetime earnings and income. If so, the greater equality that minimum wages or wage compression create at any point in time may be accompa-nied by more inequality viewed from a life-course perspective. This, of course, depends ultimately on whether egalitarian wage structures or job protection legislation do in fact promote more unemployment. The evi-dence suggests that the Nordic countries have been highly successful in combining low unemployment with extensive job security and wage equal-ity. In contrast, this is far from the case in most Continental European coun-tries such as France, Italy, and Belgium (OECD 1999; Esping-Andersen and Regini 2004).

A good example of such ambiguities is found in married women's labor force participation, which varies substantially across countries. As already suggested, maternal employment can have decisive effects on IGM through its ability to reduce poverty. The key issue has to do with how precisely female employment is distributed. High maternal employment rates at the bottom of the income distribution should promote upward mobility, since the marginal effect on total family income is likely to be considerable. Most countries exhibit huge female participation gaps in terms of education, but this is not the case in the Nordic countries, where participation varies little across social strata. Raaum and his colleagues (2007) argue that the intergenerational correlation in family earnings depends greatly on female employment at the top of the social hierarchy. Since mothers in high-income households work less in the United States and the United Kingdom than in Scandinavia, country differences in intergenerational income transmission are smaller than otherwise would be the case. Variations in female labor supply can be attributed, at least in part, to policy differences, including the wage penalty for part-time work, the way couples are taxed, the design of maternity leave schemes, and the price, availability, and quality of child care. An implication is that policies that promote women's labor force participation may also yield positive effects in terms of intergenerational income mobility, in particular if the effect is strongest at the bottom of the household income distribution.

In expenditure terms, health care is one of the core pillars of the welfare state. There is ample evidence linking health in childhood to socioeconomic status, and also linking childhood health to later outcomes (see, for example, Blanden and Gibbons 2006; Eriksson, Bratsberg, and Raaum 2005; Case and Paxson 2006). It is well established that poor child health is strongly correlated with family poverty, and the adverse health effects of low income are likely to cumulate over children's lives. Studies such as those by Anne Case, Angela Fertig, and Christina Paxson (2005) suggest that an important share of the intergenerational transmission of socioeconomic status works through the impact of parents' income on children's health. Tor Eriksson and his colleagues (2005) report that in Denmark the intergenerational earnings elasticity falls by 25 percent to 28 percent when controlling on parental health status and that the correlation with parents' earnings decreases when controlling also for children's health. Hertz (2007) estimates that the relation between parental income and health status explains 8 percent of the intergenerational correlation of income in the United States (see also Case, Lubotsky, and Paxson 2002). The analyses of Esping-Andersen and Wagner (2010) find similar strong effects of offspring health on IGM in all the countries included in their study. Poor health explains typically between 5 and 10 percent of the variance in offspring's income mobility.

If health is potentially a key factor in the intergenerational correlation of income and education, can we identify institutional settings that minimize health inequalities and can we be sure that they contribute to greater IGM? The factors underlying health inequalities are still hotly debated, including the role of health care versus material circumstances and behavioral factors. The scope for health care to reduce health inequalities may be limited in most rich countries, though less so in ones where access to care for the poor is particularly constrained. The United States, for example, is unusual in the extent to which income affects access to health care, and Janet Currie and Jonathan Gruber (1996) find a clear impact of the expansion in Medicaid eligibility on children's chances of seeing a doctor. Better health care for poor families is an important element in the broader package of measures required to improve the prospects of disadvantaged children and could contribute to reducing intergenerational poverty persistence. The fact that Esping-Andersen and Wagner (2010) find few country differences in the impact of health may have to do with the fact that all the countries under study boast comprehensive and universal health care systems. Leaving aside access to health care, it is, however, less obvious how policy can best tackle the impact of health inequalities on IGM.

Although housing policy constitutes another significant element of the welfare state, its potential role in IGM is less obvious. One issue that has received considerable attention in the literature is the potential effect of living in a "bad" neighborhood. Although the reigning consensus in IGM research is that neighborhood effects pale in comparison to family effects, some studies suggest that local conditions can help explain the intergenerational transmission of income (OECD 2008). Solon, Page, and Duncan (2000), analyzing PSID data on school attainment, conclude that neighborhood factors contribute at most 20 percent to the factors that siblings share. Raaum, Salvanes, and Sorensen (2003), using Norwegian census data, find that neighborhood correlations are small compared to sibling correlations for both education and long-run earnings. Considering the rather weak influence of neighborhood conditions on IGM, it is unlikely that differences in housing policy have much of an effect overall.

In contrast, family policies are of potentially great relevance. Generous child allowances can have a substantial marginal effect on family budgets, especially in low-income households. The design of parental leave schemes and the provision of affordable child care help reconcile motherhood and employment. And as we shall examine in more detail later, universal high-quality early child care should help equalize both cognitive and noncognitive development and thus school readiness.

There is a good deal of evidence that family structure affects the linkage between socioeconomic outcomes of parents and children. Björklund and Chadwick (2003) find that sons of divorced couples are less mobile than their peers from intact families, and they ascribe this to differences in educational attainment. Children from single-parent households do less well than they "should," given their parent's income, and Gordon Anderson and Teng Wah Leo (2006) argue that income transmission is stronger in "intact" families than in single-parent households. It is possible, however, that the observed negative effects of single parenthood are related to social selection into single parenthood to begin with. In this case, the real issue is not family structure but the characteristics that determine such (Piketty 2003). Compared to the United States, where the adverse effects of single motherhood are well documented (albeit controversial), there has been little such research for European countries. Esping-Andersen and Wagner (2010) estimate the effects of single motherhood on both educational attainment and adult income; having controlled for mother's education and financial hardship in the family, they find no significant effects of single motherhood in any of the countries included in their study (Denmark, Norway, Italy, France, Spain, and the United Kingdom).

An important issue in this respect is the changing social gradient of marital behavior. While high-status women have traditionally been less likely to marry and more likely to divorce, the trend in many countries (especially in North America and Scandinavia) is now exactly the opposite: single motherhood and partner instability is increasingly concentrated among low-educated women. This may produce compounding and potentially polarizing effects in terms of children's life chances (McLanahan 2004; Esping-Andersen 2009). If Timothy Biblarz and Adrian Raftery (1999) are correct in arguing that it is not single motherhood as such but rather its association with low incomes that affects children adversely, then the role of family policy—and, more broadly, welfare state income support— would appear to be of key importance for equalizing life chances. If, on the other hand, the adverse consequences of divorce and single motherhood are related to a nurturing deficit, then the provision of affordable, high-quality child care services would seem to be relevant.

Birth order and the number of siblings might also influence mobility. Lena Lindahl (2002) reports that the intergenerational earnings elasticity decreases with birth order for a given family size in Sweden; this is especially so at the bottom of the earnings distribution. The intergenerational association in earnings is also likely to be strongest for children without siblings (Björklund et al. 2004; see also Sigle-Rushton and McLanahan 2004).[5] Such effects could be ascribed to different causes: there are more mouths to feed, which means added constraints on the family budget, and there are more children to nurture, which means that each child receives less. Esping-Andersen and Wagner's (2010) cohort analyses also include estimations of sibling size effects. Here, interestingly, it was found that the negative effect of sibling size remains significant (and quite strong) across all the postwar birth cohorts in France, Italy, Spain, and the United Kingdom, whereas in both Denmark and Norway it disappears with the cohort born between 1958 and 1967. To the extent that the latter effect captures welfare state effects, it is unlikely to be related to child care services— their expansion only began seriously in the 1970s and 1980s. The more plausible hypothesis, then, is that it has to do with family allowances and income support.

The Importance of an Early Childhood Focus

There is a growing consensus in the literature that conditions in the earliest phases of childhood are particularly important for subsequent life chances. It is well established that ages zero through six years are decisive for children's cognitive skills, sense of security, and motivation to learn, with developmental psychologists agreeing that the basic learning abilities are most intensely developed during this period (Danziger and Waldfogel 2000; Duncan and Brooks-Gunn 1997). Substantial differences in children's cognitive abilities by parents' socioeconomic status emerge at early ages and carry through to subsequent achievements in education and earnings (see, for example, Cunha and Heckman 2007). Heckman's work has been particularly influential in demonstrating that investing in early childhood is a cost-effective policy, with early childhood development programs having a pronounced positive impact on school achievement and other outcomes that substantially outweigh the costs.

If most agree that early childhood conditions are key, we are less certain about which conditions matter most. There is little doubt that family income in early childhood and poverty in particular have strong effects on later outcomes such as educational attainment and earnings. Family "culture" also seems important in influencing parenting behavior and child stimulation (de Graaf, de Graaf, and Kraaykamp 2000; Esping-Andersen 2007). This is captured in Heckman's "learning begets learning" model: kids who start well subsequently learn more easily; kids with a poor start are likely to be handicapped for life (Carneiro and Heckman 2003). The finding that differences in the design of education systems seem to matter only marginally for mobility may reflect the importance of childhood circumstances in the ages *prior to* compulsory schooling.

This finding has major implications for the role of social institutions in IGM. The extent and intensity of child poverty vary substantially across industrialized countries, and this may be related to observed variations in later outcomes, including education and earnings as well as social problems such as truancy, school dropout, and criminality (see Duncan et al. 1998; McCulloch and Joshi 2002). Social policy can help minimize, both directly (through income transfers) and indirectly (by supporting maternal employment), the incidence and duration of family poverty. The role of maternal earnings may be especially important for single-mother families. Targeting intensive health, nutrition, and other supports on particularly deprived families can be readily justified within the same frame from an IGM perspective as well as for its own sake.

We should also keep in mind that it is during the earliest years that children are most privatized and rely primarily on family inputs. The time that parents dedicate to their children, as well as the kind of dedication they bring to bear, varies hugely across families (Sayer, Gauthier, and Furstenberg 2004), and some evidence suggests that nurturing patterns are polarizing (McLanahan 2004; Esping-Andersen 2009). Although it is difficult to imagine how policies might alter parenting behavior, inequalities in families' learning culture can be neutralized, or at least diminished, if institutions ensure that childhood stimulation is more homogeneous across all children. Any first-grade teacher can readily identify the children who attended (good-quality) child care and kindergarten institutions.

All this suggests that welfare states that furnish comprehensive, high-quality preschool care are also likely to produce a homogenizing effect in terms of children's school preparedness. Indeed, the core evidence that underpins Heckman's work comes from early intervention programs in the United States. Using cross-national comparisons, Esping-Andersen (2004b) finds some indirect support for the thesis: he shows a significant decline in social inheritance effects (focusing on children from low-educated parents) for the Nordic countries (but not elsewhere) within the child cohorts that first came to benefit from universal, high-quality child care. Of course, these very same cohorts also benefited from the largesse of the family allowance system and, more generally, from very low child poverty, which once again makes the precise welfare state effects difficult to disentangle. Schütz and her colleagues (2005), in their cross-sectional comparison across countries, report an inverted U-shaped relationship between family background effect and preschool enrollment, which suggests that early education reduces the extent to which family background shapes life chances. OECD (2008) concludes that good-quality care in early childhood, the preschool years, and also the school years is an essential tool for promoting inter-generational mobility.

It is important, in highlighting the role of "learning culture," to distinguish between cultural resources and aspirations: any cultural explanation needs to be able to account for the expansion seen in educational participation and gender differences in those trends. Differences in broader economic resources, not merely income, may create uncertain and stressful environments that significantly reduce the possibility of creating environments or micro-cultures that are learning-friendly. This is not inconsistent with the rational action perspective, which sees families acting in a subjectively rational manner, and explanations couched in terms of cultural values and resources. The former assumes that actors have goals and alternative means of pursuing these goals and that, in choosing their course of action, they tend in some degree to assess probable costs and benefits. From this perspective, as Breen and Goldthorpe (1997 [2001]) argue, insofar as class-specific norms may be identified, we can recognize them as guides to action that have evolved over time out of distinctive class experiences. Where this form of explanation fails, we may seek alternative explanations in terms of class differences in the value placed on educational outcomes.

Although Cunha and Heckman (2009) stress the value of early investment, they acknowledge that the early years are far from being determinative of adult outcomes. As Orla Doyle and her colleagues (2007) argue, the economic case for early investment does not preclude later investment but rather directs attention to dynamic complementarities. A further example of policy-relevant choices and complementarities is provided by recent research on the relative importance of "primary" and "secondary" effects on educational attainment (Erikson and Jonsson 1996; Jackson et al. 2007). Primary effects are all those effects, whether of a genetic or sociocultural kind, that are expressed through the association between children's class backgrounds and their levels of academic performance. Secondary effects are those that are expressed through the educational choices made by children from differing class backgrounds, within the range that their performance allows. As Michelle Jackson and her colleagues (2007) argue, a major policy issue is the relative weight attached to policies aimed at overcoming the resource and informational constraints that affect the educational choices of those from less-advantaged backgrounds, as opposed to policies aimed at helping them from an early age to develop the relevant academic abilities more successfully. Although focusing on primary effects is in principle the more radical approach, questions can still be posed about relative cost-effectiveness in light of the substantial wastage of *already developed* academic ability and the potential impact of measures designed to offset the economic costs to poorer children when attempting more ambitious educational courses.

Conclusions

Research on intergenerational mobility still has far to go in its quest for genuinely causal explanations. To be sure, we have made headway in terms of understanding the relative importance of genetics as distinct from social inheritance; we have come to understand that neighborhood effects play, at best, a secondary role; and we are beginning to zero in on the key role that early childhood conditions play in later attainment. There is universal consensus that the family of origin is central, and we have been able to pinpoint quite well the salience of both family finances and family sociocultural characteristics. But the relative impact of both of these factors remains unclear, and we still have no understanding of whether the two produce important interaction effects.

There is also a broad consensus that social institutions matter, but here we are very far from being able to pinpoint any concise causality. Education systems were traditionally hypothesized to have what we might term a quasi-causal effect: it was broadly assumed that a genuine democratization of education would guarantee selection based primarily on merit rather than the lottery of birth. To be sure, contemporary research has not discarded the role of educational institutions altogether; it is well documented that some features—tracking systems in particular—do influence the pathways from origins to destination in important ways.

A finding in contemporary research that needs to be highlighted is the general persistence of IGM patterns, both historically and across nations.

With very few exceptions, the impact of origins on educational attainment, income, and class mobility appears to be as strong today as it was in our parents' and grandparents' times. But the exceptions are important. First, they cluster in Scandinavia; Sweden, in particular, stands out, although this may simply be because comparative researchers focus more on Sweden than on any of the other Nordic countries. Second, the evidence suggests that the noticeably greater mobility found in Scandinavia is of rather recent vintage. Focusing on the importance of early childhood, we also need to highlight the importance of the causal chains uncovered by James Heckman's work in particular. This work, too, emphasizes variance rather than seemingly preordained persistency: the life chances of children most at risk can be substantially improved with the help of high-quality intervention policies.

Both of these "highlights" within recent scholarship provide fertile clues to how we might better grasp the potential influence of social institutions in general, and the welfare state in particular. Beginning with the latter, the evidence points clearly to the salience of three factors: health, cognitive stimulation, and noncognitive stimulation. The lack of universal access to quality health care makes the United States a very exceptional case, and we might plausibly hypothesize that this constitutes one important reason why the United States performs comparatively poorly on many mobility indicators. As far as both cognitive and noncognitive development are concerned, the "externalization" of early childhood stimulation yields truly impressive effects for later achievements—if, that is, the externalization occurs in high-quality child care institutions. This insight can be generalized: if early stimulation is decisive and yet depends almost exclusively on familial inputs, it would seem logical that variations in parenting intensity and talent should account for much of the social inheritance effects we observe. It follows that *universal*, high-quality early childhood care attendance should produce equalizing effects in terms of children's subsequent school preparedness.

The contributions of Heckman and others stress the impact of family "culture," which is promising for potential welfare state effects, from family policy in general and child care institutions in particular. The fact that the Scandinavian countries stand out as exceptional and that this is of recent vintage may be attributable to their international leadership in securing early child care based on identical high-quality standards for all children. Yet here there is a counterfactual case—namely France, which, after the Nordic countries, boasts Europe's highest rates of preschool child care but nonetheless displays less social fluidity than comparable countries. For future researchers, Finland provides a different kind of empirical test because there, since the 1990s, governments have changed policy direction by providing greater incentives for mothers to stay home with their preschool children.

Welfare states also affect the income distribution. In fact, it is difficult indeed to untangle welfare state effects that operate through child care provision from those that operate through income equalization and, especially, poverty reduction: the two developed in tandem within the Nordic countries. Since we still do not have any clear and consistent conclusions regarding the relative salience of family finances and "culture," we are also poorly positioned to formulate more precise hypotheses regarding rival welfare state effects. To complicate matters further, we should also take the argument of Erikson and Jonsson (1996) seriously—namely, that the decline of social inheritance in Sweden is also a function of an incomparably aggressive equalization policy in the education system. Their argument can nonetheless be questioned, since a similar educational reform was not put in place in either Denmark or Norway. In other words, the welfare state offers a promising starting point to explain the phenomenon of Scandinavian exceptionalism *and* its recent vintage. As in IGM research generally, the chief challenge is to establish the relative salience of money, culture, and the interaction of the twain.

What research strategies have the greatest potential for understanding better the impact of welfare state institutions? One avenue would be to focus on specific barriers to mobility and the ways in which public policy could reduce them (see, for example, Jencks and Tach 2006). A complementary strategy, stressed earlier, would be to compare across different countries over time, measuring trends in different aspects of IGM and relating these to variations in institutions and policies. This strategy has been particularly fruitful in research on income inequality and poverty, and despite the need for care in interpreting summary indicators and the many difficulties in relating variations in them to institutional factors, it is an indispensable component of IGM research for the future. As Björklund and Jäntti (2009) argue, theory suggests many causal processes, and different theoretical models offer different predictions about, for example, the relationship between intergenerational mobility and cross-sectional inequality or the impact of public education programs. Such models are often far too complex and demanding for estimation and testing. As they argue: "By offering a rich set of stylized facts, empirical research can tell us what mechanisms are important, which can in turn sharpen future theoretical research" (Björklund and Jäntti 2009, 495). The review of the evidence presented in this chapter offers many examples, perhaps the most striking being the "surprises" in the ranking of countries in terms of the intergenerational correlation in earnings, as well as the U.K. debates about trends over time in different indicators of IGM and how they (and their interrelationships) are to be interpreted.

The challenges we face in pushing this strategy forward are substantial. The first is to improve the information base in terms of the coverage, reliability, and interpretation of measures of IGM. Very substantial progress has been made in that respect over the past quarter-century, but as we have seen, the number of country cases that can be reliably compared, both with each other or over time, across the different dimensions of intergenerational mobility is still too limited. The second challenge, in aiming to identify precisely the aspects of welfare state intervention that make a difference, is that the leap from institutions or policies to IGM is too great—we must have better analytical tools that link institutions to mobility processes if we are to pinpoint the key mechanisms at work.

Notes

1. Our remarks regarding community and neighborhood effects reflect the current state of research in general. There exist, to be sure, studies that bring out highly negative effects of special situations, such as William Julius Wilson's (1987) work on the ghetto underclass phenomenon in the United States.
2. These analyses control for financial hardship in the childhood family, immigrant status, number of siblings, and the labor supply of the offspring.
3. The relatively low intergenerational correlation in the case of Australia and Canada is sometimes attributed to the role of immigration and immigration policies, but Abdurrahman Aydemir, Wen-Hao Chen, and Miles Corak (2009) show that for Canada the elasticity between father's and son's earnings is no different among immigrants than among the population at large.
4. Note, however, that inequality is being measured in the studies mentioned in relation to household income rather than earnings. Dan Andrews and Andrew Leigh (2009) show a significant positive relationship across ten countries, but based on predicted parental earnings (using fathers' occupation and current earnings by occupation).
5. Timothy Biblarz, Adrian Raftery, and Alexander Bucur (1997) and Biblarz and Raftery (1999) have also examined differences across family types in the intergenerational transmission of occupational status.

References

Aaronson, Daniel, and Bhaskar Mazumder. 2008. "Intergenerational Economic Mobility in the United States, 1940 to 2000." *Journal of Human Resources* 43(1): 139–72.

Anderson, Gordon, and Teng Wah Leo. 2006. "Intergenerational Educational Attainment Mobility and Family Structure." Paper presented to the twenty-ninth general conference of the International Association for Research in Income and Wealth. Joensuu, Finland (August 20–26, 2006).

Andrews, Dan, and Andrew Leigh. 2009. "More Inequality, Less Social Mobility." *Applied Economics Letters* 16(15): 1489–92.

Aydemir, Abdurrahman, Wen-Hao Chen, and Miles Corak. 2009. "Intergenerational Earnings Mobility Among the Children of Canadian Immigrants." *Review of Economics and Statistics* 91(2): 377–97.

Biblarz, Timothy, and Adrian Raftery. 1999. "Family Structure, Educational Attainment, and Socioeconomic Success: Rethinking the 'Pathology of Matriarchy.'" *American Journal of Sociology* 105(2): 321–65.

Biblarz, Timothy, Adrian Raftery, and Alexander Bucur. 1997. "Family Structure and Social Mobility." *Social Forces* 75(4): 1319–39.

Björklund, Anders, and Laura Chadwick. 2003. "Intergenerational Income Mobility in Permanent and Separated Families." *Economics Letters* 80(2): 239–46.

Björklund, Anders, Tor Eriksson, Markus Jäntti, Oddbjørn Raaum, and Eva Österbacka. 2004. "Family Structure and Labor Market Success: The Influence of Siblings and Birth Order on the Earnings of Young Adults in Norway, Finland, and Sweden." In *Generational Income Mobility in North America and Europe*, edited by Miles Corak. Cambridge: Cambridge University Press.

Björklund, Anders, and Markus Jäntti. 1997. "Intergenerational Income Mobility in Sweden Compared to the United States." *American Economic Review* 87(5): 1009–18.

———. 2009. "Intergenerational Income Mobility and the Role of Family Background." In *The Oxford Handbook of Economic Inequality*, edited by Wiemer Salverda, Brian Nolan, and Timothy Smeeding. Oxford: Oxford University Press.

Björklund, Anders, Markus Jäntti, and Gary Solon. 2005. "Influences of Nature and Nurture on Earnings Variation: A Report on a Study of Various Sibling Types in Sweden." In *Unequal Chances: Family Background and Economic Success*, edited by Samuel Bowles, Herbert Gintis, and Melissa Osborne Groves. New York: Russell Sage Foundation.

Black, Sandra E., Paul J. Devereux, and Kjell G. Salvanes. 2005. "Why the Apple Doesn't Fall Far: Understanding Intergenerational Transmission of Human Capital." *American Economic Review* 95(1): 437–49.

Blanden, Jo, and Stephen Gibbons. 2006. *The Persistence of Poverty Across Generations: A View from Two Cohorts*. Bristol, U.K.: Policy Press.

Blanden, Jo, Alissa Goodman, Paul Gregg, and Stephen Machin. 2004. "Changes in Intergenerational Mobility in Britain." In *Generational Income Mobility in North America and Europe*, edited by Miles Corak. Cambridge: Cambridge University Press.

Blanden, Jo, Paul Gregg, and Stephen Machin. 2005. "Educational Inequality and Intergenerational Mobility." In *What's the Good of Education?* edited by Stephen Machin and Anthony Vignoles. Princeton, N.J.: Princeton University Press.

Bonke, Jens, Azhar Hussain, and Martin Munk. 2006. "A Comparison of Intergenerational Earnings Mobility Studies Based on Danish Register Information." Working paper. Copenhagen: Danish National Institute of Social Research (SFI).

Bowles, Samuel, and Herbert Gintis. 2002. "The Inheritance of Inequality." *Journal of Economic Perspectives* 16(3): 3–30.

Bratberg, Espen, Øivind Nilsen, and Kjell Vaage. 2007. "Trends in Intergenerational Mobility Across Offspring's Earnings Distribution in Norway." *Industrial Relations* 46(1): 112–29.

Breen, Richard. 2004. *Social Mobility in Europe.* Oxford: Oxford University Press.

Breen, Richard, and John Goldthorpe. 1997. "Explaining Educational Differentials: Towards a Formal Rational Action Theory." *Rationality and Society* 9(3): 275–305. (Reprinted in *Social Stratification: Class, Race, and Gender,* edited by David Grusky [Boulder, Colo: Westview Press, 2001].)

Breen, Richard, and Jan O. Jonsson. 2005. "Inequality of Opportunity in Comparative Perspective: Recent Research on Educational Attainment and Social Mobility." *Annual Review of Sociology* 31: 223–43.

Breen, Richard, Ruud Luijkx, Walter Muller, and Robert Pollak. 2009. "Nonpersistent Inequality in Educational Attainment: Evidence from Eight European Countries." *American Sociological Review* 114(5): 1475–1521.

———. 2010. "Long-Term Trends in Educational Inequality in Europe: Class Inequalities and Gender Differences." *European Sociological Review* 26(1): 31–48.

Carneiro, Pedro, and James Heckman. 2003. "Human Capital Policy." In *Inequality in America,* edited by James Heckman and Alan Krueger. Cambridge, Mass.: MIT Press.

Case, Anne, Angela Fertig, and Christina Paxson. 2005. "The Lasting Impact of Childhood Health and Circumstances." *Journal of Health Economics* 24(2): 365–89.

Case, Anne, Darren Lubotsky, and Christina Paxson. 2002. "Economic Status and Health in Childhood: The Origins of the Gradient." *American Economic Review* 92(5): 1308–34.

Case, Anne, and Christina Paxson. 2006. "Children's Health and Social Mobility." *The Future of Children* 16(2): 151–73.

Chadwick, Laura, and Gary Solon. 2002. "Intergenerational Income Mobility Among Daughters." *American Economic Review* 92(1): 335–44.

Charles, Kerwin Kofi, and Erik Hurst. 2003. "The Correlation of Wealth Across Generations." *Journal of Political Economy* 111(6): 1155–82.

Conseil de L'Emploi, des Revenues et de la Cohesion Sociale (CERC). 2004. *Child Poverty in France.* Paris: CERC.

Corak, Miles. 2001. "Are the Kids All Right? Intergenerational Mobility and Child Well-being in Canada." *Review of Economic Performance and Social Progress,* vol. 1. Montreal: Institute for Research on Public Policy and Centre for the Study of Living Standards.

———, ed. 2004. *Generational Income Mobility in North America and Europe.* Cambridge: Cambridge University Press.

———. 2006. "Do Poor Children Become Poor Adults? Lessons from a Cross-Country Comparison of Generational Earnings Mobility." Discussion paper 1993. Bonn, Germany: Institute for the Study of Labor (IZA).

Corcoran, Mary. 2001. "Mobility, Persistence, and the Consequences of Poverty for Children: Child and Adult Outcomes." In *Understanding Poverty,* edited by Sheldon Danziger and Robert Haveman. New York and Cambridge, Mass.: Russell Sage Foundation and Harvard University Press.

Couch, Ken, and Dean Lillard. 2004. "Nonlinear Patterns in Germany and the United States." In *Generational Income Mobility in North America and Europe,* edited by Miles Corak. Cambridge: Cambridge University Press.

Cunha, Flavio, and James Heckman. 2007. "The Technology of Skill Formation." *American Economic Review* 97(2): 31–47.

———. 2009. "The Economics and Psychology of Inequality of Human Development." Working paper 5/2009. Dublin: University College Dublin, Geary Institute.

Currie, Janet. 2001. "Early Childhood Intervention Programs." *Journal of Economic Perspectives* 15(2): 213–38.

Currie, Janet, and Jonathan Gruber. 1996. "Health Insurance Eligibility, Utilization of Medical Care, and Child Health." *Quarterly Journal of Economics* 111(2): 431–66.

d'Addio, Anna Christina. 2007. "Intergenerational Transmission of Disadvantage: Mobility or Immobility Across Generations? A Review of the Evidence for OECD Countries." Social, Employment and Migration working paper 52. Paris: Organization for Economic Cooperation and Development.

Danziger, Sheldon, and Jane Waldfogel. 2000. *Securing the Future: Investing in Children from Birth to College.* New York: Russell Sage Foundation.

de Graaf, Nan Dirk, Paul de Graaf, and Gerbert Kraaykamp. 2000. "Parental Cultural Capital and Educational Attainment in the Netherlands: A Refinement of the Cultural Capital Perspective." *Sociology of Education* 73(2): 92–111.

Dearden, Lorraine, Stephen Machin, and Howard Reed. 1997. "Intergenerational Mobility in Britain." *Economic Journal* 107(440): 47–66.

Doyle, Orla, Colm Harmon, James Heckman, and Richard Tremblay. 2007. "Early Childhood Intervention: Rationale, Timing, and Efficacy." Working paper 5/2007. Dublin: University College Dublin, Geary Institute.

Duncan, Greg, and Jeanne Brooks-Gunn, eds. 1997. *Consequences of Growing Up Poor.* New York: Russell Sage Foundation.

Duncan, Greg, Wei-Jun Yeung, Jeanne Brooks-Gunn, and James Smith. 1998. "How Much Does Childhood Poverty Affect the Life Chances of Children?" *American Sociological Review* 63(3): 406–23.

Erikson, Robert, and John H. Goldthorpe. 1992. *The Constant Flux: A Study of Class Mobility in Industrial Societies.* Oxford: Oxford University Press.

———. 2010. "Has Social Mobility in Britain Decreased? Reconciling Divergent Findings on Income and Class Mobility." *British Journal of Sociology* 61(2): 211–30.

Erikson, Robert, and Jan Jonsson. 1996. *Can Education Be Equalized? The Swedish Case in Comparative Perspective.* Boulder, Colo.: Westview Press.

Eriksson, Tor, Bernt Bratsberg, and Oddbjørn Raaum. 2005. "Earnings Persistence Across Generations: Transmission Through Health?" Unpublished paper 35/2005. Oslo: University of Oslo, Department of Economics.

Ermisch, John, Marco Francesconi, and Thomas Siedler. 2006. "Intergenerational Economic Mobility and Assortative Mating." *Economic Journal* 116(513): 659–79.

Esping-Andersen, Gøsta. 2004a. "Unequal Opportunities and the Mechanisms of Social Inheritance." In *Generational Income Mobility in North America and Europe,* edited by Miles Corak. Cambridge: Cambridge University Press.

———. 2004b. "Untying the Gordian Knot of Social Inheritance." *Research in Social Stratification and Mobility* 21: 115–39.

———. 2007. "Sociological Explanations of Changing Income Distributions." *American Behavioral Scientist* 50(5): 639–58.

———. 2009. *The Incomplete Revolution.* Cambridge: Polity Press.

Esping-Andersen, Gøsta, and Marino Regini. 2004. *Why Deregulate Labor Markets?* Oxford: Oxford University Press.

Esping-Andersen, Gøsta, and Sander Wagner. 2010. "Learning About Intergenerational Mobility from the EU-SILC Module 2005." Working paper. Barcelona: Universitat Pompeu Fabra, Department of Sociology.

Fortin, Nicole, and Sophie Lefebvre. 1998. "Intergenerational Income Mobility in Canada." In *Labor Markets, Social Institutions, and the Future of Canada's Children,* edited by Miles Corak. Ottawa: Statistics Canada.

Goldthorpe, John, and Michelle Jackson. 2007. "Intergenerational Class Mobility in Contemporary Britain: Political Concerns and Empirical Findings." *British Journal of Sociology* 58(4): 525–46.

Goldthorpe, John, and Colin Mills. 2008. "Trends in Intergenerational Class Mobility in Modern Britain: Evidence from National Surveys, 1972–2005." *National Institute Economic Review* 205(1): 83–100.

Gottschalk, Peter, Sara McLanahan, and Gary Sandefur. 1994. "The Dynamics and Intergenerational Transmission of Poverty and Welfare Participation." In *Confronting Poverty: Prescription for Change,* edited by Sheldon Danziger, Gary Sandefur, and Daniel Weinberg. Cambridge, Mass.: Harvard University Press.

Gregg, Paul, Susan Harkness, and Stephen Machin. 1999. *Child Development and Family Income.* York, U.K.: Joseph Rowntree Foundation.

Hanushek, Eric, and Ludger Woessmann. 2005. "Does Educational Tracking Affect Performance and Inequality? Differences-in-Differences Evidence Across Countries." Working paper 11124. Cambridge, Mass.: National Bureau of Economic Research (NBER).

Harbury, Colin, and David Hitchens. 1979. *Inheritance and Wealth Inequality in Britain.* London: Allen and Unwin.

Harding, David, Christopher Jencks, Leonard Lopoo, and Susan Mayer. 2005. "The Changing Effect of Family Background on the Incomes of American Adults." In *Unequal Chances: Family Background and Economic Success,* edited by Samuel Bowles, Herbert Gintis, and Melissa Osborne Groves. New York: Russell Sage Foundation.

Heckman, James, and Lance Lochner. 2000. "Rethinking Education and Training Policy." In *Securing the Future,* edited by Sheldon Danziger and Jane Waldfogel. New York: Russell Sage Foundation.

Heineck, Guido, and Regina Riphahn. 2007. "Intergenerational Transmission of Educational Attainment in Germany: The Last Five Decades." Discussion paper 2985. Bonn, Germany: Institute for the Study of Labor (IZA).

Hertz, Thomas. 2007. "Trends in the Intergenerational Elasticity of Family Income in the United States." *Industrial Relations* 46(1): 22–50.

Hertz, Thomas, Tamara Jayasundera, Patrizio Piraino, Sibel Selcuk, Nicole Smith, and Alina Verashchagina. 2007. "The Inheritance of Educational Inequality: International Comparisons and Fifty-Year Trends." *B.E. Journal of Economic Analysis and Policy* 7(2): article 10.

Hirvonen, Lalaina. 2006. "Intergenerational Earnings Mobility Among Daughters and Sons: Evidence from Sweden and a Comparison with the United States." Unpublished paper. Stockholm: Stockholm University, Institute for Social Research.

Holmlund, Helena. 2006. "Intergenerational Mobility and Assortative Mating Effects of an Educational Reform." Working paper 4/2006. Stockholm: Stockholm University, Swedish Institute for Social Research (SOFI).

Hout, Michael. 2003. "The Inequality-Mobility Paradox: The Lack of Correlation Between Social Mobility and Equality." *New Economy* 10(4): 205–7.

———. 2004. "How Inequality May Affect Intergenerational Mobility." In *Social Inequality*, edited by Kathryn M. Neckerman. New York: Russell Sage Foundation.

Jackson, Michelle, Robert Erikson, John Goldthorpe, and Meir Yaish. 2007. "Primary and Secondary Effects in Class Differentials in Educational Attainment: The Transition to A-Level Courses in England and Wales." *Acta Sociologica* 50(3): 211–29.

Jäntti, Markus, Bernt Bratsberg, Knut Roed, Oddbjørn Raaum, Robin Naylor, Eva Österbacka, Anders Björklund, and Tor Eriksson. 2006. "American Exceptionalism in a New Light: A Comparison of Intergenerational Earnings Mobility in the Nordic Countries, the United Kingdom, and the United States." Discussion paper 1938. Bonn, Germany: Institute for the Study of Labor (IZA).

Jäntti, Markus, Eva Sierminska, and Timothy Smeeding. 2008. "The Joint Distribution of Household Income and Wealth: Evidence from the Luxembourg Wealth Study." OECD Social, Employment and Migration working paper 65. Paris: Organization for Economic Cooperation and Development.

Jencks, Christopher, and Laura Tach. 2006. "Would Equal Opportunity Mean More Mobility?" In *Mobility and Inequality: Frontiers of Research from Sociology and Economics,* edited by Samuel Morgan, David Grusky, and Gary Fields. Stanford, Calif.: Stanford University Press.

Karoly, Lyn, Rebecca Kilburn, and Jill Cannon. 2005. *Early Childhood Interventions.* Santa Monica, Calif.: RAND Corporation.

Klevmarken, Anders. 2004. "On Household Wealth Trends in Sweden over the 1990s." Working paper 395. New York: Bard College, Levy Economics Institute.

Lee, Chul-In, and Gary Solon. 2006. "Trends in Intergenerational Income Mobility." Working paper 12007. Cambridge, Mass.: National Bureau of Economic Research (NBER).

LeFranc, Arnaud, and Alain Trannoy. 2005. "Intergenerational Earnings Mobility in France: Is France More Mobile Than the United States?" *Annales d'Économie et de Statistique* 78: 57–77.

Leigh, Andrew. 2007. "Intergenerational Mobility in Australia." *B.E. Journal of Economic Policy and Analysis* 7(2): article 6.

Lindahl, Lena. 2002. "Do Birth Order and Family Size Matter for Intergenerational Income Mobility? Evidence from Sweden." Working paper 5/2002. Stockholm: Stockholm University, Swedish Institute for Social Research (SOFI).

Liu, Haoming, and Jinli Zeng 2009. "Genetic Ability and Intergenerational Earnings Mobility." *Journal of Population Studies* 22(1): 75–95.

Maurin, Eric. 2002. "The Impact of Parental Income on Early School Transitions." *Journal of Public Economics* 85(3): 301–32.

Mayer, Susan. 1997. *What Money Can't Buy.* Cambridge, Mass.: Harvard University Press.

Mayer, Susan, and Leonard Lopoo. 2005. "Has the Intergenerational Transmission of Economic Status Changed?" *Journal of Human Resources* 40(1): 169–85.

———. 2008. "Government Spending and Intergenerational Mobility." *Journal of Public Economics* 92(1–2): 139–58.

McCulloch, Andrew, and Heather Joshi. 2002. "Child Development and Family Resources: An Exploration of Evidence from the Second Generation of the 1958 Birth Cohort." *Journal of Population Economics* 15(2): 283–304.

McLanahan, Sara. 2004. "Diverging Destinies: How Children Fare Under the Second Demographic Transition." *Demography* 41(4): 607–27.

McLanahan, Sara, and Gary Sandefur. 1994. *Growing Up with a Single Parent.* Cambridge, Mass.: Harvard University Press.

Meghir, Costas, and Martin Palme. 2005. "Educational Reform, Ability, and Family Background." *American Economic Review* 95(1): 414–24.

Menchik, Paul. 1979. "Intergenerational Transmission of Inequality: An Empirical Study of Wealth Mobility." *Economica* 46(184): 349–62.

Morgan, Stephen, and Young-Mi Kim. 2006. "Inequality of Conditions and Intergenerational Mobility: Changing Patterns of Educational Attainment in the United States." In *Mobility and Inequality: Frontiers of Research in Sociology and Economics,* edited by Stephen Morgan, David Grusky, and Gary Fields. Stanford, Calif.: Stanford University Press.

Mulligan, Casey. 1999. "Galton Versus the Human Capital Approach to Inheritance." *Journal of Political Economy* 107(S6): S184–224.

Nicoletti, Chetti, and John Ermisch. 2007. "Intergenerational Earnings Mobility: Changes Across Cohorts in Britain." *B.E. Journal of Economic Analysis and Policy* 7(2, Contributions): article 9.

Organization for Economic Co-operation and Development (OECD). 1999. *Employment Outlook.* Paris: OECD.

———. 2009. *Growing Unequal.* Paris: OECD.

Oreopoulos, Philip, Marianne Page, and Ann Huff Stevens. 2006. "Does Human Capital Transfer from Parent to Child? The Intergenerational Effects of Compulsory Schooling." *Journal of Labor Economics* 24(4): 729–60.

Österbacka, Eva. 2001. "Family Background and Economic Status in Finland." *Scandinavian Journal of Economics* 103(3): 467–84.

Page, Marianne. 2004. "New Evidence on the Intergenerational Correlation in Welfare Participation." In *Generational Income Mobility in North America and Europe,* edited by Miles Corak. Cambridge: Cambridge University Press.

Pekkala, Sari, and Robert E. B. Lucas. 2007. "Differences Across Cohorts in Finnish Intergenerational Income Mobility." *Industrial Relations* 46(1): 81–111.

Pekkarinen, Tuomas, Roope Uusitalo, and Sari Pekkala. 2006. "Education Policy and Intergenerational Income Mobility: Evidence from the Finnish Comprehensive School Reform." IZA discussion paper 2204. Bonn, Germany: Institute for the Study of Labor (IZA).

Piketty, Thomas. 2003. "The Impact of Divorce on School Performance: Evidence from France, 1968–2002." Discussion paper 4146. London: Centre for Economic Policy Research (CEPR).

Raaum, Oddbjørn, Bernt Bratsberg, Knut Røed, Eva Österbacka, Tor Eriksson, Markus Jäntti, and Robin Naylor. 2007. "Marital Sorting, Household Labor Supply, and Intergenerational Earnings Mobility Across Countries." *B.E. Journal of Economic Analysis and Policy* 7(2): article 7.

Raaum, Oddbjørn, Kjell Salvanes, and Erik Sørensen. 2003. "The Impact of a Primary School Reform on Educational Stratification: A Norwegian Study of Neighbor and School Mate Correlations." *Swedish Economic Policy Review* 10(2): 143–69.

Sayer, Liana C., Anne H. Gauthier, and Frank F. Furstenberg. 2004. "Educational Differences in Parents' Time with Children: Cross-National Variations." *Journal of Marriage and the Family* 66(5): 1152–69.

Schütz, Gabriela, Heinrich Ursprung, and Ludger Woessmann. 2005. "Education Policy and Equality of Opportunity." IZA discussion paper 1906. Bonn, Germany: Institute for the Study of Labor (IZA).

Shavit, Yossi, and Hans-Peter Blossfeld, eds. 1993. *Persistent Inequality: Changing Educational Attainment in Thirteen Countries.* Boulder, Colo.: Westview Press.

Sigle-Rushton, Wendy. 2004. "Intergenerational and Life-Course Transmission of Social Exclusion in the 1970 British Cohort Study." Discussion paper 78. London: London School of Economics and Political Science, Centre for Analysis of Social Exclusion.

Sigle-Rushton, Wendy, and Sara McLanahan. 2004. "Father Absence and Child Well-being: A Critical Review." In *The Future of the Family,* edited by Daniel Moynihan, Lee Rainwater, and Timothy Smeeding. New York: Russell Sage Foundation.

Solon, Gary. 2002. "Cross-Country Differences in Intergenerational Income Mobility." *Journal of Economic Perspectives* 16(3): 59–66.

———. 2004. "A Model of Intergenerational Mobility Variation over Time and Place." In *Generational Income Mobility in North America and Europe,* edited by Miles Corak. Cambridge: Cambridge University Press.

Solon, Gary, Marianne E. Page, and Greg J. Duncan. 2000. "Correlations Between Neighboring Children in Their Subsequent Educational Attainment." *Review of Economics and Statistics* 82(3): 383–92.

UNICEF. 2007. "Child Poverty in Perspective: An Overview of Child Well-being in Rich Countries." Innocenti Report Card 7. Florence, Italy: UNICEF.

Waldfogel, Jane. 2006. *What Children Need.* Cambridge, Mass.: Harvard University Press.

Whelan, Christopher, and Richard Layte. 2006. "Economic Boom and Social Mobility: The Irish Experience." *Research in Social Stratification and Mobility* 24(2): 193–208.

Whiteford, Peter, and Willem Adema. 2007. "What Works Best in Reducing Child Poverty: A Benefit or Work Strategy?" Social, Employment and Migration working paper 51. Paris: Organization for Economic Co-operation and Development (OECD).

Wilson, William Julius. 1987. *The Truly Disadvantaged: The Inner City, the Underclass, and Public Policy.* Chicago: University of Chicago Press.

Wolff, Edward. 2004. "Changes in Household Wealth in the 1980s and 1990s in the United States." Working paper 407. New York: Bard College, Levy Economics Institute.

———. 2007. "Recent Trends in Household Wealth in the United States: Rising Debt and the Middle-Class Squeeze." Working paper 502. New York: Bard College, Levy Economics Institute.

Index

Boldface numbers refer to figures and tables.

mechanisms of persistence in the
United States and United Kingdom,
29–30, 55–57; assumptions and limitations in analyses of, 38, 40–41;
conceptual framework for analyses
of, 30–32; data and variables for
analyses of, 36–38; descriptive
statistics for pathway variables in
earnings regressions, **39–40;** double
decomposition analysis, 48–53; estimation methods used in analyses
of, 32–36; estimation results, 41–53;
family income as measure of outcomes, 53–54; family income persistence across countries, **62;**
individual earnings persistence
across countries, **41;** men, detailed
decomposition results for, **58–59;**
men, double decomposition using
education pathway for, **49–50;** men,
sequential decomposition analysis
for, 42–45; offspring family income,
63; pathway variables, **37;** robustness
check on British education measures,
64; robustness tests, 53–55; sequential models for American men, **43;**
sequential models for American
women, **46;** sequential models for
British men, **44;** sequential models
for British women, **47;** women,
detailed decomposition results for,
60–61; women, double decomposition using education pathway for,
51–52; women, sequential decomposition analysis for, 45–48
Meghir, Costas, 346
Menchik, Paul, 340
methodology: comparative, advantages of, 2, 6–7, 176–77; measuring
intergenerational mobility, 32–33;
principal components analysis,
180–81; status attainment models,
use of, 117–18; wealth data, challenges of analyzing, 117
Mexico, 132n2
Milligan, Kevin, 91, 215
Mills, Colin, 342
mobility, intergenerational. *See* intergenerational mobility

monetary gifts to children, 289–92,
320; by age and wealth of parents,
295, 297; average income and
wealth of parents who make, **308;**
for children's education, 318–19;
children's housing and income, 319;
by country, in 2004, **294;** cross-
country variation in, 293–304; data
regarding, 292; descriptive statistics
of U.S. sample, **324;** equality of
within the family, 311–14; grandchildren and, 319; linear regression
model of, **301–2;** multi-child households giving to all children in the
household, **312;** multivariate model
results for the short- and long-term,
314–19, **321–23;** over time in the
United States, 304–11; over time in
the United States to all children,
305; over time in the United States
to one child, **306;** over two, eight,
and fourteen years, linear regression results for, **316–17;** by parent
age, in 2004, **297;** parent characteristics, by country in 2004, **296;** parents' income and wealth and, 318;
by parent wealth, in 2004, **298;** persistence of by high-giving households, **309;** ratio of nineteenth and
seventy-fifth percentiles to median
and each other, **310;** to a seventeen-
or eighteen-year-old child in school
over the next six years, **307;** social
expenditures and, 297–98; taxation
and, 303; within-household equality
of giving to children over time in
the United States, **313–15**
Morgan, Stephen, 348
multidimensional model of social
mobility: classes, definition of, 145,
147, **148–49,** 150; conclusions from,
165–66; contours of reproduction,
155; cross-national variation in
social reproduction, 156–58; data
for, 145, **146,** 166–67; fit statistics for
selected models, **167;** immobility by
country and type, **153;** immobility
parameters by country and type of

in economic outcomes and, 226–30; multidimensional mobility model, conclusion from, 166; transmitting intergenerational associations through, 10–11; welfare (*see* welfare state institutions and policies)

Raaum, Oddbjørn, 67*n*20, 332, 335, 337, 351–52
Raftery, Adrian, 353, 359*n*5
Reed, Howard, 265
Rege, Mari, 212
relative mobility. *See* social fluidity
reproduction. *See* intergenerational persistence
Riphahn, Regina, 265, 347
Roemer, John, 78, 229
Romani, Annette, 259*n*19
Rosenzweig, Mark, 104*n*5, 242, 247, 249, 250
Ross, Karen, 289
Rumberger, Russell, 132*n*1

Salvanes, Kjell, 212–13, 332, 346, 352
Schjølberg, Synnve, 210
Schoeni, Robert, 289
Schulz, Wolfram, 269
Schütz, Gabriela, 283*n*14, 345, 355
Shapiro, Thomas, 111, 114
Shavit, Yossi, 344–45
Siedler, Thomas, 337
Smeeding, Timothy, 8, 10, 18
social fluidity, 21*n*2, 153–55, 161–64, 341–43
social institutions: intergenerational mobility and, 331–33; welfare state institutions (*see* welfare state institutions and policies)
social mobility. *See* intergenerational mobility
social reproduction. *See* intergenerational persistence
socioeconomic scales, 140
socioeconomic status (SES): children's life chances and, 1; gender differences in transmission of, 261 (*see also* education, children's cognitive ability and parents'; gender); low

family income in early childhood, impact of (*see* early childhood family income and adult attainment); persistence of across generations (*see* intergenerational persistence); school readiness and (*see* income-related gaps in school readiness)
Solon, Gary, 5, 41, 68*n*24, 75, 81–82, 96, 265, 331–32, 336–37, 352
Sombart, Werner, 138–39
Sørensen, Aage, 111
Sorensen, Erik, 332, 352
Spain: college degree, percentage of the population with a, 320; co-residency rates in, 303; earnings mobility in, 335; monetary gifts to children in, 293, **294,** 303; parent characteristics in, **296;** poverty and mobility in, 340; social expenditures in, **299**
Spilerman, Seymour, 132*n*2
Stabile, Mark, 105*n*12, 215
state, the: intergenerational persistence, role regarding, 228–29; role of in influencing economic mobility, American and Canadian opinions regarding, 79–81; transmitting intergenerational associations through, 10–11; welfare (*see* welfare state institutions and policies)
status attainment models, 110, 117–25, **126–31**
Stevens, Ann Huff, 346
Sure Start program, 177–78
Sweden: children's cognitive ability and parents' gender and education, 265–66; class mobility in, 342–43; earnings mobility in, 335; education and intergenerational mobility in, 344, 349, 358; as exception to persistence of mobility patterns, 357; genes and intergenerational correlation in earnings in, 332; as ideal-type mobility regime, 143–44 (*see also* multidimensional model of social mobility); immobility in by type of immobility, **160,** 161; immobility parameters and type of

Vaage, Kjell, 210, 212–13
van der Lippe, Tanja, 261, 281, 282n4, 283n15, 283n17
Vogel, Claudia, 303
Votruba, Mark, 212

Wagner, Sander, 339–40, 343, 351–53
wealth: cross-national comparison of intergenerational impact, 122–23; data and methods for a study regarding intergenerational impact of, 115–18; distribution of in the United States and Germany, **116;** full status attainment models, **126–31;** future research on intergenerational impact of, 124–25; intergenerational effects in Germany, 121–22; intergenerational effects in the United States, 118–22; intergenerational effects of in the United States and Germany, 113–15; intergenerational impact of, 109–10, 123–24, 340–41; monetary gifts to children as intergenerational transfer of (*see* monetary gifts to children); summary of hypotheses regarding intergenerational impact of, **113;** as a transformative asset, hypotheses regarding, 111–13

welfare state institutions and policies: child care (*see* child care); for children in low-income families in the United States and United Kingdom, 177–78 (*see also* income-related gaps in school readiness); class mobility and, 342–43; early childhood, targeted at, 353–56; for early childhood in low-income families in the United States and Norway, 209–10, 226–30 (*see also* early childhood family income and adult attainment); earnings mobility and, 335–38; impact of parental wealth on children's opportunities and, 114–15; intergenerational mobility and, 347–53, 356–59; linking institutions and outcomes, 333–34; monetary gifts to children and, 290–91, 297–98; social expenditures in selected countries, **299;** transfer payments to low-income families in Canada, 92–93; welfare dependency, factors promoting, 349–50
Whelan, Christopher, 343
Wilson, William Julius, 359n1
Woessmann, Ludger, 283n14, 345
Wolfe, Barbara, 262, 264–65

Zeng, Jinli, 332
Zimmerman, David, 5, 75